In Defense of Chaos:
The Chaology of Politics, Economics and Human Action

L.K. Samuels

Cobden Press • Apple Valley, CA

Copyright © 2013 by L.K. Samuels
Published by Cobden Press
20258 Hwy 18
Apple Valley, CA 92307
(480) 684-2651
www.fr33minds.com
Illustrations: © istockphoto.com/Simone Becchetti
All Rights Reserved, Published 2013
Printed in the United States of America
This book is printed on acid-free paper.
ISBN 978-1-935942-05-4

L.K. Samuels
In Defense of Chaos: The Chaology of Politics, Economics and Human Action
ISBN 978-1-935942-05-4
1. Chaos Theory   2. Political   3. Socioeconomics
I. Title   II. Samuels, L.K.

Printed in the United States of America
First Printing, 2013

In Defense of Chaos:
The Chaology of Politics, Economics
and Human Action

Contents

Foreword: vii

1. *The Beginning: In Defense of Chaos and Complexity*
   The Origins of Chaos—To Solve Unsolved Mysteries—What is Chaos Anyhow?—Where is the Control?—The Serenity of Order—Self-Organizing Systems/Complex Adaptive Systems—Evolution vs. Entropy—Death of Determinism and Positivism—Chaology and Economics—Predictability: The Future Leaves No Footprints 1

2. *System Failure: The Boomerang Effect*
   The System Failure Phenomenon—Reconfiguring Dynamics—The Political Systems of Command and Control—Boomerang Effect Mechanics—Political Remedies and Global Warming—Losing Control of the Steering Wheel—Government Conspiracies—Planned Chaos—Central Planning and Linear Modeling—Forced Assimilation—Mechanics of Failure—Foreign Boomeranging—Environmental Blowback 27

3. *Infinity, Equality and Imperfection*
   The EPR Paradox: Uncertainty and Indeterminism—Flaw Linear Regression—Uncaused Phenomena and Political Causality—The Impossibility of Exact Results—Imperfections and Inequality—The Illusion of Reform—Spaghetti Coding/Loop 61

4. *Strange Attractors and Subjective Value*
   A Strange Attractor in Economics—Subjective Value—Information Theory and Accurate Information 78

5. *Social Chaology and Weak Structures*
   Transgressions of Emperor Nero—Weak Structures – Bad Chaos—Edge-of-Chaos Disequilibrium—The Devil's Footpath—The Planned Chaos of Mao Tse–tung—An Institution of Legalized Violence—The Licensing Effect—The Complexity of Disorder and Violence—Foxes Guarding the Henhouse 89

6. *Social Chaology and Strong Structures*
   Absolute-based Architecture—Emergence and Reductionism—The Entanglement of Distant Parts—The Canopy of Altruism—Termite Architecture—The Synergic Mode—Political Reductionism—Volitional Structures—Monolithic Church and State—Economic Engines at the Edge of Chaos—Three Strong Structures – Business, Family, Social 115

7. *Social Upheavals and the Legalization of Violence*
   The Rule of Law, the Government of Men—Violence Breeds Violence—The Attraction of Consent—Coercing the Conscience—Pathogenic Systems—"Live–and–Let–Live" Systems—Empowerment and the Dangers of

Democracy—Dividing and Destroying the Community—The Warm Glow of Charity—Truth Distortion of Dystopia—My Way or the Highway – A Story of Planned Chaos—Competing Governments – The Collective Violence of War—Political Flatliners—Chaos Dynamics Versus Atrophy   145

8. *Decentralization and Simplicity*
   The Swiss Confederation—The War Factor—War and Decentralization—Single Point of Failure—The Soviet Colossus—Spontaneous Decentralization—Decentralized Decision Making—The Decentralization of City-States—They Who Would Decide—Invisible Systems and Patterns—Beyond the Reach of the Authorities   191

9. *Self-Organizing Systems*
   History of Self-Organizing Systems—The Living Organism of Economics—Stateless and Self-Organizing Societies—Pirate Societies and Autonomous Zones—Modern Stateless Societies and Somalia—Agriculture, City-States and the Roman Republic—The Over-Organizing Gene—Fleeing to Virgin Lands – Westward Ho—Self-Healing and Biological Uniqueness—Market Failure and Succeed by Failure—Government Failure—Fractalized Information   225

10. *Swarm Intelligence and Dynamics*
    Complexity with No Central Processor—Swarming Birds of Precision—Errors, Choice, and Randomness—Self-Organization vs. Compulsion—Big Things Fail in a Big Way—Roads Gone Wild   259

11. *Control, Order, and Chaos*
    Immeasurable Universe—Spartans: Becoming a Slave to Slaves—Gangs: Controlling the Uncontrollable—The Fear of Losing Control—A Manicured World—The Crosswalk Principle—Order Without Law   279

12. *Paradoxes and Inconsistencies*
    Connections to Paradoxes—Diversity vs. Unity Paradox—Paradox Theory—Ruler's Paradox—The Political Anarchist Paradox—The Paradox of Power—The Autopoietic Paradox—Short-Term, Long-Term Inconsistencies—Paradoxes in the Economics Arena—Other Ironies, Curiosities and Paradoxes—Foreign Aid Conundrum—Preservation Laws That Fail to Preserve—Upside-Down Behavior   297

13. *Evolution and Order Without Design*
    Round Soap Bubbles—Order Without Design—Survival of the Most Adaptable—Mindless Intelligence and Entropy—Evolution not Revolution   335

14. *Chaology and Market-Based Economics*
    Division of Knowledge—Open Source: A Network of Dreams—Linux: The Accidental Revolutionary—The Austrian School of Economics—The Strong Eat the Weak: Monopolies—Game Theory—The Cooperation of Trade—Economic Systems: Marxism—National Socialism and Fascism—The Fascism of Mussolini—Keynesism—Mercantilism   351

Index   391

Foreword

"How do you hold a moonbeam in your hand? How do you keep a wave upon the sand?" These words from *The Sound of Music* bring out the elusive nature of chaos. In life, most things cannot be captured for long. It is like trying to encapsulate time itself.

Starting from an accident in a computer software program to predict future weather, scientists in every discipline began to see something fascinating in how the chaotic systems played on the dynamic stage. They discovered hidden order in chaos and hidden chaos in order. Not long after that revelation, chaos theory as a promising new science was born.

For me, it all began back in the late 1980s. A dear friend, Dagny Sharon, made me aware of this new science, along with its socio-economic and political implications. She insisted that the mechanics of chaos theory had the possibility of completely changing the world as we knew it. And in that friendly discussion, she suggested that chaology had the potential to prove scientifically that the flexible, open-ended systems of a free society indeed work, compared to the closed, inflexible and anti-evolutionary systems often employed by governments. At the time, I simply pondered the possibilities of an obscure science.

Then along came Michael Crichton's book *Jurassic Park*, and later the movie, which encouraged me to delve deeper into theories that offered a better explanation of how both the universe and society truly operate. Soon after that, I discovered James Gleick's *Chaos: Making a New Science* and other books. I began to put words to paper around 1992 when I found myself stranded in the small desert town of Inyo-Kern, waiting for an auto mechanic shop to replace my broken transmission. I wrote for days, and so began my excursion into writing a book on a subject that almost seemed to defy description. Those early writings in the desert eventually became the first chapter of this book

The internet was of little help in the beginning, because it lacked the wealth of information required to research chaos and complexity science. But by 2007 and 2008, the internet and its resources had exploded with a cornucopia of related material. In early 2011 I sent my manuscript to two professional editors for publishing.

Although I had minored in journalism, my background did not seem to lend itself to writing a book on science, politics and economics. While the editors peppered me with questions about syntax, sources and logic, I searched for an understanding publisher. Fortunately, I found a think tank eager to be my publisher—Cobden Press of the Moorfield Storey Institute, founded by James Peron. Writing is a lonely endeavor, but what makes it possible is support of friends, family and colleagues.

I would like to thank a number of my cheerleaders—my wife, Jane Heider, who went through the book determined to clean up all of my grammatical indiscretions; Prof. David R. Henderson, who looked over a number of chapters, especially the one on economics, giving me many valuable suggestions; my editors Jackie Estrada from San Diego and Elizabeth Brierly from the San Jose area, and my final proofer, Linda Blumenthal.

This odyssey has led me to one major conclusion: chaology and complexity science will change the way we think. With more knowledge about the workings of this new science, humanity will be set free to consider and pursue every conceivable possibility.

1 The Beginning—Defense of Chaos and Complexity

Chaos is the law of nature; order is the dream of man.
—Henry Adams, historian

There is no detailed blueprint, only a set of laws with an inbuilt facility for making interesting things happen. The universe is free to create itself as it goes along.
—Physicist Paul Davies, *The Cosmic Blueprint* (1988)

Why do things behave the way they do? Why do planets wobble, stars fluctuate, and galaxies bend? Why is the universe speeding up instead of slowing down? Why is observable matter in the universe clustered together in galaxies instead of being evenly spread out across vast reaches of space?

Closer to home, how did simple molecules of the primordial soup produce the first cell, on a lifeless rock revolving around a thermonuclear sun? Or more fundamentally, how can evolutionary processes go against the laws of thermodynamics—a condition in which entropy demands that the universe must eventually grind down to a cold state of disorder and disorganization? And if entropy is always increasing, how can biological systems self-organize and achieve a higher order of complexity? These are just a few of the perplexities and paradoxes that have emerged from the fascinating field of chaos science: chaology.

The Origins of Chaos

For centuries, mathematicians and physicists ignored or overlooked any strange anomaly they encountered. They could hardly be blamed. They did not have powerful analytical tools to figure out why so many of their experiments resulted in erratic and inexact outcomes. They had no course of action other than to see randomness as just "white noise," like static radio signals, or to conclude that their experiments had simply gone bad. In less publicized cases, scientists would actually smooth over, or "linearize" results, to make outcome fit theory, which geologist Thomas Chrowder Chamberlin referred to as "pressing of the theory to make it fit the facts and a pressing of the facts to make them fit the theory."[1] This "confirmation bias" would start to change once the power of computers and mathematician James A. Yorke had arrived on the scene.

A professor of mathematics and physics at the University of Maryland, Yorke had read an obscure but fascinating article penned in 1963 by meteorologist Edward Lorenz. Published in the Journal of Atmospheric Sciences, Lorenz's article discussed the curious outcome from a computer program designed to chart and study weather systems. While working at Massachusetts Institute of Technology (MIT), Lorenz had built one of the first computer modeling programs to simulate weather patterns. One day in 1961, Lorenz wanted to replay one particular sequence of his model. This time he decided to cheat: he started in the middle of the sequence instead of at the beginning. When he came back to the computer, the pattern had diverged wildly and evolved into an entirely different outcome from that of the original data. Dumbfounded, Lorenz started to search for the problem. He soon discovered why. In order to save paper, he had printed his report using three decimal places, not the usual six. Instead of typing in the normal 0.506127, he had input 0.506. Little did he know that this simple mistake would eventually usher in a new science so significant that mathematician Robert Devaney would refer to this science, chaos theory, as "the third great scientific revolution of the 20th century, along with relativity and quantum mechanics."

In his research paper, Lorenz attributed the deviations to an effect in which small initial conditions may lead to large changes—sensitive dependence on initial conditions—later to be known as the "butterfly effect." And yet this consequence of chain reactions was hardly unknown to the general public. Even an English nursery rhyme from the Middle Ages alluded to the danger of little problems metastasizing into big ones, cautioning:

> *For want of a nail, the shoe was lost; for want of a shoe, the horse was lost; for want of a horse, the rider was lost; for want of the rider, the battle was lost; for want of the battle, the kingdom was lost. And all for the want of a horseshoe nail!*

A more famous example is the loss of the U.S. Space Shuttle Challenger, because of the failure of a tiny, synthetic rubber O-ring seal on the solid rocket booster.

Lorenz had discovered scientific evidence to prove that dynamic systems are sensitive to initial conditions. In more concrete terms, a butterfly flapping its wings in Tokyo could influence a hurricane in the Gulf of Mexico a month later. Effect was not proportional to cause. A ball hit twice as hard will not necessarily fly twice as fast. Naturally, this shocking revelation flew in the face of traditional linear theory, which said that motion output is directly related to input force. But there was more to come. Years later, when chaologists started to debunk linear systems, they discovered a whole array of problems that chaos theory might solve. Lorenz had been instrumental in starting a new age of inquiry, but the world would have to wait over a decade before someone rediscovered Lorenz.

Unfortunately, Lorenz's article had been published in a meteorology publication and garnered little interest. Not until Yorke found it and applied his mathematical skills did other scientists take notice. In reexamining Lorenz's computer model, Yorke discovered to his surprise that the universe is fundamentally disordered. Chaos is ubiquitous, not at all rare. In 1975 T.Y. Li and Yorke co-wrote a now-famous paper concerning one-dimensional systems, *Period Three Implies Chaos*, which showed a stable oscillating between three values. The paper jolted the physics community. It implied that "mathematical chaos" is not only stable, but possesses a sort of structure. This marked the birth of the modern chaos theory and complexity science. Yorke is now credited with giving this new science of chaos its name.

Why was this discovery so revolutionary? Why would anyone care about some mathematical equations showing chaos to be found everywhere and residing in everything? Average people in the street already knew that chaos ruled their lives. On a daily basis, people struggled with a disorderly and dysfunctional world that often defied logic. So what was the big deal?

It was a big deal to the scientific community. As science journalist James Gleick wrote in his immensely popular book, *Chaos: Making a New Science*, "Where chaos begins, classic science stops."[2] And indeed, the traditional scientific foundation had been shaken to its core. The reason was obvious: Conclusive mathematical evidence that chaos is ubiquitous meant that the entire scientific world had been based on a false premise. Immediately, this dethroned the static, mechanistic world of Isaac Newton and his era of enlightenment. The whole notion of "deterministic predictability"—of a fixed, replicable state of reality which, when called upon, obeys—was found to be completely invalid. This so-called fuzzy logic of complexity and chaos had overthrown centuries of ironclad theorems based on machine-like calculations. The universe could no longer be considered a single dimension, chock-full of straight lines or acting in the fashion of an industrial assembly line. Scientific methodology would have to be reconfigured and scientists could no longer ignore unsolved mysteries of chaotic systems.[3]

To Solve Unsolved Mysteries

But why did scientists begin to look beyond orderly systems in the first place? Actually, they had little choice. Studies, research, and experiments kept coming up with inconclusive outcomes.

One of the most famous anomalies was the mystery surrounding the orbit of planet Mercury. In 1859, an astronomer noticed that Mercury's perihelion changed slightly during each orbit. It had been assumed that the planet's strange gravitational variations were caused by an unidentified nearby body, most likely an undiscovered planet. Most astronomers believed that Mercury's unsteady patterns could not be a factor. Orbits of planets were considered immutable and regular. So astronomers solved the problem by predicting a mysterious planet to compensate for Mercury's eccentric orbital behavior. They named the planet Vulcan, but obviously, it has never been found, it was never found.

Another example: For centuries, British cartographers had mapped the coast of England, only to find one glaring inconsistency that continued to confound them and scientists. After charting smaller areas of the coastline and then adding up the numbers, they would get a total coastline measurement of over 8,000 miles. There was only one little problem: The British coastline had already been calculated to be only 5,000 miles long. To the mapmakers, it appeared that a finite coastline area of Britain was being bounded by a variant line. This phenomenon became the subject of many mathematical theories, until the introduction of the Mandelbrot set, which established the self-similarity of fractals—which is an illustrated journey into the heart of chaos.

Meanwhile, ecologists were continually baffled by extreme declines and increases in animal populations. In Alaska, Pacific salmon saw substantial declines in population during the 1920s, 1960s, and 1970s, but for some reason, they always rebounded. The reasons were never clear. Similarly, ecologists studying sea otter populations along the coasts of California and Alaska could not detect any conclusive explanation for sharp fluctuations in populations.

The mysteries kept piling up. Frustrated ornithologists could not figure out how, when swarming, birds would spontaneously fly into precise formations. Physicists experimenting with and attempting to understand fluctuations in a particle chamber repeatedly failed to predict what subatomic particles would do. Medical researchers studying heartbeat data discovered that hearts do not beat in precise intervals; surprisingly, dynamic irregularities appear normal for healthy hearts. When close measurements were taken of the swinging action of a pendulum—the very heart of a clock—unpredictability was clearly evident. After using high-speed computers to study the pendulum, scientists discovered that even the movement of the pendulum did not behave like a normal linear system. Over long periods, calculations of time predictions broke down completely. The pendulum had a blot of imprecision. Like most systems, this high-precision machine had fallen into a chaotic pattern of locally unpredictable behavior.

In all fields of study, scientists struggled to make predictions with crateloads of handwritten data and graphics, and often found themselves facing a dead end. No longer could they keep "smoothing over" irregularities. With the advent of the computer age, the "fudge" factor was becoming a less viable option. Scientists were confronted with the impracticality of inventing variables just to force a calculated result—feeling an urgency to explain the discrepancy between theory and experiment. In short, the dynamics of instability had to be recognized.

By the 1970s, a small circle of scientists in such fields as astrophysics, microbiology, chemistry, particle physics, meteorology, and botany came to realize that certain aspects of their disciplines defied predictions, patterns, and order. They came face to face with irregularities they could not explain, due mainly to the complexity of almost unending numbers of variables. And early on, some of the scientists, such as Mitchell Feigenbaum, a mathematical physicist at Los Alamos National Laboratory, realized that not only is randomness important to study, but that it is, perhaps, a factor that should be elevated to the status of a science. In the 1970s, he began mapping chaos, determined to unravel the seemingly intractable random behavior of chaotic systems.

For Feigenbaum, it started after playing with a cheap calculator. He sensed that something was flowing from the random numbers on his machine. They represented a rhythm, more than just pure mathematical units, perhaps something that embodied the fingerprints of God, but far too complex for human beings to understand. In a flash, he saw that chaos pervades every aspect of physical existence. With more study, he discovered from these rhythms that when orderly systems disorganized into chaos, patterns would develop. It was so precise that the pattern was defined by a number, 4.669, now known as the "Feigenbaum constant."

Feigenbaum was the first to formulate a mathematical constant to plot the cause of chaos. Eventually, other rhythms were discovered, and soon these causes became known as "strange attractors." When entered into computers as mathematical formulae, strange attractors would produce beautiful, colorful, and infinitely complex psychedelic images reminiscent of the Haight-Ashbury hippie days of the 1960s. They were christened "fractals."

With the advent of high-speed computers, scientists began to explore this new world. They were able to input data and perform previously impossible calculations. With this new tool, they could now plot complex systems. The world had entered THE CHAOS ZONE.

What Is Chaos, Anyhow?

So what exactly is chaos? It is not, obviously, a prerequisite to warfare, bloody riots, or crime-infested inner cities spiraling out of control. Such violent episodes are usually the backwashing effect of arbitrary controls imposed on society, or bitter turf battles between warring political factions. The Taoist philosopher who developed the concept of *yin* and *yang*, Lao Tsu, addressed this conundrum back in 600 B.C., writing: *Why are the people rebellious? Because the rulers interfere too much…Why do the people think so little of death? Because the rulers demand too much of life.*"[4]

First and foremost, chaos is the engine of nonlinear change, an unfolding emergence, often with neither detailed blueprints nor mankind's permission. But, paradoxically, the theory of chaos is actually a theory about order and mathematical algorithms that encompasses unpredictable and complex systems.

One way to look at chaos theory is to consider the workings of a roulette wheel. The bouncing ball represents randomness and uncertainty, but the rest of the system is deterministic—stable structures composed of a solid, mahogany bowl, an aircraft-grade aluminum wheel, and chrome-plated ball pocket separators. Only the final destination of the roulette ball is unknown—the attractor. Some have attempted to measure the height from which the roulette ball is dropped, the speed of the spinning wheel, and the dimension of the table. In theory, if the numbers were plugged into a differential equation, the right answer should be easy to calculate. But it does not work that way; the measurements are too small to gauge, and there are too many other variables to allow for an accurate prediction—which together add up the exact recipe for chaotic systems.

Others have depicted "mathematical chaos" in more academic terms. In Stephen H. Kellert's book *In the Wake of Chaos*, he defines chaos theory as "the qualitative study of unstable aperiodic behavior in deterministic nonlinear dynamical systems."[5] Definitely a mouthful, but a better definition of chaos is difficult to pinpoint, for both scientists and laymen alike. In fact, some have referred to chaos as an unsolvable paradox in which chaos and order seem to be dissimilar and similar at the same time. Physicist Joseph Ford, in *The New Physics*, made this observation, referring to chaos as "a paradox hidden inside a puzzle shrouded by an enigma," which is, interestingly, paraphrased from Winston Churchill's description of a perplexing Russia.[6]

Chaos theorists primarily seek to understand the dynamics of change and how it relates to the universal behavior of complex systems. They research the types of changes that are unpredictable, erratic, and patternless, such as roiling fluids, turbulent clouds, irregular heartbeats, raging wildfires, market fluctuations, and confusing military battles—everything that traditional scientists avoid as being either too complex or unworthy of research.

And as traditional scientists have begun to reexamine these unexplained phenomena, they have found more puzzles in what some have referred to as "ordered chaos." For instance, in physics, "Why is it that simple particles obeying simple rules will sometimes engage in most astonishing, unpredictable behavior?" asks M. Mitchell Waldrop in *Complexity*.[7] Or why does order sometimes spontaneously arise from chaotic situations, and vice versa? Why does chaos erupt within seemingly perfect, ordered structures? What power, divinity, or even mindless intelligence is behind these processes—like the nebulous origins of the first galaxies? Or are we just observing chaos and order simply trying to reach some type of equilibrium—what chaos scientists call "the edge of chaos?"

Gleick takes a different approach, asserting that "to some physicists chaos is a science of process rather than state, of becoming rather than being."[8] Simply stated, chaos appears to be the instrument by which most changes occur.

Some partisans of chaology go a step further, contending that order comes from chaos, and chaos from order—a sort of cosmic yin and yang bound together by some unknown force, but repelled by another. Others have claimed that order and chaos have a symbiotic relationship, in which each needs the other to survive, as though they were negatively and positively charged particles, or matter and anti-matter. Or better yet, as with the Heisenberg's uncertainty principle of either particle-like or wave-like electrons, chaos and order are like "the man and woman in the weather house. If one comes out the other goes in." This description refers to the indecisive nature of subatomic particles—either wave-like or particle-like, but never both simultaneously. As more scientists scrutinized chaotic systems and complexity, it became apparent that the rules had changed. In fact, under the prism of chaos, the mere act of playing the game had a way of changing the rules. Except within narrow limits, predictability was now seen as an almost impossible feat. The comfort of feeling in control of one's own situation was no long assured.

Where Is the Control?

We all want control in our lives. But are controls and order available at our fingertips? Consider the scary implications of the meltdown in the reactor at Three Miles Island Nuclear Generating Station in Pennsylvania on March 28, 1979. The control room had over a thousand gauges, lights, and dials with which to monitor the reactor. Despite this massive array of instrumentation, and excellent safety and feedback systems, nobody really knew what was happening to the reactor, long after piercing horns and sirens had alerted the engineers.

Actually, nothing was wrong with the nuclear reactor. Workmen cleaning a minor filtering device had somehow set off the alarm. In typical chain-reaction mode, the system started to drain cooling water away from the nuclear core when a small valve failed to close. Although the core had overheated to 4,300 degrees Fahrenheit, conflicting information convinced the engineers to shut down the emergency water system—the worse possible reaction.

For two days, operators thought they had solved the problem, until shockingly, they detected radioactive gases inside the plant. They could not believe it. "We had a mindset that said we had these marvelous safety systems which had back-ups of back-ups," said Bob Long, a supervising engineer at Three Mile Island. "It was hard for people to really come to grips with the reality that severe damage had occurred."[9]

When the astronauts of America's Apollo 13 mission (April 11-17, 1970) arrived back on Earth, they were stunned to learn of the seemingly unrelated, minor events that had led to the oxygen tank explosion which had almost cost them their lives. Before going into space, the astronauts had been subjected by NASA's engineers to a series of mock problems, simulating improbable malfunctions. But none of the simulated malfunctions had come close to what occurred in flight. After learning what had crippled their spacecraft, the astronauts said that they would have refused to go on the voyage if they had known

The Beginning—Defense of Chaos and Complexity 9

that such problems could actually happen.

Similar to the crisis fictionalized in Michael Crichton's *Jurassic Park*, almost unnoticeable and immeasurable events—called micro-events—can significantly affect the outcome of seemingly unrelated events. In the case of Three Mile Island, a series of minor mistakes increased the instability of a system that had been considered foolproof. The control room operators were in an automated, information-rich environment with many dials at their fingertips. And yet there was a meltdown in the information feedback loop and a misplaced confidence. As the runaway reactor veered out of control, the engineers leaned back in their control chairs and believed their information to be accurate and their emergency response methods successful. Like many, they believed that they had everything under control.

The Serenity of Order

One can glance up into a starry sky and feel a sense of peace and serenity, secure in the belief that tomorrow will be no different from today. In reality, no day is the same as another—a scientific impossibility. To some, it might appear that human beings are caught in boring routines—dragging their bodies to work, hauling out the trash cans weekly, and turning over their income tax paperwork to the IRS before the deadline. But such linear tranquility is misleading.

Order is not universal. In fact, many chaologists and physicists posit that universal laws are more flexible than first realized, and less rigid—operating in spurts, jumps, and leaps, instead of like clockwork. Chaos prevails over rules and systems because it has the freedom of infinite complexity over the known, unknown, and the unknowable. One best-selling science fiction author, Terry Pratchett, assigned a pejorative spin to stability, observing that, "Chaos is found in greatest abundance wherever order is being sought. Chaos always defeats order because it is better organized."[10]

But how rare is order? Complexity scientists often like to use the example of a deck of shuffled playing cards. Since gambling relies on a thorough, random shuffle, the cards are dealt in no special order. Four aces would be a good poker hand, potentially a winner, but the probability of this occurrence is quite slim. The odds of dealing four aces in a poker game are one in about 270,000 shuffles. Order has a low probability.

So what is order? Linguists might describe it as a methodical and systematic arrangement that organizes things in a geometrical or hierarchical way, biased toward uniformity or regularity. But according to the basic principles of ontology, any entity that exists cannot be identical to another entity. True uniformity is impossible. In fact, if the universe were based on pure order, it could not exist. It would be a closed, dead-end system, since change is a major constant of the universe. In short, without the interaction of chaos, there would be no creative process in which to create the universe. Literally, we owe our very existence to the interaction of chaotic conditions and complexity. Otherwise, we would all be floating in an entropic "heat death" of nothingness.

Self-Organizing Systems or Complex Adaptive Systems

As more physicists, mathematicians, and scientists have delved into nonlinear, dynamic systems, they have come up with one astounding conclusion: The universe appears to be guided by a set of fairly simple physical laws that can create amazing complexity. But despite this awe-inspiring complexity, they've found no specific blueprint or any predetermined system. Further, they have realized that not only are stable and predictable systems uncommon, but they are "incredibly scarce" in the universe. More exciting, they've found that chaotic and complex systems have enough adaptability to govern themselves better than do orderly ones commanded by external forces. Suddenly, a whole new subfield, complexity science, has arisen, dedicated to the understanding of "self-organizing systems," also known as "complex adaptive systems."

Complex adaptive systems are based on self-organizing systems that optimize their own functions. Considered autonomous, they have a natural and almost organic tendency for self-improving and self-organizing. John H. Holland, the originator of the "genetic algorithm" computer program, refers to this self-learning process as "the hidden order" in which stability emerges in everything from the indomitable drive of animal migration to the persistent hexagonal-shaped structure of every snowflake.[11] Many economists use the term "spontaneous order" to describe the self-organizing phenomenon in marketplaces, where stability is abundant. Biologists see "self-assembly" in biological and chemical systems, from the subcellular level to entire ecosystems. And still others, such as theoretical biologist Stuart Kauffman, point to "autocatalytic processes" and "autopoiesis" to explain the origins of life. In all these cases, a deeply hidden order emerges from inside an organism, not necessarily from outside forces.[12]

Naturally, the revelation that systems organize on their own sat poorly with the apostles of social sciences—especially political scientists who base their theories on imposing external controls to achieve selected political goals. They are accustomed to thinking about government-produced certainties, not ambiguous probabilities. In their linear calculations, humanity must be physically forced to follow the guiding light of political leaders or flavor-of-the-month ideologies. The economy and human actions must march in step with legislative or dictated law, no matter what the outcome. Yet natural systems do not operate this way.

Political systems are self-destructive constructs. They possess a de-evolutionary or cannibalizing nature, locked firmly within closed-ended structures, micromanaged from top tiers, and endowed with an overwhelming capacity to crank out external controls in assembly-line fashion. With clockwork precision, these systems manufacture rules and a legal apparatus which in turn erect artificial barriers to prevent the optimizing processes of evolution and information fluidity. Instead of embracing self-determination for subgroups, they live off the energy of all autonomous organisms within their territory. And if that resource becomes depleted, they go after those in other, neighboring lands.

Chaos theory and complexity science demonstrate that in a constantly evolving environment, individual agents require unfettered leeway to adapt. Without flexibility, the obstructive walls of regulations, taxes, edicts, laws, licenses, and so forth can only hamstring, starve, or destroy upstart organisms. In economics as well as in biology, this premise has been shown to be scientifically accurate. With mathematical modeling, physical chemist Ilya Prigogine proved that systems need to dissipate their energy to create new systems of higher order. He won a Nobel Prize for chemistry in 1977 for this discovery concerning "non-equilibrium thermodynamics." In *Order Out of Chaos*, Prigogine illustrated how open-ended systems (dynamic, far-from-equilibrium systems) will leap spontaneously into higher organization—challenging the "dead heat" of entropy, negating the certainty of determinism and confirming the irreversibility of time.[13] He argued that the dynamics of dissipation were necessary for self-organizing structures to work off the products of their instabilities. Not only did these "dissipative structures" resist entropy but they also expanded their energy output. Prigogine's research sent shock waves across the scientific community, because it contradicted certain aspects of entropy.

Evolution vs. Entropy

Evolution and entropy share a problem: they contradict each other. Entropy, according to the second law of thermodynamics, is the natural tendency of the universe toward disorder. The big machine of the universe is grinding down, leaking energy through energy sinks, as gears wear away gears, eventually reaching a nearly uniform absolute cold of deep-space emptiness. This process contradicts evolution, which states that lower forms give rise to increasingly higher levels of organization and complexity.

One of Prigogine's greatest achievements was to bridge the gap between natural science and social science. A number of experts have applied Prigogine's theories to the field of economics, arguing that command-and-control systems usually debase the economic lives of citizens. Such rigid structures embrace entropy, by artificially dissipating the energy of any autonomous system or subsystem that might challenge their authority. The imposition of government obtrusion obstructs the evolutionary and dynamic process that may lead to more complex organisms.

To illustrate this point, consider the case of an entrepreneur organizing a small company to sell hand-held police scanners or receivers in Belgium. These devices can monitor civil or military frequency ranges. The owner of the new enterprise might earn a living by selling the device to commuters who want to avoid heavy traffic resulting from accidents, natural disasters, terrorist attacks, or other emergencies. To initiate this microbusiness, the owner might purchase the scanners in bulk from Japan or Taiwan, open a small office, hire a salesperson or two, arrange for some accounting software, and vacuum the carpets at night. But the entrepreneur has one big obstacle: It is illegal to use police scanners in Belgium. There, as in much of Europe, most things are illegal until Parliament decides to legislate their legality.

In many nations, new start-ups must be bonded costing hundreds of thousands of dollars, must go through long permit and licensing application processes, and must endure laws that make it difficult and expensive to fire incompetent staff. And because of culture and laws, the ability to raise early-stage financing is daunting, if not impossible, for those without many resources. If the company fails, as 30 to 50 percent of start-ups do, the legal and financial penalties would be intimidating. The World Bank often charts such difficulties, reporting that it takes 152 days to start a business in Spain, but only five days in the United States. It can take up to 288 days to enforce a contract in England, 425 days in India, and 1,390 days in Italy.[14] Perhaps this explains why, in 1997, *The Economist* claimed that the informal, off-the-books economy in developed countries was growing at three times the rate of growth in the official economy.[15]

Surviving initial conditions is vital for emergence. There can be no kickstart for new systems when they are discouraged or outlawed. But political systems generally impose protective and dominating barriers to prevent upstarts from competing. Many small, seat-of-the-pants businesses with few resources—such as Apple Computer and the Disney Brothers Studio—would never have gotten the chance to establish a foothold in a static environment. What became the billion-dollar fast-food restaurant franchise Carl's Jr. was started in 1941 as a street-corner hotdog pushcart. Political systems inhibit evolution and adaptation; they are the worst example of energy-dissipating entropy in action.

Under Prigogine's theories, external controls are the death knell to newly born organisms. In his models, a sort of "instability bubble" develops under linear systems, blocking the means to dissipate energy. And if this bubble—called the "bifurcation point"—bursts, there are two stark possible consequences. The organism will either collapse back into disorder, or take a higher road of increased order. For instance, after the turbulent war for American independence, the new nation organized into an innovative system that instilled higher stability. If George Washington's Continental Army had been captured, the colonies might have fallen into an unstable political stew of discontent and conflict, until the end of European colonialism.

The Death of Determinism and Positivism

Cracks in the predominance of linear, deterministic systems had actually developed long before the age of computers and chaos theory. In the early twentieth century, a new breed of physicists pioneered the science of quantum particles. Albert Einstein's relativity and Werner Heisenberg's quantum mechanics challenged the very notion of matter and space as absolute entities. But it was Heisenberg's discoveries that put a stake through the heart of determinism and the philosophy of positivism, showing the complete unpredictability of the subatomic world under the uncertainty principle.

Writing about the microscopic world of electrons, Heisenberg wrote: "The more precisely the position is determined, the less precisely the momentum is known."[16] With these seemingly innocent words, Heisenberg inadvertently attacked the core premise of causality and determinism. Predictability was no longer completely tethered to causality. The philosophical implications were profound.

In the Copenhagen interpretation of quantum mechanics, Heisenberg and Niels Bohr argued that on the elementary physical level, the universe is a collection of probabilities, and that the universe does not exist in a deterministic form. Even if scientists were able to construct instruments to produce infinitely precise measurements, they would still be unable to predict the exact path of each subatomic particle. Einstein was so offended by this interpretation of a random cosmos that he famously remarked: "I cannot believe that God would choose to play dice with the universe." Whereas, Bohr retorted: "Einstein, don't tell God what to do."

The real deathblow to determinism came when scientists posed one simple question: How can the future be predicted if one cannot accurately measure the present? Predominant from the sixteenth to nineteenth centuries, determinism and positivism represented the old, classical physics of Isaac Newton, in which the material world was thought to be precise, knowable, and predetermined. Reinforced by the successes of the Industrial Age, positivists saw the universe as a gigantic, smoothly operating machine. The Newtonian mechanistic paradigm held that "the laws of nature completely specify the past and future down to the finest details," explains Heinz R. Pagels, an American physicist from the New York Academy of Science, in *Cosmic Code*.[17] He writes that classical physicists mistakenly believed that "the universe was like a perfect machine: once we knew the position of its parts at one instant, they would be forever specified."

Newton had envisioned a perfect world with mechanical precision, reflecting the belief in an all-knowing god who micromanaged nature to the nth degree. These early scientists were looking for certainty in a world that was anything but certain. The famous French mathematician Pierre-Simon Laplace (1749–1827) took the extreme position that if enough facts and figures were known, it was possible to forecast events ahead of time and to "retrodict" the past.[18]

Auguste Comte, the founder of nineteenth-century positivism, took this a step further. He wanted to use science-based sociology to create a superior state of civilization, seeking to reengineer mankind and force it to obey laws just as strict as the physical laws of motion and gravity. In this way, more evils could be eliminated in an effort to improve the human condition. John Stuart Mill referred to Comte's philosophy as "despotism of society over the individual."

But the chains of determinism and positivism were broken with the arrival of quantum mechanics in the 1920s. Although highly controversial, quantum

The Beginning—Defense of Chaos and Complexity

mechanics was no flash in the pan. What Heisenberg and other physicists theorized did work extremely well in laboratory experiments. In essence, quantum mechanics proved that Newton's determinism of infinite precision had instead the consistency of a pinball machine and a roller derby wrapped into one. The world was not deterministic after all, but rather "indeterministic." Nobody knew it, but the seeds of chaos theory had been sown.

Quantum mechanics also provided scientific evidence that the material world is based mostly on randomness, and that probability can be established only as a statistical aspect of physical phenomena. The position and momentum of subatomic particles are just probabilistic descriptions of future trajectories. This is not to imply that predictable conditions are impossible. Scientists are capable of predicting the future of certain phenomena, within narrow limits, such as the timing of weather patterns, volcanic eruptions, and solar eclipses. For example, with modern sensory devices, seismologists were able to forecast a disastrous earthquake that hit the city of Haicheng in Northeast China in 1975. Four other quakes in China were also successfully predicted, giving hope that these natural disasters could now be predicted beforehand. This sense of conquering nature did not last long. On July 28, 1976, a magnitude 7.8 quake hit Tanqshan, China, without warning, despite the use of similar equipment and methods.

Any one person is unlikely to experience a catastrophic event throughout his life—on a probability basis. It is comforting to see the sun rise every morning, but even such a daily occurrence is not 100 percent guaranteed. Nothing is. Uncertainty is inherent, because of the constant flux between the two extremes of unstable and stable dynamics at the "edge of chaos"—a sort of tightrope walker's balancing act, in which systems flux back and forth in disequilibrium. This is a place where innovation nibbles at the current state of affairs, anarchy battles stagnation, complexity mingles with simplicity, and adaptation gives birth to spontaneous unknowns in a process where things evolve to evolve.

Chaotic conditions are a consequence of complexity. William of Ockham (c. 1288 – c. 1348), of Occam's Razor fame, showed he understood this problem when he told people to keep things simple and to refrain from making convoluted mountains out of nondescript molehills. He suggested that people should not create complex explanations for simple phenomena. His sage advice was: "Entities should not be multiplied unnecessarily." Even Aristotle had his own theory about cutting away complexity, writing that "the more perfect a nature is, the fewer means it requires for its operation."

The minimalist nature of simplicity often works well, because as a system becomes more complex, it behaves more unpredictably. Even worse, a complex system might break down at an utterly obscure single point of failure, requiring parts that are inaccessible or obsolete, along with the engineering skills to figure out what is wrong. It can be readily argued that success lies in the simplicity of the interactions among a system's components. As with heavy industrial equipment, the more moving parts, the more potential for breakdowns. As the old motherly saying goes, "Don't buy fancy cars with all of those fancy gizmos. They'll just break down and cause nothing but heartache." And it is true. Vehicles with more elaborate gadgets such as automatic headlights, rain-sensing wipers, power-heated memory mirrors, power moon roofs, and cruise control do malfunction at greater rates, simply because there is more to go wrong.

And yet in a paradoxical rub, the simplest of systems often present extraordinarily difficult problems of predictability—for example, calculating the direction and height of a bouncing ball. Scientists can predict the ball's movement, but only on a probability basis that may be far off the mark. The reason usually cited is that deterministic systems are so sensitive to measurements that their output appears random. Small effects can and do have spectacular or devastating outcomes, not only in weather but also in the economic and political realm.

Chaology and Economics

The field of economics is not exempt from the consequences of chaos and complexity. Marketplaces are indeterminate; value is subjective; and outcomes are subject to interpretation. Economic forecasting is just as nebulous, being based on the probability of statistical information that may or may not be accurate. As the comedian Jim Hightower once joked: "The amazing thing to me is that people who laugh at Gypsy fortune-tellers take economists seriously."

Despite the difficulty in understanding the complexity of markets and consumers, economics is often viewed as though it were something that could be physically touched, handcuffed by police, or made to sit down on command. Incredibly, individuals and companies making up markets are compelled to perform in ways that contradict the optimizing mechanics of greater choices and options. The business of trade becomes politicized and centralized, measuring people and situations with one yardstick. Markets are put under a collective sword and commanded to achieve mandated goals that ignore aggregated choice. Under an increasingly global economy, each individual is an independent subsystem, a one-person agent acting on a wide variety of choices together with 6 billion other agents—making it impossible to understand much of the overlapping and jumbled complexity, except in broad, brush-stoke terms.

Take the example of how people spend their money. Why would anyone purchase a round, gray pebble in a box with printed instructions explaining how to care for a piece of granite? Yet in 1975, the originator of the Pet Rock, Gary Dahl, bought tons of Rosarito Beach stones for a penny a piece, and packed them in wood shavings inside a gift box modeled after a pet carrying case. Newsweek considered it a nutty craze, but Dahl sold enough rocks in a box to make him a millionaire.

In the 1980s, Ken Hakuta did something similar. He discovered a cheap, strange novelty item selling in Japan. It had no practical application, but with his import-export business, he decided to buy some for the United States market. The object looked like a small octopus. It was sticky and rubbery, and when it was thrown against a wall or window, it would slowly wobble down to the floor. He named it the Wacky WallWalker. Within a few months, his little toy became a wildly popular fad, selling over 250 million units and earning Hakuta over $20 million.

Tastes are truly subjective. From Hula Hoops to Lava Lamps, seemingly impractical consumer goods make innovators wealthy. Nobody has the ability to predict such outcomes. Economic indicators are clouded by a fickle public. As futurist Peter Schwartz wrote, "Information is always contaminated by people's beliefs and is never really complete."

Because information is often biased, outdated, or inadequate, command-based systems rely on obtuse information to produce blunt solutions. Wielding force like drunken revelers, political systems gamble on the singularity of direction to fix a multiplicity of problems, woefully ignorant that one size does not fit all. Blinded by political ideologies, they rarely act to solve underlying problems. Karl Hess (1923-1994), a former presidential speech writer, noted this condition, observing, "Politicians occasionally do the right thing—but only after they've exhausted all the alternatives."

A host of distortions are inevitable in command-based systems. When external controls are imposed on a complex system already built on prior consent, the integrity of its structure is jeopardized. Systems can be managed, but not entirely controlled, by outside forces. If these controls are mandated—as with the prohibition of alcohol in the United States—individual agents will actively sabotage the system, go underground, or circumvent the law.

This is not rocket science. Market chaologists understand that unintended consequences befall the best of intentions on a recurring basis. Nations struggle daily with unstable conditions, mostly because of past, misguided policies. Every system, public or private, has an inbred tendency to engender the exact opposite of intended goals. If an agency has a policy to uplift the impoverished, almost inevitably the outcome will be the downtrodden being mired in even greater poverty. This is exactly what occurred after President Lyndon Johnson launched his popular campaign of "total victory" for the "War on Poverty" in 1964.

On the surface, Johnson's programs appeared noble in their quest to eliminate economic hardship for the poor. But ever since Roman times, political systems have found it advantageous to play the bread-and-circuses game. The Johnson administration excelled at these festivities, concocting a massive welfare program to eliminate poverty once and for all. Johnson submitted, and Congress enacted, more than one hundred major proposals for his anti-poverty agenda. Of course, with aid to poverty now nationalized, long-established groups dedicated to assisting the poor—community groups, churches, charities, and nonprofits—were pushed to the back burner.

So what happened? After over forty years and $8.9 trillion spent, the poverty rate has remained steady.*[19]* According to the U.S. Census Bureau, the poverty rate in the United States was 12.1 percent in 1969. It jumped up and down, until it peaked at 15.2 percent in 1983. By 2004, it was at 12.7 percent. Poverty did not decline as promised: it actually increased. The only things that shrank were citizens' wallets, as tax rates ballooned to pay for unsuccessful social-engineering programs.

And how much government assistance did the poor get? According to Peter G. Peterson, Secretary of Commerce under President Nixon, in *From Running on Empty*, "In 2002, out of $1.2 trillion in federal, state and local benefits, the poor received roughly $140 billion, according to the Census Bureau. That's about 12 cents of every full benefit dollar."[20] Interestingly, most nonprofit charities spend 75 percent to 85 percent of their money on program activities. However, in 1965, before government's federalization of charity had started, "70 cents of every dollar spent by the government to fight poverty went directly to poor people."[21]

Not only did the poor get a small percentage of government funds earmarked to fight poverty, but according to Peterson, "social-welfare programs no longer redistribute wealth in favor of low-income households. Total federal benefits to the affluent are at least as substantial as those to the needy. Among Social Security beneficiaries, for instance, households with incomes of $150,000 or more received, on the average, checks that are twice as large as those of households with incomes of less than $15,000."[22]

But who actually pays the highest percentage of their wages in taxes? It turns out that in California, the poorest of the poor bear the highest tax burden. But California is often cited as having done more than most states to address tax fairness. Still, according to the Matthew Gardner, executive director of the nonpartisan Institute on Taxation and Economic Policy in Washington, D.C., many states, including California, have a regressive "upside-down tax system. The more you earn, the less you pay in taxes." The California Budget Project agreed, asserting that "the poorest fifth of taxpayers in California pay 11.7 percent of their annual income for state and local taxes, which include income, sales, and excise taxes. In contrast, the richest 1 percent of taxpayers fork over 7.1 percent of their income. In the case of middle-income earners, they pay 9.5 percent of their income.[23]

Nor did government-operated education fare any better. Literacy rates were higher in 1840 than they are in 2011, despite the fact that government schooling systems were almost nonexistent for the first hundred years of United States history. Between 1800 and 1840, literacy in the Northern United States increased from 75 percent to 90 percent, and in the Southern from 60 percent to 81 percent, according to Sheldon Richman in *Separating School and State*.[24] In fact, by 1850, Massachusetts had a literacy rate of 98 percent. John Adams once observed that it was easier to locate a comet in the sky than to find an uneducated man in America.

But in 2011, not only have literacy rates plunged, but a high percentage of public school teachers fail to pass basic skills and subject matter tests that are often required for employment. "In Virginia, nearly one-third of aspiring teachers did not pass the Praxis test of basic skills in reading, writing, and math" in 1998.[25] Also in 1998, approximately 1,800 would-be teachers in Massachusetts took a first-ever high school level teacher's test. The failure rate was 59 percent. Equally stunning is the fact that the cities found doling out the most money per student—Washington, D.C., and New York City—produce the lowest scholastic results per graduating student, ranking near the bottom on almost every level of performance. The results from government-managed education have almost become a mathematical constant—the more money spent, the worse the performance.

Voted by the New York State Education Department as New York State Teacher of the Year in 1991, John Gatto points out in *The Underground History of American Education* that literacy rates have plunged in America since the 1930s. His example is the fourth-grade reading test given to U.S. military draftees. During World War II, 96 percent of draftees passed the simple test; 81 percent passed during the Korean War, and only 73 percent during the Vietnam Conflict.

In 1993, the National Adult Literacy Survey determined that only 3.5 percent of the American adult population were capable of literary skill adequate for traditional college study, compared to 30 percent in 1940.

The education establishment is repeatedly confounded when it is revealed that college graduates' reading proficiency continues to decline. "It's appalling—it's really astounding," said Michael Gorman, president of the American Library Association. "Only 31 percent of college graduates can read a complex book and extrapolate from it. That's not saying much for the remainder." Back in 1992, that figure was 40 percent of college graduates.[26]

A more ominous sign is the cheating scandal uncovered in 2011 in Atlanta, Georgia, where 178 public school teachers and principals were caught in a widespread scheme to cheat on the state-mandated Criterion-Referenced Competency Test.[27] The 800-page investigative report discovered that the cheating was systematic and was occurring in close to 80 percent of the schools examined. In many cases, teachers admitted to being intimidated or forced to help students cheat on the standardized tests. The report stated that "a culture of fear, intimidation and retaliation existed in Atlanta Public Schools, which created a conspiracy of silence." In one instance, "a principal forced a teacher to crawl under a table during a faculty meeting because that teacher's [students'] test scores were low."[28]

Superintendent Dr. Beverly L. Hall, who had been named the 2009 National Superintendent of the Year, became the center of the cheating scandal. According to the New York Times, "Dr. Hall's administration punished whistle-blowers, hid or manipulated information and illegally altered documents related to the tests, the investigation found."[29]

Even comedian Jay Leno took a dig at the scandal, joking: "You know who gets hurt by something like this? The kids. The kids are the ones who get hurt, because they're never going to learn how to cheat on their own."[30]

As government continues to intervene in education, the system loses its adaptive quality. It can no longer remain an independent structure of education, but becomes rather a systematic entrenchment of the political status quo, destined to fail at educating. Command-based systems inevitably collapse into unintended consequences of disastrous proportions. One of the biggest reasons for this is the problem of predictability.

Predictability—The Future Leaves No Footprints

Political theory would be fine in a perfect world, but in an uncertain one, it is a dangerous gamble. As historian William Durant wrote, "Inquiry is fatal to certainty."

The inquiring eye of science has demonstrated that long-term predictability is nearly nonexistent. One of the main obstacles to predicting the future is that information comes in extremes—either too much or too little. There is little middle ground.

Obviously, making predictions is difficult when information is not available. But the lack of accurate and meaningful information is not the only obstacle. It is a lack of perception of what the information should and can be. Often, one does not know what one does not know. Albert Einstein voiced this concern, and considered that the theories of physical reality extend further than observable events, although his theory of relativity is observer-centric.

In his conversation with Heisenberg in 1926, Einstein contended: "It is the theory which decides what can be observed."[31] In a sense, this statement is correct. Without knowing what to look for, how could anyone find what is not currently observable? To be able to predict, one must have some knowledge about what can be predicted. But uncertainty means that things could happen that are completely below the radar screen that occur in a way that nobody, in their wildest dreams, could have guessed. The problem has always been, not what *is* there, easily identified, but what is *not* readily observable. This is what makes predictability extremely unreliable. Ironically, it was his private conversation with Einstein that helped Heisenberg come up with certain aspects of his uncertainty principle.

The other extreme is just as problematic. Information overload can also lead to a paralysis in which nobody is certain of anything, because of mountains of often contradictory data. Stacks of papers published in fine print mix poorly with busy schedules and timetables. But this is the exact condition that legislators must endure on city, county, state, and federal levels. They are inundated with hundreds of pages of proposals, codes, and regulations on a daily or weekly basis. They rarely have the opportunity or patience to read and consider each and every page to glean potential consequences. In fact, most never read the bills that come across their desks. Instead, an overworked staff is responsible for analyzing piled-high volumes of nearly indecipherable bills and budget items. However, their primary duty is not to decipher future consequences to solve economic and societal problems, but rather to protect the political aspirations of their boss and to provide for their own job security.

In 2001, Congress passed the U.S.A. PATRIOT Act in response to the September 11 terrorist attacks. According to Congressman Ron Paul of Texas, the final revisions of this act that came out of the U.S. Senate were unavailable. He desperately tried to locate a copy. Congress would not wait, and instead voted for this bill without having seen the final version. In fact, Rep. Paul has disclosed that several Congressional colleagues told him personally that they believed the bill to be dangerous to civil liberties, and that they opposed it. And yet, they voted in favor of it, sight unseen, fearful of what their constituents might do, back home.

In some cases, bills are voted into law even before they have been written. During the 2009 budget meltdown in California, State Senator Abel Maldonado freely admitted, "We need to stop passing bills and budgets that aren't even written. We frequently vote on budgets in 'draft form,' meaning the language has not been finished."[32]

In 2010, U.S. Speaker of the House Nancy Pelosi, in a bout of honesty during debate over President Barack Obama's healthcare reform bill said, "We have to pass the bill so that you can find out what is in it, away from the fog of the controversy." With blindfolds tightly affixed, most lawmakers don't have the faintest idea what a bill actually says or what it will do.

As if that were not enough, Pelosi had proposed and seriously considered using the "deem and pass" tactic on that bill, which would have allowed it to become law without any Congressman actually having cast a vote. This gambit was not used after all for the passage of "ObamaCare," but many politicians argued that both parties had been guilty of this sort of political maneuvering in the past. The point now becomes obvious. What is the purpose of a legislative branch? If legislators don't read bills, write them, or vote for them, how can elected officials be considered representatives of the people?

Even when legislators are determined to do what is right, they are confronted by a wall of self-contradictory data and unpredictable consequences. And they are unlikely to make heads or tails out of economic trends, statistics, or changes. Political systems are primarily based on acquiring the reins of power, not on understanding the daily or long-term economic interactions of citizens. Pandering to voters counts more than sensible legislation; re-election money adds up more than the laws of supply and demand; and political expediency is more important than economic data. In the end, even those in the political landscape realize that nobody can declare precisely what effect a particular law will have in the future. Nonetheless, they toe the official party line and hope for economic conditions to favor the political party currently in the driver's seat. They know they are groping in the dark like everyone else. They know that the future leaves no footprints.

This lack of predictability is one of the major reasons that enacted laws have a high probability of resulting in the exact opposite of what the instigators had intended—a dynamic phenomenon called the "boomerang effect," sometimes referred to as the law of unintended consequences. Interestingly, the CIA coined their own word to refer to bad results from covert operations: blowback.

*****

The emergence of chaology is just the beginning of a new age of discovery. The knowledge gleaned from this new science will expand our understanding of how we think about science, society, and the clusters of individual parts that make up our world. Chaology will touch every field of study and eventually will redefine life and society, providing empowerment, connectivity, and self-governance.

1 John R. Platt, "Strong inference," *Science* 146 (3642). doi:10.1126/science.146.3642.347, 1964. Quote originally came from Chamberlin's article "The Method of Multiple Working Hypotheses," first published in the *Journal of Geology* in 1897.

2 James Gleick, *Chaos: Making a New Science,* Penguin Books (Non-Classics), 1988.

3 It is now acknowledged that the first person to understand chaos as a "dynamical instability" was the physicist Henri Poincaré (1854–1912) in the late 19th century. His references to chaos as a lack of order in systems that still obey particular laws laid the foundation for modern chaos theory.

4 Lao Tsu, *Tao Te Ching*, chapter 75. He also wrote that "The more prohibitions there are, the poorer the people will be."

5 Stephen H. Kellert, *In the Wake of Chaos: Unpredictable Order in Dynamical Systems*, University of Chicago Press, 1994.

6 Joseph Ford, *The New Physics*, Chapter 12: "What is Chaos, that we should be mindful of it?" edited by Paul Davies, Cambridge University Press, 1992.

7 M. Mitchell Waldrop, *Complexity: The Emerging Science at the Edge of Order and Chaos*, New York: Simon & Schuster, 1992.

8 Gleick, *Chaos: Making a New Science*, Penguin Books (Non-Classics), 1988.

9 "Meltdown at Three Mile Island," PBS Special for T*he American Experience,* WGBH Educational Foundation, A Steward/Gazit Production, Inc. Films, 1999.

10 Terry Pratchett, *Interesting Times*, HarperTorch, 1998.

11 John H. Holland, *Adaptation in Natural and Artificial Systems: An Introductory Analysis with Applications to Biology, Control, and Artificial Intelligence*, The University of Michigan Press, 1975, reprinted in 1992 under the MIT Press. Prof. Holland is considered the father of genetic algorithms, which are computer programs that evolve to optimize solutions.

12 Stuart Kauffman, *At Home in the Universe: The Search for the Laws of Self-Organization and Complexity,* Oxford University, 1995.

13 Ilya Prigogine and Isabelle Stengers, *Order out of Chaos*, New York: Bantam Books, 1984.

14 Sunil Jetley, "How Tough Is It to Start a Business in India Compared to That in America or China?" *India Daily,* August 10, 2005.

15 "Shadow economy growth is making life difficult for tax collectors and economists." *The Economist*, May 3, 1997.

16 Werner Heisenberg, *Über den anschulichen Inhalt der quantentheoretischen*

Kinematik und Mechanik, Z. Phys. Volume 43, 172-198, 1927. Physicists often call the uncertainty principle by its more descriptive name —the "principle of indeterminacy."

17 Heinz R. Pagels, The Cosmic Code: Quantum Physics as the Language of Nature, New York: Bantam, 1984.

18 Retrodiction is often used by scientists to test a theory. It is the act of making a prediction about a past event.

19 Jenifer Zeigler, *$9 Trillion Didn't End Poverty—What to Do?* September 2003, Foxnews.com. According to Zeigler, "In the past 40 years, we have spent at least $8.9 trillion (in constant 2003 dollars) on the 'war on poverty.' Isn't it time that one of the candidates admit we cannot spend our way out of poverty?" Zeigler is a welfare policy analyst at the Cato Institute.

20 "10 Partisan Myths," *Newsweek*, July 12, 2004.

21 Michael Tanner, *Replacing Welfare*, Cato Institute policy report, December 1996.

22 Peter G. Peterson, Running on Empty, reviewed in Newsweek, July 12, 2004.

23 George Avalos, "Poor in California bear greatest tax burden," *Contra Costa Times*, MediaNews, April 13, 2007. To be fair, high-income earners pay the lion's share of the California income tax, but only because they make more money.

24 Sheldon Richman, *Separating School and State: How to Liberate American Families*, Future of Freedom Foundation, 1994.

25 Dr. Abigail Thernstrom, Prof. of History at Harvard University, article from the Manhattan Institute, New York, Dec. 2003.

26 Lois Romano, "Literacy of College Graduates Is on Decline," *Washington Post*, December 25, 2005.

27 Christina Samuels, "80% of Atlanta schools cheated on testing, investigators find," *Seattle Times*, July 5, 3011.

28 Dorie Turner and Shannon McCaffrey, *Associated Press*, "Report: Atlanta superintendent knew about cheating," July 6, 2011.

29 Kim Severson, "Systematic Cheating Is Found in Atlanta's School System," *New York Times,* July 5, 2011.

30 Jay Leno, *The Tonight Show*, NBC, July 7, 2011.

31 Abdus Salam, *Unification of Fundamental Forces*, two 1968 lectures by W. Heisenberg, Cambridge University Press, 1990.

32 Abel Maldonado, "What went wrong, and how to fix it," *Monterey County Weekly*, May 28, 2009

2 System Failure: The Boomerang Effect

The more complex a system is, the more numerous are the types of fluctuations that threaten its stability. —Prigogine and Stengers

Science is competent to establish what is. It can never dictate what ought to be. —Ludwig von Mises

Science is organized unpredictability. —Freeman Dyson, physicist

Why did the shooting of hundreds of Russian protesters in 1905—an incident known as Bloody Sunday—produce the opposite of its desired effect, and significantly increase opposition to the Czar? Why did the unemployment rate for the disabled rise a few years after President George H. W. Bush signed the Americans with Disabilities Act (ADA) in 1990—a law enacted to improve working conditions for the disabled?[1] And why did illegal entry continue to increase after the U.S. Congress passed a series of reforms in 1992 designed to curb immigration from Mexico? After all, the decision–makers in Washington, D.C. had tripled the budget of the Immigration and Naturalization Service (INS), bringing it to $4 billion, and had doubled the number of border patrol agents, to 7,000. But the new law seemed only to do the exact opposite of its proponents' intent, contorting to a sort of "political jiu-jitsu," as coined by political scientist Gene Sharp.[2]

What these backfiring missteps reveal is that nature always sides with hidden flaws and uncertainty. As so aptly stated by Murphy's Law, "if anything can go wrong, it will." Things don't always go as planned, because complex systems operate in a specialization-vacuum mode in which information is often encapsulated—preventing or distorting feedback. Complexity clouds or camouflages what resources should be used, as well as what determines "the legitimate values of the system," contends systems scientist and professor C. West Churchman in *The Systems Approach*.[3]

In other words, bad information inevitably leads to bad choices. Worse still, most information is usually highly decentralized, based on the localized conditions, which makes feedback almost meaningless to systems dependent upon linear-inclined centralization. Even if a thread of information is particularly accurate, the possessor has little way of knowing its priority or importance. Complexity has the propensity to overload systems, making the relevance of a particular piece of information not statistically significant. And when an array of mind-numbing factors is added into the equation, theory and models rarely conform to reality. That is because the more complex the structure, the more vulnerable it becomes to system failure. But the complexity by itself is not the catalyst in which a system might crash. Rather, it is how the complexity emerges in a system that determines whether that system will do what it was intended to do or morph into an unworkable organization clogged by bottlenecks and blockages. Does the system emerge through a natural course of events vetted by trial and error, or does it emerge by artificial means that detach the system from its external, self-assembled process?

In 1936, the man most often credited for popularizing the concept of why things backfire, sociologist Robert K. Merton, referred to this phenomenon as "the law of unforeseen consequences." In an influential paper, "The Unanticipated Consequences of Purposive Social Action,"[4] Merton identified five sources of unanticipated consequences. The first two are the most relevant: ignorance and error. The third one, "imperious immediacy of interest," is a situation in which someone is so eager to do something that he will purposely ignore any possible failure from side effects. The next one involves America's old-fashioned Protestant work ethic. Labeling this concept "basic values," Merton wrote that asceticism "paradoxically leads to its own decline through the accumulation of wealth and possessions." The final source is the "self-defeating prediction." This unintended consequence occurs when predictions of possible future change cause people to alter their ways. Similar to a scientist's altering of an experiment simply by observing it, the prediction in and of itself can change the course of history, taking it to new, but unexpected alternatives.

In *Systemantics: How Systems Work and Especially How They Fail,* pediatrician John Gall took a hard-hitting approach to explaining why many large-scale international organizations fail. Gall contended that "the larger and more complex the system, the less the resemblance between the true function and the name it bears."[5] He maintained that "complex systems are beyond human capacity to evaluate," and that as they grow in size, they tend to oppose their stated function and begin to "encroach."

One of Gall's most ironic examples was the federal government's policy to subsidize farmers in order to prop up food prices, while simultaneously issuing food stamps to the poor because food prices are too high. Throw in the bizarre policy of funding the efforts of the National Institutes of Health to battle obesity, and it would appear that some sort of "mad politician disease" had contaminated Washington, D.C.

But Gall's greatest revelation was that complex systems tend to function as "problem reprocessing machines." When systems are unable to make progress (i.e., when they fail), administrators and central planners find it convenient to transform persistent problems into problems of another type, so as to make them almost undetectable to economic indicators. In other words, they misguide or relabel what the system was originally set up to do, validating the old adage, "Bureaucrats do not change the course of the ship of state—they merely adjust the compass." In this way, a failure can be redefined as having been a success, which coincidentally has the effect of preserving jobs for the bureaucracy and "staffocracy." Or, to put it in a more skeptical context, every system will do what it must to justify its own existence. In many cases, the biggest successes of government are actually failures that don't instantly materialize.

But relabeling failure as success has other problems. The double-edged sword cuts both ways. Actually, reaching the ultimate goal risks loss of one's source of income. If crime could be completely eradicated, would there still be a need for police? If fires no longer plagued mankind, would anyone require the services of firefighters? And if every possible crisis were to be amicably resolved, would the system of governance become obsolete and needless? Systems walk a fine line between success and failure. Too much of either one can lead to undesirable consequences. This aphorism perfectly reflects the "[Clay] Shirky Principle" whereby "institutions will try to preserve the problem to which they are the solution."

John Gall is best known for his Gall's Law, which states, "A complex system that works is invariably found to have evolved from a simple system that worked. A complex system designed from scratch never works and cannot be patched up to make it work. You have to start over with a working simple system."

Similarly, another popular law that explains why systems continuously fail has been attributed to science fiction writer Jerry Pournelle: the "iron law of bureaucracy." Pournelle argues that in "any bureaucratic organization there will be two kinds of people: those who work to further the actual goals of the organization, and those who work for the organization itself." The tendency is for the second type of person to gradually take control, moving the group in a direction counter to the organization's stated goals. After all, organizations are organized for the benefit of the organizers.

Another book dealing with failure is *Why Most Things Fail: Evolution, Extinction and Economics*, by Paul Ormerod,[6] who taught economics at the Universities of London and Manchester. Inspired by recent advances in evolutionary theory and biology, Ormerod writes:

> *Failure is pervasive. Failure is everywhere, across time, across place and across different aspects of life; 99.99 percent of all biological species that have ever existed are now extinct. More than 10 percent of all the companies in America disappear each year.*

Delving into the concepts of creative destruction and adaptive evolution, Ormerod argues that for an entity lacking the ability to evolve to meet new challenges, failure is almost unavoidable. He maintains that the best-laid plans do not provide a perfect equilibrium, but instead trap biological species and human systems within a continuity that's locked down and static. This situation makes long-term predictions almost useless. And the principle behind this is obvious: What you can't predict, you can't avoid. Although corporate executives plan ahead extensively, plants and animals do not. Yet companies are just as vulnerable to sudden extinction as was the dodo bird.

The System Failure Phenomenon

With almost surrealistic consistency, governmental policies, business projects, and everyday plans routinely backfire in grotesquely spectacular but often karmic ways. This particular phenomenon is now recognized as the "boomerang effect."

So what causes such boomerang effect episodes? Primarily, it is a system failure pumped up on steroids. These failures surface when new variables are forced into the dynamic mix of a complex system, often boomeranging into a result opposite of the expectation. This effect is similar to adverse side effects often seen in the medical field, except that undesirable outcomes may not mirror an exact opposite. For instance, the rationale behind the United States' invasion of Iraq in 2003 was to destroy weapons of mass destruction, liberate the Iraqis from a brutal dictatorship, and put the country on a stable, democratic footing. There was no talk of stopping a civil war, since no infighting existed prior to the invasion. And yet, the U.S. intervention into the Iraqi political arena precipitated a civil war between Sunni and Shiite factions, a side effect that nobody had been trying to prevent, since the corresponding aftermath had not been a predesigned objective.

System Failure: The Boomerang Effect

Under complexity science and system theories, boomerangs occur when systems and subsystems become disoriented and disturbed after new variables are forcibly inserted into a working system.[7] It is analogous to forcing water and oil to mix—two substances that will resist the change and eventually separate into incompatible layers again. New variables tend to compromise a system's state of balance, pushing it toward an extreme and preventing a counterbalancing disequilibrium from coming into play. Futurist R. Buckminster Fuller referred to this balancing act between opposing forces as "compression" and "tension" under the term he coined "tensegrity."

Chaologists regard "systems" as self-maintaining networks that emerge when particular elements weave together, form common patterns, and display certain properties and behaviors. Similar to the mechanics of biological evolution, most systems emerge under their own autonomous means, known as autopoiesis. They respond to their environment by constantly evolving to adapt to external challenges.

So, what would happen if something were to interfere with a system's natural autopoiesis process—invading or blocking its self-operating activities? The probable outcome would be a system failure. With little or no means to self-adjust, a complex internal system would be unable to discover the counterbalancing dynamics that made its existence possible in the first place. For instance, luminous balls of plasma—stars—operate under two opposite, but counterbalancing dynamics: gravity and nuclear fusion. If suddenly a new variable were thrust into the mix, stars might not operate as they do today. In other words, there is no preset blueprint to create what has never been attempted before.

The same goes for weather. In climatology, temperature instability is the driving factor for weather conditions. In order to develop thermal differentials (or "convection cycle") that hurricanes need for creating violent storms, they require warm water below and cooler air above. Temperature equilibrium is unable to feed the engine that drives weather. All complex systems exist in perpetual disequilibrium, between attractive and repulsive forces.

But there is more. Since complex systems are riddled with unknown factors, microscopic interactions, and often unforeseeable forces, the reaction to new ingredients can inadvertently energize something unwanted, resembling the random scattering of balls across a billiards table after the break shot. That is because a complex system, according to chemists George M. Whitesides and Rustem F. Ismagilov, has "multiple pathways by which the system can evolve."[8]

Reconfiguring Dynamics

When a system must digest new variables or energy, it has to reconfigure its structure to alter its long-term behavior. At this point, systems tend to overcompensate, fluctuating in wild swings to dissipate the new energy while attempting to return to its original operating structure. A cascading failure is highly probable during this self-reconfiguration toward stability, because of the incompatibility of the new with the old. Either bifurcation causes a new system to emerge, or the old system dies. In either case, the outcome is often unexpected or unwanted; when applied to human society, an expletive is commonly uttered in frustration, as in, "Some damn fool has broken another law of unintended consequences!"

But why is the boomerang effect so ubiquitous? Primarily because complex systems' properties are not fully explained by adding up their component parts. Generally speaking, complex systems are interdependent and adaptive, with networking automata and homeostatic feedback loops, but paradoxically, they tend to display both heterogeneous and homogenous elements—meaning that they exhibit both diverse and uniform traits. That is because complexity consist of a welter of interacting nodes and overlapping functions whose combined complexity approaches the level of infinity. These interconnected systems and subsystems not only display paradoxical behavior but appear, at times, to have little in common with each other. Hence the term, "complexity systems."

Chaologists who study human society as a complex system—a discipline known as "social complexity" or "social chaology"—tend to gravitate toward the research of systemic failures so commonly found in command-and-control systems. Unlike others complex systems, political systems peddle the totality of dominance, seeking to forge a mechanistic society, preconceived and premeditated, all without the benefit of synergic emergence, autopoiesis, or open dissipative structures. Instead, a political system will latch onto already established social systems, and mandate top-down edicts that are often at odds with its own bottom-level body politic. In this sense, "boomerang effect" describes unwanted consequences that surface when political authorities overrule the natural, self-organizing mechanism of human society.

In a political and psychological context, the boomerang effect often occurs when people react against a physical force depriving them of their freedom to choose. Psychological experiments have shown that restricting a person's self-determining choice can cause a negative emotional state, culminating in anti-conformity defiance. This threat to volition induces some people to value that which is forbidden, although without the limitation, they might never have become interested in the prohibited matter. According to "reactance theory," when people feel that their actions are being unjustly threatened, they will behave in such a way as to regain control by avoiding compliance. In the end, the boomerang effect presents a no-win situation; compliance to rules is reduced while the public feels compelled to engage in possibly dangerous or anti-social behavior.[9]

The Political Systems of Command and Control

The reclusive American novelist Thomas Pynchon wrote, in *Gravity's Rainbow*: "If they can get you asking the wrong questions, they don't have to worry about answers." Those working in political systems excel at "spinning" the issues, misdirecting the public debate, cloaking hidden agendas behind hidden agendas, and introducing questions framed in such a way as to allow only for one-sided answers. In such a sterile environment, politicos are predisposed to ask only questions they want answered. By manipulating the meaning of language, political structuralists can make their dogmatic worldview more palatable to the public. As with any system based on deception, governing hierarchies have a vested interest in getting their subordinates to believe in the "desirability as well as the necessity of political systems."[10]

This is why politics is a revolving door. But this revolving door is usually rigged. Political systems are set up to game society with the skill of a carnival huckster. No matter for whom you vote, the government always wins. The institutionalized abuse found in governmental systems always remains intact, despite endless changes of leadership. The changing of the political guard is mostly symbolic. The promise of change is used merely to secure public approval and compliance. People must be made to feel that they have a voice, in order to prevent demands for real change. And if real change somehow makes it to the forefront, it usually comes in the form of increased government size, debt, spending and scope.

In democratic countries, elections provide a forum for budding political cognoscenti to charge "misconduct" against those currently piloting the ship of state. And such misconduct is easily identifiable because it is inherent in all political systems, based on monopolistic practices. As Charlie Reese, a former columnist for the *Orlando Sentinel*, pointed out: "Politicians are the only people in the world who create problems and then campaign against them."[11]

These reformers, strutting around as though they are outsiders, tout "change we can believe in" and solemnly promise to sweep clean the rampant corruption tainting every corner of government. But according to Ukrainian author Leonid S. Sukhorukov: "Politicians are all the same. They promise reforms then reform their promises."

Some politicians, usually those in the temporarily out-of-power party, resort to high-sounding principles and anti-government sentiments, promising to curtail the concentration of state power. But this approach is pure, sleight-of-hand, shuffling of cards. The question never asked: Why do the titanic policies of political commanders always collide with every iceberg in the ocean, regardless of who captains the ship?

Not only do political ships of state crash and sink regardless of leadership, but their crews are apt to be frolicking aboard while their vessels slip to a watery grave. Replacing one sinking politician with another during times of crisis is like stocking a new line of candy bars in a broken vending machine. Little can be done by politicos to alter a broken system that nobody can readily change. But the masses are led to expect big changes from the next crop of political aspirants. In some ways, this attitude resembles a spouse who remains loyal to an abusive relationship. No matter how abusive the system, the populace can be easily manipulated, mesmerized or intimidated by those with the power to make offers that few dare to refuse.

The machinery of government emits an aura of dominance and organizational prominence that prods people to do things they would not normally do. From the egotistical Napoleon marching his army into the cold interior of Russia, to the charismatic Jim Jones urging his flock to drink poisoned Kool-Aid at his communal settlement in Guyana, most political leaders glisten with faux promises of greatness. And such promises inevitably degenerate into limited access of movement, information and wealth creation; which affords only the wealthy the potency to live their dreams in a highly intrusive and regulated environment.

But what makes political systems so prone to failure? Some point to the fact that these systems are awkwardly rigid, saddled with egotistical personalities, and besieged by worries that others are jockeying to wrestle away their precious job. In sharp contrast, most other complex systems—immune systems, insect colonies, cells, biospheres, ecosystems, the brain, evolutionary processes, artificial life, and so forth—exhibit a natural tendency to adapt, evolve, and cooperate "in parallel, constantly acting and reacting to what the other agents are doing."[12] But political systems need not adapt; they simply need to know how to acquire and maintain top-down, vertical hegemony. After all, political monopolies have no pressing need to be successful.

Although representative democracies have several scales of organization—local and provincial jurisdiction—based on John Locke's "consent of the governed" and federalism, they are problematic. Individuals have little say or control over the direction of political systems, with their enormous complexity. The "fractal sharing" of political authority rarely scales down to the foundational core, individual electors. Instead, like an ever-expanding Big Bang universe, "the political scaling of authority" always accelerates into a pyramid-peaking *apparat* of elitism and consolidation of power, hurling the consensus of the many farther into the outer reaches of obscurity. And as the politically charged universe of intrusive rules, edicts, and laws expands, the sovereign authority of individual agents shrinks—inciting frustration, hostility, and volatile conditions.

Professor Butler Shaffer, author of *Calculated Chaos*, has devoted most of his professional life to analyzing the deficits of political systems. Teaching at Southwestern Law School in Los Angeles, Shaffer wrote in 2004 that "vertically-structured political systems are not only incapable of generating social order, but invariably produce disorder. In a complex world, only unstructured, spontaneous practices are capable of generating order, a truth that can be glimpsed by comparing marketplace economic behavior with systems of state planning."[13]

Social chaologists acknowledge that political systems have the unique characteristic of encroaching upon self-assembled social systems on a massive scale, treating society as if government were its affable twin brother. In sharp contrast to the *modus operandi* of swarm dynamics, political bodies are ill-equipped to protect the integrity of their components and lack the collective wisdom for synchronization. Instead, highly layered command-based systems invade, institutionalize, and indoctrinate society with centralized directives, straitjacket bureaucracies, and self-serving officialdom. These systems hungrily feast on what others have created, cannibalizing other people's resources like a tribe of pragmatic headhunters. With a thirst for resources, they send "swarms of Officers to harass our people and eat out their substance," as was expressed in the American Declaration of Independence. As if that were not enough, command-based systems leak energy and grind down to molasses-slow speed, behaving more like the proverbial deer caught frozen by oncoming headlights than a fast-reacting force to resolve a crisis.

Even leading intellects from the eighteenth century recognized these political traits. One French economist, Vincent de Gournay (1712-1759), had numerous confrontations with his nation's political system and its regulatory infrastructure. After butting heads with French bureaucrats, he observed that they "are not appointed to benefit the public interest, indeed the public interest appears to have been established so that the offices might exist."[14] Closed-ended and fixed, political systems have little capability to do anything, other than repeatedly fail to achieve their stated objectives. They become mired in a complex web of ham-handed status quo, special-interest string pulling, self-survival instincts, and political maneuvering that magnifies friction and shatters cohesion. These traits become far more pronounced when political systems attempt to collectivize and criminalize society in a gambit to pit people against each other. And these personal in-fighting slugfests are not for the fainthearted.

One would think that any system that continued to perpetuate poor achievements of such staggering proportions would simply die and become extinct like any other biological system that failed to be self-supporting. But parasitical systems need not be successful in their own right; they only require a way to become attached to healthier systems. With the power to make others subservient to their needs, political self-seekers are free to systematically milk friend and foe as though society were a cash-cow repository. Even in modern democratic regimes, political systems tend to mimic the mannerisms of organized crime, prepared to brandish the instruments of physical force—the gun in the room—if all other avenues fail to provide what they want.

But the greatest reason for political system failures is the illusion that governmental officials can correctly target and control future events. Their operators not normally being known as masters of clairvoyance, political systems are regularly used in attempts to resolve intricate problems in society, as if those running them had intimate knowledge of a precise and stationary certainty. Butler Shaffer argues that "the state endeavors to reinforce the impression that it is *controlling* that which determines events."[15] Obviously, it can't and doesn't.

Political systems are likely to misidentify fast-moving causes and their solutions. One reason for this is that most governments are all too willing to sacrifice long-term solutions for short-term fixes. But the most common reason is that political leaders are neither storehouses of knowledge nor far-sighted visionaries. And when they go after either real or imaginary crises, they face an uphill battle. That is because problems and possible solutions do not remain stationary; they move, fluctuate, and mutate. Since it is difficult to hit a moving target, a legislated or dictated action usually fails to pinpoint the intended target and thus misses its mark by a wide margin. If course, that is because the original cause or causes will have darted out of range. Not only will this lack of precision ensure the failure of legislative laws, but it has the potential to bring about far worse problems: pursuit of the wrong targets.

Boomerang Effect Mechanics

The mechanics of the boomerang effect embody the fact that increased complexity leads to increased instability and decreased reliability. The law of unintended consequences cannot be revoked. Logically, one thousand pages of detailed verbiage enacted for a particular law will create more entangled interaction and therefore provoke more breakdowns, misunderstanding, and disorder, than a one-page law. Clearly, simplicity has a greater chance of success than complexity. Fewer moving parts will result in less breakage, deterioration, and failure.

For instance, the U.S. Constitution is a model of brevity, clarity and readability. Originally written on four large pages, this document equates to only seven to ten pages long, typeset to today's standards, with another seven to ten pages of amendments. The U.S.A. PATRIOT Act, signed into law after the September 11, 2001 attacks on the World Trade Center and the Pentagon, has 342 pages.[16] The European Constitution signed in 2004 but subject to ratification by member states, is an almost unreadable tome of legal language running around 300 pages with another 400 articles[17] of legalese—appendices, comments, and declarations, which has since been expanded to hundreds of additional pages.[18] The European Constitution is over 60,000 words versus a modest 4,400 words for the original U.S. Constitution, without amendments.[19] The "No Child Left Behind Act of 2001" legislation exceeds 1000 pages.[20] The "ObamaCare" healthcare reform law of 2010 is a whopping 2,500-plus pages that calls for 99-plus new federal board, commission, and agencies.[21] And according to *Time* magazine, "The federal code (plus IRS rulings) is now 72,536 pages in total," which is massive compared to what the magazine calls the "statist French" who have "a tax code of 1,909 pages."[22]

When government attempts to achieve narrow, precision-based results in a dynamic environment, the outcome can only be a wild, shotgun spray of side effects—wounding many innocent bystanders in the process. The truth of the matter is that nobody actually controls a massive, slumbering behemoth like government. It is far easier to put government in motion than to achieve specific control over its direction. The real trick is to get out of its way when it begins to steamroll across the lawn and into people's homes.

Consider the numerous results of well-funded government programs that are designed to help society. One particular program—the treatment of recidivism—is conducted in prison systems to make prisoners become better citizens. Billions have been spent to reduce the recidivism of convicted and imprisoned criminals. These expensive programs are designed to rehabilitate prisoners so that they will not engage in the same criminal activity after they have been released back into society. But in a scathing 2007 report by California Inspector General Matthew Cate cited evidence that the billions spent to reduce recidivism had boomeranged. In that report, Cate documented a complete breakdown in the prison recidivism program. He reported that "the recidivism rates for prisoners enrolled in two of the largest in-prison substance abuse programs were actually higher than those of a control group that did not receive the treatment."[23] In other words, the billions spent since 1989 in California to rehabilitate prisoners and get them off drugs actually made them more inclined to abuse drugs after they were released from prison. In response to the report, Governor Arnold Schwarzenegger appointed a new director and changed the name of the program.

Political Remedies and Global Warming

Groucho Marx came up with a memorable witticism concerning the contorted nature of politics. He quipped, "Politics is the act of looking for trouble, finding it everywhere, diagnosing it incorrectly, and applying the wrong remedies." Amazingly, a comedian was more accurate at exposing the inner workings of the political system than were many ivory-tower political scientists.

A good example of Groucho Marx's interpretation of politics can be seen in the hot, politically turbulent debate concerning the causes of so-called global warming. In typical fashion, politicians, media pooh bahs, and bureaucratic commissions have misidentified the problem and are working feverishly to apply the wrong remedies. The ecological-political establishment, led by former Vice President Al Gore, claims that man-made carbon dioxide (CO_2) is the main culprit in global warming and that new government policies and taxation must be put into place before the world suffers catastrophic flooding, severe droughts, rising sea levels, lasting hunger, and economic chaos. Some alarmists actually predict the end of humanity within a couple of decades.

System Failure: The Boomerang Effect

But the father of chaos theory, Edward Lorenz, saw climate as "a complex, non-linear, chaotic object" that defies long-term prediction. In a 1963 issue of *Journal of the Atmospheric Science*, Lorenz wrote, "Prediction of the sufficiently distant future is impossible by any method, unless the present conditions are known exactly. In view of the inevitable inaccuracy and incompleteness of weather observations, precise, very-long-range weather forecasting would seem to be non-existent."[24]

Moreover, ice-core samples dating back up to 600,000 years give conflicting evidence about whether mankind is responsible for warming climates. All records of ice cores, including those drilled at the Vostok site in Antarctica, show that increases in CO_2 lag behind warming spells, by an average of 800 years. This pattern suggests that rising temperatures are responsible for the rise of CO_2 levels in the atmosphere, not the reverse. Leading archaeological climatologist Ian Clark, a professor of earth sciences at the University of Ottawa, disputed that CO_2 is warming the climate, along with more than 17,000 other scientists.[25] Professor Clark pointed out that "you can't say that CO_2 can drive climate; it certainly did not in the past... CO_2 clearly cannot be causing temperature changes; it is a product of temperature—it's following temperature changes."[26]

Even the father of scientific climatology, and professor emeritus at the University of Wisconsin, Reed Bryson, has called man's contribution to global warming "tiny," comparing it to the likes of "an elephant charging in and you worry about the fact that there is a fly sitting on his head."[27]

So why is there such a wide disparity of opinions? Who is right? Since climatology is a complex system, scientists must consider a host of changing parameters and interdependent variables that can generate interactions of unforeseeable consequences. Consider the climatic determinants: ocean currents, cosmic rays, magnetic fields, sun spot activity, solar radiation, axial tilt, earth's wobble, vegetation coverage, solar winds, humidity, cloud cover, water vapors, ocean memory, hothouse emissions, aerosol particles, dust storms, evaporation, convection, and volcanoes, to name a few. There are so many interlocking and overlapping systems and subsystems that a computer model would be hard-pressed to pinpoint one overwhelming factor for global increases in temperature, unless someone plugged in fudge factors (parameterization). And yet, the political appointees at the United Nations Intergovernmental Panel on Climate Change (IPCC) submitted a report on February 2, 2007 stating with "more than 90 percent confidence" that mankind is the main culprit for the global warming, due to increases of anthropogenic CO_2.[28]

Another way to look at the long-range predictability of climate is to compare it to the three-body problem. Scientists are able to determine the position and velocity of two celestial objects with fair accuracy—for instance, the earth orbiting the sun. But throw another body into the mix, and the predictability of their motion is impossible to forecast (except in certain special cases). Under complexity science, the more interacting factors, the more unpredictable and irregular the outcome. To be succinct, the greater the complexity, the greater the unpredictability. With up to fifty or more factors involved in climate change, how is it possible to make exact analytical calculations? This is why chaology relies on the properties of probability to estimate future events.

To some extent, mankind's industrialization of the world must have an effect on climate. But under complexity science, where so many variables are in a state of flux, the probability that one factor has a 90 percent responsibility for a particular action or reaction is extremely remote. Carbon dioxide is a trace gas, a minor component of the earth's atmosphere—approximately 0.039 percent. And of that infinitesimal amount, human-induced CO_2 makes up less than 1/20, depending on the data source. Under the basic laws of probability, such a small amount of anthropogenic CO_2 should have an almost negligible effect on climate. The butterfly effect theory asserts that small variations in initial conditions can have large-scale outcomes, but the probability of ever reaching a "peak proportional outcome" almost totally responsible for a worldwide catastrophe is marginal. Under classical probability theory, the chance of an event occurring is defined as:

> *The ratio of the number of cases favorable to the event, to the number of all cases possible.*

Not only does anthropogenic CO_2 warming have a low probability, but valuable time and money has been wasted in pursuing the wrong target.

So, what is the right target? With so many interweaving variables, an all-inclusive answer would be almost impossible to calculate. Some scientists, including astrophysicist Nir Shaviv, have pointed to solar activity combined with the activities of cosmic rays and cloud formation. After all, the sun accounts for 99.8 percent of the solar system's mass. One solar flare can release as much energy as a billion one-megaton nuclear bombs.[29] In fact, the 2005 data from NASA's Mars Global Surveyor and Odyssey missions reveal that the ice caps near Mars' south pole had diminished for the past three summers, concurrent with the heating up of other planets. Habibullo Abdussamatov, head of space research at St. Petersburg's Pulkovo Astronomical Observatory in Russia, said in 2007 that "the Mars data is evidence that the current global warming on Earth is being caused by changes in the sun."[30] Interestingly, experts made similar dire predictions of an impending ice age during the cooling trend from 1940 to 1975.

Although some climatologists have pointed to natural long-term climatic cycles, others suggest that methane might play an important role. Until recently, scientists believed that the main sources of methane were flatulent cows, belching pigs, and dead vegetation. But conventional belief has been recently turned on its head. According to Frank Keppler, an environmental engineer at the Max Planck Institute for Nuclear Physics in Heidelberg, Germany, his research team has recently discovered that living vegetation also releases methane into the atmosphere.[31] The *New Scientist* reported in 2006 that this source of methane is "no small amount either—between 10 and 30 percent of all the methane pumped into the atmosphere. One reason why we may have missed this 'minor detail' is that we know of no physiological reason why plants should make methane."[32]

Ironically, this new discovery creates even more confusion in government's attempts to stop, regulate, or stabilize global warming. The problem is that living trees are considered an excellent and natural way for nature to soak up CO_2. Under the Kyoto protocols, nations are permitted and encouraged to plant more forests to mitigate man-made emissions of CO_2. But methane is a more potent greenhouse gas than CO_2. It is very likely that planting more trees could, at least in the eyes of those advocating action to prevent global warming, produce more heat on the earth. Complexity strikes again.

Another flip-flopping effect that surfaced from governmental programs to stop global warming occurred in England. In 2001, the British parliament introduced a tax on vehicles according to their CO_2 emissions. This legislation was enacted to encourage drivers to switch over to diesel-powered vehicles, since these produce 21 percent less CO_2 than gasoline-powered vehicles produce. And sure enough, consumers voted with their wallets and bought more diesel cars. By 2005, diesel ownership increased by over 20 percent. But political leaders had failed to realize that those diesel-powered vehicles "emit more particulates, which can cause respiratory and heart problems." Two scientists, physics professor Hadi Dowlatabadi and Eric Mazzi at the University of British Columbia in Vancouver, Canada, decided to study the effect of this policy. The conclusions were revealing. "They estimated that the switch to diesel will reduce total CO_2 emission between 2001 and 2020 by up to 7 megatonnes, but raise particulates by 12 kilotonnes, causing 90 extra deaths each year."[33]

Political systems have a soft spot for the Chicken Little *panique du jour*. Whether the world is allegedly coming to an end because of Islamic terrorists, human-induced global warming, avian flu pandemics, flesh-eating bacteria, Ebola fever, outbreaks of SARS, or weapons of mass destruction, political officials and sycophants have a vested interest in scaring the public to death in order to maintain a firm grip on society. This is a far cry from the primary purpose of an organizational system—to provide the means to satisfy the parts that make up the whole. With few exceptions, the upper echelons of political systems feel a duty to herd the lower ant-heap stratum toward a predetermined direction, to ward off so-called imminent threats. Unfortunately, these political opportunists usually frame their argument in ideology, not facts or the scientific method. And if the lower-level peons blindly march in lockstep, the boomeranging repeatedly litters the beaten path with ruined lives and bankrupted economies. Whatever direction politics takes the issue of global warming, it is almost assured that this supposed crisis will politicize science, enrich the well–connected, increase the authority of governments, and do little to cool the globe.

Losing Control of the Steering Wheel

It is common for political maestros and reigning pundits to step where wise men fear to tread. With reckless abandon, short-sightedness, and a flair for extravagant spending of other people's money, there is no end to what political commissars will compel, in the name of the common good.

Officials running one city in Southern California decided that they knew how to take control of the financial steering wheel: make money by becoming a public insurance company. In 1993, the city council of Gardena, a Los Angeles suburb of 60,000, put into motion a plan to establish the Municipal Mutual Insurance Company. In their reports to their citizens, they expected to rake in large profits for the city by selling coverage to other municipalities, plus the plan would lower the city's insurance bill.[34] Predictions were off a little. By 2005, the company was under state supervision while the city officials were considering declaring bankruptcy, raising taxes, or closing down whole city departments. As the debt ballooned to over $25 million, there was no money to fix potholes, sewer lines, or any other infrastructure. Frustrated shopkeepers and citizens thought about leaving the city.

The city council had originally thought that it would be a snap to turn government investments into substantial profits by issuing bonds. According to their predictions, the city would have $50 million in business within a few years, with over a million in profits. City Hall's calculations were dead wrong. The venture lost money from day one. Even several large underwriters solicited by the city balked at the proposal, considering the venture far too risky. Finally, a determined city council reworked their rules and offered to pay $500,000 in fees to lure an underwriter. It worked, but the city could not persuade other cities to purchase insurance coverage, which was required to pay off the bonds. When that venture failed, the city offered home loans to residents, a program which also failed to produce good results. The city lost over $900,000 in the first year of that operation. Eventually, the city had to refinance its debt load by increasing its debt amount, which, one city official joked, was like using one credit card to pay off another. Despite the losses, the underwriter earned millions in consulting and refinancing fees, while citizens were left with the feeling that they had been conned.

Not one person was indicted for the city's insurance company failure. The former mayor, a schoolteacher, mentioned that he wished he had been "more sophisticated in the ways of business." Years earlier, a group of alarmed businessmen had warned the city fathers about the problems of dabbling in insurance, implying that they were opening a can of worms. One local insurance salesman told Gardena's city manager that they were "going down the wrong path."[35]

Gardena's financial troubles represent again how political high priests will believe they can accomplish any miraculous feat, until a binge of spectacular failures hits the newsstand. But for those alarmed by seeing such patterns week after week, these debacles by authorities cannot be explained away as having been simple incompetence.

Government Conspiracies

There are countless examples of incompetence and outright corruption in command-based political systems—as common as dandelions sprouting in a fallow farm field. They are so rampant that many outraged citizens arrive at one possible conclusion: it must all be a government conspiracy of epic proportions. Generally, it is not. Conspiracies require competency. Government agencies do not come close to the professional millisecond precision of *Mission Impossible* that is needed to pull off savvy conspiratorial feats. Most people can barely run their own lives, let alone orchestrate a secret international conspiracy.

The boomerang effect best explains why slapstick comedians are not the only ones to foolishly shoot themselves in the foot. The nature of government is to do what is wrong for the wrong reason at the wrong time, while believing in its own exalted sainthood. Even Albert Einstein once wrote that "any government is certain to be evil to some extent."[36]

Command-based systems simply have a strong addiction to act in a self-destructive manner by feeding on their own flesh and that of those within reach. Analogous to the natural process of dry-rot, political bodies do not generally or intentionally plot seditious activities to devour the greatness of a country or its people. It just seems that way. Rather, they cast about for a means to live off the public treasury at the expense of others. And in that pursuit, they sing alongside the choir of good intentions and doublespeak that always seems to glorify government largesse.

While those running political systems often encourage feeding frenzies at the public trough in order to gain voter popularity, the citizenry find it difficult to resist the lure of getting something for nothing. Thinking that the public treasury has unlimited funds, high-minded idealists overwhelm the populace with delusions of grandeur. Soon, the common belief has become the fallacy that every social and economic affliction can be eradicated, if only enough resources were allocated or the right people were elected. As more pockets are picked clean and economic activity is restrained, corruption supplants honesty. As have-nots begin to outnumber haves, political instability overpowers natural order. The system of governance becomes too complex and unmanageable for all the freebies promised to be delivered. Good intentions or not, political systems degenerate into a prolific breeding ground of civil strife, back-stabbing hypocrisy, high-level malfeasance, and potential dictatorship, all struggling to remain afloat in choppy waters. This effect is probably the root cause for the popular aphorism, "The road to Hell is paved with good intentions."

Planned Chaos

Often attributed to Ludwig von Mises of the Austrian school of economics, the concept of the boomerang effect is most conspicuous when physical force is applied in large doses. When Gandhi's followers were beaten mercilessly by English police during the early 1930s in India, the result was opposite of what had been expected by the government. British officials thought that beatings would stop the nonviolent protests. Instead, the police violence caused the movement for India's independence to surge across the entire nation, and it eventually weakened British resolve.

In *Why Government Doesn't Work*,[37] Harry Browne (1933-2006) attributed the boomerang effect to what he calls the "dictator syndrome": the mistaken view that a piece of legislation that a person supports will accomplish its intended purpose, as though a particular individual citizen possessed any dictatorial or omnipotent powers. Such notions are extremely naïve, considering the haphazard and botched manner in which potential laws are enacted. Whatever emerges from the process will likely resemble a bastardized version of the original idea, if not its very opposite, bringing to mind Otto von Bismarck's observation that to retain respect for laws and sausage, one should not look too closely at how they are made. And he was right. All too often the legislative panacea disintegrates into a confusing and disorderly jumble—a sort of man-made chaos that fails to adhere to any physical law, such as the laws of thermodynamics or the general theory of relativity. This type of human-crafted chaos is often referred to as "planned chaos," a term coined by von Mises, who understood that order comes from complex "adaptive" systems, while unstable conditions surge from complex "structured" systems.

Interestingly, the Soviet Union observed this overplanned, man-made chaos in its own socialized backyard, during the 1980s. The official government newspaper *Pravda* published a report in 1988 bemoaning the poor condition of the country's socialist economy. The paper editorialized: "Not one of the 170 essential sectors has fulfilled the objectives of the Plan a single time over the last 20 years...this has brought about a chain reaction of hardship and imbalance which has led to 'planned anarchy'....the disequilibrium has affected every pore of our economy, and has become legendary."[38]

The "planned anarchy" that destabilized—and eventually brought down—the Soviet Union was exacerbated by central planners' determination to move society in a particular direction. Often under a hex of myopic hubris, political policymakers lack the empirical clarity that can prevent systems from becoming hopelessly lost, while cranking out collateral damage along the way. That is because political structures have a natural impetus to steer society with short-term blinders, resulting in long-term "mission drift."

Central planners are ambiguous about the dangers of mission drift. They will have departed the crime scene long before the chalked outlines of victims' bodies appear. By the time historians discover the incriminating evidence, it will be too late to prosecute the perpetrators. Once government has dug in and bankrolled Taj Mahal monuments and entitlement programs, nothing on earth can pry them loose. Governmental programs never die; they just change their names.

Central Planners and Linear Modeling

Central planners regularly stumble under the influence of politicalization, polarization, and institutionalization—a recipe for disaster, especially when trying to micromanage socioeconomic programs for large, interdependent populations. With centralization as the guiding blueprint, government-inspired projects are designed to precise parameters, instead of being designed to allow complex systems to evolve within an event-driven architecture. Viewing society as "infinitely malleable," central planners work with static and invariant simulations, gathering data from scripted and approved sources and eventually coming up with conclusions derived from assumptions already built into the system.[39]

Expecting predictable and infallible results, state planners routinely find themselves shooting in the dark, and out of touch with the public. Vertical hierarchies resist taking into account real-world trial-and-error verification or observational testing made by outside-the-box skeptics. Further, modeling usually mimics only particular, isolated phenomena, while harboring a hidden bias against certain repeatable observations. But even if planners were to consider heuristic data, which statistics would they highlight and input into their simulations? After all, they are cherry-picking data within their scope of pre-established parameters, categories, and expectations. Anything outside their comfort zone that appears remotely unorthodox is simply culled.

But there are other problems with modeling. Political agencies spend an inordinate amount of time writing and rewriting policies with little practical content. They engage in long discussions and issue vague policy decisions, but the process diverts from the essential question: What is the problem? A problem cannot be solved if it is never confronted directly. Then again, maybe solving problems is never the real intent. The New Zealand economist Brian Easton has mused over this dilemma, concluding that it is easy for the public sector to officiate backward scenarios where "policy defines the problem."[40] That is, the official rule book is written in such a way that problems are always unsolvable, because they are always misidentified—the perfect recipe for system failure. Easton attributed this phenomenon to Gilling's Law, which states: "The way the game is scored, shapes the way the game is played."[41]

System Failure: The Boomerang Effect

Consider some of the poorly designed projects that have marred central planners' reputations. In 2005, the U.S. Congress passed the Transportation Equity Act, which earmarked more than $223 million for a "'bridge to nowhere' that would connect Ketchikan, Alaska, to an offshore island where 50 people live...."[42] (The proposed Gravina Island Bridge would have replaced a ferry that charged $6.00 per car and took 15 to 30 minutes to cross.)

In the Soviet Union, central planners excelled at designing infrastructure projects with little economic viability. The Baikal-Amur Mainline Railway (BAM), a 2500-mile railroad line from Central Russia to the Pacific Ocean, was one of the most costly construction projects in postwar Soviet history. To date, the railroad has endured nothing but huge losses. The plan was to open the frigid and unpopulated eastern sector of Siberia to economic development. "According to the experts, the railway has expected load capacity of less than 10–15 percent."[43]

Another grandiose Soviet-era project was to divert the course of the Amu Darya and Syr Darya rivers through an extensive canal system for agricultural development. It slowly caused the Aral Sea to lose three-fifths of its water, destroyed a large fishing industry, and rendered much of the nearby land infertile due to windblown toxic salt and fertilizers. The United Nations has called this failed water project man's greatest ecological disaster. Soviet central planners wanted to transform Uzbekistan into a major agricultural center, concentrating on cotton, at the expense of all other crops. Besides the overuse of pesticides, the region experienced massive soil erosion, because those operating the collectivized farms failed to practice crop rotation. Many fields became barren, too contaminated to grow anything. According to the PBS television series *Journey to the Planet*, "dried-out canals scar the landscape. Deprived of water, river traffic is nonexistent—abandoned cargo boats litter the shoreline—mute testimony to a misguided agricultural policy. And a river—once wider than the Mississippi—never reaches its natural destination in the Aral Sea."[44]

Then there was the city of Magnitogorsk in the southern Ural Mountains of Russia, a gigantic industrial center built from scratch to satisfy Stalin's determination to showcase Soviet achievements. Stalin's first Five-Year Plan and the deaths of 30,000 gulag prisoners resulted, conveniently enough, in a mining and steel manufacturing city of 450,000 inhabitants. Although the center was constructed next to a mountain of pure iron ore, the surrounding areas had no coal or wood, and the shoddily built railroad system could accommodate only trains traveling no faster than 10 kph. But the real blunder was that after a little more than ten years, the iron ore ran out, and Magnitogorsk was left in economic and ecological ruin. In sharp contrast, the mining boomtowns of the American West were built as needed, and most were erected with easy-to-transport wooden-framed shacks and canvas tents, as everyone knew that the supply of gold and silver ore was exhaustible.

Another one of Stalin's prestige construction projects was the White Sea–Baltic Sea Canal, designed as a shipping canal to join the two seas and end at the key port of Leningrad. But something went wrong with the design. By the time of its completion in 1933, the canal was almost completely useless. For some strange reason, the canal was built too narrow and shallow (10 to 12 feet deep) to carry seafaring freighters or military vessels. Only small barges could navigate its limited waterways. The numbers vary widely, but the massive loss of life during the canal's construction has been estimated at between 100,000 and 1 million forced laborers.

Forced Assimilation

Inherently, political systems and central planners fear randomness and unexpected patterns that spontaneously well up and evolve from subordinate systems. The fear is justified. Throughout the centuries, political authorities have dreaded societal changes and perspectives that appear out of nowhere. They realize that amorphous situations are ubiquitous. Control must be applied in order to gain a stranglehold over mankind's natural affinity for living without restraints, and to prevent related behavior. And to enforce this conformity, political systems do not hesitate to regulate, outlaw, and even commit genocide on, nomadic and aberrant people living within the political system's borders.

In 1871, the British enacted the Criminal Tribes Act, which classified hundreds of nomadic and semi-nomadic tribes in India as criminals. The mere fact of belonging to one of the listed tribes automatically made one a criminal. In Turkey, government officials have repeatedly imprisoned famous musicians for singing songs in the banned Kurdish language. In centralized states, any people living by their own self-governing rules are seen as uncontrollable and potential troublemakers. The same holds true for ethnic minorities, indigenous natives, newly arrived foreigners, and offbeat religious and culture groups. Central authorities are notoriously eager to force assimilation and standardization on anyone who does not fit within the national framework of race, religion, or ideology.

Even U.S. President Franklin D. Roosevelt, considered the lodestone of modern liberalism, had a hostile prejudice against the Japanese people, which perhaps helps explain the internment of 120,000 Japanese-Americans in U.S. concentration camps during World War II. As early as 1925, Roosevelt, in a newspaper column, called the Japanese in California a "nightmare" that raised the specter of racial intermarriage. Referring to this mixing of blood as repugnant, he wrote, "the mingling of Asiatic blood with European or American blood produces, in nine cases out of 10, the most unfortunate results."[45]

Above all, central planners have a strong penchant for charting courses toward conformity and equalitarian outcomes. They fear what an impulsive public might do if left to their own devices. An aggregation of individuals might arrive at attitudes that are politically unsavory or incorrect. Citizens might express beliefs that are diametrically opposed to the aims of planners and social engineers. Because most complex systems evolve through an unstructured process of spontaneous order, openly decentralized and resistant to outside control, planners find such methodology unappealing and unworkable. Instead, they search for commandable applications to facilitate their preconceived, cure-all solutions. And unfortunately, many of these applications are based on politically motivated objectives that have nothing to do with satisfying the general public. There is nothing worse to central planners than a public who does not recognize problems that politicos view as apocalyptic and in immediate need of a fix.

But there is another dilemma with linear modeling and central planning. If a problem appears to be solved and is no longer detectable as a problem, was the trouble successfully mitigated, or had the planner simply made a bad prediction in the first place? Or perhaps the reason the problem no longer appears is that some other factor came into play to push it into another realm—similar to what police experience when they crack down on street-corner drug pushers who eventually move their drug-peddling operations to another corner. Most likely the problem has not been solved, but has merely been transformed into something else or moved to another location.

One of the greatest shortcomings of central planners is that their faith in people's capabilities is razor-thin. They do not trust people to solve their own problems or manage their own lives. To planners, the solution for anything must stem from legality-based legislators, generously paid experts, top-notch advisers and lobbyists, or highly paid attorneys. To compensate for their poor opinion of the current status of society, planners feel compelled to remold and recast human behavior so that it fits a particular linear diagram. Such standardization allows state coordinators to optimize the means by which governmental agencies can categorize, regulate, and tax society. In this way, planners become promoters of "design-dependent systems" instead of "evolution-driven systems."

Computer modeling and other planning tools are vital for an industrialized and technologically advanced society. Advances in "pattern-oriented modeling" have helped us to understand the interplay of bottom-up modeling processes. But as Heisenberg's uncertainty principle attests, techniques such as modeling are methods to examine possible scenarios that can shed light on possible courses of future events.

After all, a model is not the system; it is just a particular representation that may or may not be correct. It is common knowledge that academic experts have a poor record of predicting the future in their own field of study—they are unable to distinguish the forest from the trees. As one popular aphorism goes, "Specialists learn more and more about less and less until finally they know everything about nothing." Butler Shaffer contends that "model-building provides no more than a possible theory to be tested against reality."[46]

What *can* go wrong *will* go wrong, because political objectives are so narrowly defined. Without a great breadth of elasticity, a system has countless ways in which to crash and burn, since only one pathway has been designated, by legislated or dictated law, as the correct flight plan. It takes no great statistician to figure out the low probability of an errant political objective landing successfully in one precise landing spot. With so many possible routes in which to fail, government programs seem to boomerang every which way.

Mechanics of Failure

Every organization has within its deep-seated core the seeds of its own destruction. Even success can carry its own kernels of kryptonite. The secret to prosperity is not to activate self-destructive forces. But political structures excel at selecting questionable seeds, planting them in contaminated soil, and then wondering why they sprout into thorny thistles that prick the flesh of society. Many ask why?

First, the self-perpetuating and stasis-driven bureaucracy must interpret hundreds or thousands of pages of the law, often self-contradictory and unintelligible. Second, the new legislation will probably conflict with old. Third, the people who administer and manage the dusty cobwebbed halls of the bureaucracy are inclined to be hostile to new legislative arrivals. They must relearn what they had known so well for so long. And fourth, at some point the whole applecart will be upset when changing conditions make well-inten-

System Failure: The Boomerang Effect

tioned laws ridiculously obsolete and possibly dangerous. There is no shortage of examples.

One such spectacular debacle flared into a widespread crisis when California policymakers attempted to repeal the laws of economics in 1996. By a unanimous vote, the California legislature approved Assembly Bill 1890 to supposedly deregulate the electricity industry. Fluent in Orwellian doublespeak, these legislators had actually *reregulated* the power industry, capping retail electricity prices (price controls) and preventing power-acquiring utilities from signing long-term power supply contracts. Without the ability to purchase long-term contracts, utilities were at the mercy of the more expensive and volatile daily "spot" market. Plus, power suppliers and the utilities had to trade power through the Power Exchange—a state-run program.

Called a "man-made" crisis by *Newsweek*, the power industry came crashing down at Sacramento's doorstep in 2000. With little warning, brownouts and blackouts rolled across an energy-starved state in the middle of a hot summer. Wholesale power prices soared, bankrupting all three major power suppliers. To stop the financial hemorrhaging, Governor Gray Davis stepped in and decided to dabble as a commodity broker himself. Through a state agency, California bought billions of dollars of long-term energy contracts at some of the highest energy prices ever recorded at the time—over $59 billion in long-term contracts. It became the perfect bureaucratic storm.

The California energy regulations backfired to such an explosively self-destructive extent that the crisis might be more appropriately dubbed "the Frankenstein effect." Despite the monstrous part played by lawmakers and Governor Davis, several self-righteous politicians proposed nationalizing California's power utilities, arguing that the private sector and market manipulators were to blame for the energy mess.[47] But, before anyone could author a bill to put the private sector under state ownership, the boomeranging was not done running its zigzag course.

When the summer of 2001 turned out to be cooler than expected, energy demand dropped dramatically, and California suddenly found itself with a glut of energy. This curious episode prompted state officials to sell excess power at a loss. To the chagrin of legislators and taxpayers, the California government had to start selling energy for as little as $1 per megawatt-hour, although the government had entered into long-term electricity contracts at an average of $138 per megawatt-hour.[48]

The taxpayers were fit to be tied. California officials were doing the exact opposite of following sound economic advice; they were buying high, selling low, and losing millions of taxpayer funds. California's Controller, Kathleen Connell, averred that the contracts were so poorly written that the state would likely waste billions of taxpayers' money. Moreover, the contracts had loopholes that protected energy sellers from price fluctuations in the market.

Sacramento Bee columnist Dan Walters touched on this issue of government's inherent inefficiencies and ineptitude, stating that "unlike political issues, the energy is not a static matter, but rather one that mutates with time." He further wrote, "a fluid power market and hidebound, process-oriented politicians are a bad mix, which is probably why they performed so poorly, why they have been outsmarted by fast-moving power traders,...and why they should get out of the business as fast as humanly possible."[49]

In other cases, there appears to be little rhyme or reason as to why something boomerangs. Even seemingly innocuous laws are not immune to this effect. Since 1999, the city of Washington, D.C. has had a program to reduce car accidents. The stated intention was simple: Installing cameras at busy intersections would stop impatient drivers from running red lights, thus preventing intersection crashes and saving lives. For years, everyone in Washington believed just that—problem solved. To all concerned, the program was wildly successful, generating more than 500,000 violations and $32 million in fines, from cameras at 45 intersections.

That all changed when the *Washington Post* hired three traffic specialists to review the data. They were shocked to discover that the traffic cameras were failing to reduce accidents. "The analysis showed that the number of crashes at all locations with cameras more than doubled, from 365 collisions in 1998 to 755 last year [2004]."[50] In fact, fatal crashes and injuries shot up 81 percent. The results were not isolated. In the city of Fort Collins, Colorado, the number of accidents has steadily increased since cameras were installed in 1997. And in Philadelphia, the increase of accidents has shot up 10–20 percent since the cameras began to generate $100 citations. Nobody seems to know why.

One of the most famous boomerangs occurred after passage of the Smoot-Hawley Tariff Act in June of 1930. Championed as a way to bring down unemployment, the law instead caused the exact opposite. Within five months of its passage, unemployment skyrocketed from 6.3 percent in June of 1930 to 16.3 percent in 1931, and then to 24.9 percent in 1932. Unemployment rates stayed in the double digits for the entire decade of the 1930s.

After the stock market crash of 1929, federal lawmakers became fearful of high unemployment figures. Throughout most of its history, America had experienced critical labor shortages. There were never enough workers to

System Failure: The Boomerang Effect 53

meet demand. Two months after the crash, the unemployment rate jumped to 9.5 percent, but soon declined. By June of 1930, unemployment stood at 6.3 percent. But politicians still considered the rate unacceptable and passed The Smoot-Hawley Act. The law imposed record high tariffs on over 20,000 imported goods. Congress incorrectly believed that the law would make citizens buy only American-made goods, which in turn would create more manufacturing and farming jobs.

In protest, over a thousand economists sent a letter to President Hoover asking him to veto the bill; he refused. They argued that high tariffs on foreign goods would backfire and cause retaliation by other countries. The economists were right. The law provoked a storm of foreign measures that resulted in higher tariffs on American goods. It was as though the governments of the world had declared war on trade. The unintended consequences were severe — international trade drastically declined, causing unemployment rates to rise worldwide. The U.S. unemployment rate eventually peaked at 24.9 percent in 1933.

Another classic example of boomeranging occurred when forced busing of school children was instituted, with the goal of achieving racial equality and ending racial segregation in schools. During the 1970s, many intelligent people thought that the only way to remedy past racial discrimination in America was to forcibly transport children of one race to a school attended by children of another race. Federal judges ordered busing to counteract the longstanding "separate but equal" policies, which had been anything but equal in government-operated schools. But what were the results of over thirty years of redesigning American society on mandated policies to improve race relationships in classrooms?

By the twenty-first century, most experts on both sides of the issue had come to the realization that forced busing was counterproductive and had been a dismal failure. According to a 2003 report by the Civil Rights Project at Harvard University, desegregation of U.S. public schools peaked in 1988. After that year, schools became more segregated. "The desegregation of black students, which increased continuously from the 1950s to the late 1980s, has now receded to levels not seen in three decades." The report further stated that the proportion of black students at majority white schools was now at "a level lower than in any year since 1968."[51]

The negative backlash to mandated integration in schools was inevitable. Using social engineering tools to force racial interaction can only weaken the interdependence that instills mutual cooperation and social bonds. Simply put, people do not like being shoved around—even for the noblest of causes. Nobody wants to participate in programs devoid of any self-activated or decision-making authority. Without the opportunity to consent, parents were confronted by barriers which they perceived were preventing their children from getting a good education. They searched for loopholes and discovered different pathways that frustrated government social planners and the courts. They did what anyone would do when dissatisfied with an unyielding system: they voted with their feet. They moved out of the desegregated school districts ("white flight"), enrolling their children in private schools, and in "gifted" or "magnet" programs, or they engaged in home-schooling. The result: Predominantly white schools slowly became predominantly black schools, to the point that they were now more segregated than they had been prior to the historic *Swann vs. Charlotte-Mecklenburg County Board of Education* case in 1971.

Another backfiring blunder involved the case of gasoline additives such as methyl tertiary butyl ether (MTBE). This oxygenate was pushed by the Environmental Protection Agency (EPA) and mandated by Congress in 1990, to cut automobile-emissions pollution. What Congress did not realize is that underground gas tanks and pipes often leak, and that MTBE moves quickly through the soil and fails to break down naturally. Thus, mandated as a way to protect the air, the MTBE additive instead polluted underground wells and water supplies in many communities.

Ironically, the Environmental Protection Agency's own scientists had warned that MTBE could have unintended consequences. The EPA's management ignored those warnings, yet later announced that MTBE may be a potential human carcinogen at high doses.

It would appear that since so many laws boomerang, the phrase "creating good laws" is more of an oxymoron than a reality. The only outcome that consumers can depend on is getting the sticky side of a sucker's lollypop.

Foreign Boomeranging—Blowback

Some of the most infamous boomerang effects have occurred in the Middle East as a result of the United States' efforts to control the internal politics of oil-producing nations. Nicknamed "blowback" by the CIA, unintended negative consequences often occur when intelligence agencies attempt to advance U.S. interests. For instance, under Operation Ajax, the CIA engineered the toppling of a democratically elected government in Iran to bring back the repressive Shah regime in 1953. This action helped set in motion a radical Is-

System Failure: The Boomerang Effect 55

lamic movement that eventually kicked out the Shah, and has since created an environment hostile to U.S. interests in that country.

In neighboring Iraq, the United States interfered in the internal affairs of a foreign nation, helping Saddam Hussein rise to power through U.S.-backed assassination plots and funding of the Ba'ath Party. In 1980, not long after becoming the president of Iraq, Saddam initiated the invasion of Iran. Eager to oppose Iran's new government, the United States provided the Iraqi government with military intelligence and equipment, including the means to create biological weapons of mass destruction—some of the same weapons that contributed to the second Bush administration's motive for invading Iraq in 2003.

In *Blowback: The Costs and Consequences of American Empire*, Chalmers Johnson details numerous unforeseeable consequences that resulted from U.S. government foreign policy in the Middle East and Southeast Asia. Arguing that "a nation reaps what it sows," Johnson describes blowback as "the likelihood that our covert operations in other people's countries could result in retaliation against Americans, civilian and military, at home and abroad."[52]

Many see the September 11, 2001 attacks on the World Trade Center and other American targets as payback by Islamic extremists. During the Soviet Union's invasion of Afghanistan (1979–1989), the mujahideen—Muslim guerrilla "freedom" fighters—along with Osama bin Laden, had accepted U.S.-funded military equipment to fight the Russians. But during the 1991 Persian Gulf War, many in the Muslim community turned against their former U.S. allies, enraged over "infidel" American troops being stationed on sacred Saudi Arabian soil. Other perceived insults included economic sanctions against Iraq that killed hundreds of thousands of Iraqi citizens, and unconditional U.S. favoritism toward Israel. Johnson wrote, "Ever since, bin Laden has been attempting to bring the things the CIA taught him home to the teachers."[53]

Although coalition forces had quickly kicked Saddam Hussein's army out of Kuwait during the first Gulf War (1990-1991), American military bases continued to operate inside Saudi Arabia with no plans to withdraw. Many Islamic militants considered the long-term presence of U.S. forces as undermining Saudi Arabia's perception as a sovereign, independent nation. Taking into account Newton's third law of motion— for every action there is an equal and opposite reaction—attacks against American targets by Middle Eastern terrorists are simply a "you hurt me, I hurt you" act of revenge for past U.S. intervention. One cannot expect to escape the stinging wrath of hornets after having disturbed their nest.

One of the main stated reasons for the preemptive strike on Iraq by United States military forces was to rid the world of terrorism. But according to a 2005 report released by the National Intelligence Council (NIC), the CIA director's think tank, Iraq had replaced Afghanistan as the training ground for the next generation of "professionalized" terrorists. The report indicated that Iraq had become a fertile breeding ground for the recruitment of terrorists and for "enhancing technical skills." In other words, in a classic example of the boomerang effect, the presence of the United States in Iraq and Afghanistan was fueling insurgency, rather than smothering it.

NIC Chairman Robert L. Hutchings said that Iraq "is a magnet for international terrorist activity." In a classic showcasing of blowback, David B. Low, the NIC national intelligence officer for transnational threats, indicated that these terrorists would eventually spread out and expand terrorism. Low pointed out "the likelihood that some of the jihadists who are not killed there will, in a sense, go home, wherever home is, and will therefore disperse to various countries."[54] Obviously, the invasion and occupation of a secular Iraq has fueled the threat of Islamic terrorism, instead of the original intent to extinguish it. To add insult to injury, a 2006 State Department report noted that terrorist attacks worldwide shot up more than 25 percent that year, killing 40 percent more people than in 2005. In other words, the U.S. government is making enemies faster than it can kill them—making the world a more dangerous place for Americans, both at home and abroad.[55]

Michael Scheuer, a 22-year veteran of the CIA and chief of the Osama bin Laden tracking unit at the Counterterrorist Center, argues that the U.S. will continue to be attacked by foreign terrorists because of remaining grievances over past acts it has perpetrated. In his book *Imperial Hubris*, Scheuer stated that "foreign policy is about protecting America. Our foreign policy is doing the opposite."[56]

Environmental Blowback

The boomerang effect can pop up anywhere, especially in the complexity found in ecosystems. A good example occurred in Yellowstone, the 2.2-million-acre national park established in 1872. Described by Michael Crichton in his novel *State of Fear*, an ecological disaster arose when park rangers thought they could preserve Yellowstone's beauty and wildlife by actively interfering with its ecological system.

System Failure: The Boomerang Effect

When President Teddy Roosevelt visited the park in 1903, he witnessed a landscape brimming with wildlife. He and the Park Service were determined to keep it that way. But not long after laws were put in place to keep Yellowstone in its original, pristine condition, all hell broke loose. By 1913, the park had changed completely. Believing that its highly prized elk were on the road to extinction, rangers instigated a campaign to rid the park of predators and rescue the elk. They shot and poisoned the wolves, and prohibited American Indians from their traditional hunting of the animal. This began a chain reaction that dramatically increased the elk herds, marring the ecology. The elk ate the willow seedlings, which should have grown to become willow saplings, which beavers would have used for food and for building dams. Without beavers, the meadows dried up, pushing out trout and otters. Soil erosion increased. The abundant herds of elk ravaged Yellowstone, altering its biodiversity. To reverse the damage, park rangers were forced to shoot elk by the thousands, but the delicate mix of plant and grass ecology failed to return.

But other man-made disasters were just waiting for the right conditions in the park. Misdiagnosing the forest's health, Yellowstone rangers had practiced the policy of "fire suppression" for over a century. In their effort to prevent the natural process of wildfires, the Park Service had allowed the build-up of dead trees and debris to become a powder keg in search of a spark. Finally, in 1988, over one-third of the park burned, with a fire so unnaturally hot that the ground became sterile—meaning that the forest would not grow back unless people reseeded the land.

Despite the Park Service's dedicated effort toward good stewardship of Yellowstone's habitat, they had interfered with and destroyed the very thing they had intended to save. They failed to understand the complexity of ecological systems, especially those systems whose complexity reaches infinity.

1 According to Murray Weidenbaum of the Center for the Study of American Business: "One survey reported that the portion of men with disabilities who are working dropped from 33 percent in 1991 to 31 percent in 1995." ("The Disabilities of ADA Regulations," *Intellectual Ammunition*, November/December 1998).

2 Michelle Malkin, "Recent Research by Wayne Cornelius and Claudia Smith at the University of California at San Diego Suggests That Heightened Controls May Have Simply Encouraged Illegals to Stick Around Once They Get Here," *Reason*, March 1999.

3 C. West Churchman, *The Systems Approach*, New York: Delacorte Press, 1968.

4 Robert K. Merton, "The Unanticipated Consequences of Purposive Social Action," *American Sociological Review*, Vol. 1, Issue 6, Dec. 1936.

5 John Gall, *Systemantics: How Systems Work and Especially How They Fail*, Quadrangle/New York Times Book Company, Inc., 1977.

6 Paul Ormerod, *Why Most Things Fail: Evolution, Extinction and Economics*, New York: Pantheon Books, 2006.

7 System theory was introduced by biologist Ludwig von Bertalanffy in the 1940s. He authored *General Systems Theory* in 1968.

8 George M. Whitesides and Rustem F. Ismagilov, "Complexity in Chemistry," *Science*, April 2, 1999, pp. 89-92.

9 Sharon S. Brehm & J. W. Brehm, *Psychological Reactance: A Theory of Freedom and Control*, New York: Academic Press, 1981.

10 Butler Shaffer, "The Insanity of the State," www.LewRockwell.com, Feb. 23, 2007.

11 Charlie Reese, "The 545 People Responsible," *Orlando Sentinel*, March 7, 1985.

12 M. Mitchell Waldrop, *Complexity: The Emerging Science at the Edge of Order and Chaos*, Simon and Schuster, 1992: quote is attributed to John H. Holland.

13 Butler Shaffer, "The Reactive State" www.LewRockwell.com, Nov. 30, 2004. Some of the material based on Shaffer's *Calculated Chaos: Institutional Threats to Peace and Human Survival*, San Francisco: Alchemy Books, first edition, 1985.

14 Baron de Grimm and Diderot, *Correspondence littéraire, philosophique et critique, 1753-69*, 1813 edition, Vol. 4, pp. 146 & 508; cited by Martin Albrow, *Bureaucracy*, London: Pall Mall Press, 1970, p. 16.

15 Ibid, Shaffer.

16 Timothy Egan, "Sensing the Eyes of Big Brother, and Pushing Back," *New York Times*, Aug, 8, 2004.

17 Lisbeth Kirk,"European Constitution to be signed in Rome today," *EUobserver*, Oct. 29, 2004. Source: http://euobserver.com/18/17657.

18 James M. Banner Jr. "Don't blame Ireland," *Los Angeles Times*, June 25, 2008.

19 There are 4543 words in the U.S. Constitution if signatures are counted.

20 Rehema Ellis, NBC News correspondent, "No child left behind," *The Daily Nightly*, MSNBC.com, Sept. 8, 2008. Source: http://dailynightly.msnbc.msn.com/_news/2008/09/09/4373338-no-child-left-behind.

21 Michael D. Tanner, "The Real Impact of the New Health Care Law," *Cato's Letter*, Fall 2010, vol.8, no. 4) Tanner explains that nobody can identify the exact number of boards, commissions and agencies in the law because in many places the government is "authorized to create more agencies and commissions and boards: a sort of infinitely expanding federal bureaucracy."

22 Fareed Zakaria, "Complexity Equals Corruption," *Time*, Oct. 31, 2011, p. 27.

23 Editorial, "$1 billion, for nothing" *Sacramento Bee*, Feb. 25, 2007.

24 Edwin N. Lorenz, "Deterministic Nonperiodic Flow," *Journal of the Atmospheric Sciences*, Vol. 20, Issue 2, March 1963, pp. 130-141.

25 Oregon Institute of Science and Medicine's Global Warming Petition lists 17,200 scientists skeptical of man-made global warming. Part of petition: "There is no convincing scientific evidence that human release of carbon dioxide, methane, or other greenhouse gasses is causing or will, in the foreseeable future, cause catastrophic heating of the Earth's atmosphere and disruption of the Earth's climate." Petition started in 1998.

26 Documentary: *The Great Global Warming Swindle*, 2007, WAG TV, England.

27 "Rebel with a Klaus," *Investor's Business Daily*, Editorial and Opinion, June 22, 2007.

28 Elisabeth Rosenthal and Andrew C. Kevkin, "Science Panel Calls Global Warming 'Unequivocal,'" *New York Times*, Feb. 3, 2007.

29 NASA feature report, "Antimatter Factory on Sun Yields Clues to Solar Explosion," Sept. 2, 2003, NASA website – Goddard Space Fight Center.

30 Kate Ravilious, "Mars Melt Hints at Solar, Not Human, Cause for Warming, Scientist Says," *National Geographic News*, Feb. 28, 2007.

31 *New Scientist*, "The Lungs of the Planet Are Belching Methane," Jan. 14, 2006, p. 13.

32 *New Scientist*, "Red Faces All Round," Jan. 14, 2006, p. 3.

33 *New Scientist*, "Carbon Tax Turns Into A Health Risk," Jan. 20, 2007, p. 21.

34 Marc Lacey, "Gardena Finds a Way to Lower Insurance Bills: Its Own Firm, *Los Angeles Times*, Sept. 16, 1990.

35 Quoted in Richard M. Ebeling, *The Impossibility of Socialism*, Future of Freedom Foundation, 1990.

36 Andrew Robinson, "Einstein On and Off the Soapbox," *New Scientist*, April 14, 2007, p. 51.

37 Harry Browne, *Why Government Doesn't Work*, New York: St. Martin's Press, first edition published in1995, second edition 2003, p. 19.

38 Quoted in Richard M. Ebeling, *The Impossibility of Socialism,* Future of Freedom Foundation, 1990.

39 Llewellyn Rockwell, Jr., "Best-Laid Plans," Mises Daily (blog by the Ludwig Von Mises Institute), posted March 31, 2003.

40 Brian Easton, *The Commercialisation of New Zealand*, Aukland, New Zealand, Auckland University Press, 1997, p. 245.

41 Gilling's Law was coined by Brian Easton, named after a professor of accountancy, Dr. Don Gilling.

42 *USA Today*, "Bridge to Irresponsibility," posted Oct. 23, 2005; experts say that the Gravina Bridge will cost over $315 million.

43 Oleksandr Zahorny, "BAM: The Way to the Future or the Road to Nowhere?" *The Ukrainian Observer*, no. 184, 2003.

44 PBS story on Uzbekistan *Journey to Planet Earth*, Stories of Hope TV series produced by Hal and Marilyn Weiner, 2005.

45 Jonathan J. Bean, "R. C. Hoiles, Civil Rights Pioneer," *Orange County Register*, Nov. 25, 2007.

46 Butler Shaffer, "The Global Warming Jihad," www.LewRockwell.com, April 12, 2007.

47 Some energy companies did take advantage of a flawed system as concluded by the Federal Energy Regulatory Commission—FERC.

48 Karen Gaudette, "California Selling Off Surplus Power," *Associated Press*, July 19, 2001.

49 Dan Walters, "Lawmakers Lack Timing in Work on Power Crisis," *Sacramento Bee*, July 22, 2001.

50 Del Quentin and Derek Willis, "D.C. Red-Light Cameras Fail to Reduce Accidents," *Washington Post*, Oct. 4, 2005.

51 Erica Frankenberg, Chungmei Lee, and Gary Orfield, *A Multiracial Society with Segregated Schools: Are We Losing the Dream?* Civil Rights Project at Harvard University, Jan. 16, 2003.

52 Chalmers Johnson, "Blowback," *The Nation*, Oct. 15, 2001.

53 Chalmers Johnson, *Blowback: The Costs and Consequences of American Empire*, New York: Macmillan/Holt Paperbacks Books, 2004, originally published as a hardback in 2000, p. xi.

54 Dana Priest, "Iraq New Terror Breeding Ground," *Washington Post*, Jan. 14, 2005.

55 Matthew Lee, "Iran Tops List of State Terror Sponsors," *Denver Post*, May 1, 2007.

56 Michael Scheuer, *Imperial Hubris: Why the West is Losing the War on Terror*, Dulles, Virginia: Potomac Books, Inc., 2004. This book was originally published without identifying the author.

3 Infinity, Equality and Imperfection

Chaos seems to provide a bridge between the deterministic laws of physics and the laws of chance, implying that the Universe is genuinely creative and that the notion of free will is real. —Paul Davies, *physicist*

God plays dice with the universe, but they're loaded dice. And the main objective of physics now is to find out by what rules were they loaded and how can we use them for our own ends. —Joseph Ford, *physicist*

The effort to understand whether the universe is finite or infinite has always been a bewildering task. The ancient Greeks attempted similar endeavors, but often found themselves impotent to come up with a definitive answer. The more clever ones realized that they were treading on the shadowy realm of paradoxes, since theories of either a finite or an infinite universe presented conflicting problems. But the one unanswerable question that stirred the most heated debate went as follows: if the universe were finite, what would happen if you stuck your hand out at the edge? Where would it go?

The complexity of a system may be so great that a warehouse of high-speed supercomputers could never discover an accurate, repeatable pattern—no matter how much computing power were applied. So why are chaologists so intrigued with the mind-bending mysteries of infinity?

It goes back to Einstein. The fabric of space and time is elastic and infinite—there are no absolute measurements of space and time. Einstein added a fourth component—the space-time continuum—to coordinate his system with the other three dimensions, uniting time and space and making everything relative. Einstein's theories put an end to simultaneity of absolute time and space, concluding that the flow of time differs depending on one's reference point and gravitational mass. In other words, time varies depending on the distance from objects with mass. Since gravity slows time, the passing rate of time moves more slowly on the surface of the earth than in outer space. This is why it is hard to get clocks to agree, and another reason that accuracy of measurement is difficult to obtain.

Under the old, linear way of thinking, time flowed with perfect uniformity according to Newtonian laws of motion. Classical physics required causality and locality. But the science of quantum physics seemed to require neither, demonstrating that just by knowing the result of a measurement (on the microcosmic level), we could determine its outcome. Although quantum scientists argue that order comes about only through measurement, actually making those measurements is a tricky business. Theoretical physicist Stephen Hawking acknowledged this problem in *A Brief History of Time*: "one certainly cannot predict future events exactly if one cannot even measure the present state of the universe precisely!"[1]

Hawking got it right. Without the ability to accurately quantify what we are trying to gauge, trying to make pinpoint predictions is an exercise in futility. When scientists perform measurements with Angstrom spatial scales or picosecond time scales, it becomes all too apparent that things can be measured only to a certain extent. Time and space are both infinitely large and infinitely small. The ancient Greek philosophers known as the Atomists believed that matter is composed of an infinite number of indivisibles. For instance, imagine walking across a 20–foot–long room to reach the kitchen. If you were to go half the distance first, then half of that distance, and repeat the process continuously, you would never reach your destination.

Pi has similar qualities. This mathematical constant, used to determine the circumference of a circle, is sometimes referred to as "the secret number of infinity," since it is a never–ending, never–repeating string of numbers. Mathematicians refer to such numbers as "irrational," because no matter how accurately you calculate the circumference of a circle, it will never be quite accurate enough. It could be said that the impossibility to make highly precise measurements gives chaos its predominant role in the universe.

But the inability to measure accurately is not the only problem in the geometry of space. In the field of astrophysics, researchers understand that the universe is not uniform, especially when they are confronted with the nagging problem of "dark matter," which some experts have estimated to make up a still-undetectable one-fourth of the mass-energy of the observable universe. The overall picture got a lot fuzzier when "dark energy" was calculated to account for 74 percent of the total mass–energy of the observable universe.[2] With that in mind, scientists theorize that a mere 1 percent of the universe is visible to humans.[3] Other scientists now put that figure at around 4 percent.[4] Nonetheless, it's hard to measure what you can't see.

Further, there may not be one set of measurements; some experts insist that the universe has multidimensional personalities. For instance, under the principles of wave–particle duality, subatomic particles can switch back and

Infinity, Equality and Imperfection 63

forth between wavelike and particle-like properties, transforming into endlessly expanding ripples, extending infinitely into space. The two forms act differently, but they are simply two aspects of the same entity—two sides of the same coin.

Under the laws of quantum mechanics, "zero–point energy" treats particles such as quarks and electrons as point–like objects that take up no space and yet have "infinite mass and infinite charge." Scientists have found ways to calculate an electron's true mass and charge, but they do so by stopping at an arbitrary distance just short of zero. This bizarre method is officially known as "renormalization." Particle physicist Richard Feynman had a better description for it, dubbing the method "a dippy process."[5]

Other difficult-to-measure oddities abound. The curvature of space–time, known as gravity, behaves differently in different pockets of the universe. As any schoolchild knows, the infinite density of black holes breaks down the laws of physics. Notoriously chaotic, black holes represent the most extreme conditions of space—where time and space are so warped that they flip positions. "Time becomes space and space becomes time," as astronomer Geza Guyuk put it.[6]

The infinity of space–time underscores the fact that physical laws are often indeterminate and that they play in nature's inescapable game of chance, bending and warping to create ever new and unexpected phenomena.

The EPR Paradox: Uncertainty and Indeterminism

Taking a mechanistic view of nature, Einstein had serious problems with the uncertainties that quantum physics brought to the science table, although he was involved in defining those very uncertainties. By the mid–1930s, he began searching for ways to demonstrate the inconsistencies of the new science of the subatomic world. Einstein wanted to keep the quantum genie tightly bottled up in the atomic world, because it represented a breakdown of determinism in nature. And such breakdowns were popping up all over the quantum landscape.

With probability interpretations in mind, Niels Bohr's principles of "complementarity" assert that when measurements were made on subatomic particles, they would exhibit either particle–like or wave–like properties, placing a fundamental limit on what we may know about nature. Then Heisenberg further muddied the water with his uncertainty principle, which mathematically limits the accuracy of measuring the position and momentum of any quantum object. But the weirdness factor hit the roof with "quantum entanglement," and to a lesser degree, "quantum superposition." Bohr and Heisenberg insisted that photons could explore all possible paths simultaneously, overlapping and occupying the same space at the same time, without limit.[7]

Immediately, quantum entanglement became the poster child of the bizarre. The principle claimed that an atomic or subatomic particle could exist in two locations at the same time, acting as one, each twin instantaneously communicating with its ghostly doppelganger. As if that was not enough weirdness, it was postulated that such swapping of information could span the entire universe. But this would violate Einstein's Special Theory of Relativity, which states that no signal can travel faster than the speed of light. At this point, Einstein thought he had quantum mechanics over an incongruent barrel.

But more came out of this dialogue than had been expected. In the case of quantum superposition, many researchers began to imply that an observer would have no idea of the phase state of any object. In fact, as quantum theory suggests, a particle could be in all possible states simultaneously; only when one would take a peek at a photon, causing the wave function to collapse by measuring it, could the object be limited to a single possibility. This was too absurd for classical physicists. They declared war.

Einstein and two colleagues, Boris Podolsky and Nathan Rosen, went after the strange conclusions of the new science, attempting to prove that quantum mechanics was an incomplete physical theory. In 1935, they authored a thought–experiment paper on what soon become known as the Einstein, Podolsky and Rosen Paradox (or the EPR Paradox). Einstein was searching for proof that the angular spin of objects before the separation of protons was already determined, but merely unknown until the observer had observed it. If this were true, then measurements would simply tell us what was already well defined and predetermined by nature. But to the standard interpretations of quantum theory, such things are not merely a matter of ignorance. The rate or direction of a proton spin is not determined until it has been measured. Quantum scientists argue that we determine the kind of reality that will be revealed through the experiment we select. This is analogous to the "Schrödinger's cat" thought experiment, in which it can be inferred that the cat is both alive and dead until the box is opened.[8]

Generally, quantum mechanics deals with possibilities, rather than actualities, meaning that little can be determined beforehand. This is another reason that Bohr and Heisenberg declared, in the Copenhagen Interpretation, that the madhouse of quantum physics is categorically unsolvable.

So what happened? Although the debate continues, there is strong experimental evidence supporting the theories of quantum mechanics, nonlocal correlation, and a probability–based universe. Quantum mechanics has been regularly declared one of the most successful theories of nature ever devised—the application of which made possible such things as transistors, computer chips, lasers, and superconductivity.

Even the bizarre principle of quantum entanglement has been mostly upheld, through a number of mathematical theorems and experiments. In 1969, John Bell, a specialist in nuclear physics and quantum field theory, attempted to solve the EPR Paradox. Considered one of the most important theorems of the twentieth century, Bell's Inequality appears to have verified that instantaneous communications, or what Einstein skeptically dubbed "spooky action at a distance," can, in fact, occur. The "nonlocality principle," was upheld, meaning that neither objects nor events need a close physical connection to interact. In *Scientific American*, David Z. Albert and Rivka Galchen affirmed Bell's conclusions, in no uncertain terms: "the universe we live in cannot be local."[9] Causality was seriously wounded, since all possible causes must be identifiable in the physical world, in order to be scientifically investigated or considered to have an effect. There appear to be at least two different sets of physical laws; causality sometimes applies, but at other times, it does not.

Even without Bell's Inequality, other factors have damaged the reputation of direct cause and effect. According to Stephen Hawking, the uncertainty principle implies that the universe is "full of tiny virtual black holes, which appear and disappear again." This alone invalidates much of what we think of as causality and determinism. Why? Because these subatomic black holes could swallow up particles and information forever, breaking the chain of events. As Hawking argues, "the future of the universe is not completely determined by the laws of science, and its present state...."[10] It would appear that God indeed plays dice with the universe and He is probably surprised to see what happens.

Next came a series of experiments in the laboratory. One of the first to test Bell's Theorem was Alain Aspect, of the Institute of Optics at the University of Paris. The Aspect Experiment concluded in 1982 that nature actually prefers to act from a distance! Using high–speed switching mechanisms and photons produced by mercury vapor, Aspect and his collaborators found that arbitrarily far–apart phenomena can still share a quantum link.

In another remarkable experiment, conducted in 1997 by physics professor Anton Zeilinger and other researchers from the University of Innsbruck, quantum entanglement was reaffirmed. Zeilinger's team was first to demonstrate "quantum teleportation" between two separately entangled photons, transmitting information instantaneously over a distance that could have been light years.[11] This and other experiments have lent credence to the principles of nonlocality and an indeterminate universe. It is now generally understood that accuracy is prevented not by the limited precision of measuring tools, but by the lack of establishing a "probability distribution" by which the measurement is specified. In other words, researchers can learn only what their instruments are capable of measuring.

Flawed Linear Regression

Scientists, especially mathematicians, have long understood that just a handful of interacting variables can produce permutations running into the thousands. Edward Lorenz, a mathematically trained meteorologist, was the first to stumble upon chaotic systems and the problem of understanding the virtually countless ways variables might interact.

With some of the first computer–modeling software, meteorologists were actively researching atmospheric change, convinced that someday, a numerical analysis would enable accurate, long–range weather forecasting. Their results were lackluster, and the problem appeared internal. They were searching for a precise computer formula that would sweep away the annoying randomness of weather data. But their analytical weather modeling failed, and there seemed to be no solution. With the arrival of high computation power and the Butterfly Effect theory, weather forecasters gained some comfort. "We certainly hadn't been successful at doing that anyway," Lorenz said, "and now we had an excuse."[12]

Fortunately, Lorenz had a hunch that the statistical method known as "linear regression" was flawed. Analogous to Columbus accidentally discovering an unknown continent, Lorenz came across a new science in his explorations, but soon found himself in unfamiliar territory. After additional research, Lorenz came to the realization that seemingly inconsequential data could have important consequences. "A small numerical error," writes James Gleick, "was like a small puff of wind—surely the small puffs faded or canceled each other out before they could change important, large–scale features of the weather."[13] Yet in Lorenz's particular system of equations, small errors proved catastrophic.

Even after Lorenz's discovery of "deterministic chaos" in the 1960s, most meteorologists were still at a loss as to why their models were running amok. While still under the influence of linear equations, they kept getting poor results. Irregular outcomes were blocking any hope of finding what they had originally sought: predictability and perfection. Their job was not to explore the mysteries of infinity, but to make dependable weather predictions.

Today, thanks to chaos theory, unless a meteorologist is clairvoyant, weather forecasters understand that there is little certainty in long–term weather reports. As Gleick contended "Beyond two to three days the world's best forecasts were speculative, and beyond six or seven days they were worthless."[14] Computer models can predict short–term weather patterns, but even these are only probabilities. The problem is that constant changes in humidity, wind, temperature, clouds, and dozens of other factors increase the complexity beyond the capacity of even computer models. The number of possible data is infinite.

Understanding the lack of predictability is crucial in a universe governed more often by the laws of chance than by predesigned patterns. Many in society trust predictions of future events as gospel. And in treating probability as reality, they find it perfectly justifiable to command others to do their bidding within political, social, and economic structures. Government policies may be predicated on faith, dogma, or on some vague credo, but they are not based on precisely known outcomes or certainty of information. *Pure speculation* would be a better portrayal, since the future cannot be fully determined by past patterns. While past events do offer some direction, they commonly resemble a roadmap printed in an obscure foreign language.

Uncaused Phenomena and Political Causality

Politicians pander to causality. It is a matter of their survival. They must identify a cause in order to propose a solution, leading to an endless litany of oversimplified and gimmicky quick fixes—flaunted to impress countrymen with their concern to *do something*. And doing something, anything, increases the chance of that politician staying in a position of authority. But conditions always change, and ill-conceived populist remedies have a nasty habit of going awry. Eventually, some type of Band–Aid fix must be applied to cover up a festering crisis. But temporary patches are often worse than the wound. At this point, political stalwarts are apt to blame others for situations caused by their own meddling. Whatever actually caused the crisis is immaterial; the crucial element is for the authorities to scare up a plausible scapegoat.

Political maestros have a vested interest in what philosophers call "hard determinism." If there was never a real choice in the first place, politicos need not take responsibility for their actions. Wars and atrocities were not their fault; the war was necessary, and predetermined by past consequences and administrations. They could not have changed the future if they had wanted to; they were obeying an unbroken chain of prior occurrences, merely following orders. The principles of realpolitik would argue that nothing is wrong with taking Machiavelli's amoral advice introduced in *The Prince*. Any act of inhumanity against the populace can be easily justified and legitimized. Those in the political arena could simply argue that the ends justified a preordained means.[15]

Under the theory of hard determinism, uncaused events are supposedly impossible, and the unbreakable chain of causality links each and every event with every other event, unalterably and with no genuine alternative. The concept of free will does not apply. And yet, a remarkable number of scientific experiments have found that temporally ordered sequences are anything but determinate.

In 1961, Calus Jönsson at the University of Tübingen was the first to perform a double–split experiment with electrons. This experiment did more than reaffirm the principle of wave–particle duality. It suggested the possibility of time–reversed phenomena. As early as the 1940s, Richard Feynman, one of the scientists working on the Manhattan Project, indicated that particles such as positrons, the antimatter counterpart of electrons, might have properties that give them the ability to travel backward in time. The results of the double–split experiments appeared to show just that, baffling scientists. The photons seemed to somehow "know" beforehand whether scientists were planning to take measurements. It was as if the photons were being tipped off before the experiment—as if information might be flowing backward in time.

In 1964, a milestone experiment with proton accelerators, conducted by James W. Cronin and Val L. Fitch from Princeton University, found convincing evidence that time reversals are in fact rather messy (they received the Nobel Prize in 1980 for their discovery). This finding was important, since time reversal was assumed to be perfectly symmetrical; that is, if time did slip into reverse gear, everything would move backward in the same order that it had occurred. But the experiment proved that if time does leap backwards, it does so asymmetrically and unequally.

In 1998, additional experiments at the European Organization for Nuclear Research (CERN) and the Fermi National Accelerator Laboratory (Fermilab) again dispelled absolute causality. Their antimatter experiments upheld Cronin's and Fitch's research, proving that "when certain particles go backward in time, their behavior is somewhat different from what it is when they go forward."[16] Whether or not time can actually flow backwards in a traditional sense is a minor point. The remarkable story here is that the arrow of time appears to be asymmetrical, not predestined in either direction. These experiments on the world of subatomic physics suggested that the universe is teeming with uncaused phenomena of almost invisible micro–events that distort spatial and temporal properties. These events could easily disrupt any semblance of a direct linkage between cause and effect—creating instead a loose web of causation.

Moreover, these findings are consistent with Feynman's theory of quantum electrodynamics in which all probable paths in time and space interact to select a final trajectory for a particle, meaning that there are many possible paths to a location.

The Impossibility of Exact Results

Scientists have been confounded routinely by chaos theory, because they have wanted to discover a hidden order where nobody thought it existed. But the duty of scientists is to observe and measure all sorts of phenomena—the scientific method—and attempt to both explain and repeat them. But measurement methods can be quite problematic. For instance, in theoretical physics, some of the most cherished concepts are well understood and accepted, but when they're put to the test, the outcome can be surprising. In other words, these general theories break down when precise results are demanded. Under the properties of infinity, measurements can never be perfected—we could never reach an absolutely accurate datum. Calculations of eclipses, particle movements in cloud chambers, and spacecraft guidance are merely approximations.

Even the motion of planets, once considered the epitome of predictability and regularity, has a flighty nature. In 1992, Gerald Sussman, a professor of electrical engineering and Jack Wisdom, a professor of planetary sciences, both at MIT, completed a detailed calculation of the motion of the solar system's nine planets. Calling planetary orbits "chaotic," these scientists found that planetary positions, just 4 million years in the future, could not be predicted with any certainty.[17] Using the Digital Orrery and the Supercomputer Toolkit, they were able to confirm a high level of "chaoticity" throughout our planetary system. (The Digital Orrery is a special computer designed by Sussman to perform orbital–mechanics experiments.)

Sussman and Wisdom's study also confirmed an earlier work by astronomer Jacques Laskar, of the Bureau des Longitudes in Paris, who indicated back in 1989 the abundance of irregular behavior in the solar system. According to Laskar's report, "The amount of chaos is quite high: the positions of the inner planets become effectively unpredictable in just a few tens of millions of years."[18] Even Earth's orbit is not fixed in space. The basic ellipse gradually rotates at the current rate of 0.3 degrees per century. True, the sun dominates the gravitational forces that affect celestial mechanics, but the other planets exert influences too. Earth's irregular precession is due to perturbation from other planetary bodies in our solar system, with the greatest gravitational influence coming from Jupiter.

One of the first to identify a combined chaotic but deterministic system was Henri Poincaré (1854–1912), a nineteenth–century French mathematician and theoretical physicist often claimed to be the father of modern chaos theory. While working on the most famous question of classical mechanics—the "three–body problem" (a subset of the "N–body problem")—Poincaré attempted to find solutions to the motion of more than two orbiting bodies in the solar system. The problem had eluded mathematicians for over 150 years. Scientists could not seem to predict the trajectory of three or more moving objects. The two–body problem had already been solved, by Newton. But when a third body was added to the equation of motion, such as an asteroid tumbling in space between Mars and Earth, scientists could find no closed analytical solution. Everything is moving in space; everything is relative to everything else, making it so complicated that any method defies calculation.

Scientists had no analytical means to determine the precise, mutual gravitational interaction of more than two masses. When Einstein became involved with this problem in his attempt to understand motion and gravity, he came across something so radical that most in the scientific world refused to take him seriously.

So what was so radical? Einstein had assaulted classical physics by asserting that under special conditions, some laws of physics do not act as they should, contending that time and space are not always constant. This was a bombshell to the scientific community. But Einstein had not abandoned classical physics entirely. His theories also assumed the universe to be "static" and homogeneous, under his theory of the "cosmological constant." However, with the discovery that the universe is expanding (Big Bang Theory), parts of his relativity theory were shown to be incorrect. Eventually, Einstein realized his mistake and called his cosmological constant his "greatest blunder."

The originator of the now famous "Poincaré Conjecture," Poincaré was unable to solve the three–body problem with mathematics. He was aware of the unpredictability associated with some equations of motion, but he failed to figure out why. He did prove that there was no general solution to the problem.

The three–body problem illustrates that even with more accurate measurements and calculations, the law of diminishing returns will allow some things to be predicted only a little longer. In a sort of reversal of the Butterfly Effect, a big increase in accuracy often reduces the time available for a prediction. This is what makes weather forecasting increasingly unreliable, as weathermen struggle to predict further into the future. The "sensitive dependence on initial conditions" causes all sorts of embarrassing errors for climatologists.

The same can be demonstrated for economic forecasting by the Federal Reserve, reports by Wall Street gurus, and the economic statistics that pour out of the U.S. Commerce Department. These predictions must also brave the slings and arrows of outrageous misinformation, inaccurate measurements, and constant revision. Rarely does anyone come up with precise numbers for future interest rates, monetary inflation, or gross national product.

Uncertainty is unsettling, because it leads to the obvious fact that perfection is more than just elusive—it is physically impossible. Even matter and antimatter are not that similar. The Cronin and Fitch experiment in 1964 also demonstrated that antimatter particles are not exact mirror images of each other. The pair of scientists discovered that K–mesons and anti–K–mesons were slightly different—violating the fundamental symmetry principle. The scientific community was doubtful.

By 2001, other experiments found a second fundamental difference between the behavior of matter and antimatter. It occurred at the $177–million Stanford Linear Accelerator Center (SLAC), where more than 600 scientists from nine nations sent electrons and positrons colliding, at near the speed of light. They were not disappointed. After they examined 32 million pairs of decaying B–mesons, the verdict came in: matter and antimatter particles are indeed asymmetrical.[19] Again, more evidence that subatomic particles are unique and imperfect.

Imperfection and Inequality

Consider imperfection. How many times have we heard that no two snowflakes are exactly the same? And similarly, that everyone's fingerprint, cornea, or DNA sequence is different? Such statements beg the question: if no two things are exactly the same, how can anything conform to perfection and equality?

Both perfection and equality are impossible in the physical world. Nothing is identical; nothing is equal. Manufactured guns leave distinct scratch patterns on bullets, to the delight of police investigators. The fluctuating orbit of an electron around a water molecule makes each molecule unique. Nature abhors equality and perfection. As the Greek philosopher Heraclitus once said, "No man ever steps in the same river twice, for it is not the same river and he is not the same man."

If on Monday, every person in the world were handed $1 million, by Friday, very few would retain that exact amount. Change is ubiquitous. Most people who win millions of dollars in the lottery spend their winnings very quickly. According to psychologist Stephen Goldbart, research shows that most lottery winners lose their winnings within five years.[20] In fact, some financial experts have indicated that up to 80 percent of U.S. lottery winners file for bankruptcy within five years.[21]

Despite the absence of physical equality in nature, political systems engage in grand endeavors to dictate perfection and equality in a universe devoid of both. In their egalitarian and quixotic quest to redistribute wealth, they rob Peter to pay Paul, which only creates a state of dependency, not of equality. Any attempt to impose equality can only bring about more inequality. Rev. William J. H. Boetcker expressed this same insight in 1916, writing, "You cannot strengthen the weak by weakening the strong."

Various sociopolitical movements are oriented to the nostrums of "social justice," favoring entitlements for all those with economic disparity. They struggle for what is scientifically impossible: equality of outcome. They want everyone to end up with the same amount of wealth—billions of people all possessing the same numerical affluence. Under their interpretation of nature, economic disparity can be eliminated and replaced with utopian equality among all members of society.

Nothing is innately wrong with helping the unfortunate, but social justice reformers seek to do so by hurting the fortunate. Such no-win policies will simply implant more inequality, resentment, and undesirable distortions.

Worse still, the advocates of enforced equality seek to impose their concept of perfection on a human psyche that tends to strive for more options, not fewer. Antagonistic toward a choice–driven society, these perfectionists presume that people can be made faultless if they have no other alternative. Without the disorderly clutter of choices, society would finally be able to do away with infectious temptations and antisocial behavior. In fundamental ways, the evangelists of equality try to change human behavior, as if they were a new bride confident in her ability to alter the habits of an untrained husband. In a nutshell, equality and perfection are not only impossible to imitate or even define, but incapable of performing to a perfectionist's standards.

But equity pushers just can't leave the field of socioeconomics undisturbed. Economies and consumers, are regarded as dispensable guinea pigs expected to perform dazzling feats of societal makeover while being lured into social–engineering mazes. The hard sciences are generally left alone. Legislators do not usually mandate laws to alter the laws of physics—although some misguided Illinois legislators attempted to legally change the value of pi in 1894. Policymakers do not regulate the orbiting distance of electrons to reduce the velocity of light to a safer speed. They don't tell mathematics to diversify primary numbers to accommodate multiculturalism. Nor do they command the human cell to be kinder and gentler. But for some reason, they feel obligated to play the role of God in society.

These artificial laws and mandates are enacted and enforced as though central policymakers had perfect knowledge of all variables, at any given moment in time. Of course, nobody can comprehend every variable—future, past, or present—or foretell exact consequences. It's possible that a particular deterministic law could be in tune with a socioeconomic situation at the moment of enactment, but will surely become obsolete, or even dangerous, over time. Ironically, in governing systems laws are often proposed that have already become antiquated before the bill ever reaches a final vote. At other times, newly enacted laws often overdo the very thing they had intended to undo.

A good example of incompatible legislation resulting in bad side effects can be found in the "price support" laws for dairy products in California. The pricing for dairy products has been heavily controlled since the 1940s. At the time of their enactment, the California legislature clearly failed to anticipate the effects of modernization. Unbeknownst to political stalwarts, milk production increases during the long hot days of summer. When combined with better milking machines, supplies often overwhelm demand, flooding the consuming market. Normally, some type of average–based equilibrium swings back into play when prices are free to fluctuate. But California legislators wanted to dominate the pricing mechanism by enacting laws to prevent dairy products from being sold below cost.

But these dairy price support laws did more than control market prices. Legislators also stipulated that it was illegal for dairy farmers to give away their products to charities and nonprofit organizations. Incredibly, politicians made it a crime to freely give milk to children and the poor. The outcome was not hard to predict: a fleet of milk tankers routinely dumped thousands of gallons of unspoiled milk into rural fields, year after year. They had no choice. They were obligated to follow these statutory laws. Eventually, food banks, soup kitchens, and charities sued over the spilled milk, and certain sections of these laws were overturned by the courts during the 1990s, allowing food banks to give out milk and cheese to children and adults.

Without the intervening of price–support laws, dairy farmers would have done what farmers usually do, when confronted by bumper crops. They would have lowered prices to get rid of excess inventory, even if they'd had to sell below cost. It may seem too simple to allow dairymen to determine their own pricing structure, but simplicity is often a better working method than inflexible regulations by fiat.

The Illusion of Reform

It is naïve to think that policymakers would simply repeal their own labyrinthine webs of overweening laws. Apologies and regrets would imply incompetence or error. The political path of least resistance is to deflect blame and appoint a committee to find superficial straw men. And when investigative reports are released, the probability is low that the legislators who crafted the short–sighted laws in the first place will set them right in the second. Even if the underlying causes were understood—which is highly unlikely—there are few incentives or political capital to be gained from finding a long-term solution.

More can be accomplished by the illusion of solution—reforms that temporarily mitigate the symptoms. However, without striking substantively at the root of the problem, the most likely outcome is a chain reaction of bad laws breeding worse laws. Most political reforms only exacerbate the original problem, shift greater control to the elite, provide fewer choices, and widen the gulf between the governing and the governed. In addition, attempts at political reform will usually fail, because the reforming mechanism itself is endogenous—that is, the only ones with the ability to make the changes are the insiders who originally enacted the problematic laws.

The disastrous effects of most legislation do not appear immediately. It takes time for their effect on complex systems to flare up, but when it does, it does so explosively. For instance, environmental laws enacted during the Clinton administration prohibited the use of bulldozers or fire retardants in "wilderness areas." This edict seemed reasonable, until the summer of 2000, when massive wildfires raged across the western part of the United States. The well-intended environmental laws hamstrung firefighters across the west, resulting in the worst fire season in fifty years, with over 6.6 million acres burned.

Firefighters near Clear Creek, Idaho, had to stop fighting the fire to allow the government time to study ways to protect sensitive plants from firefighting crews. The result: the Clear Creek fire expanded to over 200,000 acres and burned the plants to ash. Even aircraft assisting in fighting the fire were often ordered away from ecologically sensitive areas, despite heavy fire rampaging through the area. In one case, firefighters were ordered to stop pumping water from a small stream because it might harm the endangered bull trout. The creek eventually boiled away, killing the trout.[22]

Deterministic laws had made the wildfire situation worse. Congress failed to anticipate the fiery maelstrom that could be caused by such harsh, inflexible legislation. There is no reason to believe that the Clinton administration wanted to destroy what they professed to preserve, even though their actions seemed to conflict with their pro-environment creed. Actually, their only crime was that they could not conceive how their actions might achieve results opposite to their intent. Habitually, politicians consider themselves "problem solvers," although they rarely read the laws they pass.

Many policymakers have the mistaken belief that perfection is attainable and sustainable. This notion is responsible for Hitler's eugenics experiments to beget the super Aryan Man (*Homo aryanus*), and for the Soviet Union's re-education camps which sought to forge a flawless Soviet Man (*Homo sovieticus*). But perfection requires uniformity, invariant people, and permanent conditions—all obviously unattainable because of the uniqueness of time and matter.

The quest for perfection leads to increasing demands for standardization and codification, despite the poor performance of most legislative policies. The vast majority of laws on the books represent attempts to mitigate prior failed attempts. Most political reformers get caught in a cycle of unwanted consequence. Instead of starting over with a blank slate, lawmakers head back to the drawing board to over-load and over-design a system they don't understand. Of course, this repeated intervention simply mutates into greater confusion and distortion—the Spaghetti Loop Effect.

Spaghetti Code or Loop

"Spaghetti code," a derogatory programmers' term, refers to computer instructions so complex and entangled that they are almost impossible to decipher, even by the original software developer. Under deadline pressures, desperate programmers often fail to change the original coding, and instead write subroutines as makeshift patches.

But quick–and–dirty software patching is a short–term solution and often creates kludge, a word coined in 1962 to mean "an ill–assorted collection of poorly matching parts, forming a distressing whole."[23] Without explicit rules for code hygiene, software tends to become awkward and error-prone. When programmers attempted to write more subroutines to fix awkwardly designed software, additional errors would crop up. In an effort to understand the bigger picture, some programmers would chart the subroutines. The results were devastating. The diagrams often revealed confusing logic streams that resembled a bowl of cooked spaghetti noodles—revealing that the chain of causality had been badly garbled, or even disconnected.

Some chaologists refer to the bewildering results from thousands upon thousands of convoluted and mismatched laws as the "Spaghetti Loop Effect"—a sort of Gordian Knot that can never be unraveled. In a political context, this principle relates the difficulty in coping with a baroque array of countless overlooping laws that defy common sense. Even the most adroit political leader would be hopelessly lost if he or she were to try to untangle such a chaotic potpourri.

The Spaghetti Loop metaphor spotlights the systemic weaknesses found in all political systems. If programmers are incapable of crafting perfection through the precise language of machines, how could sociopolitical systems ever come close to achieving perfection through the nebulous language of human beings?

Spaghetti Loop represents the dilemmas of infinity and its never-ending quality to be beyond the beyond. If the uncertainty of infinity proves anything, it proves that we must question our grasp of reality.

1 Stephen Hawking, *A Brief History of Time*, New York: Bantam Dell Publishing Group, 1988, p. 59.
2 Gary F. Hinshaw, WMAP by the National Aeronautics and Space Administration (NASA) on April 30th, 2008. "WMAP Cosmological Parameters Model: lcdm+sz+lens Data: wmap5," Data on NASA's website at http://lambda.gsfc.nasa.gov/product/map/dr3/params/lcdm_sz_lens_wmap5.cfm.
3 Robert Sanders, "Dark Matter' Forms Dense Clumps in Ghost Universe," *UC Berkeley News*, Nov. 5, 2003.
4 Peter N. Spotts, "New findings on dark energy back discarded Einstein theory," *Christian Science Monitor*, January 6, 2010.
5 Charles Seife, *Zero: The Biography of a Dangerous Idea*, NY: Viking, 2000, pp.191-209; Brian Green, *The Elegant Universe: Superstrings, Hidden Dimensions, and the Quest for the Ultimate Theory*, NY: Vintage Books, 1999.
6 Donna Vickroy, "Expert Sheds Light on Black Holes," *Daily Southtown*, Feb. 28, 2007. Interview of Dr. Geza Gyuk, director of astronomy at the Adler Planetarium.
7 Nick Herbert, *Quantum Reality: Beyond the New Physics*, New York: Anchor Books, 1985, p. 38.
8 "Schrödinger's cat" is a thought experiment devised by physicist Erwin Schrödinger in 1935. Often viewed as a paradox, it represents the incompleteness of the Copenhagen interpretation of quantum mechanics. Under quantum superposition, where all possible states of a system can co-exist, what state would Schrödinger's cat be in? It would depend on an earlier event. If the cat were put in a box with a device that might shatter a flask of deadly radiation, the cat would be found either alive or dead. But under the Copenhagen interpretation of quantum mechanics, the cat is simultaneously alive and dead.
9 David Z. Albert and Rivka Galchen, "Bell's Theorem and the Physical World, *Scientific American*, Feb. 18, 2009. This story is a supplement to the story "Was Einstein Wrong?: A Quantum Threat to Special Relativity."
10 Stephen Hawking, "Does God Play Dice?" public lecture series, written in 1999, www.hawking.org.uk.
11 D. Bouwmeester, J.W. Pan, K. Mattle, M. Eibl, H. Weinfurter, and A. Zeilinger, "Experimental Quantum Teleportation," *Nature*, 390, pp. 575–579, 1997.
12 Nigel Calder, *Magic Universe: The Oxford Guide to Modern Science*, Oxford University Press, USA, 2003, p. 133.
13 James Gleick, *Chaos: Making a New Science*, Penguin Books (Non-Classics), 1988, p. 17.
14 Ibid.
15 This idea can also be first attributed to Plato from around 360 b.c. Machiavelli's *The Prince* did not contain the phrase "the ends justify the means," but nonetheless enjoined such a policy.
16 Malcolm W. Browne, "Where Does the Time Go? Forward, Physics Shows," *The New York Times*, December 22, 1998.

17 *Science*, "Chaotic Evolution of the Solar System," July 3, 1992, p. 56.
18 Jacques Laskar, "A Numerical Experiment on the Chaotic Behaviour of the Solar System." *Nature*, 338, pp. 237–238, 1989. References in article made to Robert Matthews' *Unraveling the Mind of God: Mysteries at the Frontiers of Science*, London: Virgin, 1992.
19 *Physical Review Letters*, July 26, 2001, press release.
20 Kelly St. John, "Big Lottery Winners Know a Lot About What Not To Do," *San Francisco Chronicle*, Feb. 16, 2002.
21 Jack Canfield, *The Success Principles: How to Get From Where You Are to Where you Want to Be,* Harper Paperbacks, 2006, p. 74.
22 William F. Jasper, "Scorched Earth," *New American*, 2004, vol. 16, no. 21.
23 Jackson Granholme, "How to Design a Kludge," *Datamation*, Feb. 1962, pp. 30–31.

4 Strange Attractors and Subjective Values

Facts and theories are natural enemies.—Johann Wolfgang von Goethe

Scientists are always searching for predictability and repeatable patterns. In so doing, they must inevitably deal with the clash between theory and experiment. But some experimental results are so revolutionary that the conclusions they lead to often fall on deaf ears.

David Ruelle, a Belgian–French mathematical physicist at Institut des Hautes Études Scientifiques (IHES), and Floris Takens, a Dutch mathematician at the University of Groningen, Netherlands, wanted to understand the dynamics of rushing water, where eddies and swirls appear and disappear without warning. As they looked closer at this phenomenon, they kept running into something that was drawing order out of disorder. They had no idea that they were peering deep into the heart of chaos. Unexpectedly, they began to unravel some sort of unknown, stabilizing factor within the irregularities of fluid motion.

After considerable study, they submitted their findings to a prominent scientific journal, but the research paper was soundly rejected. The editor wrote back to the mathematicians, and according to Ruelle, explained to them "what turbulence in fluid really was." Disappointed, Ruelle and Takens had to publish their now famous article—"On the Nature of Turbulence"—by themselves, which they did in 1971.[1]

Not only were Takens and Ruelle's conclusions slow to be accepted, but many professionals simply could not understand what they were trying to say. Implying that disorder could be channeled, these two scientists had to recruit an armful of metaphors with which to explain their findings to a baffled science community and public. At first, they compared these strange phenomena to the hidden order found in a gyroscope, which maintains orientation during times of erratic motion. Another image they used was that of a metal ball freely rolling around in a wooden bowl until it finally comes to a fixed point at the bowl's bottom. What made this all occur, they contended, was a counterbalancing force that was attracted to the trajectory of objects and conditions.

This stabilization phenomenon was not unknown. Scientists had grappled with the aberrant behavior of chaotic systems for centuries. They even had a disparaging name for it: "monster curves"—as if the anomalies were wild beasts ready to pounce on unsuspecting villagers and inflict incalculable damage. Actually, these strange behaviors were simply general tendencies in systems that oscillate between extremes. Not until scientists graphed them on computers, did they discover beautiful geometrical designs—fractals.

When Takens and Ruelle studied these stabilizing forces, they wanted only to understand the mysteries of turbulent fluid. Instead, they stumbled upon a whole new theory that applied to many disciplines. They had found that over long periods, erratic behavior often displays patterns not obvious in the short term. They even gave a name to this bizarre phenomenon: "strange attractors." One of the best descriptions came from broadcaster and author Benjamin Woolley, who contended, "An attractor is a state towards which a system is drawn."[2]

One of four attractors in chaos theory, the strange attractor contains a subtle, mostly nondeterministic force that displays patterns of order over time. Since the universe is fundamentally disordered, strange attractors provide an approximate picture of what has happened, but not of what will definitely happen. Strange attractors reveal a messy equilibrium of endless repetition, infinite detail, and unrepeatable initial conditions. And when these random–event data are compiled, computers can draw an identifiable geometric image, thanks to Benoît Mandelbrot's mathematical innovation, the Mandelbrot Set (more about this shortly).

The most famous strange attractor is the Lorenz attractor, introduced by meteorologist Edward Lorenz. He applied simple differential equations for fluid convection to the never–ending disturbances found in the atmosphere. With the assistance of early computer systems, Lorenz's seemingly random data plotted the likeness of butterfly wings. This symmetry pattern coincidentally evokes the symbol representing infinity, which is exactly what strange attractors represent: a rough world of infinite self-similarity and self-referencing properties.

From that point onward, scientists started to unearth other strange attractors in a clutch of other fields, including population dynamics, ocean currents, neural networks, movement of celestial bodies, coupled chemical reactions, brain waves, and heartbeats.

A Strange Attractor in Economics

Perhaps one of the most important and unrecognized strange attractors involves the human interaction of economic choice. Every day, consumers assign value to the things they need or want. How they determine this marginal utility has always confounded economists. Nevertheless, individual agents are the ones in the economic market trenches, scrambling to decipher the value of goods and services in a world fraught with scarcity. I refer to this strange attractor as "valuing."

The valuing attractor is truly perplexing. Why would anyone pay thousands of dollars for a Mickey Mouse wristwatch that originally sold for $3.25 in 1933? Even certain cheap plastic toys given away with breakfast cereal fetch hundreds of dollars today. For everything from old lunch boxes to Duncan yo–yos, there is a wide range of value, little of it attributable to its cost of manufacturing or its actual utility.

Used cars are particularly difficult to gauge value, since so many questions about their true condition are unanswered. Antiques vary wildly in uniqueness, condition, and price. Home prices move up and down with the economy, but less so if they are located in highly desirable areas, such as on beachfronts. And then there are invaluables: photo albums of long-deceased family members, keepsakes from past teenage flings, a wedding ring of a departed spouse.

Newly manufactured products are just as challenging to determine value. Without consumer support, products will simply gather dust on the store shelves and could eventually end up repackaged and shipped off to discount stores. For consumers, it does not matter how much a product cost to manufacture and distribute. When the Coca-Cola Corporation introduced their sweeter New Coke in 1985, the company had to practically give the reformulated soda away, when the public refused to buy it. Consumers also ignored the 1958–1960 Edsel, despite Ford Motor Company having spent over $400 million for its development and publicity.

One of the first scientists to study price and valuing was the French mathematician Benoît Mandelbrot. An employee of IBM in 1963, Mandelbrot decided to study the market fluctuations of cotton prices. Wondering whether some long–range patterns might appear, he searched for order where none was thought to exist. Naturally, his theory was ignored. Most economists were never able to make heads or tails out of past prices for commodities, and discarded them as random numbers lacking merit. With the improvement in computers' power and memory, Mandelbrot discovered that cotton prices did hide order within their complexity. Going over more than sixty years' worth of data, he found that curves representing daily price changes of cotton matched those representing its monthly price changes. He even coined the term "fractal," and popularized it through his book *Fractals: Form, Chance, and Dimension*.[3] To this day, the Mandelbrot Set is widely used in studying patterns in the stock market and other investments.

Valuing is important because it reinforces chaos theory's contention that hidden order is ubiquitous in all dynamic systems, making accurate predictions nearly impossible. Valuing also relates to open systems in which reciprocal relationships are established within surrounding boundaries—exchanging matter, energy, and information. In fact, some economists had already discovered the indeterminate nature of value by the late nineteenth century. They noticed that valuations made by human beings were often too transient to pin down, and that therefore, value must have something to do with the wandering eye of the beholder. They labeled this economic theory "subjective value."

Subjective Value

First advanced in 1871 by Carl Menger, an economist from the Austrian school and the author of *Principles of Economics*, subjective value theory posits that invariably, consumers will select those things that will yield them the greatest satisfaction. Accordingly, the price consumers are willing to pay is a product's genuine value, irrespective of costs in its manufacture or government-imposed price constraints. This means that the value of an object is not inherent, but lies in the mind of an individual who wants it. For instance, for a person stranded in the sizzling–hot desert, a glass of water might be worth more than a bag of diamonds. Value changes continually, as needs and desires fluctuate; personal decisions are hard to predict since people differ as to what pleases them. Value is truly subjective. One person's trash is another person's treasure.

In sharp contrast, Karl Marx's "labor theory of value," widely popular throughout the mid–nineteenth century, veered down the same old Newtonian cul–de–sac. Under Marxist interpretations, the value of a commodity is directly related to the labor required to produce or procure it. If the central government were to calculate the prices for cameras, computers, or furniture, by the labor theory of value, the cost of past labor would be the sole determining criterion. No other factors would apply; consumer participation, marginal utility, and buyer's satisfaction would have no part in the equation.

Marx constructed an ideological framework to determine value, arbitrarily carving pricing into stone. Under these unyielding determinants, the bustling of society is excluded from any decision–making processes. Without the annoying presence of options, command–control systems are free to ignore "biopolar feedback," which allows positive and negative data to fluctuate in response to change. Obviously, central planners find it more convenient to dictate value and disinformation according to moralistic or ideological objectives. But this is not the way to verify or discover the informational accuracy of consumer demand.

Information Theory and Accurate Information

So, what is information? Some argue that information resembles a "fluid lubricant," coated with a chaotically acting membrane that allows data to pass from transmitter to receiver. Others see information as the building blocks of matter and energy that can trigger the actions of strange attractors. No matter how information is described, most information scientists contend that only unfiltered accessibility of data allows people to clearly understand the nature of their world and the universe. Of course, nowadays it is almost impossible to completely obstruct or censor information. Current Internet technology re-routes information anonymously, allowing different approaches to open up in a way that almost exhibits a crude form of electronic self–awareness.

However, many political systems still block information, being generally averse to letting nonpolitical systems dictate their own terms and events. Command and control structures clearly understand that an unrestricted flow of information can easily unmask state–induced incompetence and deception. Most political systems are extremely fearful of data that show what's truly happening. Joseph Goebbels, Nazi Germany's Minister of Propaganda from 1933 to 1945, revealed this fact when he said, "truth is the greatest enemy of the State."

The co-founder of Twitter, Isaac "Biz" Stone, understood the power of uncontrolled access to information. Before the 2011 pro-democracy uprisings in the Arab world, Stone had foreseen the global implications of his invention. Since 2009, Stone had been proclaiming that "Twitter is not a triumph of technology, it is a triumph of humanity." In a speech in San Francisco in 2010, he outlined his vision further, describing Twitter as "a tool for times of revolution and strife, a service that can break news, bring down tyrants, and salve the wounds of the forsaken."[4] Stone was describing the revolutionary concept of the movement of uncensored information for everyone—a sort of unlimited swarming of shared knowledge.

Although the usual suspects attempting to restrict information flow reside mostly among nondemocratic nations, a growing number of representative democracies are toying with legislation to censor the Internet. One nation, Australia, announced plans in 2008 to systematically block Internet access to child–pornography web sites. At first, that seemed innocuous. But civil libertarians wondered whether the plan had a hidden agenda. Was the political system scaremongering the public to get them to accept a wider spectrum of censorship? Or was it the old bait–and–switch tactic to justify stronger governmental actions unrelated to the original fear?

When the Australian regulators started to compile a list of illegal web sites, purportedly to "protect the children," the list was quickly leaked to the press. Not surprising to free speech activists on the blogosphere, most of the web sites had no relationship to kiddy porn. For instance, the blacklist targeted "a slew of poker sites, YouTube links, regular gay and straight porn sites, Wikipedia entries, euthanasia sites, websites of fringe religious groups such as satanic sites, fetish sites, Christian sites, the website of a tour operator and even a Queensland dentist."[5]

Although the Australia officials promised that the mandatory filters would block only illegal child–porn sites, the whistleblower web site WikiLeaks was added to the banned list after it posted the list of banned sites. Apparently, the act of listing banned web sites for public viewing is, itself, banned. As one irate blogger at the web site Classically Liberal sarcastically remarked, "People must not be allowed to know what they aren't allowed to know." In fact, in the case of Australia's censorship laws, the punishment for informing the public about who is on the banned list is ten years in jail. Although the WikiLeaks server and operations are located in faraway Germany and Sweden, that did not stop Australian censorship regulators. In less than a week, eleven German police officers conducted a night raid at the home office of the volunteer in charge of the WikiLeaks server, confiscating computers and searching for the password to disable the web site.[6]

But this particular case of censorship has a far more sinister side. Since it is a crime to publish or post which sites have been blacklisted, nobody knows for sure who is considered illegal. Nor are the web sites themselves informed of their legal status, since that would be giving out illegal information. If an innocent web site owner or blogger decided to link to a secretly banned site, what would happen? Would their site be banned and blocked, too? And how far up the ladder of linked web sites would the censorship go? It did not take long to find out. According to the *Sydney Morning Herald*, regulators at the Australian Communications and Media Authority "threatened the host of on-line broadband discussion forum Whirlpool last week with a $11,000-a-day fine over a link published in its forum to another page blacklisted by ACMA — an anti-abortion website."[7]

So, what does this say about the importance of uncensored information? For chaologists and information theorists, it means that trying to restrict the flow of information causes needless complexity, confusion, and conflict. Moreover, information is link-dependent, meaning that it is nothing but linked and networked messages that communicate with other information. If any link can be blocked, banned, or altered because it has a relationship to other sources of information, the whole system can become compromised and corrupted, ending accuracy's role as a constant. The integrity of information would be undermined. Without unfiltered information, society can be easily misled, as there would no longer be any foundation upon which to place trust.

Through politicization, information is invariably molded to convey a particular message — usually to the detriment of competing information. And that basic message recycles around defense of the status quo, preserving the existing state of affairs. But according to Claude Shannon, the father of Information Theory, information is not associated with meaning, and it has the ability to be "an agent of change." In this sense, information performs a balancing act between choice and constraints, certainty and uncertainty, patterns and randomness.

John Archibald Wheeler, an American theoretical physicist who collaborated with Albert Einstein, refers to information as the "new physics of science," where "everything is information." The coiner of the term "black hole," Wheeler proposes that information theory is built upon "elementary particles of binary units, or bits," that are analogous to the packets of energy described in quantum physics.[8] To chaologists, communication is merely the means to receive and decode information, regardless of the message. To accomplish this, the data must be part of an open-ended system without political-advocacy filters, dogmatic padlocks, or state-funded firewalls; otherwise the data would be limited, compromised, or would fail to contain accurate information. The same goes for economic systems: markets are informational highways, paved with links allowing its members to converse directly with those who want to exchange lower value for higher value in the consumer bazaar.

Without a two–way data stream, there is simply no objective way to allocate resources, because there is no accurate way to gauge what is actually occurring in the economy. Too much restriction on informational feedback was a major factor contributing to the downfall of the Soviet Union. The socialist authorities simply did not know what was going on in their own backyard, nor could they figure out how to fix the problem. They lacked what Austrian economist and philosopher Friedrich Hayek dubbed "unique information." Further, they were not armed with the proper tools. Soviet economists had been trained as engineers and planners. The concepts of unplanned processes and spontaneous order were not in their dog–eared lexicon. With a limited toolkit, these central planners were like carpenters equipped only with hammers; everything began to look like a nail.

Chaologists take a favorable approach to stochastic processes, in which the set of likely outcomes could be drawn from any of several possible, evolving realities. For instance, large numbers of people will often take an unplanned dirt shortcut between two buildings, perhaps at a campus, while the official landscaped concrete pathway experiences less traffic. Central planners would say that paths shouldn't just happen; they should be predetermined. But why can't they just happen? Why not build the path where the users actually want to go? Some refer to this obsession with orchestrating prearranged routes as "path dependency."

Unfortunately, most ideologies are path–dependent. Ideologues strive to "lock in" systems and societies to the "proper" course of action—whatever that might entail. They have no qualms about prohibiting individual agents from making autonomous decisions concerning which direction to move. In this way, authoritarian doctrines resemble monolithic religions, ever vigilant to restrict their flock from inquiring about other denominations or wandering away from long–established precepts. Allowing congregation members to make low–level choices is dangerous, since they might be tempted to take the wrong route, one that wasn't preordained. The ability to choose is seen as both hazardous and a waste of time. For those addicted to path–dependency, the more complex the belief system, the more heresy there is to counteract.

Chaos theory and complexity science rely on the availability of options to discover observable patterns as practiced in the scientific method. Similar to the unfettered movement of strange attractors, the ability to have multiple choices allows individual agents to demonstrate value patterns without external guidance.

And when the aggregate of self-determining value is added up, one by one, accurate data can come to the forefront—at least momentarily. This is the true value of having feedback indicating what people really want. What other way could there be to reveal accurate information?

Unfortunately, those caught up in command–based systems fear the erratic and uncontrolled nature of choice–driven valuing. Preoccupied with controlling and manipulating society, they see the self–prioritizing flow of information as a threat to their authority. In their mindset, the economy and society must perform in a way that they view as suitable for their ideological or leadership precepts. The authoritarian mindset sees truth as a slippery target, and therefore extremely difficult to hit with their stockpile of well–planned mandates. In everything from rent control to minimum wage laws, from land–use laws to usury laws, command–based systems strive to assign absolute values, as if they could be etched into stone for all eternity.

The scientific world knows better. The essence of chaos theory is that nonlinear systems never completely settle into an absolutely fixed equilibrium. Under the theory of relativity, Einstein took the position that everything is relative to someone else's position. The ebbing and flowing tide of value is relative to the observer. In a sense, individual human action resembles subatomic particles guided by uncertainty—creating value by a subjectivity that may never be known. Even if someone were to attempt to freeze value, value would still speed toward its own destination.

Economists have long realized that hog–tying price to an arbitrary value simply forces its market to flee underground. This situation can be readily seen in cities where rents are artificially set below market value. The result is almost a ritual. The landlord usually arranges an under–the–table deal to compensate for underpriced rent. Naturally, this deal is off the record, which makes it even more difficult to gauge true value or rentals in a rent–controlled city.

Regardless of the many attempts to control value by fiat, it remains constant only to its nature. And any attempt to force either value or choice to do otherwise will merely lead to manmade instability and great social distortions—what I refer to as "bad chaos."

1 David Ruelle and F. Takens, "On the Nature of Turbulence," *Communications of Mathematical Physics* 20, (3): pp. 167–192, 1971.

2 Benjamin Woolley, *Virtual Worlds: A Journey in Hype and Hyperreality*, Oxford: Blackwell Publishers, 1992, p. 88.

3 Benoit B. Mandelbrot, *Fractals: Form, Chance, and Dimension*, New York: W.H. Freeman, first edition,1977.

4 Farhad Manjoo, "Tweet Now, Revolt Later," *Slate*, posted April 15, 2010, http://www.slate.com/id/2250991/

5 Ahser Moses, "Leaked Australian Blacklist Reveals Banned Sites," *The Sydney Morning Herald*, March 19, 2009.

6 Ryan Singel, "German Cops Raid Home of WikiLeaks and Tor Volunteer — Update," *Wired*, March 25, 2009.

7 Asher Moses, "Banned Hyperlinks Could Cost You $11,000 a Day," *Sydney Morning Herald*, March 17, 2009.

8 Heather Wax, "Information Technology Raises New Question on Everything," *Science and Theology News*, March 1, 2003.

5 Social Chaology and Weak Structures

The attempt to combine wisdom and power has only rarely been successful and then only for a short while. —Albert Einstein

Coercion cannot but result in chaos in the end. —Mahatma Gandhi

Since time immemorial, human history has been awash in horror stories of death and destruction. The more reputable historians are able to sift through the human carnage and write compelling narratives about the underlying causes of violent social upheavals. But many of the ancient interpretations were biased and evaded the truth. Sadly, the writers from antiquity often had to be discreet or cryptic when pointing an accusing finger at those responsible for inciting social disorder.

In a world where brutish victors wrote history and where uncensored writing was a fanciful notion, many ancient historians and scribes sought safe harbor by blaming upheavals on unstable conditions, foreign barbarians, or wrathful gods. Only after political storms had blown past and half–hearted eulogies had been forgotten could historians finally assign culpability to the obvious delinquent—the 800 pound gorilla who seeks to be crowned with Caesar's laurel wreath of power and glory.

History is the stuff of "social complexity." Social chaologists pore over the annals of history to understand why structural weaknesses in society lead to its self–cannibalization. Why is politics so dominance-inclined, diktat–based, and failure–prone? To some social chaologists, this conflict–ridden tableau appears to have been built into the system. After all, few systems operate so disjointedly and unwieldily, drunken with the fanatical lure of power, systemized by a coterie of "controlaholic" heavyweights, desperate to be loved but willing to unleash the dogs of fear and war upon their own people.

Some argue that political systems are premised on a pathological dominance that disfigures the many, to ennoble the few. Indeed, the apparatus of government has always been an exclusive tool for the elite, regardless of which political system is in place. This fact alone compels government-centric adherents to oppose any semblance of an independently armed citizenry. To the political elite, statecraft is predicated on the notion that society is theirs to put into some type of hegemonic order. It is immaterial whether this institutionalized order actually helps society or instead puts it into a chokehold that slowly squeezes the air out of life. To the authorities, supremacy is always the primary objective.

Political structures are excessively paternalistic, and to maintain them requires a high level of energy. The massive amounts of energy they consume are unsustainable and invite political meltdowns, bailouts, and fallout. On the other hand, proponents of complexity theory take the paradigm–shattering view that less is more. They understand that, paradoxically enough, the complexity of simplicity is the key to the emergence of systems, repeatable patterns and the social glue that holds community together and creates order. Anyone can make simplicity complicated; it takes a true genius to make the complicated simple.

Social and cultural self–organizing systems are interdependent but are structurally unorganized so as never to be locked into a permanent position or role. Yet, paradoxically, they maintain a strong degree of stabilizing internal control. They invoke self–dampers that maximize their operations with the energy at hand; that is, they self–organize by optimizing the "free energy" found within their system. In sharp contrast, invasive-based political systems spend energy to command what they rarely control.

Some complexity theorists have dubbed the fuel behind the self–ordering process "organizational free energy," which seems to correlate not only to John Locke's "principle of least authority" but to the software–based "principle of least power." By the 1960s, computer scientists had discovered the benefits of the power of dispower. Yes—they came to realize that the way to optimize a computer language is to select, ironically (or "counterintuitively"), the least powerful solution. Simplicity was the key to success. The less powerful the language, the more options available for stored data—a principle nicknamed KISS (Keep It Simple, Stupid). This less–power aphorism is remarkably compatible with John Locke's interpretation of limited government, where the power of authority should be so diffuse that no one man or group can gain a larger share than another. This minimization of power is elegantly described by French writer Antoine de Saint–Exupéry, who observed, "A designer knows he has achieved perfection not when there is nothing left to add, but when there is nothing left to take away."

Social Chaology and Weak Structures 91

But proponents of diffuse authority are usually relegated to the back lots of irrelevancy. The most attention is lavished on politically ordained celebrities who treat societal actors as disposable, mere extras from Central Casting whose lives were never worth owning. With an air of arrogance, the strong and the political elite see power as a birthright. Yet, in an ironic twist, it is the strongest of the strong who tout heartfelt devotion to the weak. They chant the same liturgy: government exists to protect the weak from the strong—although the strong are usually the ones in charge of institutions that cause the weak to grow weaker. In reality, the politically impotent plebes understand their deficiencies, and seek "impunity from power," rather than a democracy that is power.[1]

Many social chaologists acknowledge that the pitfalls of political structures are uncontainable. These systems are the primary disrupters of order, smothering or muzzling grassroots emergence. The politics of control and manipulation can only have a degenerative effect on civilization and stability. When larger systems dominate smaller ones, society and its members must face a host of bad choices, debilitating harm, and dicey outcomes. Once the leviathan has been released, few can really control its movements.

So once the damage has become visible, historians can point to the inevitable source of the criminality: the "structured order" of politics, rather than an "unstructured order" of the people. To the gullible, this is a shocking revelation. How could any system entrusted with maintaining order destroy the very thing it had sworn to uphold? One of the most poignant cases of such delinquency ever recorded was that of Roman Emperor Nero Claudius Caesar Drusus Germanicus.

Transgression of Emperor Nero

An egomaniac with a flair for the dramatic, Nero had his share of troubles governing Rome during the first century A.D. After a series of unsuccessful attempts to assassinate his own mother, the emperor turned his attention to the ugliness of Roman slums. Possibly one of the earliest advocates of redevelopment, Nero pushed to rebuild major portions of Rome. But the Roman Senate ardently objected to his costly plan of street widening, slum removal, and beautification.

Although the origin of the great Roman fire of 64 A.D. was never completely determined, most citizens accused Nero of ordering the fire to clear room for his ambitious vision of Rome, which he planned to rename "Neropolis." But could Roman officials set fire to their own city? Historian Tacitus (56–117 A.D.) thought so, writing that during the blaze, Nero had "mounted his private stage and, reflecting present disasters in ancient calamities, sang about the destruction of Troy." Later historians were more direct, indicating that Nero sang merrily with his lyre, as flames devoured the city.

In a city of one to two million inhabitants, outbreaks of fire in wooden–constructed Rome were daily occurrences. But this was no ordinary fire. According to Tacitus, gangs of thugs stopped citizens from fighting the fire, causing it to rage out of control and burn two–thirds of Rome. As the rumors spread of his involvement, the emperor ordered an official investigation, which led to accusations that an obscure Jewish religious sect—the Christians—had conspired to burn the city.

Public suspicions of Nero's duplicity were validated when he built a 300–acre palace and garden near the spot where the fire had started, the same area where the Roman Senate had refused to let him start his urban redevelopment program. In all likelihood, the emperor's lust for death and chaos caused him not only to burn down most of Rome, but eventually to murder his mother and pregnant wife. This is the true legacy of planned, manmade "bad" chaos.

Weak Structures: Bad Chaos

Bad chaos rears its offensive head when external controls overpower the internal affairs of autonomous systems. In a sociological context, this stranglehold chokes the self–directing functions of society. Although unrecognized by the general public, command–based systems are constantly at war most members of society. This perpetual political warfare represents the opaque barricade that separates the governed from the governing, and accounts for the strife over who will be assigned the role of superior or subordinate.

Because the two are diametrically opposed to each other's sphere of self–interest, conflict will affect every course of action. Like a drunken teenager in a fast sports car, the political adherents don't care as much about direction as about commanding the steering wheel. Usually indifferent, most members of society merely seek a free ride, but they often find themselves at destinations not of their choosing. This divergence is inherent in myopic systems that are consistently inconsistent. One reason is that it is impossible for a monopolistic structure to impose actions on any two individuals that will generate an equal outcome—inevitably, one will benefit more, and one will suffer more. Over time, citizen alienation tends to increase, especially when politicos tighten their obsessive–compulsive grip on the steering wheel.

If one peels back the onion layers a bit more, the undesirable chaos of conflict and discord can be found to run far deeper than simple antagonism between warring groups. William Durant, historian and the author of *The Story of Civilization*, put mankind's true disposition into crystal–clear perspective: "If man asks for many laws it is only because he is sure that his neighbor needs them; privately he is an unphilosophical anarchist, and thinks laws in his own case superfluous."

It is only human to instigate some type of control over what is considered inferior. But some people try to control everything within their reach—fervid to run the show and call all the shots. Thomas J. Schumacher, a psychotherapist from New York, has dealt with this personality disorder, writing that control freaks need to diminish others in order to feel better about themselves: "They need you to feel helpless, so they will not feel helpless."[2]

This insatiable appetite to control others presents command–based systems with the opportunity to consolidate power structures and to punish anyone who gets out of line. They do so by convincing everyone that the structures are needed, and that some entity must limit the so–called defective activities of others.

But political systems exhibit other weaknesses. Even before complexity theory arrived on the scene in the 1990s, a number of political scientists and economists in the 1960s began to dabble with nonlinear systems that bordered on sociopolitical cha-ology. Yale economist Charles E. Lindblom and economist A. O. Hirschman indicated that human beings have limited capacities to solve problems. To them, comprehensive policymaking by governments would always fail because of conflicting values, information inadequacies, and general complexity beyond our intellectual capacities. In later works, Lindblom described actual policymaking as "disjointed incrementalism" and "muddling thought." He suggested that things are accomplished not through centralized planning but through bit-by-bit, evolutionary, baby steps of often unplanned changes.[3]

Then there is W. Brian Arthur, one of the authors of *The Economy as an Evolving Complex System II*, a faculty member at the Santa Fe Institute, and winner of the Schumpeter Prize in Economics in 1990. He muses over whether mankind can ever achieve optimal decision–making in any system, political or economic. Referring to "deductive rationality" as something that breaks down under extreme complexity, Arthur uses a chess game analogy to illustrate the true magnitude of complexity. If every atom in the universe had been involved in the computing effort of a supercomputer, crunching numbers since the Big Bang, it would still be impossible to identify the optimal move at the beginning of a chess match. Arthur suggests that when systems are complex or ill–defined, inductive reasoning is a better tool for understanding future events. And that is because multiple outcomes put into motion a "rationally bound" world, where patterns unfold in a changeable environment.[4]

Edge–of–Chaos Disequilibrium

The "edge of chaos" is a sweet spot where a system is neither exactly orderly nor completely disorderly. All systems navigate across a wide zone between stability and instability. Neither extreme elicits a round of resounding applause. Too much order causes a system to stagnate toward the ossification of death, while too much chaos causes systems to become ensnared in the meaningless randomness of anarchy. The balance is a disequilibrium that encompasses both worlds.

When this happy disequilibrium is achieved, it can inspire cooperation, mutual self–interest, creativity, and prosperity of breathtaking proportions. This is the "good" chaos in which societal structures are free to act consensually in a direction of their own choosing, analogous to the decentralized decision–making found in swarm dynamics. It also exhibits a pluralistic, open-choice approach that provides unobstructed channels for new synapse–like pathways to challenge the old without the unwanted side effects of stagnation or anomie. But when this balancing connectivity is severed by outside forces, bad chaos is sure to follow. So the question that becomes paramount is: why the incongruity?

Social disorder thrives on structural deficiencies. Deterministic structures erected by ruling systems are organized to govern toward preplanned outcomes. Social planners design to design, but almost always from lofty heights, in order to save humanity from itself or to control human behavior. They act as though they have already anticipated future events, and become agitated when the laws of unintentional consequences violate their foreordained conclusion. Most political systems find existing societal foundations and traditions inconvenient, because these elements might prevent them from imposing more stringent restrictions. They want faultless outcomes, where they need not learn what happens after things occur. Favoring deterministic systems, they are not equipped to compensate for unexplainable errors, random defects, and messy outcomes. The property of emergence, in which things happen in ways that are unanticipated by the designer, is nowhere to be found in the central planner's toolbox.

Social chaos theory posits that in open systems—where both input and output are relatively unrestrained—societies remain healthy, dynamic, and stable. But under closed systems, society is compromised by life–threatening political inhibitors. Analogous to cholesterol clogging up arteries, calcified societies prevent the free flow of people, innovation, and information, with plaque–like obstacles restricting the socioeconomic life–blood of society. As the body of society begins to atrophy and vital organs shut down, its members lack ways to escape the approaching disorder. The system suffers a sclerotic hardening, in which all functions slow to a trickle at every level. Demoralized and frustrated, central planners are reduced to the level of delinquents and schemers, ever on the prowl to exploit the weak, the politically unconnected, and the trustworthy. They have few qualms about victimizing others before being victimized themselves, because the new social order will spin ethics inside out, punishing honesty while rewarding dishonesty. Society soon collapses into an ungovernable and uncooperative mess—bad–to–the–bone chaos.

The Devil's Footpath

Any political malady can kill off the cooperative and ethical behavior of society while encouraging a violent and aggressive culture. In the BBC documentary *The Devil's Footpath*, director June Arunga set out to discover why the African continent was so rich in natural resources, yet so poor in terms of the lives of its peasants. During her 5,000–mile, six–week excursion, she unearthed an unsettling dread that overwhelmed many Africans: a fear of being beaten and even tortured by the authorities.

While in Sudan, Arunga encountered a truly dysfunctional, unstable society. She explained, "Imagine living in a place where if someone wants your property, instead of renting or buying it, they decide it is cheaper to kill you, and then proceed to make a law that entitles them to do this unabated, and guess what, you can't turn to the government for justice because these guys are the police and the army! So all you can do is run for your life."[5]

Arunga observed that the small political elite in Sudan possessed all the wealth and power. There were apparently no independent institutions to protect the peasants' right to their land. And without such safeguards, there was no functioning economy.

When it comes to governments in Africa, Ghanaian–born economics professor George Ayittey asserts that they "suck the vitality out of the people," so he denounces them as "vampire states." This he defines as "a government which has been captured or hijacked by a phalanx of bandits and crooks who use instruments of the state to enrich themselves, their cronies and tribesmen and exclude everybody else." During a PBS interview with Bill Moyers, Ayittey reported that government corruption had become so perverse that one head of state, Sani Abacha of Nigeria, launched a predawn raid on his own central bank and trucked billions of dollars out of the country.[6]

"The richest in Africa are African heads of state and ministers," Ayittey reported. "How did they make their money? They made their money by raking it off the back of their suffering people. That is not wealth creation. It is wealth redistribution."[7]

The Planned Chaos of Mao Tse–tung

Governmental and economic transgression is only one form of bad chaos. Chairman Mao Tse–tung of the People's Republic of China discovered other ways to make run–of–the–mill encroachments resemble the virtuous deeds of saints. In an effort to keep a watchful eye on every citizen, Mao's government did more than procure secret dossiers on each individual. Mimicking the policies of the U.S.S.R., the authorities set up thousands of street committees to control the lives of ordinary people.

One of the more sinister techniques undermined societal cohesion and community trust by barring the flow of information. Street committees required written reports whenever citizens spoke to each other. The reports would be compared. If they did not match, an official investigation would be launched to pinpoint the liar and to determine whether counter–revolutionary activities were underway. In short order, citizens realized that it was safer to wave to a friend or neighbor than to strike up a conversation. Without an open forum for interpersonal communications, there was no pressure valve for venting feedback to peers. Chinese society began to implode under a paralysis of isolation. The normal synergism of working together for common goals was supplanted by the poison politics of combative disunity.

Throughout most of Mao's reign, an incessant turbulence stalked the Chinese people. From the Cultural Revolution to the Great Leap Forward, Chinese citizens experienced social and political upheaval.

Considered a civil war between rivaling Communist factions, the Cultural Revolution (1966–1976) was an upsurge against the bureaucrats of the Chinese Communist Party. Responding to Mao's call for continuous revolution, armies of mostly youths organized into Red Guard units, took control of the cities, and toppled the older Communist leadership in almost every province. Students were encouraged to attack the old structure—teachers, administrators, parents, even old temples and artwork. Millions were imprisoned, expelled to reeducation centers or work camps as slave labor, tried in kangaroo courts, humiliated as enemies of the people, and publicly executed.

These political purges were brutal, but were no less shocking than the starvation of 20 to 30 million Chinese in the "Great Leap Forward." In an attempt to increase industrial and agricultural output, the government imposed a Five–Year Plan (1958–1963). To accomplish this grand plan, nearly 700 million people were collectivized into over 26,000 farming communes with over 600,000 backyard steel furnaces. But problems quickly developed. Political decisions overrode common sense. If the communal leaders complained about impossible production quotas, they could be charged as a "bourgeois reactionary" and shipped off to prison. So, local leaders exaggerated their reports of future farm production, flooding central planners with erroneous claims, which caused officials to believe that China was going to experience a huge food surplus. In response, the Chinese central planners sold food to Russia, ordered more fields to lie fallow, and let crops in the field go unharvested. Ironically, as the shortage of food became more critical, the authorities encouraged farm communes to melt down their farm equipment, to satisfy the government's industrialization plan to increase the production of steel.

The national drive was so strong that even those in schools and hospitals abandoned their work to smelt iron, even though the backyard steel was too inferior to be of any use. Also aggravating the crisis was a shortage of fuel. Because backyard furnaces had consumed much of China's coal output, there was not enough for the railroad system to transport supplies to needy destinations. After three years of economic chaos, the central planners finally realized that China was paralyzed in the grip of a full–fledged famine.

Mao eventually admitted his role in the disorderly fiasco, confessing, "The chaos caused was on a grand scale and I take responsibility. Comrades, you must all analyze your own responsibility. If you have to shit, shit. If you have to fart, fart. You will feel much better for it."[8]

An Institution of Legalized Violence

Command–based systems take the form of institutions with a monopoly on legalized violence within a given geographical area. Through either guns or paper ballots, these systems have acquired control over those who have tolerated interference in their lives. Frequently, critical mass is reached on a Richter scale of dissatisfaction, triggering violence if the populace cannot find other avenues for change.

Under democratic institutions, citizens have achieved more peaceful means to dump unresponsive leadership and unpopular governmental policies. But the fact remains that every command–based system, including democratic ones, has the authority to inflict violent reprisals upon any individual agent who fails to follow its dictates, rendering such political systems utterly puissant. In essence, the amount of applied violence is often the only factor distinguishing dictatorships from democracies or constitutional republics. Although government has the means to tuck you into bed at night, it can just as well suffocate you with the pillow.

Without robust regulations on the machinery of government, political structures mimic misbehaving children unrelenting in their infantile endeavor to do whatever they please. During a 1977 ABC Television interview with Barbara Walters, Fidel Castro was questioned whether there was freedom in Cuba. With complete confidence and anarchistic flair, Castro smiled broadly and affirmed that, "I can do anything I want."

In extreme cases, this defiant behavior takes on more ominous character, especially when policing agencies are permitted to lash out at the unfaithful, in mass "democides." Even institutions sworn to written or oral constitutions often turn impotent during so–called emergencies, allowing state–sponsored terror to dominate particular segments of society with impunity. And that is because governing systems are always looking to exploit some crisis, real or imaginary. As President Obama's White House Chief of Staff, Rahm Emanuel, said in an honest, offhand tone, "Never let a serious crisis go to waste."

The role and function of society are always precarious. But one factor is always the same: the stronger the governing system, the more weakly functioning the society. To maintain power, all political systems must conceal from the citizenry the unpleasant side of institutionalized violence. The masking is devious. Compulsory systems seduce society with grandiose promises to fund all sorts of public goodies and private lifestyles. In actuality, political divas fool the citizenry into playing a master–slave role. Political systems are always on the prowl, to exchange free bread for chains and shackles. They are more than willing to substitute public assistance for private independence. But free lunches have devastating consequences other than the loss of options.

Dependence on governmental handouts undermines people's self–responsibility and their self–governing urges to take care of themselves and others in the community, which can easily block social bonding. Ironically, the National Park Service warned about this sort of destructive behavior, when humans started to feed bears and other wildlife in parklands. Park rangers argued that to give handouts to wild animals not only made them dependent on the not–so–dependable tourists, but dissuaded them from foraging for themselves. But worse, if the charity stopped or became infrequent, bears would often go on a rampage, breaking into homes and vehicles as if they now had a permanent right to man–made food. Human civilization could take a lesson from the National Park Service's wildlife policies.

The Licensing Effect

For social chaologists, whether public policy is deemed well–intentioned or evil–inspired is immaterial. Good intentions rarely make good laws. Those who do evil almost always think they are doing good for goodness' sake. Nobody sees himself as evil. As Will Smith, the American actor, once quipped, "Even Hitler didn't wake up going, 'let me do the most evil thing I can do today.' I think he woke up in the morning and using a twisted, backwards logic, he set out to do what he thought was 'good.'" Friedrich Hayek took this idea a step further, writing: "It is indeed probable that more harm and misery have been caused by men determined to use coercion to stamp out a moral evil than by men intent on doing evil."[9]

There is little to prevent do–gooders and their actions from unexpectedly metamorphosing into holocaustic bloodbaths, especially when considering the "licensing effect." Under this effect, people can rationalize bad conduct, if they first do something good. Whether in dieting, consumer choice, or politicking, the licensing effect permits people to be wicked after they have performed something deemed good.

According to Dale Miller, a psychology professor at Stanford Business School, "With licensing, the first act doesn't commit you, it liberates you." This liberating euphoria permits the human psyche to do what it supposedly is against. Miller's experiments uncovered business managers who publicly declared their lack of bias in hiring minorities, for instance, but in practice showed a strong prejudice against minorities. Since these managers had declared their support for minorities, they were now free to be extremely biased.[10]

A major study by a sociologist at the University of Arizona exposed the twisted dilemmas and unintended consequences of the licensing effect. The 2007 study provided clear analytical evidence of the ineffectiveness of involuntary diversity training in the workplace. It would be reasonable to presume that by the late twentieth century, encouraging diversity within the workplace had become an easy sell. But after reviewing 31 years of data from 830 mid-sized and large corporations, sociologist Alexandra Kalev concluded that involuntary diversity training was "ineffective and counterproductive."

How counterproductive? The figures are shocking. A comprehensive review of data revealed that those businesses' mandated diversity training exercises for their managerial staff were followed by a "7.5 percent drop in the number of women in management." For black female managers, the decrease was 10 percent, with a 12 percent drop for black men. "The effect was similar for Latinos and Asians."[11] So what is going on?

This study shows that mandatory enforcements routinely backfire, because they are set up with unrealistic and artificial expectations. Real change comes when people voluntarily modify their opinions. Any other way makes people feel that they have been imposed upon. Professor Kalev confirmed this reality by noting: "When attendance is voluntary, diversity training is followed by an increase in managerial diversity."[12]

When companies with government contracts are put under the gun to teach diversity, managers get the impression that, having taken a course, they've performed their good–citizen duty. They've been trained by experts to be a lean, mean antidiscrimination machine. And yet, the sacrifice they made in taking the compulsory training shouts out for compensation. They have been put upon to do something good. They have spent long, boring hours in the classroom. They can now subconsciously overlook or avoid the hiring of minorities. In Kalev's words, "Forcing people to go through training creates a backlash against diversity."[13]

Many corporations also bring diversity training into the workplace for legal protection. In this case, the training becomes an exercise in public and legal relations, instead of reaching toward true, long–term change. After all, companies understand that their diversity training bestows some legal protection, if later they are hit by a discrimination lawsuit. In short, preventing lawsuits is more important than efficacious training. Bill Vaughn, cofounder of Diversity Training University International, confirms what the study foreshadowed. "If they are doing it for legal protection, they don't care whether their training is successful."[14]

The licensing effect affords us an explanation for a time–honored way to justify violating principles. For instance, if someone is always condemning greed, he is now entitled to a binge of overt self–indulgence. Having cleared his conscience of any avarice, he can waltz into a Mercedes–Benz showroom and splurge like a rapacious man of wealth. Further, he can brand others as greedy SOBs while taking comfort in the fact that the saintly blood of altruism flows through his own noble veins. For the virtuous, to act self–centered is impossible, as such behavior is unthinkable to the enlightened mind; therefore, narcissistic greed can run wild. Habitually, the greediest are blissfully unaware of their own selfish motives.

In an interesting article in *Psychological Science*, two researchers argued that people who feel morally virtuous have a tendency to engage in the "licensing (of) selfish and morally questionable behavior," also known as "moral balancing" or "compensatory ethics." The researchers, Canadian psychologists Nina Mazar and Chen–Bo Zhong, revealed that when people try to save the planet or do noble deeds, they become less kind to others and more likely to cheat and steal. They wrote: "Virtuous acts can license subsequent asocial and unethical behavior."[15]

The licensing effect is also found among public employee unions who act as if they still represent government employees receiving little compensation for their work. For over 150 years, that was true of American civil servants, but no longer. According to economist Chris Edwards, "As of 2008, the average federal salary was $119,982, compared with $59,909 for the average private sector employee. In other words, the average federal bureaucrat makes twice as much as the average working taxpayer."[16] Despite this disparity in pay between the public and private sectors, the political and bureaucratic classes routinely accuse opponents of greed. They condemn tax–averse corporations and taxpayers as selfish pigs obsessed with money. And yet, as columnist Steven Greenhut observed: "there are few things as greedy as running up debt and lobbying for more taxes from the peons so that an elite class can keep retiring earlier with ever–greater pension and other benefits."[17]

But this greedy disposition is just the tip of a bloating iceberg. Many government and union–operated retirement programs have no qualms about taking big risks in the stock market. Why? Because the political class always holds the winning hand. Applying a Las Vegas metaphor, Greenhut asked: How would you bet if you could keep all your gains at the casino, but dump your losses on someone else? But this is exactly how many of these public retirement systems operate. If a Public Employees' Retirement System (PERS) fails to make a profit, the taxpaying public is often responsible for making up the deficiencies. So, who are the real greedy profiteers here?

In the electoral politics realm, the licensing effect grants politicos the prerogative to flip–flop their principles. When President Richard Nixon, fervently anticommunist, visited Red China in the 1970s, political pundits came up with a proverbial apothegm: "Only Nixon could go to China." Fluent in altruistic doublespeak, those in control of command–based systems rely on the fulcrum of well–respected virtues. Since they are public servants—supposedly hired to serve up healthy scoops of community goodwill—they find themselves confronted with a license to act contrary to stated purposes. This situation supplies a politico the license to sabotage principles of good governance by becoming a player in society, instead of a referee.

After becoming a player, the governing team no longer needs to be tethered to impartiality. Without the restraints of a rules-bound referee, government officials are free to take sides and play favorites. Like professional football teams, bureaucrats, politicians and technocrats often wage strategic campaigns against those perceived to be the opposition. Taxpayers are no longer seen as cooperative partners, but as antagonistic contestants in a never–ending struggle for turf and money. In the final analysis, political systems based on compulsion must remain at perpetual war against their own plebeian kinsmen. The war causes a general breakdown of social order, and predisposition toward a government incapable of operating on a level playing field.

A first–rate example of the licensing effect occurred when in 2009, three of President Obama's key cabinet nominees were caught practicing an embarrassing double standard. The nominees, all well–respected Democrats known for their fondness for higher taxes and harsher punishment for tax cheats, were discovered to have failed to pay their taxes. One nominee, former U.S. Senator Tom Daschle, once said, "Make no mistake, tax cheaters cheat all of us, and the IRS should enforce our laws to the letter."[18]

And yet, during his confirmation hearings for Health and Human Services Secretary, Daschle admitted he had failed to pay over $128,000 in taxes in the previous three years. Another nominee, Timothy Geithner, who was confirmed as the Secretary of the Treasury, an office that oversees the IRS, had failed to pay $34,000 in taxes for the previous four years.[19] Another nominee, Nancy Killefer, failed to pay unemployment compensation taxes for her family's nanny. A fourth one, Congresswoman Hilda Solis, ran into trouble when it was revealed that her husband had failed to pay fifteen outstanding state and county tax liens since 1993.

A year later, in 2010, another such tax–cheating scandal burst on the political scene. U.S. Congressman Charles Rangel, chairman of the Committee on Ways and Means—the key tax–writing committee—had to step down from his post for a spate of ethical violations. One charge was that he "failed to disclose properly $500,000 in assets on his annual financial–disclosure forms." In another charge, investigators were reviewing whether he had failed to pay taxes on an offshore rental property. It appeared that Rangel might have hidden the rental income from the IRS.[20] The Committee on Ways and Means has jurisdiction over all taxation, tariffs, and other tax–raising measures.

During the hearings, Congressman Rangel, who had failed to pay the full extent of his tax liabilities for seventeen years, continuously insisted that he was "not corrupt." On December 2, 2010, Congress censured him for having committed eleven counts of ethical misconduct. Although anyone else would have gone to jail, Rangel's punishment was limited to standing before Congress while being rebuked by the House Speaker. He kept his U.S. Congressional seat. Evidently, most politicians feel entitled to different rules from those which govern their citizens.

This is not simply a case of outright hypocrisy. Lawmakers see no inconsistency in advocating inconsistent stances. They can easily hold two opposing opinions simultaneously without noticing the pungent odor of hypocrisy. They are above their own laws, because, as they see it, they have made great sacrifices in order to enact those laws. They did good, so, in their minds, it is perfectly legitimate to now be bad. Violating particular laws is their reward for having made society better. This being a double standard never seems to invade their frame of mind—until they get caught. None of these political bigwigs offered to pay their taxes until they were offered a cabinet job. It is easy for those crafting the laws to advocate tax increases, when they do not intend to pay them.

Interestingly, there were so many tax gaffes during Obama's cabinet nominations that pundits joked that most politicians must be violating tax laws, since what are the odds, otherwise, that the President would only nominate tax cheats.

An argument can also be made for an "inverse licensing effect." If people think they have done something bad, they are more inclined to compensate by doing something good to ease their conscience. In the realm of economics, even successful businessmen and investors have confessed to pangs of guilt after have made great gains in the marketplace. Perhaps that is why some of those flush with money feel an impulse to contribute hard–earned cash to worthy charities.

The Complexity of Disorder and Violence

As overall complexity increases, so does the likelihood of instability. In a modern world of fast–track mobility, command–based systems are incapable of gathering, documenting, or absorbing society's seemingly random behavior, especially the microscopic activities of subsystems operating under the radar.

Political systems stumble about blindly, as infinite movements of information, people, and products ebb and flow on their own timetable—or lack thereof. Systems can function smoothly only if they are well oiled and resilient to challenges. Obviously, closed systems and open systems are polar opposites. Closed–ended systems have no compatibility or interconnectivity, almost ensuring failure. To believe that a linear system could be successful in the long term is like believing in the potency of pixie dust or that a tornado could be tamed.

Because of the unclear nature of complexity, command systems are unqualified to do any but the simplest of tasks. When the U.S. government decided to test security at one of its nuclear–weapons facilities, it was obligated to notify the operators before the test. Even with the advance warning, staff at the nuclear facility failed the open–book test where "50 percent of the time the test-terrorists succeeded." Embarrassed, the U.S. Energy Department demoted the man in charge of the testing team.[21] Likening governing systems to a "mentally retarded giant," syndicated columnist Charley Reese wrote: "Government is inherently incompetent, and no matter what task is assigned, it will do it in the most expensive and inefficient way possible."

Nonetheless, political systems do excel at one thing; they are skillful at disengaging the populace. Since compulsion is akin to an impregnable concrete wall, governments have become skillful at fortifying against any meaningful sharing of decision–making powers with the general populace. Even the voting process is limited, as political honchos are under the spell of licensing, influence peddling, and other self–serving appetites. In reality, the politically astute are beholden to the world–view that they are intelligent, and the rest of the world is cluttered with ignoramuses. The elite practitioners of statecraft have little faith in allowing society free reign to work out internal problems on a personal, nonviolent, one–to–one basis or by a network of nongovernment organizations (NGOs). To state supremacists, centralization and conformity are the only methods to resolve problems. And to accomplish this, they must use punitive laws, power plays, and compulsion.

Obviously, governance by gun is anathema to a stable and healthy society. The main duty of any managerial or administrative system is to defend its members from all sorts of harm, including violence, abuse, and fraud. But if a system itself engages in the activities that it purports to oppose, it has lost its moral underpinnings. To avoid the label of "hypocrite" and the associated stigma, moral standard–bearers must engage in moral conduct. The public expects doctors, for example, to abide by the Hippocratic Oath, which calls for "doing no harm." Government ministers must keep their word and live by example.

Hypocrisy is related to compulsion. Political officeholders who explain to their children during bedtime storytelling that violent behavior is unacceptable are often the ones who, during business hours, orchestrate aggressive, iron–fisted policies. And when society grows increasingly unruly over the countless inconsistencies, those engrained in the political landscape are usually clueless. They see no inconsistency arising from political, but hypocritical, actions. When citizens ask why some chosen people can legally steal, lie, and cheat, when nobody else can, the rhetorical reply is, as newspaper columnist George Will once quipped, "*Dirigo, ergo sum*—I boss people around, therefore I am."

Political leaders and their sycophants fear that nothing will ever get done unless they grab the helm and steer by their own infallible moral compass. Believing that society's true destiny must lie within a single trajectory, they think they know how to chart the stars for all members of society, especially for those who underperform. But this linear mindset is more complex than just fretting about an idle citizenry. Most power brokers arrogantly hold to the myopic notion that the people can never be trusted to do the right thing.

If the citizenry balks at varied flavor–of–the–year social engineering programs or media scares, fangs and claws will be unsheathed. And if some people still stubbornly refuse to cooperate, they might find themselves trapped in a close encounter of the violent kind. R. Buckminster Fuller, the inventor of the geodesic dome, understood this menacing drawback to political systems, remarking, "The end move in politics is always to pick up a gun."

Waves of social turbulence are the trademark of those who repeatedly fail to live up to standards of moral conduct. Without standards, it is almost impossible to differentiate the good guys from the bad guys. Criminal elements, law enforcement, and political dignitaries too often appear to have donned the same black hat. After all, Machiavelli professed that "politics have no relation to morals." Any distinctions become difficult to recognize, because behavioral patterns of political leaders are breathtakingly consistent with those of psychopaths and hoodlums. Russian novelist Leo Tolstoy took this caustic theme to heart, arguing that "Government is an association of men who do violence to the rest of us."

One of America's most gifted political theorists, Lysander Spooner (1808–1887), pointed out the common traits of all those who deprive others of their property. To Spooner, the only difference between highwaymen and tax collectors was that the freelance thief robs his victim once and goes on his merry way, while the political prowler does so habitually. To a varying degree, most political systems are "kleptocracies," secured with the legal jurisdiction to take what they want—a "license to steal." The Russian human rights activist Sergei Kovalyov labeled the Russia Federation under Putin a "bandit society."[22] Other, less flattering critics refer to such activity as "state–sanctioned theft," or merely "forced labor." A phrase that has gained popularity during the Obama Administration is "gangster government," in reference to the state.

If taxpayers were to refuse to cooperate with gangster governments, retaliation would be assured, from the barrel of a gun. Of course, this same reaction would be expected from any disappointed mugger confronted by an uncooperative victim.

No wonder governments get poor grades from the public. But do most people regard government as a band of pirates, or do they trust government? In a 2007 study conducted by the progressive Democracy Corps, the opinion research institute found that "by 57 percent to 29 percent, Americans believe that government makes it harder for people to get ahead in life instead of helping people." As for government waste and inefficiency, the same poll revealed that "an emphatic 83 percent say that if the government had more money, it would waste it rather than spend it well."[23] This sour attitude toward the authorities stunned the pollsters and advocates for effective government.

A 2010 poll by Pew Research Center showed that nearly eight out of ten Americans distrust the federal government, saying they had little faith in the government's ability to solve the nation's problems. At the time of the poll, this public antagonism toward government and Washington was at its highest in nearly a half–century.[24]

Those who put faith in do–good government are continually confounded by sweet–talking politicians who leave behind toxic legacies, undermining the public confidence in government. Many do–gooders earnestly want to believe in political systems that can be made to behave, and that will make high–minded repairs to a flawed society. And yet when the man on the street gets strong-armed by bureaucracies, he figures that whichever political party wrests controls of the ship's rudder, good government is not the destination. In this sense, it could be argued that "good government" is an oxymoron, an invention that's workable only in theory. One twentieth–century philosopher and theorist for "autarchism," Robert LeFevre, heartily agreed, musing that "there is no such thing as good government, only good excuses."

Foxes Guarding the Henhouse

Political leaders and their minions are the proverbial foxes guarding the henhouse. Having been elevated to the top tier of the food chain, they find it almost impossible to avoid taking advantage of their position. Given enough authority, they will take on gangster–like personas while making power retention their prime goal.

This fox–controlling–the–henhouse phenomenon can occur in every form of governance. It is not limited to authoritarian governments. Nations boasting of democratic values regularly lose their bearings and drift sideways with "mission creep." The term "managed democracy" was coined to describe nations going through the motions of freedom while practicing instead a strange hybrid of heavy–handed control and uncoordinated openness. This political contradiction has plagued and paralyzed a wide swath of nations, including Russia and many of the former Soviet satellites.

In other cases, a foxy government could find advantages in overseeing a democratic henhouse that contributes to a dysfunctional milieu—described by some as "hyperdemocracy." This is a condition where everyone has a say–so, to the point where nobody does. The *San Francisco Weekly* denoted this phenomenon in a story explaining the reasons for what was plaguing its city. They suggested that hyperdemocracy was a disorder that could transform a progressive society "into the democratic equivalent of death by a thousand cuts; as everybody gets a voice, democracy votes accountability down. When everyone's in charge, no one is." And because nobody seems to have much say–so, the state becomes the greatest influence–peddler.

But the real secret behind political systems is that the fox not only guards the henhouse, but has had a hand in designing it. This situation would explain the lack of incentives for political systems to be serious sentries for the public good. Since the political apparatus was originally fashioned to pick the pockets of the defenseless for the benefit of well–fed gatekeepers, citizens are usually relegated to victimhood. Across the globe, citizens have a high probability of being attacked by their own security forces or ill–treated by their own authorities—the same entities sworn to defend and protect their citizenry. One such citizen was Donald Scott, a Malibu millionaire from Ventura County, who quickly discovered just how vicious certain agencies of the government can be.

In late 1992, Scott's wife, Frances Plante, was awakened by the sound of their door being broken down. Masked men pointed high–powered weapons at their human targets. Pleading for her life, Plante screamed, "Don't shoot me, don't kill me!" Recovering from cataract surgery at the time, Scott nevertheless found a gun and ran to his wife's defense. Three shots rang out and Scott died instantly.[25]

The Donald Scott incident was no ordinary robbery and killing. The early–morning intruders belonged to an elite narcotics task force from the Los Angeles County Sheriff's Department and five federal law enforcement agencies, including the National Park Service, Border Patrol, and National Guard. With a "no–knock" warrant, the 32–man task force was looking for an alleged 4000–plant marijuana plantation. After an extensive search, they found no illegal drugs; Scott did not even smoke cigarettes. According to a report from Ventura County District Attorney Michael Bradbury, the police had lied to obtain the search warrant. In addition, the raid was said to have been motivated by law enforcement's desire to seize the valuable property under asset forfeiture laws.

For years, the National Park Service had attempted to acquire Scott's multi–million–dollar ranch, without success. As proof, the District Attorney's report mentioned that the raiding party had taken along a parcel map with a handwritten message noting the $800,000 price tag for the adjacent 80–acre property, sold recently.

Scott's widow filed a $100–million wrongful–death lawsuit. Finally, after eight years, the federal and L.A. County law enforcement agencies settled out of court for $5 million, fearful of a jury's verdict during a time of widespread revelation of illegal shootings, perjured testimony and planted evidence. Scandals had become so frequent that public mistrust of the authorities was causing juries to doubt the word of police officers in courtroom testimony. Despite the out–of–court settlement, the L.A. County Sheriff's Department maintained that they had done nothing wrong, that the shooting was completely justifiable, and that the raid had not been botched. The property was eventually lost to foreclosure for back taxes to the Internal Revenue Service.

Social Chaology and Weak Structures

Scott's plight was not an isolated case. Asset forfeitures increased at an alarming rate throughout the 1990s, with over 30,000 homes, cars, boats, and businesses seized. Forfeiture laws allowed every level of government to snatch private assets without the legal processes of an indictment, court trial, or conviction—rights that exist only if someone is charged with a criminal offense. And if a citizen was foolish enough to try to stop the confiscation, law enforcement agencies often used deadly force with impunity.

In 1989, Ethel Hylton was arrested at Houston Hobby Airport after drug-sniffing dogs pointed to her luggage. Agents found no drugs, but they did find over $39,000 in cash, which they never returned.

In May of 1992, police were stopping black men in poor sections of Washington, D.C. to "routinely confiscate small amounts of cash and jewelry." Most of the property was never even recorded by the police department. One resident called it "robbery with a badge."[26]

An Iowa woman accused of shoplifting a $25 item had her $18,000 car seized.[27] A drugstore owner in Detroit had money taken from his cash register and store safe by narcotics officers, although no drugs were found at his shop.

In 1992, investigative reporters from the television program *60 Minutes* checked out complaints that the Drug Enforcement Administration (D.E.A.) had confiscation squads stationed at major airports. The newsmen discovered that in every case where an airplane patron had bought a ticket for cash, a DEA agent had come out and seized all the money in the person's pockets.

Brenda Grantland, a leading asset–forfeiture defense attorney, wrote, in her book *Your House Is Under Arrest*, that much of the forfeited property goes to law enforcement officials for a fraction of the value of the property taken. For instance, the New York District Attorney James M. Catterton got an impounded BMW 735i for only $3,412. It had been taken from an alleged drug dealer.[28]

Taking forfeiture laws to their logical extremes, government attorneys in 2006 tried to confiscate the gold caps from the mouths of two men under investigation on illegal drug charges in Tacoma, Washington. The government argued that gold caps, known as "grills," qualified as seizable assets. A judge halted the procedure just as the two men were being escorted to the dental clinic in a police van. The past president of the Washington Association of Criminal Defense Lawyers, Richard J. Troberman, was flabbergasted when he heard about the case. "It sounds like Nazi Germany when they were removing the gold teeth from the bodies, but at least then they waited until they were dead."[29]

According to the Forfeiture Endangers American Rights Foundation (FEAR), almost any offense can lead to property theft by government agencies. With over 200 federal forfeiture statutes on the books, government authorities could seize private property for almost any reason: "making a false statement on a bank loan application, killing an endangered species of rat on your land, collecting feathers of migratory birds such as sea gulls, or failing to report to the IRS the purchase of over $3000 in money orders within 24 hours or a cash sale involving over $10,000."[30]

In a major exposé published in the *Orange County Register*, editorialist Mark Landsbaum revealed that new California policies gave the state government a license to steal. Under current law, "if you have forgotten about a bank account or haven't received dividends or cast a proxy vote for stock you own, after three years the state can seize such technically 'abandoned' assets, sell them and spend the cash." Originally, the lost–and–found governmental department had to wait sixteen years before it could seize abandoned property, and if owners of the lost assets later filed a claim, they would be repaid with interest. That all changed. Not only is the California Controller's Office without a department to track "abandoned money," but it no longer "even bothers to contact owners by mail once it acquires their money, stocks or other valuables."

Although the Controller's Office referred to the lost assets as "revenue," a number of the victims began to sue. A trial judge ordered the state agency to "give constitutional notice before seizing property," to pay interest on past seized property, and to rewrite regulations to prevent similar travesties. Unhappy with the court decision, the controller appealed, and obtained a stay of enforcement. In a backward and devolving approach to protect the interest of citizens, the law in California requires the state controller only to notify some people—not everyone—*after* the seizure, *not before*.

One victim, Chris Lusby Taylor, lost $3 million of his Intel stock when the state seized his property without his knowledge. Flight attendant Nancy Pebble–Gonsalves of Riverside lost her retirement fund to the state of California during the TWA bankruptcy reorganization. During the trial, the Controller's Office maintained that it could not find the owner. Judge Kleinfield wrote in 2003, "California is taking the flight attendant's stock in her airline on the basis, basically, that she cannot be found, even while she is standing in court shouting, 'Here I am! Here am I! Give me my money!' And the state of California turns a deaf ear, pretending it cannot hear her."[31]

*****

Weak social structures can lead to the death knell of society, destroying wealth, crushing confidence, sapping the energy of those who would help society but find themselves powerless to fight entrenched hierarchies. In the end, weak social structures invite the chaos of conflict, revolution, and war, pitting groups against each other, each enticed by what their conquests might bring.

1 Robert A Nisbet, *The Sociological Tradition*, New York: Basic Books, 1966.
2 Thomas J. Schumacher, "Dealing with Control Freaks," *Zimbio*, April 10, 2007.
3 A. O. Hirschman and C. E. Lindblom, "Economic Development, Research and Development, Policy Making: Some Converging Views," *Behavioral Science*, July 1962, 211–222.
4 W. Brian Arthur, (Ed.), *The Economy as an Evolving Complex System II* (Santa Fe Institute Studies in the Sciences of Complexity Lecture Notes), Westview Press, 1997.
5 Vincent Miller, "Celebrating Anniversaries for ISIL and Rand," *Freedom Network News*, December 2005, p. 7.
6 George Ayittey, *Africa in Chaos: A Comparative History*, New York: Palgrave Macmillan (St. Martin paperback edition), 1999, p. 179.
7 PBS *Anchor Interview* by Bill Moyers with George Ayittey, July 24, 2005.
8 Jonathan D. Spence, *The Search for Modern China*, W. W. Norton and Company, Inc. 1st edition, 1990, p. 582. Speech by Mao Tse-tung at the Lushan Conference, July 23, 1959.
9 Friedrich von Hayek, *The Constitution of Liberty*, Chicago: University of Chicago Press, 1960.
10 Iris Kuo, "'Licensing Effect' seen in Dieting, Charity, Hiring," *San Jose Mercury News*, January 30, 2006.
11 Shankar Vedantam, "Most Diversity Training Ineffective, Study Finds," *Washington Post*, Jan. 20, 2008.
12 Ibid., Vedantam.
13 Ibid., Vedantam.
14 Ibid., Vedantam.
15 Kate Connolly, "How going green may make you mean: Ethical consumers less likely to be kind and more likely to steal, study finds," Guardian, March 15, 2010. Original source: *Psychological Science*, "Do Green Products Make Us Better People?" Nina Mazar and Chen-Bo Zhong at the University of Toronto, published online, March 5, 2010.
16 Chris Edwards, "Public Sector Unions and the Rising Costs of Employee Compensation," *Cato Journal*, Vol. 30, No. 1 (Winter 2010).
17 Steven Greenhut, "Pension crater much deeper," *Orange County Register*, April 11, 2010. For 2009, the average federal civil servant's pay and benefits rose to $123,049. For private workers, the figure rose to $61,051, according to the Bureau of Economic Analysis. Dennis Cauchon, "Federal workers earning double their private counterparts," *USA Today*, Aug. 8, 2010. Greenhut is a director of the Pacific Research Institute's Journalism Center.
18 Sen. Tom Daschle, *Congressional Record*, May 7, 1998, p. S4507.
19 Chris Cillizza, "How Killefer Hurt Daschle, *The Washington Post*, Feb. 3, 2009.

20 Brody Mullins, "Eventual Return to Powerful Post Is Unlikely," *Wall Street Journal*, March 4, 2010.

21 Charley Reese, "Republic Sing," King Features Syndicate, posted in LewRockwell.com, Feb. 20, 2006, source: http://www.lewrockwell.com/reese/reese264.html.

22 Douglas Birch, "Old Dissidents Still a Voice In Russia, But Fading," *Washington Post*, May 30, 2009.

23 Stan Greenberg, "Democrats are back — but" *The American Prospect*, June 18, 2007.

24 Liz Sidoti, "Poll: 4 out of 5 Americans Don't Trust Washington," *Time*, April 19, 2010.

25 Brenda Grantland, *Your House Is Under Arrest: How the Police Can Seize Your Home, Car, and Business Without a Trial—And How to Protect Yourself*, Institute for the Preservation of Wealth, Burnside, MN., 1993.

26 Gary Fields, "'Robbery with a Badge' in The Nation's Capital," *USA Today*, May 18, 1992, p.11

27 Ibid., Gary Fields.

28 Ibid, Grantland.

29 "Suspects Almost Lose Gold Teeth Caps," *The Arizona Republic*, April 8, 2006.

30 FEAR position paper, "Federal Asset Forfeiture Laws Need to be Amended to Restore Due Process and Protect Property Rights in the Forfeiture Process," posted on Forfeiture Endangers American Rights Foundation (FEAR) website in Mill Valley, CA, (www.FEAR.org), revised 2002. Under Justice Department Asset Forfeiture Chief, Cary Copeland, there were over 200 federal forfeiture statutes.

31 Ibid. FEAR position paper.

6

Social Chaology and Strong Structures

All larger organisms, including ourselves, are living testimonies to the fact that destructive practices do not work in the long run. In the end the aggressors always destroy themselves, making way for others who know how to cooperate and get along. Life is much less a competitive struggle for survival than a triumph of cooperation and creativity. —Fritjof Capra, Ph.D., physicist and systems theorist, author of *The Web of Life*.

I object to violence because when it appears to do good, the good is only temporary; the evil it does is permanent.[1] —Mahatma Gandhi

What creates strong societal foundations? What social alchemy holds society together with the firmness of concrete yet the softness of a malleable metal? What strengthens stability while eliciting the flexibility of synergetic change? To social chaologists, that adaptable substance is what prevents structures from deforming and deconstructing during stressful periods. Analogous to energy–absorbing matter, this bonding substance holds societal structures together in cooperative and coordinated ballast. This revolutionary interconnectivity material? *Individual consent.*

Obviously, without individual consent, the structural whole is prone to dysphoric breaks and decay. In sociological terms, most individuals will tend to support those structures in which they feel invested and empowered. Under self–organizing tenets, individual parts willingly cluster for mutual cooperation and to save energy. And as they freely cluster, they are averse to heavy–handedness, predatory actions, disinformation, or threats. They reserve the option to disassociate. They want policy to be consensually decided, not dictated. And they rarely expend much energy if prevented from having a decision–making voice in the organization. If they are ordered to do something without recourse, they will attempt to flee or sabotage the structure, destabilizing the entire system.

Unfortunately, most political systems fall prey to the seductive scent of the privileged and the powerful, those who are hostile toward sharing power with those they deem as subordinate. They aspire to loot the treasury, erect entry barriers against upstarts, and rummage for ways to replace competition with privilege and cooperation with outright coercion.

One recent exception to this generalization is India. The formerly caste–based nation has attempted to breach barriers and embrace politico–economic pluralism. For decades, India was hamstrung by hard–line economic and political controls and regional insurgencies. But the country has been able to unlock many of its sealed doors and emerge as an economic powerhouse. India lowered the number of its poor by throwing off a quasi–Soviet, one–party system during the 1980s, and by 2006 it had the second–fastest–growing economy in the world. According to Pradeep Chhibber, chairman of the Department of Political Science at the University of California at Berkeley, a coalition of over thirty political parties was able to move India to a more open system of governance.

This diverse political environment, along with greater economic mobility, has actually made India more stable. But what excited Chhibber was how society reacted to this greater flexibility. The increased diversity did not lead to greater chaos. "The paradox," the professor wrote, "is that the more fragmented India's politics has become, the more unified and stable the nation."[2] But such openness cannot thrive when socioeconomic structures are based on architectures of linear absolutism.

Absolute-Based Architecture

If nation–states cling to a governing architecture that's absolutist in its approach, they must come face to face with the adverse consequences of a brittle, unsteady structure. Why? Because government-imposed order is a singularity of action, a deterministic, phase-locked state that usually erects walls between the governing and the governed. Political architectures are not based on whether there will or will not be order in society, but rather on what type of so–called order is to be imposed. Letting order evolve between a stable, "phase–locked state" and an unstable, "phase–shifting state" is rarely considered.

In an episode of ABC's hit drama series *Lost*, the overweight castaway Hurley is put in charge of a newly discovered food pantry on the island where he is among fellow survivors of a plane crash. He has been ordered to inventory the food and control its distribution from an underground bunker. For a number of personal reasons, Hurley hates his new assignment and asks to be released from his official duties. His pleas are denied. Feeling trapped and frustrated, he wires the pantry with dynamite, in retaliation against a system that refuses to release him from his unwanted, mandatory duty.

As Hurley prepares to set off the explosive, another castaway discovers his plan and offers an alternative. She explains that food rationing is unfeasible and that instead, he should hand out the limited food supply to everyone freely—let the others determine how to consume or store their food. Feeling released from his involuntary responsibility, Hurley disarms the dynamite and distributes the food to the other survivors. Although fictional, this example shows how people forced into compulsory situations often will sabotage unresponsive systems, while unintentionally injuring innocent bystanders.

Such acts of sabotage must be expected when people are pushed into a corner. After all, political systems rely largely on dominance–based behavioral patterns, egotistical self–perpetuation, and obsessive–compulsive psychoneurosis. Under these preconditions, "controloid" heavyweights presume that they cannot get what they want simply by asking. That would be too simple.

Those in positions of dominance fear widespread noncompliance; therefore they resort to manipulative power plays, manufactured crises, and strong–arm policies, which further boost their sense of superiority over the societal parts. Clinical psychologists and marriage therapists see such manipulative power plays as addictive and as leading, often, to physically abusive relationships. These are techniques to get people to do things they did not want to do in the first place. And if these abusive behaviors continue, the relationship will suffer animosity, fear, and bitter separation.

Robert Nisbet, a Uuniversity of California, Berkeley sociologist, acknowledged this phenomenon in his 1953 book, *Quest for Community*, arguing that the state's progressive invasion of society was eroding the people's "natural authority" to conduct their own lives. Nisbet viewed this debilitating trend as a vortex-style breakdown, in which government absorption of people's daily functions leads to an intense disorganization, which in turn reduces societal members to a role of powerless spectators.[3]

Governmentalists are able to prey on society because most of its members are generally passive. Citizens can be coaxed, badgered or compelled into going along with whatever the higher-ups tell them. The state is usually the heavy-duty conduit for exploiting the cultural memes of society. When legislative laws are forcibly interjected into the societal mix, culture, norms and values are radically altered. Whatever a government makes acceptable can easily become embedded in the social consciousness of the masses. For instance, during the early colonial days in the Americas, the settlers were fairly open-minded in that "whites and black married each other, traded with each other, sued each other, and owned each other's labor" (*Cato's Letter*, Fall 2011, vol. 9, no. 4).

According to Robert M.S. McDonald, Associate Professor of history at the Unites States Military Academy, during this time period, "class cut deeper than race," especially in the colony of Virginia. That all changed after the Bacon's Rebellion in 1676, where poor whites and blacks and indentured servants rose up in arms against the authorities in Jamestown. After the rebellion was crushed, the gentry instituted new laws that led to "permanent, race-based slavery." Laws were passed making it illegal to emancipate a slave; Black colonists lost their right to own guns or testify in court. Slavery had become codified and legalized via the state, which pushed society toward a culture of enslavement, segregation and dehumanization of African Americans.

Emergence and Reductionism

Every system that has existed *emerged* somehow, from somewhere, at some point. Complexity science emphasizes the study of how systems evolve through their disorganized parts into an organized whole. In this process, the interaction of lower–level parts coordinates for the mutual benefit of the higher–level whole. But the approach of breaking down a system to its smallest parts—*reductionism*—is problematic. As one chaologist, Victor MacGill of New Zealand, expressed it, "We can dissect a rat and learn a lot about dead rats, but still not know much about live rats."[4]

Unfortunately, traditional science relies on an adherence to linear reductionism and thus is willing to sacrifice the parts for the benefit of the whole. Today, many scientists consider this approach aberrant, because the interconnectivity of the parts tends to be nonproportional to the sum of the whole, directly challenging the mechanistic views of René Descartes. In a sociopolitical context, this means that individual agents of society are more likely to facilitate greater cohesion and coordination on their own, than when operating in a fixed, governed whole.

Social chaologists recognize that the properties of the whole often cannot be explained or predicted by the behavior of the parts. The main principle behind this premise is fundamental and proclaimed in Aristotle's *Metaphysics*: "The whole is more than the sum of its parts." Scientists from the Newtonian age continually failed to understand this subtlety. Instead, they took simplistic approaches and found it convenient to invent micro–level theory to explain already observable macro–level phenomena. When they took systems apart for closer examination, they would treat the parts like components of machinery, and attempt mathematically to force them back into an equal whole—striving to square the hole or round the peg. To do so, they had to ignore complex, nonlinear systems or smooth over the irregularities.

But the problem with complex systems is that they generally lie beyond standard mathematical analysis. For instance, when scientists studied cellular structures, they found that chemical-based systems, such as protein folding, microtubules, and viruses, often become organized as though they had a mind of their own, showing characteristics of what some refer to as "dynamic instability." Amazingly, they appeared to be under holistic and synergetic urges that required a sort of freedom of association in order to develop. And if outside forces were to prevent this association, it would be disadvantageous to the system. Social structures operate and evolve in a similar fashion.

Because the citizenry and command–based structures are adversarial, political processes become portals for conflict–inspired showdowns. In this sense, the power to govern can easily metamorphose into the power to abuse. This corruptive role disturbs long–established societal order and cohesion, bolstering disorder and disillusionment. For instance, when Bob Teixeira decided in 2006 to innovate and fight a U.S. dependency on foreign oil, he converted his diesel–powered Mercedes to run on soybean oil. But when he was spotted with a bumper sticker reading, "Powered by 100% vegetable oil," he was pulled over, ticketed, and fined $1,000 by law enforcement officers for not having paid motor–fuel taxes.

A guitar teacher from Charlotte, North Carolina, Teixeira had spent $1,200 on the engine conversion, determined to help the environment. Instead of being hailed for his efforts, he became trapped in a legal cobweb. Although his state heavily promoted alternative fuel production and consumption, he was told that vehicles couldn't legally use biofuel unless the owner had posted a $2,500 bond. And local authorities told him he could expect another fine of $1,000 by the federal government.[5] Apparently, innovation and individual initiative are unappreciated. No good deed ever goes unpunished.

Political friction will ensure torn social cartilage, especially when those in pursuit of predesigned templates seek to push societal parts into fixed, must-be-equal wholes. Caught in a ceaseless vortex of centralization, governmental adherents see the world in a narrow, monochrome range, while underestimating its colorful complexity of society. Moreover, these devotees of governmentalism believe in the utopian fantasy that if government passes a law, the public will automatically obey, and dump their alleged bad habits. Or, if enough money is spent on a government project, problems will magically be solved. This static mindset ignores the "unseen consequences" that Frenchman Frédéric Bastiat, author of *The Law*, observed in the 1800s. Unfortunately, people concentrate too heavily on the *seen* and completely ignore *unseen* aftermaths that were not part of anyone's conscious design.

But do political perfectionists actually adhere to their own linear–derived laws? One would think so. But that would be assuming that almost everything moves in a straight line. Take a look at the usually erratic economies of Europe. For instance, under the provisions of the European Union constitution, member states cannot legally have a deficit–to–GDP (gross domestic product) ratio of over 3 percent per year. But in 2010, the financial world awoke to the shocking news that many European nations were ignoring these restrictions—breaking the law. In their projected budgets for 2009: Greece's deficit was announced as 13 percent; Ireland's, 12.5 percent; Spain's, 11.4 percent; Portugal's, 9.3 percent; and Italy's, 5.3 percent. So if governments cannot obey laws they themselves agreed upon, how can "good government" advocates expect the average citizen's behavior to be perfected through the use of statutory or regulatory laws? Simply making a rule does not produce the desired effect.

Politicos are apt to lose their bearings among messy controversies. They are prone to be perplexed by the fuzzy labyrinths of information overloads that are so prevalent with completing uncertainties. Political theater does best on dimly lit stages where recitals can be turned into shallow parodies of reality. Like Newtonian scientists of the seventeenth and eighteenth centuries, most political leaders are ill–equipped to figure out the almost immeasurable, hairsplitting nuances of how systems emerge and operate, especially when intermixed with unfixed probability. When members of society organize into groups—sports teams, church choirs, musical bands, community organizations, business enterprises—what they do and how they do it happens to generate patterns, but they move toward no equal pathway.

Systems can be shoved and forced to behave in certain prearranged ways. The citizenry can be abused through a wide range of controlling tools and imposed conformity, but mankind's natural tendencies to self-cluster and organize will remain intact. This means that if external government controls were lifted, a system's natural affinity or strange attractor would reappear. That is why external controls perpetually fail to do what they were intended to do. They conflict with the self–renewing and engrained patterns of the often unorganized parts.

Whenever it is under the influence of political institutions, the whole is at the mercy of several domineering parts. The whole is routinely pushed by agenda–driven operatives and spit–and–shine political surrogates, adroit at hoodwinking and hijacking it. The so-called governance whole never actually controls the "disparate whole." Rather, the whole is often misled and arrogated by a vocal smattering of political evangelists, gussied up in "for–the–common–good" wardrobes. It is no accident that almost all twentieth–century dictators framed their community–spirit mantras in the utilitarian ethics of the greater good for greatest number of people. The battle for the whole by the elite few ultimately excludes the vast majority of people. The whole is always inundated by realpolitik juggernauts, who, like sharks in a feeding frenzy, prey on the unorganized many, to satisfy their linear vision of society.

And yet under swarm intelligence—in which flocking birds and schooling fish move in well–organized order—the whole acts as one without any imposition. In the natural world, there are no machine–gun–toting birds or spear–jabbing fish demanding strict compliance to the intricacies of the whole. There are no specific standards. There are no external rules or punishment for heading in the wrong direction at the wrong time. Only the process of mutual influence and adaptation holds the swarm together.

The Entanglement of Distant Parts

To traditional social planners and political scientists, the general assumption is that detached parts suffer pangs of isolation. Typifying this notion is the way people behave in low–density suburbs. Supposedly, these inhabitants are trapped in an antiseptic world where the capacity to advance complex social skills is stunted.

Or at least that's the presumption that pervades popular culture. For decades, suburbanites have suffered the allegation of being socially dysfunctional, disconnected from the societal whole, encapsulated in social turmoil that could disintegrate into deep fissures among classes and races. Compared to sophisticated urbanites in high–density metropolises, suburban dwellers have supposedly lost their socializing mojo and are permeated with despair and hopelessness, dwelling in empty homes by day, and in zombie zones by night. This image is pervasive, but a myth. Detached or distant parts are not isolated; they are more than their entangled sum. It took only one study, by Jan Brueckner, a University of California, Irvine professor of economics, to dispel the urban myth of detached suburbanites.

In their 2006 study of 15,000 Americans, Brueckner and his associate unexpectedly discovered that extra elbowroom does wonders for the socializing fabric of the community and that "social interaction is higher, not lower, in the suburbs."[6] Brueckner reported that those who live in suburban areas have more friends, more interactions with neighbors, and more community involvement than urbanites. "We found that interaction goes down as population density goes up. So, turning it around, it says that interaction is higher where densities are lower," he confided. "What that means is suburban living promotes more interaction than living in the central city."

The study even proposed a mathematical formula for quantifying this phenomenon. The dictum: for every ten percent decrease in population density, the chance of weekly communication with a neighbor increases by ten percent. Brueckner is not quite sure how to explain the paradox. Maybe people are simply too close in high–density cities, and become unfriendly and distant. "One possibility," he speculated, "is that the crowding associated with a dense environment might instead spur a need for privacy, causing people to draw inward." These findings reflect Robert Frost's old adage about good fences making good neighbors. It would appear that well–defined boundaries and increased space for privacy promote the interconnectivity of societal wholes.

The Canopy of Altruism

Most political systems operate under the "altruistic" canopy of planning for "the good of the whole," although such collective measures often damage the parts that spawned the whole. But order imposed over its parts can be life–threatening to an emerging system. The spontaneous nature of nascent systems requires open–source and unobstructed creativity to inspire uniqueness. But this is the not the characteristic of systems predisposed to monopolistic, non–negotiable control. Command–based systems are arranged to block innovation and change, and to systematically inhibit new systems from self–organizing, self–repairing, or regenerating. This is similar to biological evolution, in which an existing organism has a bias against the creation of a new species, since the new organism might topple the old.

All complex systems require some way to evolve and adapt, or redesign themselves in a process of creative destruction. Some chaology theorists refer to the rising up from a dead heap as the *Phoenix effect*—a rebirth from the ashes into something unexpected. John L. Casti, renowned mathematician and resident researcher at the Santa Fe Institute, refers to the impetuousness of complexity as the "science of surprise." Casti maintains that it is only natural that complexities have the ability to defy human logic, and that there is "no *a priori* reason to believe that any of the processes of nature and humans are necessarily rule based."[7] In *Emergence: From Chaos to Order*, John Holland called this transformation "a new mathematics of perpetual novelty." A well-known innovator in the field of artificial intelligence, Holland views the edge-of-chaos process as letting systems themselves define the criteria of how they breed and operate, without external forces. And he has been quite successful in proving this scenario with genetic algorithms, a problem–solving technique that creates never-ending newness by mimicking natural selection. Although Holland's computer simulations have validated the benefits of decentralized, open-ended systems, the political world has taken little notice. Many people still put their faith into command-and-control monopolies that treat societal parts as expendable cogs in an entropic machine.

In every sector imaginable, the properties of emergence are either ignored or opposed. One of the most hotly contested debates in the United States concerns land-use controls and zoning restrictions. These bureaucratic standardization tools impede the creation of irregular architectural design and land configuration. For instance, in the California coastal town of Carmel-by-the-Sea, the century-old downtown section is famous for its clusters of cute little shops bridged by narrow passageways, reminiscent of the Old World bazaar. The city attracts thousands of tourists yearly, largely because of its quaint architecture and unique charm. And yet, under Carmel's rigid zoning restrictions, none of this would be possible today. As a result of strict urban planning in the United States, few modern shopping centers display any distinctive characteristics. Most are vanilla-flavored, monochromatic, cookie-cutter malls that could be interchangeable among cities.

The stated purpose of zoning restrictions is to segregate uses that are believed to be incompatible. But these so-called incompatible uses are usually arbitrarily set by designers caught in the wake of the latest social engineering fad. For instance, with strong zoning codes in place after World War II, central planners embraced an urban utopia craze that promoted car-dependent cities and resident-unfriendly commercial centers. The denser, mixed-use neighborhoods that were so predominant in the 1920s were shunned or outlawed.

Builders and homeowners could no longer construct apartments above commercial buildings or open up a small grocery store in the middle of a residential neighborhood. Conventional suburban and urban renewal projects had taken America by storm, with developers cranking out identical tract homes and distant shopping centers. These new cities became modern constructs of sterile dwellings on wide streets without the town centers that used to provide places for personal contact between residences.

This fad changed by the 1980s, when urban planners came up with another blueprint for organized communities, called "New Urbanism," which focused on environmental concerns. Calculators in hand, planners reverted back to dense, mixed–use communities with narrow streets and pedestrian–friendly infrastructure that had occurred organically through the process of individual choice. Everything had come full circle. Original, self–emerging buildings designed on the fly and land–use styles had gained the support of modern planners. Ironically, these top–down city planners were not about to discard their compulsory mode of operation. Residents and businesses within cities were simply redirected to follow more environment–friendly mandates that still relied on strict zoning, redevelopment plans, and the power of eminent domain.

One of the leading architects for less heavy–handed planning of cities was social activist and author Jane Jacobs (1916–2006). During the 1960s, she fought a series of New York City redevelopment projects that proposed to tear apart whole communities, replacing them with characterless apartments and commercial centers. In her acclaimed 1961 book, *The Death and Life of Great American Cities*, she urged city planners to restore life and vitality to cities. She believed that great cities did not come from the top but rather were birthed, neighborhood by neighborhood, emerging and functioning on an unplanned individual basis. She condemned urban renewal and slum clearance projects as bureaucratic visions that did not consider the preferences and aspirations of those who actually lived there. Jacobs summed up the effects of urban planning: "There is a quality even meaner than outright ugliness or disorder, and this meaner quality is the dishonest mask of pretended order, achieved by ignoring or suppressing the real order that is struggling to exist and to be served."[8]

In later books, Jacobs delved into why command–and–control systems often failed. Touching on complexity science, she revealed why self–organizing systems work far better and noted that natural systems have no grand designer or architect. In her book *The Nature of Economics*, she acknowledged that "a system can be making itself up as it goes along."

Unfortunately, the adherents of New Urbanism, also known as "Smart Growth," failed to follow Jacobs's basic principle that individual action, rather than central planning, is what makes a city vibrant and alive. Using New Urbanism as their master template, central planners simply made adjustments and repackaged their policies to fit the way they thought citizens ought to live. With a heavy dose of compulsory controls, they imposed urban design theory from the early twentieth century early, mandating it as their new standard. Instead of encouraging cities to evolve and adapt, New Urbanism made the same mistake as its predecessor: arbitrarily deciding how people should organize their lives and property.

Economist Friedrich Hayek, the foremost opponent of central planning, put this problem in perspective: "If we wish to preserve a free society, it is essential that we recognize that the desirability of a particular object is not sufficient justification for the use of coercion."[9]

Perhaps in another hundred years, central planners will be swept up in another populist wind of change and return to urban sprawl and isolated neighborhoods. With so much power at their fingertips, they need only a stiff breeze to whirl toward another urban planning route.

Termite Architecture

When it comes to open architectural structures, chaos theorists like to point to wondrously designed termite mounds and colonies. Termites are among the master architects of the animal world, creating highly decentralized, mobile, ad hoc social networks that nurture collective behavior while encouraging enterprising activity. Based on swarm intelligence and pheromonal responses, these practically blind insects construct intricate mazes of interconnecting passages, egg chambers, ventilation tunnels, and cathedral mounds, all coordinated without a grand plan but following simple, practical rules. Even in task allocation, they operate without any central or hierarchical system to direct individual participants. And as entomologists have suggested, termites interact with their environment by altering it, which in turn tends to cause their behavior to change.

One species of termites found in Zimbabwe has even more remarkable traits. These creatures have equipped their gigantic, giraffe–sized mounts with built–in air conditioning to farm their primary food source—a multicelled fungal organism. To keep the fungus healthy, the termites must control the air temperature at exactly 87 degrees Fahrenheit. They do so by opening and closing a series of heating and cooling vents, maintaining that constant temperature throughout the day. Considering that outside temperature can range from 35 degrees at night to 104 during the day, these termites have created a marvel of engineering ingenuity.

Inspired by the Zimbabwean termites, a team of architects and engineers decided to duplicate their unique heating and cooling system based on the science of "biomimicry"—technology inspired by designs in nature. "If termites can maintain an acceptable, uniform environment, why not humans?" asked one of the engineers, Fred Smith. Touted as the largest commercial and shopping complex in Zimbabwe, the 324,000 square–foot Eastgate Center was built on the environmental principles discovered by studying the termites.[10]

The Synergic Mode

So what exactly is emergence in society? What stimuli help bring about organizational structures? Some experts have likened the process to a rebirth of consciousness, in which individual agents come together and undergo a moment of possibility and transformation. Others see the possibilities of a new future, a new direction in a collective experience, where structures are supported by all those in attendance. Amy Gilley from the Institute of Architecture and Planning at Morgan State University puts this rebirthing consciousness in terms of a theatrical production: "In theater, the apparent organized system of a constrained space, the grouping together of strangers, and the focus on the actions of individuals all lead the group to experience that threshold of possibility."[11]

Other writers, such as physician N. Arthur Coulter in *Human Synergetics* (1976), have contended that the emerging whole consists of empathic parts working in unison. "In the synergic mode, a human being acts naturally so as not only to achieve his own goals, but also, whenever feasible, to promote the goals of others, with least impedance to anyone. The Golden Rule—'Do unto others as you would have them do unto you'—becomes not a moral commandment to be obeyed, but a natural and logical consequence of his mode of being, as natural as breathing, sleeping or sexual activity."[12]

British computer scientist Chris Lucas, in an Internet article, "Synergy and Complexity Science," asserted that this collaborative, win–win synergism is what adds value to the parts, and that "there are functional interdependencies present such that if a part detaches from the whole it loses fitness...because the parts have shared goals, the whole works for all of them."[13] Lucas offered an example of two men rowing across a river. If they work as a team and row in unison, there is no reason they cannot accomplish their mission. But if one stops in the middle of the river and refuses to participate, the boat will simply swirl around in circles and neither will get anywhere. Under this condition there "is no incentive for the second rower to default; he must put in equal effort if the boat is to go straight." Order is a natural outcome of cooperation, because there are no incentives to be gained by behaving uncooperatively.

But there are caveats to this vision of collective teamwork. Chaos theorists warn that the goals of individual agents must not be identical. Systems must be diverse to meet the goals of each participant. Diversity of the parts is vital to keeping the whole innovative and dynamic.

Why is this type of diversity important? Under the law of "requisite variety," it has been found that the greater the variety, the stronger the system. For example, many scientists speculate that sexually reproducing organisms are predominant in ecosystems because of their ability to merge varied genetic material. By increasing the genetic diversity of offspring, species are better able to protect themselves from new pathogens and predators that have the potential to wipe out an entire species of too–similar organisms. The Irish potato famine of 1845–1849 has been blamed on too few genetic strains, providing the potato fungus with the opportunity to infect and kill most of the potato crop. Perhaps this is why asexual reproduction is so rare among multicellular organisms.

The vitality of democratic systems rests upon the same principle of requisite variety. Political systems that embrace tolerance of individual diversity result in greater political perspectives. Systems that block diversity are predisposed to control societal parts in such a way that not all participants will benefit. To have losers is a sign of failure. To achieve synergy, the parts must generate an acceptable social whole. Democratic systems without consensus and feedback put the health and fitness of the citizenry at great risk.

Political Reductionism

All governing systems carry dogmatic and self–destructive baggage. They behave in ways that distort, divide, and dominate society instead of letting life unfold to its full potential. Political systems use single–dimensional variables in a way that produces only two possible answers: right and wrong. This linear approach argues that isolated individual parts are not applicable to the integrated societal whole, drawing the specter of politics into the realm of reductionism.

In simple terms, reductionism attempts to dissect the parts, in order to understand the whole, similar to how a repairman would fix a broken watch. Although reductionism is helpful when surgeons reattach human limbs, its importance is exaggerated when applied to the claim that if you know the components, you know the whole. Obviously, in most professions, if parts are broken or separated, they often cannot be easily reassembled or fit perfectly into one piece. The human body can be sewn and bolted back together after a horrific car accident, but as surviving patients often attest, they are never the same. Life is more than a collection of a few grams of hydrogen, carbon, and other elements found in every living organism. The dynamics of the whole are more than the arrangements and movements of its parts.

The whole has properties that its components do not. But what the science of reductionism has overlooked is that the whole is not only more than the sum of its component parts—they are diverse and unique. As Richard C. Lewontin, Steven Rose, and Leon J. Kamin contended in *Not in Our Genes*, "As one moves up a level, the properties of each larger whole are given not merely by the units of which it is composed but of the organizing relations between them...these organizing relationships mean that the properties of matter relevant at one level are just inapplicable at other levels." This suggests that every level of group interaction, from atoms to molecules to cells and so forth, have different and complex qualities that "result in products qualitatively different from the component part."[14]

The aura of reductionism has allowed political systems to cozy up to external control like fleas to a dog. This approach makes it easy for political watchmakers to compartmentalize citizens into a uniform world of detachable and equal parts. Under "mechanical reductionism," components are not only explainable, but they are treated as dead and inert national resources. The pieces need only be put back into the right order to control the workings of nature. If a man jumps from a skyscraper window, the reductionist explanation would be that death resulted from the sudden impact with the ground, totally ignoring why the person fell—whether he jumped or merely stumbled, or whether he was pushed from the window. The complexity of society is reduced to Cartesian equations in which the sum of the parts must equal the whole. At this point, all other factors become irrelevant. Physicist Fritjof Capra recognized this misplaced emphasis as "narrow perceptions of reality." He asserted that academics and government agencies are caught under this fragmented methodology by using "outdated conceptual models and irrelevant factors."[15]

Traditionally, scientists have used linear analysis to conduct research, because it provides a simple way to obtain desired results. Lewontin, an evolutionary biologist and professor of Zoology and Biology at Harvard University wrote: "Successful scientists soon learn to pose only those problems that are likely to be solved. Pointing to their undoubted success in dealing with the relatively easy problems, they then assure us that eventually the same methods will triumph over the harder ones." Of course, this is not often the case. Complexity has a habit of muddying the water. Experiments using difficult measurements are hard to reproduce in the laboratory.[16]

Complexity has always been difficult to resolve and to understand. Evolutionary biologists were among the first scientists to recognize this problem, when they dug their way toward new theories about evolution. They discovered that matter does not lack purpose. They concluded that biological systems are irreducible—they cannot be reduced to simpler or smaller forms. The interaction of living systems and stochastic processes cannot be expressed in mathematical terms or equations. Nor can these systems be understood well by cataloguing their parts like a set of Lego toy building blocks. Relationships and interconnected networking are just as important as the parts' essential natures.

Reductionism has other unpleasant warts. Many chaos theorists see it as a method that destroys information since the observer can take only a selected sample of a system that can be represented only partially. Like the tail that wags the dog, reductionism's backward approach reduces a diverse class of phenomena and limits its effects to a single cause. With command–based systems always on the prowl to magnify their authority, goal–oriented politicians find it useful to engage in single–minded hyperbole. They boil complex problems down to feel–good, single solutions: Something must be done; this is something—so let's do it. It is action for action's sake. In some ways, they are like an obsessive naval commander who orders all bulkheads in his battleship sealed to prevent water leaks. Sure, nothing gets in, but then again, nothing gets out.

Volitional Structures

No structure can stand without the integrity of those who make up its formation. Obviously, people must have chosen to support the system in which they are engaged, or they would have refrained from joining. But the potency of volitional decisions is far more significant. To join an organization or group, individual agents agree to embrace the rules, obligations, and responsibilities within the structure, contributing to a gravitation–like force which in turn weaves a stabilizing and interconnecting strength into the fabric of society. The organization is part of them and they are part of it. This connectivity is critical to the survival of a system, since interactions make up the pattern–matching and informational feedback which is then disperse to the whole.

Volitional structures have little or no relationship to the government's ability to command an orderly world. Order arises naturally from individual desires to cooperate in a mutually desirable and beneficial environment. Theoretical biologist and one of the founders of complexity theory, Stuart Kauffman, acknowledges that there is a natural capacity to produce "spontaneous order," pointing out that "Order, vast and generative, arises naturally."[17]

Disorder is more exacting, arising when coercion is substituted for coordination—preventing members in a system from determining their own destiny. History is littered with examples of excluded parts rising up to confront those exclusive few who claim they are representing the whole. The so–called religious wars that roiled during the sixteenth and seventeenth centuries dealt more with the political and religious elite overdrafting the peasants' pocketbooks than with religious intolerance. Heavily influenced by Martin Luther's Protestant Reformation, the Peasants' War in Germany (1524–1525) erupted over the imposition of heavy taxes and draconian government policies. According to Richard Marius in *Martin Luther: The Christian between God and Death*, "The peasants asked for control over their contributions to religion and tithes forced out of them as a tax to support the heavy ecclesiastical establishment. The peasants were putting forth a medieval version of the belief that taxation without representation was wrong."[18] Religion was never the primary issue; lack of peasant consent was.

Monolithic Church and State

As the authority of the Catholic Church began to disintegrate in the sixteenth century, German princes acquired the power to determine the one and only state–sanctioned religion for their regions. From the government's unilateral standpoint, only one, monolithic religion could exist within each domain, although many independent religious sects were sprouting up across northern Europe. Parishioners were completely left out of the picture. Royal decrees compelled members of unrecognized or banned religious groups to pay "church taxes" for the upkeep of the state–controlled church. Already overtaxed, German peasants were outraged at paying for a religion not of their choosing. Bloody war soon erupted, and over 100,000 peasants were slain during the Peasant War.

Across the channel, religious uprisings, political strife, and Guy Fawkes' gunpowder plots plagued England after one religion—the Anglican Church— had been established by King Henry VIII in 1534. With church and state firmly joined at the hip, the authorities were able to wriggle their way into religious affairs, tightly weaving a texture of overt corruption and bitter politicization. Under various English kings and parliaments, administrators were empowered to determine ecclesiastical law, enforce church discipline, and settle official stands on theology. Any clergyman uttering inconsistent views was subject to imprisonment. This situation was an affront to independent religious groups, whose only alternative was to flee to the New World in search of religious tolerance.

In London in 1668, William Penn (who later founded the colony of Pennsylvania) was arrested in London when he resorted to preaching outside his Quaker meeting hall, which had been barred shut. The Conventicle Act was cited in Penn's arrest, prompting George Whitehead, another Quaker, to write that the Act's purpose was to "force a general conformity to the liturgy and practices of the Church of England." In fact, Penn spent over six months in the Tower of London for authoring a religious article that displeased the authorities (doubting the existence of the Holy Trinity), a hanging offense. This was the norm. Quakers, nonconformists, and members of other religious sects were regularly jailed and punished for disobeying governmental acts, when they preached their particular view of religion. One law, the Five–Mile Act (1665), required "a further oath of allegiance to the Church and State and forbidding any non–conformist preacher to come within five miles of any corporated town."[19]

Not even the American colonies could escape this metamorphosis of church and state into one entity. In the colony of Virginia, the Anglican Church, the official state religion, compelled every citizen to pay church taxes for its maintenance. But that was not enough. The state church had to defend its monopoly. Dissenting ministers were routinely jailed for disturbing the peace. In one instance, a Baptist minister, Reverend John Weatherford, was imprisoned for five months for preaching the wrong message. Patrick Henry, an attorney, secretly paid Weatherford's bail, since the minister refused to pay one cent to the government. In a courtroom speech, Henry referred to the Anglican clergymen as "rapacious harpies" who would "snatch from the hearth of their honest parishioner his last hoecake, from the widow and her orphan child their last milch cow! The last bed, nay, the last blanket from the lying–in woman!"[20]

In post–Revolutionary War America, churches had to fend for themselves. Interestingly, many people, both during and after America's colonial period, argued that financial support by the government was necessary or the country would go godless and churchless. Ironically, Patrick Henry was one of them. He proposed a church tax that would evenly distribute government funds to all denominations. This proposal was hotly opposed and eventually defeated by a movement of disfavored denominations, Baptist ministers, Jeffersonian secularists, and freethinkers. They quickly realized that such a law would put government in a position of defining and determining the merits of what religion ought to be—not an easy task, in a politically charged and biased world.

As the moving force behind the 1786's Virginia Act for Establishing Religious Freedom, Thomas Jefferson understood the incredible corruption that would spew forth from an official marriage between power-wielding government and single-minded religions. He wrote: "Millions of innocent men, women, and children, since the introduction of Christianity, have been burnt, tortured, fined, imprisoned; yet we have not advanced one inch towards uniformity. What have been the effects of coercion? To make one half of the world fools, and the other half hypocrites."[21]

Economic Engines at the Edge of Chaos

In a relatively free and inclusive society, business activity provided the greatest stability in society, since cooperation is based on reciprocation, not on brute force. This mutualism allows the new to be exchanged for the old without resorting to strife, gunplay or revolution. That is because markets are basically open outlets for the conversion, or interchange, of a lesser value for a greater value. Such reciprocal agreements foster peaceful interdependence, because both sides have an incentive to work together.

But business activities are more than a forum for trade. They represent an area poised on the edge of chaos. An expression coined by computer scientist Christopher Langton in 1990, the "edge of chaos" is the shifting position—a sort of phase transition—that constantly leaps between the extremes of total stagnation and utter chaos. There is no fixed or stable state, only chronic perturbations absorbed in a process of transition between potential equilibriums. Marketplaces fluctuate mostly in the out-of-balance range, but remain organized in a poised state. Also known as "far-from-equilibrium," such systems constantly divide, their branches bifurcating at every point along a range, providing new beginnings or unsustainable ends. Like a malleable metal, edge–

of–chaos flexibility is what gives marketplaces their greatest strength and stability. Some refer to this phenomenon as "instability with order."

But what about achieving a perfectly counterpoised equilibrium? No such thing. By definition, equilibriums exhibit a condition in which all influences are canceled out, leaving an unmoving and unchanging system. An unchanging position would sit at the edge of the extreme range without providing any structure or leeway for things to happen. Traditional science has relied heavily on steady–state behavior that searches only for static results, not for the dynamics of process.

A model for equilibriums that behave statically was first introduced by economist Leon Walras (1834–1910), who developed a theory known as the "general equilibrium theory." Because of the influence of chaos theory, Walrasian equilibriums have come under heavy criticism. British economist and historian Mark Blaug referred to Walras' G.E. as an "almost total failure" and "an utterly sterile innovation."[22] Blaug compared Walras's equilibrium mode to "a geographical map of the towns in a country without a map of the roads between towns."[23]

Yet many neoclassical economists were infatuated with Walras' platonic equilibrium paradigm. As an adherent in the perfection of information, pricing and competition, Walras believed that creativity could be predicted by central planners and charted on a graph. Likewise, equalitarian economists thought they could find perfect balance in a world that is all but homogeneous. Part of the problem, as explained by economist W. Brian Arthur, is that "an equilibrium by definition is a pattern that doesn't change," meaning that anything that does not change can't be the epitome of perfection.[24]

Equilibriums not only misidentify the way markets operate, but bear little resemblance to ever–changing reality. For instance, financial markets continually have to deal with unknown quantities. They are set up to influence a future that is dependent on how the market might alter the present. And then there are "exogenous" changes that burst from outside the model and can cause serious disturbances, or what economists call "exogenous shock." These unexpected outside influences tend to disrupt and destabilize systems thought to be in a stable equilibrium.

It took a Belgian scientist, Ilya Prigogine, studying thermodynamics, to understand the nature of order. He revealed that far–from–equilibrium systems with dissipative, flow–through energy have the ability to produce a higher degree of structural order. This discovery meant that open systems, such as market–based economics and evolutionary processes, generate disequilibrium conditions that display a mixture of both repetitive motion (order) and non-repetitive motion (chaos). Prigogine contended: "The remarkable feature is that when we move from equilibrium to far–from–equilibrium conditions, we move away from the repetitive and the universal to the specific and unique. Indeed, the laws of equilibrium are universal. Matter near equilibrium behaves in a 'repetitive' way."[25]

Like the wavelet motion of energy and gravity, these fluctuations are generators of orderly processes. Prigogine writes in *Order Out of Chaos*: "At all levels, be it the level of macroscopic physics, the level of fluctuations, or the microscopic level, non–equilibrium is the source of order. Non–equilibrium brings 'order out of chaos.'"[26]

Because the components of a complex system never quite lock into place, market fluctuations are merely the mixing process of change within a range. Some have likened this process to the Heisenberg Uncertainty Principle, in which elementary particles literally wink in and out of existence. Market activity is similar, in that it has its own "bifurcation point," where economic activity can simply branch off toward disintegration or evolve to a higher structure of order. Some scientists have described this process in terms of matter and energy: Chaotic regions provide "evolutionary energy," while the orderly regions store "dynamic structures."

Physicist Jim Crutchfield from the University of California, Berkeley, asserts that when a peak occurs near the edge of chaos, it creates a "maximum of information." In economics, this peak represents a point at which complexity is maximized or economic change is transferable. This is the focal point of nonequilibrium conditions where energy of growth mixes with the inertia of structures. Such processes allow dissipative structures to release energy with the least amount of resistance. In the economic arena, such resistance is minimized, since a buyer and a seller have already agreed on the transfer of property, which helps mitigate disorderly change.

Nature provides a number of wonderful examples of dissipative systems at the edge of chaos, driving toward a stable and self–arranging system. One of the most dramatic, discovered by two Russian biophysicists in the 1950s and 1960s, is called the Belousov–Zhabotinsky (BZ) Reaction. What Boris Belousov unearthed, and Anatoly Zhabotinsky reaffirmed in later years, was that chemical reactions can oscillate on their own terms. This might not seem so earthshaking, but at the time, it was considered a scientific impossibility. This discovery proved that inorganic chemical compounds do not have to be dominated by equilibrium behavior. Not only did the BZ chemical reaction ap-

Social Chaology and Strong Structures 135

pear to somehow turn back on itself in a feedback loop, but it made a travesty of the second law of thermodynamics.

Naturally, chaologists got excited over this "stable state of process." During experiments, inorganic chemicals would change colors at regular time intervals—alternating between two colors. In fact, the switching of colors was so precise that it could be used to tell time. Known as the "chemical clock," this phenomenon appears to organized, rigidly, billions of molecules as a whole. Prigogine wrote: "Such a degree of order stemming from the activity of billions of molecules seems incredible, and indeed, if chemical clocks had not been observed, no one would believe such a process to be possible. To change color all at once, molecules must have a way to communicate. The system has to act as a whole. Dissipative structures introduce probably one of the simplest physical mechanisms for communication."[27]

The chemical clock phenomenon demonstrates that the messy processes of motion and change, or what Prigogine termed "dynamic equilibrium," is the staff of stability. He maintained that continuous input, and the resulting wavelike fluctuations, are "required" to maintain a stable pattern. In fact, Prigogine contended that increasing chaos in a system often becomes the engineering force behind stability. Chaos provides order. Chaotic agitation and motion are needed to create overall, repetitive order. This "order through fluctuations" keeps dynamic markets stable and evolutionary processes robust. In essence, chaos is a phase transition that gives spontaneous energy the means to achieve repetitive and structural order.

What this reveals is that economic forces are shifts in balance between what is and what will be. They are flux–derived engines that reshape and realign. Perhaps the most visible example of this apparatus can be found in stock exchanges' trading pits. Ironically, some of the largest and most conservative economic structures—billion–dollar brokerage houses, banks, and financial centers—depend on the chaos erupting across a free-wheeling platform. And yet without these engines of oscillating, temporal motion, the subjective value of money, commodities, and property could not peacefully change hands. Marketplaces are the embodiment of chaos and order in search of a disequilibrium range, and if left undisturbed, they provide the benchmark for future exchanges.

Like many disciplines, the field of economics also parallels the fundamentals of physics and systems theory. For instance, if energy cannot freely flow from one system to another, the whole system may eventually shut down as a result of increasing entropy. Without trade, there is no movement of mass, no dissipation of energy, no nexus. Change is temporal; motion is spatial. Without movement, there can be no spatial change. Without motion, biological systems become inert. The mixture of chaotic agitation and rigid order maintains the stability arising from self–arranging patterns. Stuart Kauffman of the Santa Fe Institute addressed this issue, writing that there seems to be an "extraordinary surge toward order," as if systems understand that if they fail to adapt, entropy will strangle them.

Of course, for politicians weaned on the mother's milk of control, such free–wheeling metaphysics is unthinkable. They believe that they are the ones who really control the nature of society and that they are immune to the deteriorating effects of entropy. They believe they can legislate equilibriums, forcing equality of effect upon humanity, as if dynamic, complex systems could be tamed like wild animals from the jungle.

Attempts to control a system externally tend to be lethal—because most outside controls create barriers instead of conduits for information. This wall-building bias can be the death knell to interactive systems, clogging them in an antagonistic way—where one system benefits at the expense of another.

The reason is clear: no system ever assembled has remotely approached a state of "perpetual perfection." All systems are prone to bouts of failure from the ravages of changing environments and gear–grinding wear. Systems require corrective maintenance to repair breakdowns and prevent meltdowns. But static systems, such as government–operated retirement programs (*e.g.*, Social Security) or nationalized health care, tend to have high levels of dysfunction because centralization and caked–on layers of bureaucratic makeup will try to shield society from the effects of imperfection and error. Hierarchically organized systems are inherently opposed to change, while political systems are inherently opposed to admitting error. Both prefer to ignore the changes required to fix errors, usually content to leave such matters unresolved.

Three Strong Structures

Three types of structures are most responsible for strengthening and connecting society: business, family, and social.

Business Structures

Although the stock exchanges of Wall Street provide orderly structures, Main Street in Middle America is probably a greater bastion of order, trust, and responsibility. Artisans and merchants in small shops understand the requirements for an orderly and honest system to maximize profits and productivity for the long term. Under a system of free competition, the business community realizes that patrons are at liberty to pick and choose whichever company can satisfy their needs. Merchants are at the mercy of consumers and must act in an honest and responsible manner, or suffer extinction.

A meaningful relationship with employees, consumers, and vendors is paramount to survival, which promotes honesty and responsibility. What creates a village or community atmosphere is personalization, not politicization. Large corporations tend to act stiff, rigid, and impersonal, but in the United States, far more workers are employed by small companies than big ones. Many larger businesses understand the problems of too much centralization and the resultant detached bureaucracy. They understand that bigness could distance them from both consumers and employees. For instance, when Lee Iacocca, president of Chrysler Corporation from 1978 to 1992, discovered that productivity decreased when a factory exceeded 500 workers, he attempted to break up factories to reduce the number of workers. He reasoned that smaller factories had higher productivity rates, because workers would know each other on a personal, villager–like level. In contrast, the milieu in large factories tends to be impersonal, cold, and distant, resulting in a depressing environment of less productivity.

The story of Oskar Schindler in World War II Poland exemplifies the basic decency of inclusive and personal business structures. An industrialist and a member of the German National Socialists Workers Party (Nazis), Schindler bought an enamelware factory in Poland to make a quick fortune. His chief accountant, Itzhak Stern, a Zionist, convinced his new boss to hire Jews as his workers. Schindler had little interest in the Jews' precarious situation in Nazi–occupied Poland, but had formed a father–son relationship with Stern. In the first year of operation, the number of Jewish workers in the factory increased from 7 to 150. At Stern's request, Schindler even hired old and debilitated Jews, although they lowered the factory's efficiency. As Schindler became aware of the Nazis' Final Solution, he began to feel empathy for his Jewish employees.

Originally, Schindler had concentrated on making a profitable business. Yet the structure of business, generally based on honesty, integrity, and personal responsibility, caused him to see his workers not as the hated and so–called subhuman Jews, but as ordinary, hard–working people with no substantial differences from other ethnic or racial groups. At his company, a strong community spirit had developed, which drove Schindler to risk his life and to gave away his fortune in order to help his Jewish employees escape to a rural factory in a safer area. He was a businessman, but he felt an obligation to protect those who needed his help.

In a psychological context, close contact with others creates relationships that can defy old stereotypes and attitudes of hate. To know another person is to give consideration that one would not bestow on a total stranger. Schindler knew his managers and many employees on a personal level; the upper echelon of the Nazi Party did not.

Social psychologists have been trying to understand the reasons for the Holocaust for decades, determined to discover how such atrocities could have occurred in a modern, industrialized country like Germany, and whether it could ever happen in the United States. In one such study, four psychologists at the University of California, Berkeley tried to answer that question. Their report (published in 1950 as *The Authoritarian Personality*) suggested that authoritarian upbringing with rigid, hierarchical parent–child relationships smothers independent thought, which can lead to violent behavior later in life.[28] However, this study, like many in the field of psychology, examined only the behavior of the majority, while providing little analysis of or insight into the aberrant few. For instance, in Stanley Milgram's experiments in which subjects were to administer others electrical shocks, the study concerned itself with the vast majority who obey orders, not with the few who refuse to go along with the system.

In a nutshell, Milgram's experiment asked individuals to administer electrical shocks in varying degrees to others who made mistakes in a learning task. The subject in the experiment was given the role of "teacher," and was told to increase the voltage of the shocks given to a "learner" in another room (actually the experimenter's confederate, who was not given shocks, but who yelled out as if in pain), if he continued to make mistakes.[29] What the researchers wanted to understand was how far subjects would go in obeying the researcher's orders. In *Conscience and Courage*, Eva Fogelman wrote: "Milgram found that the majority of his subjects administered severe shocks to learners—some even forcing hands onto the metal plates even after being told that these learners had a heart condition. The experiment showed that ordinary people simply doing their jobs, without any particular hostility on their part, can become agents in a terrible destructive process."[30]

The teachers and learners were strangers in Milgram's experiment and had established no personal relationships. To their dismay, authoritarian regimes often discover how personal relationships can thwart their ability to rule and punish those who disobey. In Tiananmen Square in 1989, tens of thousands of Chinese students disobeyed the law and peacefully demonstrated for greater voice in their government. Tanks and soldiers from local units of the Red Chinese Army were ordered to put down the massive protests. However, the army failed to crack down on the demonstrators. Why? The soldiers were local boys. Many recognized the people they had been instructed to hurt, or possibly kill. Finally realizing their mistake, the Chinese government recalled the local army units and mobilized distant ones from the countryside. They told these units that criminals were rioting in Beijing, killing, and damaging property. The result: These misinformed and unfamiliar army units mowed down students and citizens without a second thought.

Under business structures, merchants often deal with strangers. But since the structure is based on activities that require consent, an authoritarian mindset has a smaller chance to take hold. Whether addressing employees or consumers, it is persuasion that businesses must use to advance their product or services. Anything else would be considered coercive or fraudulent, and would likely be detrimental to the goodwill upon which businesses so depend.

Family Structures

If the individual is the atom, the family is the molecule. But the molecular structure of the family could not be born without the ability to attract others. This attraction to others is permeated not only with chaotic encounters, but is chock–full of awkward moments, unnerving heartache, and heated passion. Initially, neither side in a courtship has any inkling whether it will lead to a permanent familial structure. The unknown abounds, adding confusion to an already unclear situation. But it is the engine of chaos, the ability for atomic change to absorb structures, that permits two to become one.

Courting is dicey. Will the individuals be compatible? Will each provide something to the relationship? Or will the courtship end with a heart–wrenching "Dear John" letter? Nobody knows. Like most excursions into uncharted territory, the future is cloudy. But if the attraction is strong and mutual, the chance of a long-lasting relationship or marriage, a cornerstone of society and stability, is quite possible.

Because conditions are ever changing, structures are susceptible to breakage. Divorce provides a means for unhappy partners to break away from a soured, abusive, or dishonest relationship. Although often tragic, dissolution tends to lead to a rebirth, in the form of newer structures. Interestingly, some nations still ban divorce, allowing only for legal separation, which does not permit either side to remarry. These laws were enacted in an effort to force couples to stay together. The argument is that children of divorced parents will permanently bear traumatic and psychological scars. But strong sociological evidence indicates that children also suffer in a marriage held together only by state law. Any partnership is only as good as each partner's good intentions.

In the past, Christian–oriented governments were the primary social engineers of futile attempts to keep couples secured in a fixed relationship by prohibiting divorce—civil or religious. However, one of the oldest religions in the world—Judaism—has always maintained that it is better for a couple to divorce than to be trapped in a union of strife.

Social Structures

Individuals commonly attempt to improve their image and skills. This natural urge leads to social gatherings, for fun, enlightenment, and charitable work.

Community volunteer groups provide all sorts of stabilizing structures and connections when they donate time, meals, housing, and medical services to the underprivileged. Such charitable work connects the well–off to the impoverished. Volunteering is another form of self–clustering integration that keeps entropy at bay.

If conflict is to be found in social structures, it arises when external forces are imposed on established structures. In 1933, when the Nazi Party in Germany began to take control of every private–sector organization, many community clubs simply withered away. Every nongovernment organization was targeted, including glee clubs, youth groups, and hiking fellowships. Groups were told that the majority of their leadership had to be card–carrying members of the National Socialist German Workers Party. Further, they were ordered to hand over their treasury to the German government. Ironically, little of this money ever reached the authorities. Most clubs quickly organized lavish events and banquets in a frantic attempt to spend their funds before the deadline. They were not about to give their resources to an outsider.

True to their nature, the National Socialists organized to consolidate and centralize these social organizations, which led to the loss of the organizations' individual identities, and subordinated them to a collective anonymity. The results were conspicuous in their failure. The outside meddling put these social organizations on the road to a slow dissolution. They had become political tools of an ideological and authoritarian government that operated by different rules. For instance, one German citizen bemoaned the fact that folk music in the city of Pirmasens was dying under the politicization of music clubs, warning that this policy was causing "the falling apart of associations, a drying up of interest, and a dying out of the joy of singing."[31]

Another way to compromise and weaken social structures is to make popular, inanimate objects illegal. In 1734, an Act of Parliament prohibited the sale of hard liquor in the colony of Georgia. Reports to London had indicated that colonists of Georgia were engaged in massive and inappropriate drinking habits. The ban was in force for eight years but was rescinded because Georgian farmers stopped raising their regular crops to concentrate on more profitable moonshining. Furthermore, bootleggers from South Carolina were smuggling in hard liquor at an alarming rate. Edward Behr, in *Prohibitions: Thirteen Years that Changed America*, wrote: "This earliest Prohibition experiment revealed, in this Georgian microcosm, almost all of Prohibition's inherent failings; bootlegging and moonshining apart, Georgian juries systematically refused to convict offenders, and some colonial enforcers of the law took bribes to look the other way. Over a century and a half later, history would repeat itself on a much vaster scale."[32]

During Prohibition in the United States, organized crime and the corrupted enforcement systems victimized both social and business structures. Citizens in search of alcohol had to deal with unsavory characters who produced banned booze of questionable quality. As mobsters grew fat on high-profit alcohol sales, they soon took control of the streets, branching out more aggressively into more lucrative enterprises. One sideline operation was selling "protection." Protection rackets involved forcing businessmen to pay extortion money so that they would be safe from firebombs, broken windows, employees being beaten up, and attacks on their family members.

Society was being torn apart. Machine-gun-toting men from rival gangs would spar in broad daylight over territory. Whole police departments and city governments were in the hip-pocket of organized crime. Never before had the United States experienced such an unstable wave of crime that disrupted its normally orderly process. Few scholars dispute the root cause of this chaos: the government's attempt to stop people from drinking a brew that has been with civilization since the time of the Egyptian pharaohs.

Governmental structures often tear societal structures apart. Whether the issue is a ban on an inanimate object or an attempt to control how people live, coercive systems have the propensity to create more disorder than order.

1 Dennis Dalton, ed., *Mahatma Gandhi: Selected Political Writings*, Indianapolis, Indiana: Hackett Publishing Company, Inc., 1966, p. 43.

2 Kevin Howe, "India's Economy Grows, Lowering Number of Poor," *Monterey Herald*, Nov. 10, 2006.

3 Robert Nisbet, *The Quest for Community: A Study in the Ethics of Order and Freedom*, San Francisco, ICS Press, 1990. First edition was in 1953.

4 Victor MacGill, "Exploring the New Science of Chaos and Complexity,"— posted on his Complexity Pages website.

5 Bruce Henderson, "Driver Ticketed for Using Biofuel; Vegetable Oil Sticks Him with $1,000 Fine," *The Charlotte Observer*, June 11, 2007.

6 Jan Brueckner and Ann Largey, "Social Interaction and Urban Sprawl," research study, University of California, Irvine, October 2006 with revisions in December 2006 and August 2007.

7 John L. Casti, Would–be Worlds: How Simulation Is Changing the Frontiers of Science, New York, NY: John Wiley & Sons, 1997, p. 89.

8 Jane Jacobs, The Death and Life of Great American Cities, New York: Random House Modern Library, 1961.

9 Friedrich von Hayek, The Constitution of Liberty, Chicago: University of Chicago Press, 1960.

10 Emily Costello, "Human Architects Are Taking Inspiration from the Planet's Master Builders—Animals, Termite Towers," Science World, Sept. 13, 2002.

11 Amy Gilley, "Fractalled: The Interstitial Spaces and Frank Gehry," paper presented at the Bridges Conference, Southwestern College in Winfield, Kansas, July, 2004

12 N. Arthur Coulter, Jr., M.D., *Human Synergetics*, Englewood Cliff, N.J.: Prentice–Hall, Inc., 1976.

13 Chris Lucas, "Synergy and Complexity Science," Page version 4.83, Sept. 2006, CALResCo Complexity Writings, Internet web site. http://www.calresco.org/wp/synergy.htm

14 Richard Lewontin, Steven Rose, and Leon J. Kamin, *Not in Our Genes: Biology, Ideology and Human Nature*, New York: Pantheon, 1985.

15 Fritjof Capra, *The Turning Point: Science, Society and the Rising Culture*, New York: Bantam, 1982, pp. 25–26.

16 Richard Lewontin, *The Triple Helix: Gene, Organism, and Environment*, Cambridge, MA: Harvard University Press, 2000.

17 Stuart Kauffman, *At Home in the Universe: The Search for the Laws of Self–Organization and Complexity*, Oxford University Press, USA; 1 edition, 1995, p. 25.

18 Richard Marius, *Martin Luther: The Christian between God and Death*, Cambridge, MA: Belknap Press of Harvard University Press, 2000.

19 Catherine Owens Peare, *William Penn: A Biography*, Philadelphia: Lippincott, 1957.

20 Quote from the Parsons' Cause Trial, 1763.

21 Thomas Jefferson, 1787. *Notes on the State of Virginia*. Edited with introductions and notes by William Peden, 1982, Chapel Hill & London: University of North Carolina Press.

22 Mark Blaug, *Economic Theory in Retrospect*, Cambridge University Press, 1997, 5th edition, p. 570.

23 Mark Skousen, *The Making of Modern Economics: The Lives and Ideas of the Great Thinkers*, Armonk, New York: M.E. Sharpe, 2002, p. 217.

24 W. Brian Arthur, "Out–of–Equilibrium Economics and Agent–Based Modeling," Chapter 32, Amsterdam, The Netherlands: North–Holland, imprint of Elsevier, 2006, pp. 1551–1564, published in the *Handbook of Computational Economics: Agent–Based Computational Economics, Vol. 2*, editors: Leigh Tesfatsion and Kenneth L. Judd.

25 Ilya Prigogine and Isabelle Stengers, Order Out of Chaos, Man's New Dialogue with Nature, New York: Bantam Books, 1984.

26 Ibid. Prigogine, pp. 286–287.

27 Ibid, Prigogine, p. 148.

28 *The Authoritarian Personality, Studies in Prejudice Series*, Volume 1, Theodor W. Adorno, Else Frenkel–Brunswik, Daniel Levinson and Nevitt Sanford. New York: Harper & Row, 1950. W. W. Norton & Company paperback reprint edition, 1993.

29 Stanley Milgram, *Obedience to Authority; An Experimental View*, New York: HarperCollins, 1974.

30 Eva Fogelman, *Conscience and Courage: Rescuers of Jews During the Holocaust*, New York: Anchor, 1995.

31 Celia Applegate, *A Nation of Provincials: The German Idea of Heimat*, Berkeley: University of California Press, 1990. Original source is from *Pirmasenser Zeitung in Sopade*, 1935, 2:717–18.

32 Edward Behr, *Prohibitions: Thirteen Years That Changed America*, New York: Arcade Publishing, 1997.

7 Social Upheavals and the Legalization of Violence

In linear human systems, babies would smoothly transform into adults; businesses could effortlessly change from making candles to making electric lights; and countries could gently shift from fascist to democracy.
—Martyn Carruthers[1]

Force always attracts men of low morality. —Albert Einstein

One need not be a social anthropologist to figure out why people become distraught over overt injustice and state–induced bloodletting. When political apparatuses legalize and institutionalize violence, they invariably risk perpetual conflict, which, in turn, causes sanity to take a leave of absence. And when the people's backs are shoved against a wall, a mixture of uprisings, armed insurrections, civil wars, and revolutions arises to reshape the future.

Political systems can't help but magnify socioeconomic problems, burn societal bridges, and trigger violent reactions. The governing elite understand people's natural tendency to try to benefit themselves at others' expense. This marauder mindset gives command–and–control systems the excuse to dominate and attempt to pacify society. It allows the political class and their surrogates to unleash repressive and regulatory laws, while enjoying the generous spoils of political war with certain members of society. Of course, the plundering strips society of its innermost core of individual autonomy and interlayered cooperative behavior. Because of these assaults, societal systems must attempt to restore balance, either by throwing off energy or by reacting violently to unsolicited interventions. At some point, resistance to the interference will reach critical mass, and, like a stretched rubber band, could send spasms of uncontrollable energy in any direction. Even minor maltreatment can set off brutal disturbances.

The Stonewall Riot in New York City of 1969 provides an example of a long–smoldering powder keg ready to blow. In an era when anti-homosexual attitudes were prevalent, the police would routinely arrest patrons in gay bars and nightclubs on indecency charges, for holding hands, kissing, or wearing clothing of the opposite sex. Finally, during one raid at the Stonewall Inn in

Greenwich Village, gays fought back. In the ensuing melee, dozens of mostly gay men were severely beaten in a riot of 400 police and thousands of angry gays. Interestingly, many outraged gays threw coins at the police officers, mocking them for the notorious system of payoffs ("gayola") that leeched great sums of money from bar owners who had to pay the police to let them remain open.

Political unrest is almost assured when political pragmatists find it more convenient to compel than to accommodate. In theory, government could work, but since it has guns, it doesn't need to. Instead, society tends to be overpowered by whatever political gladiators, trends, and agendas are in vogue at the moment. And when systems of governance abandon neutrality to actively advocate pet projects, society becomes torn in its obligation to either obey its political leaders or pursue its own survival. American history is not exempt from this phenomenon. A decade after the original thirteen American colonies ratified the U.S. Constitution, the country was gripped in sociopolitical unrest. The Federalist Party had instigated a series of regressive taxes and intrusive controls that caused long–simmering resentment among the populace. The Federalists maintained a viselike grip on the nation, dominating every level of government, including local judgeships. Feeling increasingly oppressed, Americans likened their situation to a foreign invasion, but with their own government occupying the country.

In 1798, under John Adams' administration, the U.S. Congress levied another unpopular tax on houses, land, and slaves, to pay for an undeclared quasi–war against France. John Fries, a Pennsylvanian farmer, organized a rebellion of up to 400 armed men to stop tax assessors from performing their duty, often flogging, tarring, and feathering captured government tax agents. In other cases, housewives would pour hot water over tax collectors from upstairs windows, a practice that caused the levy to be known also as the "hot–water tax." Unlike the Whiskey Rebellion (1791–1794), in which American citizens were killed, dwellings were burned, officials tarred and feathered, and 7,000 armed rebels marched on Pittsburgh, the Fries Rebellion ended without bloodshed. Although found guilty of treason and sentenced to death, Fries was eventually pardoned.

As political tempers continued to rise, President Adams signed the Alien and Sedition Acts in 1798, claiming he was doing so to protect the public good, not to silence critics. Interestingly, under the Sedition Act, the presidency and both houses of Congress were protected from "any false, scandalous, and malicious" criticism, but one office wasn't—the vice presidency which, by an odd coincidence, was occupied by the Federalists' chief nemesis, Thomas Jefferson. But the Federalists' promise not to prosecute outspoken dissenters was quickly proven false, when a Vermont congressman, Matthew Lyon, wrote a newspaper letter critical of the president for "a continued grasp for power." Lyon was convicted and jailed, but won re-election from his jail cell. When finally released, he rode back to Washington, D.C. amid thousands of cheering citizens, only to find the Federalists plotting to expel him from Congress because of his new status as a convicted felon. The attempt to keep him out of Congress was unsuccessful.

A dozen or so Americans were indicted under the Sedition Act, mostly editors and publishers of Jeffersonian newspapers. Some papers were forced to shut down; others were intimidated to the point that they stopped criticizing the government. Some of the indictments were bizarre. Two men were arrested for treason after having raised a "liberty pole" with a note attached at the top, proclaiming "Downfall to the Tyrants of America." One person was indicted for circulating petitions to repeal the Sedition Act. And one of the newspaper editors arrested was Benjamin Franklin's grandson.

The Alien and Sedition Acts backfired on Alexander Hamilton's Federalist Party. Many of the laws enacted to prevent Jeffersonian leaders from gaining a prominent position in Washington only hastened the Federalists' demise. Jefferson's Democratic–Republican party gained a majority in Congress in the election of 1800, ending the Federalists as a viable political party.

But the Federalists were more than political rivals. They exemplified political warriors hell-bent on building empires with take–no–prisoners mindsets. During the 1800 campaign, the Federalists, who were well versed in political strategies, went after Jefferson with a vengeance, accusing him of cheating British creditors, committing property fraud, and stealing 10,000 pounds from a widow. The arch–Federalist journal *Connecticut Courant* wrote that if Jefferson was elected, "Murder, robbery, rape, adultery, and incest will all be openly taught and practiced..."[2]

Just as President John Adams maintained that he was protecting the common good with the Alien and Sedition Act, so do the political elite in their endeavor to manipulate the populace. With greater opportunities and wealth, they are more adept at giving the citizenry what the political elite want. And to accomplish this double-dealing, the deck has to be stacked in favor of the house. By its very nature, government is the mastermind behind the unfair tricks of the trade, absorbed with picking winners and losers, and resolved to control and direct the sequence of socioeconomic events. This is done best by playing crowd–pleasing hands, dealing out patronizing policies, favoritism and platitudes. This love-fest toward authority, or "archiphilia," allows political card sharks to rationalize any brutish act in their game of dirty tricks. And in their doing so, the ethos of controlling people for their own good can only destabilize the core of society, fractionalizing the community, distancing the populace, balkanizing and bastardizing the spirit of cooperation, and creating an atmosphere resembling a hostile takeover. Anyone who opposes this prevailing political wind is branded an uncouth renegade, insignificant gadfly, or pariah. If a foreign war is stirred into the boiling pot, peace advocates are hotly denounced as unpatriotic or traitorous, to be found only in the company of terrorists.

* * * * *

Great civilizations do not stay great forever. When they finally decline into crumbling entropic heaps, it is society's depletion of accumulated wealth and energy that precipitated their decline—not a lack of political authority. Nonetheless, most political leaders are clueless about how to stop what they had unknowingly wrought. Peering through linear lenses, they can find no way to remedy civilization's downward spiral, except to mandate stricter measures. And as they crack the draconian whip, they become mystified as to why harsher measures actually are speeding up the decline. It is no mystery to social chaologists. Destabilizing conditions become rampant when societal members surrender their independence and responsibilities and cannot act together to make a difference. Without socioeconomic interdependence, little exists to hold societal bonds together, except fear of bodily harm, the prospect of detainment, or an appointment with the hangman's noose.

Political manipulation is a means to neuter society, making people impotent, effete, and partitioned, with the purpose of muffling and muzzling the *vox populi* so that they are bereft of any hope. In the final stage, the citizenry will become so overwhelmed that they will enter a phase of "societal entropy," in which the community can only wilt under a deathwatch of unchanging evenness. Without support from the bottom, top–heavy structures must collapse into the dustbin of history, a fate that many great and not–so–great civilizations have already encountered.

The Roman Empire, the superpower of the ancient world, fell further than most have ever realized. At its height, the city of Rome bustled with an estimated two to three million inhabitants, making it the largest metropolis of the ancient world. That all changed by the early fifth century. After several waves of sacking by Germanic tribes, the city of Rome became a virtual ghost town. One historian estimated Rome's population at no more than 12,000 residents, decimated after the invaders sabotaged the city's main aqueduct. As is the way with great civilizations, the splendor of Rome had burned brightly for centuries, only to be extinguished in a puff of smoke.

The Rule of Law, the Government of Men

One way to destabilize a society is to inflate and obfuscate the laws by which people live. After all, the rule of law is made by a government of men, which often induces "over–lawed lawlessness." But this was not so clearly the case in traditional Anglo–American jurisprudence. For hundreds of years, England and America developed laws through the self–discovery process found in common law and in the principles of torts. Under procedures of common law, legal precedent was derived from judgments in real court cases, and not from speculation generated by legislative expediency and wishful thinking. Laws were discovered, not manufactured. Torts, or "wrongs," would be brought to the court to determine their validity and any possible restitution. In short, there had to be a real victim, in order to enable a ruling.

Munroe Smith, professor of Roman Law and Comparative Jurisprudence at Columbia University, provided a model of clarity in *Jurisprudence* (1909), writing, "The rules and principles of case law have never been treated as final truths, but as working hypotheses, continually retested in those great laboratories of the law, the courts of justice. Every case is an experiment; and if the accepted rule which seems applicable yields a result which is felt to be unjust, the rule is reconsidered."[3]

For instance, if smoke from a neighbor's chimney regularly invades an adjacent home, a settlement could be adjudicated to stop the trespassing or to provide compensation. But the ruling is not intended to set into stone an all–encompassing law to ban every fireplace or wood–burning stove in the land. Case law is an attempt to codify natural law into man–made laws. And yet, such court decisions do not necessarily determine future verdicts. Each case is different, and may or may not be applied to the wrongs—similar though they may be—filed by another perceived victim.

The thousands of statutory laws cranked out by political systems each year are plagued by a host of fundamental problems. Few people, if any, understand these complex laws and regulations. Nor have many people read a single volume of the more than 4,400 federal criminal laws, nor of the countless regulations that are empowered with the force of law. And yet for centuries, Moses' Ten Commandments and other ancient precepts were considered the premier legal structure for reinforcing a peaceful society.

Within the history of jurisprudence, other legal systems have coexisted with common law. One such system, now referred to as "polycentric laws," thrived, before the modern era of monopoly–sanctioned laws. Fashionable until the 1500s, polycentric laws were a set of competing or overlapping legal systems unbounded by geographical regions. They were instead based on race, religion, commerce, and kinship. Before laws were monopolized within a single paradigm, citizens had a number of choices as to which legal system under which to live. For instance, during the Roman Empire, most citizens came under Roman law, but in the outer districts, where indigenous legal systems were practiced, non–Roman laws were allowed to compete.

It was the Roman senator and historian Tacitus who penned, "The worse the state, the more laws it has." Continuously inflating statutory laws puts every citizen at risk of becoming a criminal, without the necessity of having victimized anyone. The German philosopher Max Stirner exposed government's obsession to decriminalize its own misdeeds, writing: "The state calls its own violence law, but that of the individual, crime."[4] Under the foliage of political correctness, statutory laws tend to make criminals out of those who participate in acts between consensual adults. This begs the rhetorical question: if there is no victim, where is the crime?

Charles de Montesquieu, the famous French social commentator of the eighteenth century, observed: "Useless laws weaken the necessary laws." Inflating the supply of laws cheapens all laws, creating a situation in which it becomes impossible for anyone to live without breaking a politically enacted law. To make arbitrary criminals out of normally law–abiding citizens can only lead to widening the gap between the governed and the governing.

Robert H. Jackson, a renowned U.S. Supreme Court Justice from 1941 to 1953, noted this trend in 1940, writing that a prosecutor "will pick people that he thinks he should get, rather than pick cases that need to be prosecuted."[5] Jackson warned that with so many laws on the books, prosecutors have a decent chance of finding some technical violations, especially among those who are unpopular or have the "wrong political views." Jackson went further. He noticed that the legal system was becoming partial and ideological, worrying that "There is danger that, if the court does not temper its doctrinaire logic with a little practical wisdom, it will convert the constitutional Bill of Rights into

Social Upheavals and the Legalization of Violence 151

a suicide pact..."[6] Unfortunately, criminal systems often succumb to political pressures, adopt a domineering matrix, and resemble a man with a leash looking for a dog.

The proliferation of these arbitrary laws has other consequences. In *Constitutional Chaos*, Judge Andrew Napolitano wrote that he saw a breakdown of civil order in his own courtroom, daily. State prosecutors would bribe witnesses or use material witness warrants to kidnap uncooperative suspects. All too often, the police would commit perjury, introduce false evidence, and entrap suspects. To Napolitano, the government was breaking its own laws to enforce other laws.[7]

One of the most publicized cases of prosecutorial misconduct in recent years concerned a black stripper who accused three white players from the Duke University lacrosse team of racially motivated rape at an off–campus party. The district attorney, Mike Nifong, of Durham County in North Carolina, continued to prosecute a case so flawed and unethical that he was later charged with breaking more than two dozen rules of professional conduct. According to the *Los Angeles Times*, Nifong, a prosecutor since 1978, continued to "doggedly pursue a prosecution even after it was clear early on that no eyewitnesses, DNA test or forensic evidence supported the accuser's account." It took more than thirteen months before the D.A. dropped all charges. During this period, he was seeking reelection, while he "called the defendants a bunch of hooligans who had shown 'contempt...for the victim based on her race.'"[8] The district attorney was disbarred and resigned his post in 2007. Although the Duke University athletes were innocent, the public furor resulting from Nifong's public condemnation—that the gang rape was racially motivated— caused Duke to suspend the players, cancel the team's season, and forced the coach to resign. The three players' families also piled up millions of dollars in legal fees.

Out–of–control state and federal prosecuting attorneys are only part of the problem. The entire political apparatus is geared toward taking a proactive approach to reshaping society in a particular direction. The legal system has become a tool to impose a "control matrix" on society, to create people beholden to a state–specified model. This is why lawmakers abhor legal opinions originating from a judge's bench instead of a legislator's podium. The political elite fear the loss of control if they are not able to institutionalize a monolithic legal system. They want to keep every bit of legal control within their stubby fingers. This is one reason that they shudder when juries use their de facto power to judge both the facts and the law: jury nullification.

When monarchies reigned supreme, kings enacted laws by decree. Whatever the king proclaimed would become the law of the land and had to be obeyed. Little has changed. Like absolute monarchs, legislators feel entitled to rule from the top balcony, in robes of Tyrian purple. Laws patched together down at the community-level chambers might challenge those perceived to be of a higher authority. Some legal experts have argued that statutory law is anathema to case law.

One of America's most influential jurists, Oliver Wendell Holmes, Jr. (1841–1935), understood this conflict. After years of trying to systematize law by "scientific" conceptualization, he eventually realized that the law should be a mere observation after the fact, not control before the fact. Holmes stated, "It is the merit of the common law that it decides the case first and determines the principle afterward."[9] Systems of governance habitually attempt to institutionalize one–size–fits–all laws, creating a situation in which judges are prevented from examining each case within its own context allowing each citizen his or her day in an unbiased court.

Because the laws of physics are no longer considered by scientists to be as rigid as once was thought, it is only fitting that a legal system be self–adjusting in the courtroom. Laws issued from a single authority can usurp a legal system that was meant to provide true justice. When in 1930 Mahatma Gandhi walked to the sea to gather salt, he was openly defying the British Salt Law that made it illegal for people to gather salt at the ocean. There was no pretension that gathering or eating salt was harmful to society; it was merely a government monopoly on a commodity during English colonialism. Thousands of Indians soon realized that the law was senseless and took to gathering the banned sea salt. Eventually, over 100,000 were jailed; many others fell bloodied and bruised by police and military violence. The results were stunning. By beating defenseless people who refused to fight back, the mighty British Empire was dealt a global black eye, and eventually surrendered its most prized colony.

Cranking out a slew of theoretical, government–mandated laws only harms society's stabilizing influence. Having more laws on the books simply provides the political establishment with more opportunities to lock up more alleged criminals. And since the vast majority of statutory and regulatory laws are not victim–based, violations generally entail political or administrative infractions. Even the average person in possession of a twenty–dollar bill could be subject to criminal penalties. Some 90 percent of U.S. banknotes are contaminated with traces of cocaine, up from the 67 percent reported in a study conducted in 2007.[10] Thus, under various zero–tolerance drug laws, possessing them could be considered a punishable crime.

In a society in which nobody is innocent of criminal activity of some type, citizens tend to develop hostile attitudes toward the police, government officials, and all laws in general, especially if caught in the state's tightening web of over–criminalization causality. In fact, over–criminalization on the federal level has gotten so out of control that, according to Edwin Meese III, the former U.S. attorney general (Reagan administration, 1981–1985), it has become "a violation of federal law to give a false weather report."[11]

If relatively few people were being imprisoned, this debilitating effect would be minor. But the numbers are staggering. According to the U.S. Justice Department's Bureau of Justice Statistics, the number of American adults in local, state, and federal custody rose to a record 2.1 million in 2002. In fact, 1 in 37 American adults has had prison experience. In the federal prison system, approximately 60 percent of the inmates are behind bars over drug violations. Incredibly, in 2003 the number of U.S. inmates incarcerated over drug laws exceeded the number of people in European prisons for all crimes combined.

But do victimless–crime laws actually accomplish their intended purpose? For instance, did the liquor laws during America's Prohibition days actually discourage individuals from drinking alcohol? Most researchers agree that they did not. The per-capita consumption of liquor had declined steadily since the beginning of the twentieth century, likely due to the public debate over the evils of alcohol and the high profile of the temperance movement. By the time liquor was banned in 1920, the annual death rate from alcoholism was at 1 percent per 100,000 people; however, by 1923 it had risen to 3.2 percent per 100,000, and from there it climbed steadily higher.

Not only did Prohibition accelerate the consumption of liquor, it corrupted entire law enforcement agencies. In the end, some 11,926 U.S. revenue agents out of a total of 17,816 were "separated without prejudice," since not enough proof was available for criminal prosecution. Another 1,587 were "dismissed for cause," meaning that there was proof of their having conspired with organized crime, but not enough evidence for a jail sentence.

Prohibition faltered on every level, because the general public never considered drinking alcohol a criminal offense. And without public support, laws like Prohibition will always be disobeyed or circumvented. But worse, enforcing victimless–crime laws distorts the public view of what is a good law. In a world resembling the crime–ridden social disorder and urban decay of the fictional Gotham City of *Batman* fame, the general public might not distinguish between unorthodox behavior and acts of violence. If citizens find it permissible to break anti–liquor or anti–smoking laws, they might likewise feel justified in breaking any law. In such an environment, the tendency is to lump all laws into the same basket, giving less upstanding citizens an excuse to steal, cheat, and murder. And why not? Citizens can readily see the lawbreaking antics of civil authorities daily. Clearly, disrespect for all laws will lead to a general breakdown of civil order.

Along with destroying citizens' trust in a judicial system, the inflationary spiral of statutory laws can have a destructive effect on a citizen's sense of personal authority. For instance, before the 2005 U.S. Supreme Court's ruling in *Kelo v. City of New London*, the general American consensus had been that private property is sacred. This tradition goes back to old England, where citizens embraced the old proverb, "Every man's house is his castle; even though the winds of heaven may blow through it, the King may not enter."

Government agencies have been enabled, under eminent–domain and redevelopment statutes, to demolish any private property, for any reason. The *Kelo* ruling permits local authorities to seize private property and transfer it to private developers for private profit. Besides the obvious conflict of interest, central planners can also delegate eminent–domain powers to private entities serving as legally authorized agents of the state. And authorities no longer need to prove "blight" to employ urban renewal policies. Ironically, by 2012, seven years after the Supreme Court decision, the land confiscated by the city of New London still remained barren, blighted and used as a storm debris dump. In late 2009, the private developers announced that they were no longer interested in the redevelopment project, although they stood to lease the 91-acre waterfront tract of land from the city for $1 per year.[12][13] When command-based systems intervene in the lives and property of their citizens, the psychological harm is prolonged and detrimental to the whole of society. The populace develops a nagging sense of dread that the authorities have usurped all responsibilities for their lives and that their personal authority is no longer valid. And they are right. Whenever someone seizes control over another, it is common for the captive to feel a loss of control over his or her actions. But it is more than a loss of free choice or will. Captives lose a sense of responsibility for their actions. Prior to the Civil War, slaves were subjected to this same debilitating condition. With few exceptions, they had all decisions made for them. They were bought, bred, and sold like cattle. They had no personal authority and therefore could not be held responsible for their actions—except if they were caught trying to escape.

Without personal authority, the black family structure in that period became so badly weakened that the descendants of slaves still have not recovered. Caught in an unstable world of divorce and drug use, Americans of African heritage have a disproportionately high population in prison: one in three young males is under some type of criminal justice supervision. The system of slavery not only put blacks in chains and bondage, it corrupted their very sense of individual self-worth and autonomous well-being. They lived under a rigid structure that stole their integrity, honesty, and personal responsibility.

Violence Breeds Violence

With a profound reverence for life, Gandhi taught that "violence breeds violence" and that physical coercion interferes with social order—the backbone of stability. Taking the ethical high ground, he maintained that "no action which is not voluntary can be called moral." Any action that interferes with the social network disrupts society's topology. Imposed order breaks societal synergism by tearing apart its intricate fabric of teamwork—fabric that may have taken generations to weave. Such arbitrary force makes the linking of information no longer based on accuracy, but on some other paradigm. When confined under the influence of compulsion, information can neither move down its own unplanned direction nor be true to itself. As many interrogation experts have testified, information recovered through fear or torture is rarely accurate.

Most social psychologists acknowledge that the threat or initiation of physical violence is an ineffective method for solving problems. Physicist and economist David Friedman once remarked, "The direct use of force is such a poor solution to any problem, it is generally employed only by small children and large nations."[14] And indeed, governmental systems employ a type of physical force that therapists would argue is detrimental to stable relationships. But then again, these systems are not interested in keeping relationships alive; rather, they are concerned with getting people to do what they are told.

Threatening physical violence to get participants to perform a particular action destroys the opportunity for them to make "right" or "wrong" decisions. Without choice, all decision–making functions are reduced to submission to the dictates of others, to conform regardless of content or accuracy of feedback. Tibor R. Machan, a professor of philosophy, said succinctly, "There is no morality without the freedom of choice."[15] People are thrown into a situation in which they must conduct their lives according to political rules, not from the reference point of personal ethical standards, accuracy, or honest dialogue. An environment predisposed to violence will reap a cataclysmic crop of depravity.

Back in 1968, when army pilot Hugh Thompson, Jr. landed his helicopter in the middle of the Vietnamese village My Lai, he had to make a quick, personal decision. Was he going to let American forces on the ground wipe out a defenseless village of civilians? The unwritten military objective was to rack up a high enemy body count to prove that the United States was winning the Vietnam Conflict. For some in the military high command, it did not matter whether the official death count included Viet Cong regulars, or unarmed villagers.

During this reconnaissance mission, Thompson had noticed that his fellow G.I.'s below were massacring every civilian in the village. He landed his helicopter in the line of fire and aimed his guns at the advancing American forces, determined to prevent more killing. With two of his men backing him up with heavy machine guns, Thompson ordered G.I.'s and officers to stop shooting wounded women and children, or his men would open fire on their own countrymen. He had placed himself directly between the American troops and the Vietnamese civilians. The soldiers ceased firing, obeying Thompson's orders, although he was a mere warrant officer, outranked by commissioned lieutenants leading these G.I.'s in Charlie Company.

Immediately, Thompson ordered nearby helicopters to the village and medevacked wounded Vietnamese civilians back to Quang Ngai hospital. Several hundred unarmed civilians had been killed; others mutilated. There was no enemy opposition. No American soldiers died in the military operation except one soldier who had stepped on a Viet Cong booby trap. Not surprisingly, American forces were rapidly losing the battle for the hearts and minds of the native population in many Vietnamese provinces. Children would hiss at U.S. soldiers, and Vietnamese adults would remain quiet about the whereabouts of Viet Cong guerrillas. Even the American public started to turn against the war, after the My Lai massacre made newspaper headlines.

Proving that the first casualty of war is the truth, the first report issued by the U.S. military claimed that "128 Vietcong and 22 civilians" were killed during a "fierce fire fight" at the My Lai village.

Despite his heroic actions, Thompson suffered snubs and accusations of being unpatriotic. Incredibly, according to Thompson, one angry Congressman told him that he ought to be the only serviceman punished for what had happened at My Lai.[16]

The American military had legitimate concerns about Vietnamese villagers providing support to Communist insurgents. The villagers had many griev-

Social Upheavals and the Legalization of Violence 157

ances against the central government in Saigon. They were treated like serfs, with few rights to their land, and were discouraged or even prohibited from owning guns for protection. Like most governments, the South Vietnamese government simply did not trust its own citizens.

The story was entirely different in Siam (now Thailand), where communist rebels were never able to gain a foothold in local villages. Impressed with the story of the American struggle to end slavery during the Civil War, King Chulalongkorn, Rama V, abolished slavery in his nation. This set into motion institutional support for strong private–property rights in Thai society. Not only did the vast majority of Thai people own land, but the government often provided loans to help landless farmers purchase property. When in the 1970s communist insurgents tried to agitate Thai farmers into rebelling, they discovered few willing volunteers. Acting in accordance with their true nature, the communist began to use more aggressive means, raiding villages for supplies and kidnapping young men as conscripts. With guns provided by the Thai government, villagers fought back and stopped the domino effect that had spread communism across much of Southeast Asia.

The Attraction of Consent

Clearly, people do not want to be told what to do. And if they are forced to make changes in their lives, they often react negatively or violently. The particular change is often unimportant; people simply want to be asked in advance, have the opportunity to speak their mind, and make the final decision themselves.

Consent pulls society together; compulsion pushes it apart. In a psychological context, people want to think that the ideas they embrace are their own. They are suspicious of other people's notions and the consequences that may follow. This is a universal human trait. Motivational speakers have spent considerable time affirming that people do best when they think they have come up with an idea all by themselves. And when they believe it, such people will often put themselves in harm's way to protect what they think is important— their self–crafted opinions.

Voluntaryist societies impart greater peace, since conflict is decentralized and carries little legitimacy with bystanders. Two men fighting in the street over a woman is a private matter. If one tries to seize resources from nonparticipants, he will be incarcerated and disgraced. The Hatfield–McCoy feud (1878–1891) involved two clans warring over the ownership of a pig. The private feud was confined to those who were participating. Although only a dozen family members died in the disputes, the toll could have been larger if either side had enticed local governments into the disturbance, perhaps instigating a war between West Virginia and Kentucky.

The philosopher most responsible for undermining the concept of individual consent was Jeremy Bentham (1748–1832). In particular, according to economist Paul Craig Roberts, author of *Tyranny of Good Intentions*, "Bentham believed that tyranny was no longer a problem, because people were empowered by democracy to control government. He argued that any restraint placed on government's power would limit the ability of government to do good." In fact, Bentham favored "preventive arrest," an interventionist approach that would prevent anyone who might fit a criminal profile from joining "the greatest good for the greatest number" paradise. Bentham's utilitarianism led to the slow demise of what is now referred to as "classical liberalism."[17]

Coercing the Conscience

Not until the ideology–drenched twentieth century did systems of governance attempt to coerce the conscience. In olden times, wars and conflicts were instigated by tyrants in order to snatch territory and wealth from neighboring communities. These foreign invaders were dreaded, since they kept order through ironfisted policies that could lead to a swift rendezvous with the firing squad. There was no pretense of ruling the people for their own good. Potentates rarely cared about the well–being of their newly conquered subjects. But what if the populace could be re–educated to tacitly support rulers and their policies? What if governmental systems could get the people to do their bidding without threats of intimidation or torture?

Scholars have debated long and hard whether the conscience can be coerced. The Stoic philosophers of ancient Greece thought not. They concluded that human beings usually defy those who try to change them. Even the Christian Ostrogothic king Theodoric the Great of Italy (454–526) recognized this fact, writing, "We cannot command the religion of our subjects, since no–one can be forced to believe against his will."[18] The Italian physicist and astronomer Galileo Galilei (1564-1642), held similar views about trying to educate or re-educate people, writing: "You cannot teach a man anything; you can only help him discover it in himself." Yet, in the twentieth century there was a deluge of programs to radically alter the conscience, through new indoctrination techniques.

The first mass "thought reforms," or brainwashing programs, occurred in Mao Tse–tung's China during the 1950s. The prominent American psychiatrist Robert Jay Lifton examined the results, in *Thought Reform and the Psychology of Totalism: A Study of "Brainwashing" in China*.[19] He revealed that the impact of thought reform on most victims was temporary. The process could be effective in the short run, especially with younger people. But after a few years, and left to themselves, the victims tended to doubt or dispute the attitude–changing responses put forth during the brainwashing sessions. Most people would revert to their former core values, proving that force in the long term cannot change people's behavior.

In recent years, scientists in the field of evolutionary biology have arrived at the same conclusion. Trying to figure out why we do what we do, researchers began to study human genes for clues. They came up with a startling answer: genes appear to be selfish. Richard Dawkins, in his bestseller, *The Selfish Gene*, claimed that genes are competitive and will not aid other genes at their own expense.[20] The implications are that surviving genes build and maintain human beings so as to reproduce more, similar genes. That is, evolution centers on the preservation of the gene, not of the individual.

This gene–centric view of evolution caused a controversial backlash in the late twentieth century. The uproar peaked when two–time Pulitzer Prize–winning Harvard entomologist Edward Wilson argued that genetics puts biological limitations on man's nature. In *Sociobiology: The New Synthesis* and *On Human Nature*, Wilson insisted that certain parts of human behavior are universal, and that they are encoded into our very nature through an evolutionary framework.[21] Further, he demonstrated that these traits, including entrepreneurship, creativity, conformity, spite, and so forth, are unalterable. This view flew in the face of conventional thinking. Many sociologists believed that human behavior is based on current social and environmental standards. For Marxist–leaning social scientists, man's nature is malleable: human minds are blank slates, easily rewritten to take mankind toward a perfectly just and egalitarian society. Wilson once said in an interview, "Every human brain is born not as a blank slate waiting to be filled in by experience, but as an "exposed negative waiting to be slipped into developer fluid."[22]

Wilson maintained that genetic hardwiring in human beings tends to negate the molding of individuals by outside influences. This means that regardless of equalitarian measures being imposed, the populace would eventually return to its natural, default position of a disproportionate society. Any attempts to alter this genetic programming would fail. Once, when asked about the social equality theories of Marxism, Wilson reportedly joked, "Wonderful theory. Wrong species."[23]

Research by evolutionary biologists provides evidence that human behavior and actions have strong biological structures that are difficult to change by external controls. For command-and-control systems to blindly ignore or circumvent these structures is to invite serious strife and promote the destabilization of society. Some have referred to this effort to re-educate mankind through compulsive measures as a way for some governments to "preserve disorder."

Pathogenic Systems

Command–based systems are pathogenic, by nature. Economists Andrei Shleifer and Robert W. Vishny, in *The Grabbing Hand*, referred to the self–serving behavior of governmental structures as "government pathologies." They see central–planning policies as predatory and ill–conceived, immersed in perverse political incentives that encourage a "grabbing hand," instead of a helping hand to serve the community. In their words, "Politicians do not maximize social welfare and instead pursue their own selfish objectives."[24] When political systems become enmeshed in self–centered ethos, they tend to become abusive to the general populace. As marriage therapists have pointed out, compulsive and abusive practices lead to toxic and self–destructive relationships. And not unexpectedly, structures shoved toward a particular direction invariably push back.

Unfortunately, political showdowns have the propensity to reach critical mass, forcing structures to buckle and disintegrate, thus unraveling the energy and order that had originally brought them together. Essentially, bonding encourages cooperation and coordination, as it is more energy–efficient, similar to the bonding of atoms. Inversely, when there is breakage, not only are structures ripped apart and weakened, but the situation is more costly, in terms of having to provide more energy. Thus, state–imposed order can only lead to greater social disorder. Government, like acid, has a corrosive effect on everything it touches.

When a society is caught in a coercive environment, the bonding is artificial. Some social chaologists compare this process to the problem of free radicals—the unpaired electrons that many believe to be the cause of most illness, cancer, strokes, and even aging itself. Free radicals are unstable atoms that scurry about, trying to capture electrons to gain stability. When they happen upon a stable molecule, they cannibalize it, "stealing" its electron. Mimicking little body–snatchers, they transform other molecules into free radicals and then launch themselves after new prey. Once the process is started, a cascading effect can cause substantial damage, or death, to the entire system.

To coerce is to force things together that never wanted to join in the first place. In atomic and molecular physics, if atoms fail to bond to form compounds, the structure never comes into existence. Society is no different. If individual members decide not to cluster into some sort of assemblage, it was never meant to be. All structures must adhere to the fundamental principle of "repletive bonding." Without support at the microscopic level, the whole ceases to exist in any meaningful way. The universe is based on the satisfaction of the smallest parts. To crudely paraphrase René Descartes, "If it exists, therefore it works."

By the early 1960s, a number of scientists had discovered the destructive nature of compulsive behavior, long before chaos theory and complexity science became fashionable. One of the most famous of these was astrophysicist Andrew J. Galambos, who taught thousands about the benefits of a voluntary society, under the concept of "volitional science." Employed by TRW Space Technology Laboratories, Galambos insisted that the biggest impediment to a better society is the state's sanctioning of violence. He warned, "The greatest fallacy in the entire history of the human species is the idea that it is necessary to employ coercion to eliminate disorder." Famous for early advocacy of intellectual–property rights, he understood the synergy of cooperation, summarizing, "When there is no coercion involved, the gain of one person does not come from the loss of another."[25]

Going back further, Mahatma Gandhi's "Satyagraha" movement in the early twentieth century drew on historical figures who extolled nonviolence. Influenced by Hindu tenets of *ahimsa*, the spiritual independence of Jainism, and the political essays of Henry David Thoreau, Gandhi sought to convert—not coerce—wrongdoers. He believed that injustice could not be fought "by any means necessary," and that any violent, unjust means undertaken would eventually beget an unjust end. He saw an irrefutable connection between the means and the ends, writing: "If the means employed are impure, the change will not be in the direction of progress but very likely in the opposite."[26]

Unfortunately, traditional sociology has been deficient in understanding the importance of individual action and the dangers of undue conformity. Generally, the emphasis in socioeconomics has been on the "whole" of society, and not its "parts." For instance, sociologists will examine the various causes of mass unemployment from a centralist point of view. The actual unemployed worker is of little interest since he sits on the bottom rung of the ladder. So the happiness of the whole is more important than the one, although the whole is merely an aggregate of the multifaceted many. In razor-sharp contrast, social chaologists instead focus on the "part," mindful that the butterfly effect has the propensity to turn tiny variations into disproportionate outcomes. To remedy this deficiency, a whole new social science of what I refer to as "individualogy" should be put on par with sociology.

Something similar to individualogy is being developed in the study of workplace organizations, under the subdivision of "micro-organizational behavior." Drawing primarily on psychology, this subfield seems to give equal attention to both individual and group dynamics in an organizational setting. Of course, there is already a method used by the social sciences to gage aggregate decisions by individuals—methodological individualism—but it tries not to imply any moral worth of the individual.

The science of individualogy would better explain the synergy created when the interaction of two or more agents provides a cooperative environment. This bottom-up emergence seems to be the force that allows self-organizing systems to become greater than their parts. Nonetheless, collective intelligence is solely dependent on its individual agents, not the other way around.

The common perception is that physical force and domination can bring people together into a vibrant community. And yet, everyone is familiar with the old proverb that you can lead a horse to water but you can't make it drink. Obviously, force is a poor way to engender cooperative behavior. When children are herded into large centers of mass instruction, are they left with a hunger to learn? When private property is confiscated for shopping centers by city officials and redevelopment agencies, do the former homeowners hold hands in loving gestures of community spirit and sing Kumbaya? When sons and daughters are conscripted into the military service and come home in bodybags, do parents feel part of the social contract? And when taxpayers are compelled to dump money into a leaking tax bucket of bank bailouts and lavish government spending, do they feel that society has been enriched?

When Saddam Hussein's military and police units abandoned their posts in Baghdad during the second Gulf War, the populace took to the streets and looted everything not bolted down. After years of harsh rule, the sudden absence of any authority brought out pent–up emotions that ran wild for weeks.

Some news reporters remarked that it was a fair trade. Their government had stolen so much from the citizenry that they were simply returning the favor.

"Live–and–Let–Live" Systems

Even under adverse conditions, spontaneous cooperation can bloom where least expected. During World War I in France and Belgium, a peculiar, nonaggressive behavior flourished between warring factions caught up in otherwise horrific trench warfare. Battle–fatigued soldiers on both sides secretly negotiated pacts and truces, to the consternation of higher–ups. In this "live and let live" backdrop, soldiers deliberately abstained from firing at each other's positions. If ordered to fire, they would discharge their weapons in the air, refusing to shoot at exposed enemy combatants across no man's land. Sometimes whole companies would engage in this cooperative behavior.

When superiors suspected their men of refusing to obey orders, the soldiers would take another approach and ritualize their fighting activities, firing guns and artillery at the same location within the same hour every day, subtly notifying the enemy to move to a safer location. Of course, the other side would reciprocate with the same humane tactics.[27] This "live–and–let–live" system is a good example of mankind's deep–seated desire to be nonaggressive. In most armed struggles, men are conscripted into military service, where they must either fight or face long imprisonment, or even execution. Most soldiers never have a choice. They must strike at whatever enemy is deemed to be the state's present adversary.

Mankind has an inbred appetite for cooperation. Even in the harshest conditions of war, a twinkle of synergism and humanitarianism can sometimes seep through.

Empowerment and the Dangers of Democracy

Most people wish to be consulted on things that involve them personally. This desire might explain the popularity of democratic systems, when compared to hermetically sealed societies of the past. People have an implicit need to be enfranchised, to be in the loop and have a say in who will oversee a nation–state, even if they do not oversee it themselves. But democracy itself is fatally flawed and highly overrated. Many of its ugly warts were transplanted from the malignant tissue of monarchs and tyrants. As author James Bovard quipped, "Democracy has to be more than two wolves and a sheep voting on what to have for dinner." Author and investment analyst Harry Browne took his own swipe at the drawbacks of democracy, averring: "Majority rule is three boys beating up on a smaller one."[28]

Democracy has always been a political football, a game played with biased, one–sided rules. Under democratic political processes, it is impossible to insulate the rights of the individual from majoritarian preferences that routinely seek to abridge those rights. The politics of democracy turn life into a plurality game, a sort of collective kibbutz empowered to completely replace social interaction with political interaction, while simultaneously supplanting diversity with uniformity. By currying favor with the vast electorate, governments feel justified in enacting laws that discriminate against minorities and against diversity, predicated on the notion that nations must achieve racial and cultural consistency through state–sponsored assimilation. The upshot: democracy caters to a type of monolithic and political autism. To accommodate the majority, one must inevitably hurt the minority. This is the prerequisite for majority rule. Democracies have a fondness for assaulting the awareness of differences and seeking the elimination of disparity. And within this political pantheon, public opinion becomes the tribunal. Like the heavy influence of the hammer on the nail, democratic voters fashion themselves as protectorates of monotony, guardians against choice, and the censors of unfit languages, cultures and principles.

Worse, democracies enshrine that overbearing uniformity, pressuring the dissimilar to give up uniqueness in order to belong. Democratically sanctioned actions induce a tension of unanimity in such a way that the average citizen feels that viable alternatives are inconceivable, that there simply is no outside world in which to escape.

Since politics can be defined as *power used for the pursuit of objectives unrelated to good governance*, democratic leaders have few qualms in disadvantaging the few to gain the popularity of the many. The mob mentality of democracy is based on what is electable, regardless of what is right or needed. Nonetheless, although some political decisions are extremely harmful to society, they are often overlooked by officeholders with overactive ambitions.

Constitutional laws are routinely sacrificed at the altar of public opinion, especially when put on the auction block during election year campaigning. Robert H. Jackson understood the dangers of democratically prone vicissitudes, writing from the bench in1943, "One's right to life, liberty, and property,...and other fundamental rights may not be submitted to vote; they depend on the outcome of no election."[29]

Some examples are in order. In 2004, the French National Assembly banned from public places all "conspicuous" religious clothing and signs. Despite its outwardly even–handed appearance, the law's real purpose was to outlaw headscarves worn by Muslim women. Interestingly, government officials predicted that the ban would help Muslims better integrate into French society. Muslims took a different stance, stating that the intrusive law would make French Muslims resentful and more likely to stay together in tighter communities, and would alienate parents, causing them to send their children to private schools to avoid what they saw as religious intolerance. Within a year, France erupted in ethnic civil unrest.

The 2005 riots in France started when some youths of North African ancestry were returning home from playing football. Youths from state–provided housing projects are required to carry identification papers at all times and present those when asked by authorities. They could be held for questioning up to four hours and their parents had to come to the police station before they could be released. When the youths saw a police patrol, they immediately ran away. Two of the dodging teenagers scaled a high–powered electrical fence and were electrocuted. This incident sparked a nationwide riot of mostly Muslim youths. Over 270 French districts were affected, with 8,900 vehicles torched during 20 nights of rioting.

In a country famous for its advocacy of equality, French authorities had created policies that put the Arab minority in conflict with the European majority. Despite generous welfare benefits and all the rights and privileges of French citizenship, the North African French are often plagued by high unemployment, crime, restrictive labor laws, and few opportunities. As of 2006, unemployment was as high as 50 percent for minority youth in outer–city ghettoes.[30] According to Nobel Prize–winning economist Gary Becker, French labor laws—mainly minimum wage statutes—give "insiders" with jobs a tremendous advantage over "outsiders" looking for work.[31]

The United States has had its share of racial–economic troubles. For much of American history, democracy has been a legal means for the majority to bully the minority. For instance, by 1877 all public and private establishments were forced to segregate the races in the Deep South. Alabama's state legislators made it unlawful for blacks and whites to play a game of billiards together. Other laws gave local governments the authority to determine who could get marriage licenses. The state of Mississippi wanted to do more than just outlaw interracial marriages; the state made it a criminal act to print, publish, or circulate material favoring societal equality or interracial marriage.

These state-sponsored Jim Crow laws were enacted through democratic processes and popular vote, although African Americans were often prevented from voting or registering to vote. With such prohibitive laws, some type of civil rights movement had to emerge to counter the intrusive government. It did after World War II, but not soon enough to prevent hostile emotions from spilling out into the streets. More than 750 race riots dotted the United States landscape during the period from 1964 to 1971, with over 10,000 incidents of arson that transformed whole black communities into wastelands.

Other so-called democratic nations have had worse records of abuse. The democratic nation-state of Turkey, a member of NATO, has an official policy to assimilate racial minorities by force. The Turkish government has enacted laws to homogenize society so as to develop a pure racial identity and uniformity. In many ways, this drive for perfection resembles the imposed conformity depicted by the cyborg society in *Star Trek's* Borg Collective.

So what have the Turkish legislators done? Up until 1991, the Kurdish language, whether written or spoken, was completely illegal in Turkey, although the language was in widespread use. In a nation with 15–20 percent of its population listed as Kurdish, nothing of its culture could be uttered on radio and TV broadcasts or taught in educational centers. In fact, any discussion bordering on positive aspects of Kurdish nationalism was grounds for imprisonment.

In 1991, Leyla Zana, the first Kurdish woman ever elected to the Turkish Parliament, was arrested after she took her oath of office. Wearing a headband with traditional Kurdish colors, she made a short statement in Kurdish: "I have completed this formality under duress. I shall struggle so that the Kurdish and Turkish people may live peacefully together in a democratic framework."[32] A firestorm of protest followed, with angry shouts of "Separatist," "Traitor," and "Arrest her." She was immediately placed in police custody. In 1994, after years of legal proceedings, she was finally found guilty of treason, stripped of her parliamentary immunity, and sentenced to 15 years by the Ankara State Security Court. With no outlets through which to participate in Turkey's parliamentary process, militant and paramilitary organizations turned much of southeastern Turkey into a war zone, from the late 1980s into the 1990s. The results were devastating. The war's casualties totaled over 36,000 dead; three million Kurds were made homeless; and some 3,000 villages were destroyed by the Turkish military.

Dividing and Destroying the Community

How can cooperation be expected from political systems that demand obedience over consent? How can mutual respect, goodwill, or synergy be forged, if citizens must conform to the edicts of a single–minded authority? Threats and hostile actions are poor substitutes for the successful bonding of structures. Harry Browne observed: "Any businessman can tell you that you get nowhere trying to intimidate employees; you have to motivate them to do what you want them to do."[33]

Groups have an intrinsic need for cohesion, and the individual, equally, has a need to belong. But command–based systems, interested mainly in building structures to pierce the stratosphere, ignore the fact that to reach the top, one must first secure the bottom, the foundation. In the world of atomic and molecular science, particles flow freely as they create self–organizing bonds, but they come together on their own terms. Generally, their bonding is neither conditional on external controls, nor built to support the apex. Rather, bonding is an attempt to stabilize a structure.

In chemistry, atoms come together so they can achieve lower overall energy. Bonding releases energy; breaking bonds requires energy. The formation of society is no different. Individuals naturally clump into organized groups, in order to save energy. The obvious ramification is that systems of governance have little to do with the people's natural tendency to gather and coordinate activities. People already have an innate affinity for doing that. On the other side of the coin, it is quite possible that the general public is reluctant to tear down established structures, due to the high cost of depleting energy in a breakup.

Command-based systems are more than just barriers to community nexus. They are masters of divide–and–conquer strategies. Most laws benefit a certain classification of people while simultaneously disadvantaging others. Social Security programs for the old increase the tax burden on the young. Agricultural subsidies for farmers are made at the expense of other taxpayers. Laws designed to benefit one race or group over others can foster a society where everyone mistrusts everyone else. Corporate welfare, subsidies, and bank bailouts come at the expense of the middle class and poor. Barriers and dividers clutter societal roadways, when political considerations take the front seat.

The American landscape has not always been held captive by political wonks, well–connected insiders, and heavy–handed central planners with silver–spoon pedigrees. Before the nationalization of welfare in the United

States, mutual–aid associations and private charities were ubiquitous. Stories abound of farmers in the countryside taking care of down–on–their–luck strangers. As far back as the colonial days, Benjamin Franklin and his peers set up all sorts of voluntary, beneficial social services. It seemed that American generosity knew no bounds, as ordinary citizens would take in strangers and provide them with food, medicine, and lodging at their own expense.

According to television news reporter and columnist John Stossel, 30 percent of Americans belonged to mutual aid societies, until government started to crowd them out in the 1930s. There were over 10,000 fraternal orders, with some 100,000 separate lodges, in the United States by the 1920s. Stossel wrote: "Mutual aid societies paid for doctors, built orphanages and cooked for the poor. Neighbors knew best what neighbors needed. They were better at making judgments about who needs a handout and who needed a kick in the rear. They helped the helpless, but administered tough love to the rest. They taught self–sufficiency."[34]

Journeying through America in 1831, Alexis de Tocqueville was one of the first authors to recognize the big–hearted character of Americans. He marveled over the network of voluntary associations that dotted the fruited plain. In some ways, Americans had little choice. According to historians, the American people had to empower themselves, since there was no government and few wealthy aristocrats to extend a helping hand. Nonetheless, Americans created a community of voluntary programs that impressed the world. "When an American asks for the cooperation of his fellow citizens, it is seldom refused; and I have often seen it afforded spontaneously and with great good will," Tocqueville wrote in *Democracy in America*.[35]

After crisscrossing America, Tocqueville realized that authority–controlled welfare burdens society under a paternalistic condition in which the *volk* lose their ability to care for themselves, keeping citizens in perpetual childhood. Disturbed at how the French authorities handled welfare, he was adamant that government should never usurp the functions of private charity.

Community involvement is essential for a healthy society. If local communities are discouraged from becoming involved with their own members, citizens tend to become anesthetized to the needs of others. As welfare programs become more institutionalized and centralized, the impoverished take on the features of unwanted or ignored apparitions. And when the homeless appear on street corners holding up cardboard signs pleading for work or food, most citizens simply drive by and ignore their plight.

Taxpayers feel justified in looking the other way, since government professionals are supposed to be in charge of the problem. Overtaxed citizens have already given, so conclude that nothing more is required. This perception separates the community from the lower rungs of society. And as the authorities flood society with impersonal welfare checks and punctilious controls, charitable organizations become increasingly neutralized and out of touch with the needy. The bonds break; people stand divided; and society is destabilized. The "social capital" of society is depleted. No longer can people rely fully on a network of friends and acquaintances to improve their economic well–being. According to economists Pavel Chalupnicek and Lukas Dvorak, society becomes "fractionalized" when government interferes with this social–capital networking, especially between a social group and its members.[36]

A good example of a nation that has abandoned its community spirit is Greece. In this heavily socialized Mediterranean nation, the people have developed a dog-eat-dog antisocial mindset. According to author Michael Lewis, "The structure of the Greek economy is collectivist, but the country, in spirit, is the opposite of a collective. Its real structure is every man for himself."[37]

Although Greece has had a serious budget deficit for over a decade, few self–employed pay their income taxes. Most doctors and professionals accept only cash payments from clients. Even several hundred Greek finance ministers in 2010 were accused of widespread tax evasion. Bribery and corruption are a way of life.

Like many Europeans, wealthy Greeks rarely donate to private charity, probably because they try to hide their assets since it is commonly believed that wealth can only be obtained through plunder. Ironically, a socialized economy tends to make its citizens engage in anything but community–minded and charity–driven work, the same egotistic behavior that pervaded the Soviet Union during its waning days.

For centuries, the Chinese had a different take on community involvement. According to their traditional customs, China's community leaders had developed a way to help young people succeed in life. Young men would meet with important elders of the community to propose their vision of how to become financially independent. The elder would listen to this version of a modern–day business plan, give suggestions, and select those they believed worthy to receive seed money for future business ventures. The money was provided as a gift, not a loan, and if the entrepreneur was successful, the man in later years often joined the elders, bound by tradition to contribute his money to help younger generations.

Long before the rise of chaology, Mahatma Gandhi embraced an organic view of the workings of society. He understood the follies of command–and–control structures and state–sponsored benefits. He wrote: "Government control gives rise to fraud, suppression of truth, intensification of the black market and artificial scarcity. Above all, it unmans the people and deprives them of initiative, it undoes the teaching of self–help they have been learning for a generation. It makes them spoon-fed."[38]

Further, Gandhi warned, "I look upon an increase in the power of the State with the greatest fear because, although while apparently doing good by minimizing exploitation, it does the greatest harm to mankind by destroying individuality which lies at the heart of all progress..."[39]

Compulsory systems always crowd out the traditions of charity and community. In 2007, the community bond definitely broke when Edith Rodriguez entered the public medical center known as the Martin Luther King, Jr.–Harbor Hospital, in Los Angeles. Arriving at this community hospital's emergency room with abdominal pain, she collapsed on the floor and yelled for help. But nobody came to her assistance. Videotape from a security camera showed her lying on the floor for 45 minutes, as the janitor cleaned the floor around her and staff nurses ignored her pleas. While she was writhing in pain and vomiting up blood, her husband telephoned "911" for emergency services, but the operator told him that they could do nothing, since Edith was already in the hospital's emergency room lobby. She died a short time later from complications of a perforated bowel.

Instead of punishment, the staff responsible got "letters of expectation" that explained how to treat patients in the future. The director of Islamic Project HOPE, Najee Ali, was incensed, and regarded the reprimands as a "slap in the face for the whole family, a slap in the face for the community and it shows the devaluing of Latinos and blacks...."[40]

"Here's a person crying for help. Will no one help?" said Arthur Caplan, a bioethicist at the University of Pennsylvania, during the media hype. "What kind of a society are we when we can't even render aid to someone who's in their own blood and vomit on the floor and you're mopping around them? It's a kind of morality tale of a society gone cold."[41]

Known by the locals as "Killer King," the hospital had a long history of harming and killing patients whom it was meant to serve, constantly plagued by incompetence, poor management, bureaucratic indifference, and lapses in care. For instance, a nine–year–old patient died after having gone in for treatment of two broken teeth.[42] One investigative report discovered that a man with a serious brain tumor was left untreated in the emergency room for four days before relatives transfered him to another hospital so that he could get a life–saving operation. So many violations were revealed that in June, 2007, the U.S. Centers for Medicare and Medicaid Services filed a report that not only condemned the hospital for "substandard care," but declared that "patients at King–Harbor in Willowbrook were in immediate jeopardy of harm or death."[43]

Soon after the episode, administrators from the county–operated hospital complained that they were "underfunded." But that claim had already been rebutted in a 2004, Pulitzer Prize—winning, five–part investigative series by the *Los Angeles Times*, entitled, "Underfunding is a myth, but the squandering is real." In that investigation, it was found that the hospital "spent more per patient than 75 percent of the public and teaching hospitals in California, according to a 2002 state audit that looked at fiscal year 2000."[44]

A hallmark of a civilized society is feeling secure in the availability of good medical care without the fear of playing Russian roulette from a hospital bed. When well–funded government agencies are unable to provide even minimal standards of care for society, it demoralizes the community. This profound, debilitating effect can discourage members of society from ever donating to a community–related project. Historically, when political systems are put in charge of consumer–based services or products, the structure collapses into chronic rationing, price controls, and planned disorder. In a revealing article in the *New York Times*, the reporter observed that some British citizens were so desperate to get dental care that they had become amateur dentists themselves. One Briton interviewee, William Kelly from Rochdale, had to do an extraction by snapping the tooth out by himself. What is the cause of such a system failure? The *New York Times* is explicit, writing: "It is due in large part to the deficiencies in Britain's state–financed dental service, which, stretched beyond its limit, no longer serves everyone and no longer even pretends to try."[45]

When Brits attempt to visit a National Health Service dentist, they usually have to line up with hundreds of others. They never seem to get to the front of the line before the cutoff hour, and become discouraged. The problem has become so bad that many citizens have simply given up trying to register with a public dentist and instead have let their teeth rot. A British dental nurse, Claire Dacey, disclosed that she had one "lady that was in so much pain and had to wait so long that she got herself drunk and had her friend take out her tooth with a pair of pliers."

Part of the problem is that inflexible rules are putting British dentists through the wringer. In a campaign to streamline and economize the failing system, dentists have been forced to become assembly–line workers, mandated to perform a set number of "units of dental activity" per year, which is causing dentists to quit the system. And the resulting dentist shortage is being felt mostly by the poor, who had been promised quality medical care for free.

But the unresponsive nature of bureaucracies exposes other, far more serious problems. Economist Thomas Sowell explains this in simple terms: to government employees, "bureaucratic procedure is everything and outcomes are nothing." This is exactly what occurred when ten Alameda firefighters and police stood around for an hour watching a man slowly drown in neck–high water in the frigid San Francisco Bay. The first responders chose to watch from the sidelines. Finally, a bystander, a young woman, decided to swim out and retrieve the man's lifeless body. After she pulled Raymond Zack's body ashore, firefighters tried to resuscitate him, but failed.[46]

The question is: Why did this tragedy happen? After the drowning made headlines, Mike D'Orazi, the interim fire chief, told the Alameda City Council and the news media that the firefighters and police had been handcuffed by official policy, due mostly to budget cuts. They had had to cancel water rescue training for their men. Worried about legal liabilities, the city had instituted procedures in which one official memo read: "Under no circumstances shall any member enter the water to initiate a rescue or search."[47]

This excuse revealed, in essence, the view that the value of man–made laws and policies superseded the value of life. City officials, determined to follow procedures at all cost, repeatedly claimed that they were acting appropriately, and that budgeting problems were the culprit. But according to an investigative story by *Contra Costa Times*, the city had at least $20,000 budgeted for water rescue training.[48]

When asked by an ABC–TV news reporter whether first responders would have entered the water to save a drowning child, Ricci Zombeck, a division fire chief, said he would do the right thing if off duty. But if on duty, he "would have to stay within our policies and procedures because that's what's required by our department to do."[49] In other words, Alameda firefighters and rescue teams would have let the child drown so as not to violate procedures — a sort of slap in the face to claims that public safety employees are selfless, heroic protectors of the public.

The Warm Glow of Charity

Will people reach beyond themselves and donate to worthy causes, without duress? Will they contribute to the needy, even if they get no special tax write–off advantages? Only recently have scientists discovered that the good feeling that comes when donating to a favorite charity "could be your brain patting itself on the back." That "warm glow" sensation, according to the young field of neuroeconomics, is nature's way of activating the "regions of the brain associated with pleasure." In a report in the June 15, 2007, issue of *Science*, a team of economists and psychologists discussed ways in which the brain directs how people handle money. Using brain–imaging technology, the researchers discovered that when test subjects voluntarily gave money to a food bank instead of spending it on themselves, increased activity occurred in the brain areas called the *nucleus accumbens* and the *caudate nucleus*—areas associated with the most rewarding stimuli.[50]

Paul Zak, the founding Director of the Center for Neuroeconomics Studies at Claremont Graduate University, contends that humans are "hyper–social," meaning that people are inclined to help others, even strangers. No other animal appears to have this capacity, to any extent. According to Zak, this phenomenon seems to be hardwired into the human brain. Simply stated, it feels good to help your fellow man. Furthermore, Zak's research casts doubts on the assumption that people always pursue narrow, self–interested goals. Instead, he argues that people have a physiologic "moral sentiment" which provides a balancing neurologic basis (hormonal releases of oxytocin) that echoes the theories about moral behavior and empathy that Adam Smith wrote about in *Theory of Moral Sentiments* (1759).[51]

Unfortunately, those who draft and implement government social programs have failed to understand that societal bonding is a two–way street. As most insightful clergymen can testify, it is just as important for the giver to give, as for the receiver to receive. The unselfish act of charity bonds the needy to the moneyed. Both understand that the benefactor did it voluntarily, and that awareness makes the bond even tighter. Cold money from afar fastens few, if any, societal rivets.

Truth–Distortion of Dystopia

In *The Prince* (1513), Niccolò Machiavelli is credited with introducing the concept of "the ends justify the means," which was revived by Karl Marx in *The Communist Manifesto* (1848). Marx encouraged his supporters to acknowledge that ruthless means are justifiable if the ends are historically necessary. Under this premise, truth is unimportant, as facts might interfere with what a political system has slated to accomplish.

Author George Orwell became a victim of truth distortion when he fought in the Spanish Civil War. In that war between communists and fascists, he observed that both sides were reinventing history to satisfy their ends. Orwell had originally traveled to Spain in 1936, to fight Franco and the fascists. But to his surprise, he found himself caught up in factional infighting, accused of collaborating with the fascists, put under the threat of arrest and internment, and forced to flee for his life from the Soviet Union–backed Communists, who were purging and assassinating socialist, anti–Stalin Communist, and anarchist ringleaders. Back in England, his accounts were ignored and shrugged off as fanciful distortions. Most of England's intelligentsia instead believed the official reports coming from the Soviet Union's propaganda sources. This dark experience compelled Orwell to pen *Animal Farm* and later, *1984*.[52]

The Soviet government was famous for dispensing truth like a confidence man. Communist leaders believed they had no need for accurate feedback; successfully orchestrated dogma was truth, in and of itself. If things did not run as smoothly as anticipated, it became a game to erase the old number and write in the new. As the old joke during the Soviet era went, every loyal comrade knew the future; it was only the past that kept changing. But without truthful feedback, the Soviet government was operating in utter darkness. These "dictocrats" did not know what they did not know. Eventually, the Soviet Union experienced a rude awakening.

Truth is more than an accurate account of past events. Truth anchors stable structures. In human relationships, bad faith can lead to nasty break–ups and turmoil. But generally, when citizens want to divorce their political system, break–ups are impossible. Nobody can opt out of a political structure simply by filing divorce papers at the county courthouse. Whether the relationship is bad, good, or ugly, all citizens are sealed into a permanent union within national boundaries. Without any decent options, an injured party often feels powerless, cynical, and demoralized. The feeling of entrapment by the populace weakens social structures, giving dismayed citizens no duty-to-obey attitude toward political authorities and, conversely, causing authorities to feel no loyalty toward ungrateful citizens. Worse, as sociopolitical systems collapse into dysfunction, the governing apparatus must distort the truth to a greater degree. Leaders of all political stripes understand the danger when the unwashed masses cannot be pacified, misled, or neutralized. The merchants of discontent have little difficulty in recruiting mobs of vindictive insurgents.

Honesty strengthens societal structures; lies cripple them. Structures must have integrity to stand firm. Reality is truth-based and sturdy; truth–defying contortions have little long–term durability, and crumble when exposed. Unfortunately, deceit and half–truths are the bread and butter of politics. And by serving the public a steady diet of falsehoods, politicos can feast on state–crafted banquets of subsidies, entitlements, research grants, no–bid contracts, low–interest loans, and giveaway funds. As the political establishment discovered long ago, a great deal of money can be made with lies, but little from truth.

When nations go astray, political systems and their elite surrogates continue to honor "spin fabrications" as worthy of public policy. This is why the free flow of information is an abomination to flimsy structures. Unfiltered data, no matter how insignificant, can bring down Goliath.

Under the theory of self–organized criticality, chaotic phenomena "tend to rearrange themselves to be closer to their limits." This is the opinion of physicist Ben Carreras of Oak Ridge National Laboratory in Tennessee and computer expert Vickie Lynch, who use the example of sand castles on the beach to validate their point. For instance, if a child increases the height of a castle, building each level higher and higher, at some point it will become shaky and topple over.[53] This borders on the "theory of power law distribution," in which results are distributed in such a way that the larger the effect, the less frequent the event. As a complex system grows into a megasystem, trying to reach perfection, the danger grows exponentially toward the possibility of a devastating, domino effect of failure. Inaccurate information near the edge of chaos can easily send systems over the edge. Since most political systems bathe in hidden, distorted, or fabricated information, the erroneous data become the critical tipping point that can make all the difference between system stability and system collapse. This is the prime reason that political systems are so unsteady — accurate information is anything but a constant in their command–and–control structures.

Even today, many nations continuously attempt to shut out ill–favored information. According to *Time* magazine, the People's Republic of China "employs a force of 30,000 Internet censors" in order to block access to undesirable Web sites and information, some referring to the censorship as the "Great Firewall."[54]

During the late 1970s, when the Soviet Union's economy exhibited signs of tanking instead of soaring, a group of Russian economists was determined to find out why. To their dismay, they discovered that long–term goals were not being met, and they reported to their superiors that economic growth had stagnated to a rate of zero. With figures and statistics, they expressed their concerns in the hope that something would be done to fix the problem. Something was done immediately. Many of these economists were whisked off to psychiatric hospitals, and never heard from again.[55]

The availability of feedback is far more dangerous to the leadership and cadres of a ruling regime than most realize. When governments can easily repress anyone for almost any reason, nobody really knows which subordinate leader is a loyal supporter. All feedback is then biased and distorted. Fear of deadly purges has the uncanny tendency to make devoted opponents pose as loyal supporters. In this environment, nobody can trust anybody, rocking the very core of a regime and a society.

My Way or the Highway—A Story of Planned Chaos

Generally, highways and roadways represent both linear and nonlinear movement of objects. Think about it. In a relatively free nation, any motorist can jump into a vehicle and rush headlong anywhere at any time. Despite the occasional diversions, most drivers still confine their movement inside the roadway infrastructure.

Like a roulette–wheel ball, the motorist represents a strange attractor, cruising down roads on impromptu routes and destinations sometimes unknown to the driver. Motorists are free to consume tankloads of gasoline for Sunday jaunts through the countryside, or to wander from shopping mall to specialty stores in search of bargains. This leeway of movement is immense, undirected, Wild West style, and popular.

But what if someone were to view these haphazard driving habits in an unfavorable light? What if they regarded individual drivers as poor navigators who require some guidance? How might people react to new restrictions on their driving patterns? And how would central planners rein in narcissistic motorists?

Members of society are often suspicious of grand new laws proposed by the politically savvy and government activists. Unfortunately, besides a scanty crew of short–tempered armchair skeptics, the vast majority of people have little skill in fending off the rigors of political proficiency. So, when an alleged crisis strikes a community, the veterans of past political wars mount high horses and spout their most beloved cliché: "There ought to be a law!" With the speed of a NASCAR pit crew, policymakers and special interest groups leap to the forefront, rev up their political engines, and prepare to solve another ailment of society—and then to be rewarded for their altruistic efforts.

Many government programs start by encouraging citizens' voluntary participation. After all, the authorities are merely trying to correct bad habits of misguided citizens who need to rectify their selfish and ignorant ways. How could a little nudge in the right direction hurt anyone? Being less wasteful is important for everyone in the community; some might consider it a noble cause. Of course, human nature being what it is, most citizens are unlikely to follow voluntary guidelines. They will probably default to their old, careless habits, with no substantial lifestyle changes.

Naturally, the authorities can get riled when the public refuses to adhere to their well–intentioned programs. From the authorities' standpoint, citizens are misguided souls who cannot be trusted to do their civic duty. Annoyed with being ignored, government officials see no alternative but to remove their white gloves, brandish an array of bare–knuckle threats, and impose mandates. With big fanfare and more legislative fixes, policymakers set out to enforce efficiency, requiring all motorists to notify authorities of their destinations and schedules beforehand.

Some in the public complain bitterly, but protests are feeble, since motorists are not organized. Many obey the new rules, grit their teeth, and move on with their lives. Only a few egomaniacal kooks confront the system, arguing that they are better qualified to judge where and when to drive. The more circumspect motorists quietly realize that these procedures now give the authorities the power to deny any travel requests. The smarter ones quickly emigrate.

When the law shifts into high gear, the woefully uninformed are the first to encounter a sticky web of political correctness, lawyers, and bureaucracy. They cry the loudest, turn indigent, and refuse to obey, citing some obscure constitutional right to freedom of travel. Other injured parties comply, fearing reprisals or unflattering publicity. But if a few strident dissenters resist, the enforcement agency soon ups the ante and slaps heavy fines upon violators, feeling a legitimate duty to punish all who would defy the authorities.

As resistance slowly festers, the enforcement hierocracy becomes more entrenched, institutionalized, and costly. In order to boost revenues to fight lawless motorists, penalties are increased, through additional revenue–enhancing laws. Stiffer penalties and an arsenal of tougher laws cause motorists to become more reckless in their attempts to escape capture. And with more motorists caught, processed, and incarcerated, the need arises to construct additional prisons, enlist more police officers, and hire more administrative staff.

As enforcement intensifies, an aura of paranoia grips those who feel as if they are being unfairly targeted by a mysterious but invasive conspiracy. Fear of arrest causes many to find unobtrusive ways to display their dissatisfaction. In some neighborhoods, timid drivers refuse to use turn signals during lane changes. The less daunted defiantly cheat the system, sneaking down side streets before getting back onto designated routes. Inevitably, a divisive wedge of "us versus them" polarizes society into two opposing camps: the enforced and the enforcers.

The war against drivers' inefficiency escalates. Policymakers and policing agencies work tirelessly to stop spiraling lawlessness in the street. Despite their efforts, some officials suspect that they are losing the war to a disillusioned public. This matters little to hardheaded political realists. They have already concluded that the war is completely unwinnable, but eminently fundable. With massive job creation in mind, and a desire to justify their own existence, they impose additional laws to force motorists to take prearranged routes. Immediately, they set up a cluster of alphabet–soup departments to coordinate, oversee, and manage where and when a motorist will drive. Motorists are no longer asked their route preferences, since so many have been found cheating. The public is now required to call in, to get instructions and approved destinations.

Unable to get through busy telephone lines, motorists panic. They can't procure official authorization to drive to work, visit a sick friend, go shopping, or attend social events. If by some miracle operators do become available, their information is often incomplete or outdated. Without correct information, the operators cannot verify recent career changes, newly discovered friends, or recently opened stores, and therefore can't assign destination orders. The information gap becomes a serious problem. The authorities study the problem and settle upon a solution: They hire more people to implement an intelligence–gathering agency to scrutinize every aspect of a citizen's life. With better information, they can now decipher where and when people should drive on the roads. Problem solved.

Few citizens find Peeping Tom surveillance appealing but hope it will relieve the logjam. Unfortunately, the problem only grows worse as the bureaucracy becomes mired in administrative inertia, redundant procedures, red tape, and infighting. Resigned to a world of dwindling choices, motorists struggle to find alternatives to obtain some form of mobility. They seek out the dark underbelly world of fake identify cards and authorization papers, which provide some relief.

To counter this growing threat, law enforcement agencies ratchet up their operations to stop criminal attempts to circumvent the law. They enact strong-arm tactics to discourage noncompliance. They issue fewer drivers' licenses, especially to those suspected of violating the law or of being troublemakers. To prevent recidivism, vehicles are confiscated from first-time offenders. To catch more rogue motorists, cameras are mounted at busy intersections to record violators' license plates. But when central planners discover that many drivers still alter their course *en route*, roadblocks and police are set up at many intersections. The results: the movement of people almost grinds to a halt.

Society soon becomes entangled within the *faux* complexity of gridlock, breakdowns, and chaotic consequences. Tremendous effort is spent trying to survive an increasingly rigid and corrupted system. Just finding ways to keep afloat consumes everyday life, displacing any pretense that the system ever was grounded in common sense. Eventually, the system evolves into an exclusive tool to provide traveling privileges for a select few, while organized crime does the same with under-the-table bribery. The weak become disadvantaged, while the politically connected acquire more pliable routes to their destinations, and flexible traveling hours. As always, the pragmatic opportunist is far ahead of the game. He simply bribes someone to secure preferential treatment.

The original intent, to encourage efficiency, is lost in a futile attempt to manipulate human nature to do something it was not inclined to do. In the end, a conspiracy of planned chaos and imposed order paralyzes society, as it breaks down into anthropogenic disorder, bitter conflict, and financial collapse. The true irony of this story is that increasing efficiency was never the real goal or objective—the hidden agenda was to gain a tighter grip on society.

Competing Governments—The Collective Violence of War

War causes chaos; chaos does not cause war. The political disorder released during armed clashes is merely the symptom of collective violence exerted by competing governing systems. Although multifaceted, the cause of war ultimately rests on the capacity of a structure to concentrate political authority in a way that denies autonomy to others. And when that power is consolidated within a geographical area, the political apparatus stands atop a slippery pyramid of power, exposed to volatile winds of change.

On the sociopolitical level, it can be argued that to accept the legitimacy of the state is to embrace the necessity for war. But when it comes right down to physical war and bloodshed, governments don't protect people; people protect governments.

As political philosophers have admonished throughout the ages, the power to instill goodness is the same power with which to destroy it. To unleash raw, unadulterated power is to release uncontrollable consequences for society and abutting political systems. Government in and of itself is the foremost agent for destroying order and imposing chaos. Like chemical reactions, each time a government trespasses, the breakage releases an outburst of energy that leads to disturbances across the social-political landscape.

With a natural tendency to be suspicious, goal–oriented politicos keep a wary eye on political systems that border their jurisdiction. These intrapolitical conflicts are revealing. In some ways they resemble trained roosters in cockfighting arenas, circling about, puffing up their ruff of feathers and waiting for the perfect opportunity to lunge at a potential competitor. Take the deadly antics of territory–grabbing crime syndicates that engage in unlawful activities. They, like predatory governments, aspire to enlarge their geographical turf, and beam with delight when peeking over neighbors' fences for possible goodies to plunder. This contest over political takings is perhaps the greatest cause of conflict and disharmony.

This antagonism is scalable to every level imaginable—angry mobs rioting against local authorities, guerrilla armies fighting across provinces in blood–drenched civil wars, national governments crossing international boundaries in preemptive strikes. There is no end to where or how an organized political unit will attempt to conquer rivals.

Amazingly, even radical movements that profess strong opposition to any form of government have been known to support the traditional role of governance. During anti-globalization protests at World Trade Organization conferences, self–proclaimed anarchists went so far as to demand more government controls over international trade. In 2010, during Greece's financial crisis, anarchists took to the streets to protest proposed cuts in public spending that would reduce the size and scope of government, the exact opposite of anarchists' stated goal to bring about a stateless society. Although most anarchists publicly bad–mouth violence, a number of them have planted bombs and assassinated world leaders, in bids to challenge or overthrow governments. In the final round, most agitators for political power become mesmerized by the thrill of riding in the saddle of power. And if they can seize the government's mane, the journey leads them to the same politically charged dead–end.

Whether the strife is external or internal, the politically astute understand that conflict can be a heaven–sent tool to devour the weak or rub out potential in–house rivals. Both Hitler and Stalin systematically purged thousands of old–time comrades, resulting in show trials and executions that tested ideological loyalty. But it was playing the fear card that got the ball rolling.

Fear is the greatest political parlor ploy of all time. The phobia lying behind warfare prepares society for war, a sentiment echoed by historian Charles A. Beard (1874–1948), who accused the United States of getting involved in "perpetual war for perpetual peace."[56] The mere thought of death and destruction at the hands of outsiders can terrorize a citizenry into surrendering everything they have. Historically, such fear is misplaced. According to political scientist R.J. Rummel, citizens' own governments are the greatest genocidal actors and mass killers of them all. In *Death by Government* (1994), Rummel showed that citizens have a much greater probability of dying at the hands of their own government than of foreign ones, adding credibility to the old adage that governments don't protect people; people protect governments.[57]

In a 2007 update, Rummel estimated that over 272 million innocent, non-combatant civilians were intentionally murdered by their own governments during the twentieth century.[58] Further, this "democide" was six times greater than the number killed in combat in all foreign and domestic wars. After years of research on war, collective violence, and democide, Rummel concluded that freer nations inflict less violence against their own citizens than do less tolerant ones, and that "free people never have famine." Rummel wrote, "The less freedom people have the more violence, the more freedom the less violence. I put this here as the Power Principle: power kills, absolute power kills absolutely."

President Ronald Reagan recognized the dangers of government intrusion and state–induced terrorism. Although responsible for the massive military build–up to counter the Soviet Union's Cold War threat, Reagan announced in a 1981 interview with Barbara Walters that the major threat to freedom did not come from communist governments in Russia or China, but from government in the United States.

Political Flatliners

It was probably Tim Lister, the best–selling author, business consultant, and software developer, who first identified people with rigid traits as "flatliners." Lister's critiques are directed at project managers who refuse to adapt to changing conditions. In *Extreme Project Management*, Douglas DeCarlo expanded on Lister's term and took his own running stab at flatliners, describing them as people addicted to a linear mindset who can't understand why the world refuses to conform to their plans. To DeCarlo, this compulsive way of thinking is an example of what not to do in the real world. As he put it, "Why would anyone want to change reality to conform to fiction?"[59]

Categorizing this disorder as "Newtonian neurosis," DeCarlo espouses a view that the world is deeply unpredictable and that reality instead resembles a "squiggly line." In his books and lectures, DeCarlo goes after this "linear lunacy": "Flatliners relentlessly bludgeon every squiggly line project into submission through the excessive use of project management tools, rules, templates, policies, and procedures." He also contents that continuously inserting more discipline into failing project is the equivalent of saying: "If it's not working, let's do more of it."[60]

But political flatliners are more than Newtonian-driven project managers frustrated over getting the same appalling results after repeating the same policies over and over again. Instead, they comprise a cabal of "controlaholics," bubbling over with domineering personalities and busybody agendas. They bristle with bully–like mannerisms, ready to torment opponents as if they were a fringe minority akin to Holocaust deniers. Carrying a heavy load of guilt and self–righteousness, these linearists excel at inflicting an entropy–choking clampdown on anyone who embraces spontaneity. If political flatliners are given authority, they would decompose civilization to the point where it would flatline across an EKG monitor.

Since the physical makeup of the universe—matter and energy—is almost entirely nonlinear and wavelike, political flatlining could be compared to the final stage of cardiac arrest, a phase transition in which static controls have driven humanity into a deep coma that would terminate in brain death.

This analogy can't be overstated. Under autonomic operations of the human body, it is impossible for people to take personal charge of their own body on a macroscopic level. We don't have the time or ability to manage our circulatory system at every moment. We would have great difficulty trying consciously to regulate our heartbeat or brain waves from second to second, or taking control of our immune system and zapping millions of pathogens before they can infect healthy cells. We would be overwhelmed. But this is exactly what agenda–driven flatliners propose for the political body, during their endless battle to micromanage every aspect of socioeconomic life.

Chaos Dynamics Versus Atrophy

Every living entity would die without the dynamics of motion—quickly drying up, rotting away, and being buried under the dust of entropy. But the self–ordering process of attraction and repulsion dynamics not only prevents atrophy, it also impedes the status quo.

Chaologists usually cite edge–of–chaos properties to explain how a robust stability is achieved. Disequilibrium is caused by the pendulum of order and chaos swinging back and forth in search of the most effective balance point. A common analogy is that of a tightrope walker who constantly works to maintain his stability on a thin metal wire. He does so by readjusting to account for dynamic forces. For evolutionary biologists, these acrobatic maneuvers are what make evolution possible. To them, straight–line equilibrium ultimately portends extinction.

Unfortunately, many people fail to understand the need for the friction of diversity to achieve socioeconomic disequilibrium. Flatliners envision a pie–in–the–sky utopia guaranteed by politically inspired policies, to prevent any possible risk or insecurity. They fret over the wiggly imbalances that occur when people live and work without state–mandated safety nets. They think that something is terribly wrong when humans can suffer anxiety over whether they will have enough food, clothing, education, child care, housing, medical care, and old–age assistance, ad nauseam. The fear of empty cupboards motivates equalitarian rigorists to demand enforced order and "equality of outcome."

Embarking on a holy crusade, flatliners seek to prevent people from pursuing their lives in the ways they wish to pursue them. Wealth is to be polarized, redistributed, and equalized. Choice is to be expunged, since it would allow some people to outperform others. Legislation must be implemented to halt spasmodic and unsupervised activities. And since people can't be trusted, everyone must be watched, so that nobody can accumulate an uneven share of wealth, pleasure, or knowledge.

But to shut down the pulsating dynamics of a system is to trigger the degenerating effects of atrophy and death. Think of humans as representing subatomic particles—people quantum–leaping from position to position, to take action according to how they satisfy their own nature. In this way, most systems operate in compliance with the self–organizing principles of assembly. But more important, all dynamics are disproportional; not even the pendulum swing is perfectly balanced in the long term. Most systems could not survive without two or more irregular counterbalancing forces seesawing on the edge of chaos. For instance, subatomic particles/waves of energy and matter are always in flux—molecules repel each other at small distances and attract at large distances (push–pull chaos dynamics).

Every dynamic system needs two or more opposing forces in order to function—including economic systems. For instance, what would happen if the tug–of–war between a buyer and seller were superseded by an outside influence? What if a third party of ironclad authority intervened in behalf of sellers, circumventing the normal buyer–seller dynamics? What if this outside party let sellers get any price they wanted, with little or no negotiated input from buyers? In other words, what if the buyer had no choice but to pay whatever the seller wanted? Of course, the buyer would refuse to buy, because the price would have been too high.

On the other hand, if governmental favoritism graced the purse strings of buyers, letting them extract whatever low price they desired, the outcome would be the same—no trade—as the prices demanded would have been too low. In either case, the disequilibrium between two opposing points of interests would be disrupted and few agreements would be reached.

The identical cataclysm would strike mandated labor relationships. If business owners had all the power to set wages, workers' salaries would plummet to almost nothing. If instead, workers were granted a legal monopoly to set their wages, salaries would skyrocket beyond sustainable levels. In either case, the fluxing balancing act that keeps prices in some semblance of order would cease to exist. The contrived favoritism would interfere, causing employers not to hire workers they deemed too expensive, and impelling workers not to apply for jobs they deemed too low-paying. Such an artificially distorted system would atrophy. Any system without the ability to evolve and change on its own merits is doomed to failure.

The human body is no different, in its link to chaotic dynamics. For instance, the rhythm of the human heart is not perfectly regular. And there are good reasons for this imperfection. One of them, according to some physiological researchers, is that irregular rhythms appear to imitate training principles used by weightlifters. For years, athletes realized that constant repetition of the same movement of a muscle can create harmful fatigue. Perhaps rhythmic variation in the heart is nature's way of preventing cardiac muscle fatigue.

In studies of pathology, physicians and scientists are beginning to see chaos as a prerequisite for a healthy body. Some chaologists have suggested that disease in the human body is an "acute attack of order." Others, such as biologist and theoretical neuroscientist Walter J. Freeman from the University of California at Berkeley, have argued that chaotic dynamics and activity "are essential to brain function," "ubiquitous in neural functioning," and "essential for the creation of information."[61]

In the case of epileptic seizures, Chris Sackellares, a neurologist at the University of Florida, compared brain seizures to a computer that plays the same, identical game of solitaire over and over again, until the brain has reverted to its "naturally chaotic state." In this way, many researchers have come to see an epileptic fit as the brain caught in a spasm of extreme order, which denotes that the brain is an organ that operates in a natural state of chaos.[62]

In economics, the dynamic tension between buyers and sellers has a stabilizing influence on prices. Without exception, buyers put pressure on markets to bring down prices of, for example, real estate, while sellers impel prices to move higher. The clash of priorities causes fluctuations in pricing, which, in the long run, prevents either force from becoming too dominant.

All systems need the chaotic dynamics of motion, in order to remain healthy and alive. If agenda–driven politicos were to succeed in their quest to reshape and equalize mankind, citizens deprived of control over their lives and bodies would likely search for fulfillment along violent and disruptive pathways.

1 Martyn Carruthers, "Chaos, Coaching & Therapy Part 1: Solutions for Complex Problems," internet article posted in 2003. Source: http://www.soulwork.net/sw_articles_eng/chaos.htm.

2 Adam Voiland, "Clement Moore's Anonymous Screed Against Thomas Jefferson," *U.S. News and World Report*, posted Jan. 17, 2008.

3 Munroe Smith, *Jurisprudence*, Columbia University Press, 1909, p. 21; cf. Pound, "Courts and Legislation," 7 Am. Pol. Science Rev. 361; 9 Modern Legal Philosophy Series, p. 214; Pollock, "Essays in Jurisprudence and Ethics," p. 246.

4 Max Stirner, *The Ego and Its Own* (Cambridge, UK.: Cambridge University Press 1995), p. 176, originally published 1844.

5 Robert Jackson, "The Federal Prosecutor" speech to the second annual Conference of United States Attorneys in Washington D.C., April 1, 1940.

6 Terminiello v. Chicago, 337 U.S. (1949). A prosecutor in the Nuremberg Trials in Germany, Robert Jackson's dissenting opinion opposed overturning a ruling to punish a fascist leader who incited a riot in Chicago, worrying that strong-arm tactics by militarists might become commonplace in America.

7 Andrew P. Napolitano, *Constitutional Chaos: What Happens When the Government Breaks Its Own Laws*, Thomas Nelson, 2004.

8 David Zucchino, "Duke Lacrosse Case Was Riddled With Holes, Report Says," *Los Angeles Times*, April 28, 2007.

9 Oliver Wendell Holmes, "Codes, and the Arrangement of the Law" (1871), in *The Collected Works of Justice Holmes: Complete Public Writings and Selected Judicial Opinions of Oliver Wendell Holmes*, vol. 1, ed. Sheldon M. Novick (Chicago: University of Chicago Press, 1995), p. 212.

10 Henry Fountain, "Those Hamiltons and Jacksons Carry Some Cocaine," *New York Times*, Aug. 18, 2009.

11 Adam Liptak, "Right and Left Join Forces on Criminal Justice," *New York Times*, Nov. 24, 2009.

12 "After the homes are gone," *San Francisco Chronicle*, November 28, 2009. In its lead editorial the *San Francisco Chronicle* writes: "The well-laid plans of redevelopers, however, did not pan out. The land where Susette Kelo's little pink house once stood remains undeveloped. The proposed hotel-retail-condo "urban village" has not been built. And earlier this month, Pfizer Inc. announced that it is closing the $350 million research center in New London that was the anchor for the New London redevelopment plan, and will be relocating some 1,500 jobs."

13 Linda Greenhouse, "Supreme Court Roundup; Justices Will Hear a Property Rights Case Contesting the Limits of Eminent Domain," *New York Times*, Sept. 29, 2004.

14 David Friedman, *The Machinery of Freedom: Guide to a Radical Capitalism*, Chicago, Illinois: Open Court Publishing Company, 2nd edition, 1989. Originally published in 1971.

15 Tibor R. Machan, "Anti-libertarian point refuted," *Sun Journal*, April 27, 2010.
16 Jessica Bujol, "Hugh Thompson Jr., 62; 'One of the Good Guys' Saved Civilians at My Lai," *Los Angeles Times* – Associated Press, Jan. 7, 2006.
17 Paul Craig Roberts, "No Liberty Without Habeas Corpus," December 12, 2007, posted on the antiwar.com website.
18 *Letters of Cassiodorus*, Thomas Hodgkin, trans. (London: H. Frowde, 1886), pp. 156–219.
19 Jay Lifton, *Thought Reform and the Psychology of Totalism: A Study of Brainwashing in China*, New York: W. W. Norton & Company, 1961.
20 Richard Dawkins, *The Selfish Gene*, Oxford University Press, 1990.
21 Edward O. Wilson, *Sociobiology: The New Synthesis*, Cambridge, MA: Harvard University Press, 1975.
22 Tom Wolfe, "Sorry, But Your Soul Just Died," in *Hooking Up*, New York: Picador USA, 2001.
23 Quoted in J. Getlin, "Natural Wonder: At Heart, Edward Wilson's an Ant Man," *Los Angeles Times*, October 21, 1994.
24 Andrei Shleifer and Robert W. Vishny, *The Grabbing Hand: Government Pathologies and Their Cures*, Cambridge, MA: Harvard University Press, 2002, p. 4.
25 Andrew J. Galambos, Course V-2—*The Nature of the Free World*. Other quotes come from Galambos's collected works in *Sic Itur Ad Astra: The Theory of Volition* (2nd ed.), vol.1, Coronado, CA: The Universal Scientific Publication Company, Inc., 1999.
26 Richard L. Johnson, *Gandhi's Experiments With Truth: Essential Writings By And About Mahatma Gandhi*. Lanham, MD: Lexington Books, p. 118, 2005. Forward to volume of Gokhale's speeches, Gopal Krishna Gokahalenan Vyakhyanao.
27 Tony Ashworth, *Trench Warfare 1914-1918: The Live and Let Live System*, New York: Holmes & Meier Publishers, 1980.
28 Harry Browne, *Liberty A to Z: 872 Libertarian Soundbites You Can Use Right Now!* Catersville, GA: Advocates for Self-Government, 2004, p. 51.
29 Opinion for the Court in *West Virginia Board of Education v. Barnette* 319 U.S. 624.
30 Christopher Dickey at MSNBC.com and Newsweek, "Dickery: France's Militants of the Status Quo," April 6, 2006.
31 "Riots in France -- BECKER," Becker-Posner Blog, Nov. 13, 2005.
32 Ertugrul Kurkcu, "Defiance Under Fire Leyla Zana: Prisoner of Conscience," *Amnesty International USA*, Fall 2003.
33 Harry Browne, *Liberty A to Z*, Cartersville, GA: Advocates for Self Government, 2004, p. 91.
34 John Stossel, "The Value of Private Charity," Townhall.com, Aug. 24, 2005.
35 Alexis De Tocqueville, *Democracy in America*, Book III, Chap. IV "Consequences of The Three Proceeding Chapters," Cambridge: Sever and Francis, 1863, p.

213. First published in 1835 (first two volumes).

36 Pavel Chalupnicek and Lukas Dvorak, "Health Insurance Before the Welfare State: The Destruction of Self-Help by State Intervention," *Independent Review*, Jan. 1, 2009.

37 Michael Lewis, "Beware of Greeks Bearing Bonds," *Vanity Fair*, Oct. 1, 2010.

38 *The Essential Gandhi: An Anthology of His Writing on His Life, Works and Ideas*, Edited by Louis Fischer, Chapter 28: Independence and Sorrow, New York: Random House, Inc., 1962, p 314. Original source: Prayer speech in M.K. Gandhi, Delhi Diary, November 3, 1947, Chapter 53, p. 134.

39 Ibid., Chapter 23: "Gandhi on Socialism and Communism," pp 264-265. Original source: Interview with Nirmal Kumar Bose, 1934, in D.G. Tendulkar, *Mahatma: The Life of Mohandas Karamchand Gandhi*, Volume IV, p. 15.

40 KABC-TV News, "Local Activists Call for King-Harbor Firing, Prosecution," June 17, 2007.

41 Charles Ornstein, "How a Hospital Death Becomes a Cause Celebre," *Los Angeles Times*, June 15, 2007.

42 Ibid., Ornstein.

43 Charles Ornstein, "Report Details Risks To Patients' Lives," *Los Angeles Times*, June 19, 2007.

44 Charles Ornstein, Tracy Weber, and Steve Hymon, "The Troubles at King/Drew," five-part series, "Part 2: Underfunding is a myth, but the squandering is real," *Los Angeles Times*, December 6, 2004.

45 Sarah Lyall, "In a Dentist Shortage, British (Ouch) Do It Themselves," *New York Times*, May 7, 2006.

46 Kristin J. Bender, "The drowning suicide that shook an island," *Oakland Tribune*, posted in the *San Jose Mercury*, June 5, 2011.

47 Matthias Gafni, "Contrary to what Alameda fire chief said, rescue swimmers were funded," *Contra Costa Times*, posted June, 9, 2011.

48 Ibid.

49 Ibid.

50 Robert Mitchum, "Donating to Charity Is Good for the Brain, According to Study," *Chicago Tribune*, June 15, 2007. Source: *Science*, William T. Harbaugh, Ulrich Mayr and Daniel R. Burghart, "Neural Responses to Taxation and Voluntary Giving Reveal Motives for Charitable Donations," June 15, 2007, vol. 316. No 5831, pp. 1622-1625.

51 Paul J. Zak, Angela A. Stanton, Sheila Ahmadi, "Oxytocin Increases Generosity in Humans." Public Library of Science, 2(11): e1128. doi:10.1371/journal.pone.0001128, Nov. 2007, and Paul Zak (editor), *Moral Markets: The Critical Role of Values in the Economy*, Princeton University Press, 2008.

52 Orwell published *Homage to Catalonia* in 1938 to relate his experiences in the Spanish Civil War. He attempted to show the world the betrayal by power of those committed to Stalin's Communist regime and a totalitarian mindset. It sold few copies

after its first publication.

53 Keay Davidson, "How a Butterfly's Wing Can Bring Down Goliath: Chaos Theories Calculate the Vulnerability of Megasystems," *San Francisco Chronicle*, Aug. 15, 2003.

54 Lev Grossman and Hannah Beech, "Google under the Gun," *Time*, Feb. 13, 2006.

55 The Communist Movement in the Former Soviet Union. Three Interviews," May 1997. Interview with Deputy of the State Duma, Avalianin Timiriay Georgievitch, posted on the Marxist-Leninist Translation and Reprint website.

56 Charles Beard told historian Harry Elmer Barnes in 1947 that the foreign policy of Presidents Roosevelt and Truman was "perpetual war for perpetual peace."

57 R.J. Rummel, *Death by Government*, New Brunswick, NJ: Transaction Publishers, 1994.

58 R.J. Rummel, *The Blue Book of Freedom: Ending Famine, Poverty, Democide, and War*, Nashville, TN: Cumberland House Publishing, 2007.

59 Doug DeCarlo, *Extreme Project Management: Using Leadership, Principles, and Tools to Deliver Value in the Face of Volatility* (1st ed.) (San Francisco: Jossey-Bass, 2004, p. 20.

60 Ibid.

61 Christine A. Skarda and Walter J. Freeman, "Chaos and the New Science of the Brain," *Concepts in Neuroscience*, Vol. 1, No. 2 (1990), pp. 275–285.

62 "Chaos Theory Empowers VA and University of Florida Researchers to Predict Epileptic Seizures," *Science Daily*, December 9, 1999.

8 Decentralization and Simplicity

Everything should be made as simple as possible, but not simpler.
—Albert Einstein

Simplicity is the ultimate sophistication.
—Leonardo da Vinci

Chaos often breeds life, while order breeds habit.
—Henry Adams

Simplicity in a system tends to increase that system's efficiency. Because less can go wrong with fewer parts, less will. Complexity in a system tends to increase that system's inefficiency; the greater the number of variables, the greater the probability of those variables clashing, and in turn, the greater the potential for conflict and disarray. Because more can go wrong, more will. That is why centralized systems are inclined to break down quickly and become enmeshed in greater unintended consequences. As expressed succinctly by Ward Cunningham, the computer programmer who invented the concept of the wiki engine, which allows anyone to collaboratively create, edit and link web pages: "Simplicity is the shortest path to a solution."[1]

Like the laws of physics, complexity is based on relatively few rules. Chaologists view these deceptively simple rules as the force that spawns awe–inspiring complexity. With a burst of spontaneous pattern–making, simplicity metamorphoses into natural, synergistic complexity. But what would happen if a system started out being overbearingly complex? What if every detail were spelled out, every nuance determined, every aspect centrally controlled? The system would be unworkable. If an emerging system is born complex, there is neither leeway to abandon it when it fails, nor the means to join another, successful one. Such a system would be caught in an immovable grip, congested at the top, and prevented, by a set of confusing but locked–in precepts, from changing.

Overbearing and gummed-up complexity can occur only when political factors invade collaborative working systems. The invaders are purveyors of an expanding, centralized authority, dead set on criminalizing most human activities and behavior. These political actions disempower the diversity and choice required to keep an uneven socioeconomic system in balance. One principle that seems to explain this phenomenon is the scale invariance of power-law distribution, which reveals why outcomes are mostly disproportionate and rarely equal. One aspect of this principle argues that an ever-rising, top-heavy structure must eventually collapse under its own weight. Like a pyramid-shaped sandpile, if the top continues to spike, a cascading avalanche of failure becomes inevitable, usually ending poorly, in what some social chaologists refer to as "planned chaos."

But the underlying problem of centralization is that it attempts to force many dissimilar parts into a seamless whole. Of course, nothing is identical in the physical world. No two parts are equal. This means that centralization must force cohesion of mismatched parts—a herculean task that is impossible to satisfy. Of course, this basic fact does not stop political consolidators from attempting to acquire, assimilate, and monopolize unconnected parts and make them do things they never intended to do.

A good example of the devastating effect of centralization is grotesquely evident in war-ravaged Africa. When the European powers divvied up the African continent, they carved out arbitrary political units that made little sense. Colonial authorities threw together hundreds of dissimilar tribes across a vast cultural, religious, and political divide, creating artificial states within artificial boundaries. After independence, later in the twentieth century, Africans were left with European-style governments that neither tolerated diversity nor understood the principles of self-autonomy.

Europe had westernized and modernized the old political and social structures of Africa—just as they had done with Asia. They had destroyed traditional systems that had counterbalanced the autocracy of rulers. In precolonial days, society relied on religious institutions, street merchants, trade guilds, scribes, wealthy landowners, former high officials, and the military establishment to limit the power of sultans and kings. The new European-trained ruling class discarded these traditions and instead relied on the strong-arm tactics of unabridged statecraft.

With political power up for grabs, each tribe had to jockey for control of the state apparatus, or suffer the consequences. The winning tribe had the unadulterated power to reward, punish, or liquidate other tribes within its national borders. True to their over–managing nature, the centralizing mechanics of these emancipated African nations quickly led to violent tribal, ethnic, and religious rivalry.

One of the most brutal examples occurred in the Central African nation of Rwanda. Upon achieving independence from Belgium in 1962, Rwanda held elections in which Hutus took the reins of leadership. Over 200,000 Tutsis had already fled to neighboring countries, fearing what the Hutus might do with their power. One year later, a small army of Tutsi exiles returned to Rwanda. Although unsuccessful, the takeover attempt triggered a massacre of over 20,000 Tutsis.

Animosity erupted again in 1994, during the Rwandan Genocide. Over 100 days, an estimated 800,000 to 1,074,000 Tutsis and moderate Rwandans were slaughtered by machete–wielding Hutu militias composed mostly of trained civilians. This holocaust is considered one of the most concentrated acts of genocide in human history. But what was the real cause of this tragedy? Some argue that the out–of–control centralization of the state should be put at the top of the list.

According to Linda Melvern's *Conspiracy to Murder: The Rwanda Genocide and the International Community*, the killings were not spontaneous, but planned. In Rwanda's top–level cabinet meetings, ministers discussed brutal assaults on the Tutsi population months before the massive attacks. The Rwandan government even imported $750,000 worth of Chinese machetes to hand out to Hutu militias. In covert operations, the government organized, trained, and armed death squads to implement the "final solution."[2]

To fan the flames of hate, state–sponsored news sources implemented a campaign to brand the Tutsi minority as "subhuman" beings who ought to be exterminated. One cabinet minister said that she favored getting rid of all the Tutsis because doing so would solve all of Rwanda's problems. Local government officials and state–sponsored radio stations warned Hutus that they must kill their Tutsi neighbors or be killed themselves. One Hutu remarked, "Either you took part in the massacres or you were massacred yourself."[3]

Ironically, Hutu assassins discovered an easy way to identify Tutsi targets. In 1933, the Belgian colonial administration initiated a program to standardize and centralize information on all citizens, issuing national identity cards to designate whether each Rwandan was Hutu or Tutsi. This system was retained in postcolonial Rwanda and provided crucial assistance in identifying victims for the genocide.

Eventually, the Hutu government fell, and dozens of high government officials were put on trial for crimes against humanity. One convicted war criminal was the Rwandan prime minister, Jean Kambanda, who pled guilty to the charges of conspiracy and genocide at the United Nations International Criminal Tribunal for Rwanda. He was sentenced to life imprisonment.

The United Nations, the largest concentration of governmental authority in the world, had totally failed to protect the lives of innocent Rwandans. The head of the small U.N. peacekeeping force in Rwanda, Lieutenant General Romeo Dallaire, had warned U.N. officials, three months prior to the planned extermination campaign. The Security Council declined to intervene or even to speak out against the Rwandan government's actions. Dallaire pleaded for reinforcements, but was instead ordered to defend the U.N.'s image of impartiality. In fact, the U.N. peacekeeping forces were reduced once the mass slaughter had begun. According to some reports, U.N. forces were forbidden to protect trapped citizens encircled by Hutu militia in churches and stadiums.

After a Tutsi rebel army defeated the Hutu–dominated government, some two million Hutu refugees fled Rwanda in anticipation of reprisals. They escaped to Burundi, Tanzania, Uganda, and the Democratic Republic of the Congo, thousands dying from epidemic diseases. This destabilizing factor led to another series of wars: the First and Second Congo Wars.

The Swiss Confederation

The Swiss understand the importance of decentralization. It is vital to their survival. In some ways it can be argued that there are no Swiss people in Switzerland; they possess no Swiss language or single culture. Like much of the African continent, Switzerland is a hodgepodge of 26 cantons of diverse nationalities, cultures, and four languages—French, German, Italian and Romans. In the early years of the confederation, acrid discord existed among cantons. And considering the religious bigotry between Catholic and Protestant cantons, it is a wonder that the Swiss survived the European period of religious intolerance.

Nevertheless, the independent cantons held together because they needed one another. The Old Swiss Confederation came into existence in 1291, when three forest cantons signed the Federal Charter, to announce their sovereignty from the House of Habsburg, the royal family who had claimed the area for the Holy Roman Empire. The three cantons had crafted a defense pact against any attacker, but mostly against the Habsburg family's claim over the region.

Decentralization and Simplicity

In 1315, their resolve was put to the test, when 1500 well-armed knights invaded, only to be defeated by an army of peasants, in the Battle of Morgarten Pass. After that, other neighboring regions and city-states wanted in, eager to join the loosely connected alliance of freed serfs, for their mutual protection. And when in later years the Habsburgs' overlords would venture into the Swiss homeland, the cantons would unite, and they defeated the invaders on almost every occasion.

For centuries, the Swiss had far-reaching autonomy. Each canton pursued its own foreign policy, minted its own currency, and was largely independent within its own territory. But when internal squabbling and clashes erupted in the mid-1800s, the Swiss decided they needed greater unity to withstand the military adventurism of the surrounding hostile nations. They altered their free-for-all confederacy to produce a more structured federation, adopting in 1848 a written constitution that authorized the existence of a weak central government. Despite the changeover to a federation, the country's constitution was packed with many constraints that allowed the cantons to retain self-rule, with minimal interference from the federal government.

For instance, both the Swiss presidency and vice-presidency are elected by the Federal Assembly. These positions are largely ceremonial, and are limited to one-year terms. Little importance is placed on the central authority—so little that the Swiss delight in remarking that they can rarely recall the name of their own president. One reason is that an 1891 revision of the constitution introduced a policy of popular referendums at the federal level. Under the "right of initiative," citizens can request to amend the constitution or introduce new articles, by gathering a preset number of signatures. Despite the malleable nature of the Swiss plebiscite approach, they are considered to have the most stable government in Europe.

But the primary reason for their adopting a system of strong regional self-governance and a limited central government was survival. With so many different nationalities, the Swiss understood the dangers of allowing a powerful central government to take root. They had to find a way to check their central government, in case a particular nationality gained overwhelming control of Switzerland. The remedy was to neutralize the central authority by giving it as little power as possible and granting most of the decision-making capabilities to the local cantons.

The War Factor

But how vulnerable is a decentralized nation to outside threats? Wouldn't a small, minimalist government become an easy target for a highly centralized bully–state, with a well–oiled war machine and thousands of battle–hardened troops? Wouldn't Switzerland be a pushover?

The question is legitimate. Not only do the Swiss abide by a foreign policy of non–interventionism and "armed neutrality," but they have no standing army. In fact, the Swiss are an army. For centuries, they have developed a massive defense system by honeycombing their mountains with concealed artillery, forts, and bunkers. To stop invaders, they have built into bridges, tunnels, and railroad lines Primacord fuses for instant detonation, covering from 3,000 to 6,000 designated points of demolition. They have hidden cannons in little cottages and weapons under barns, and have prearranged rockslides at narrow points in roads. The Swiss boast that they are even prepared to fight their own government if it were to capitulate to a foreign enemy.

The Swiss call this strategy the "porcupine approach," a scenario in which millions of citizens in reserve units stiffen like spines to deter foreigner invaders. Considered as some of the best marksmen in the world, Switzerland's citizen–soldiers take home their army–issued assault rifles, pistols, and ammunition, which are commonly seen in public. They are always prepared for a possible invasion. That tradition came in handy when war clouds raced across Europe in the late 1930s.

During World War II, a large German army camped at Switzerland's doorstep and waited for Hitler's order to barge inside. Germany's High Command had drawn up detailed plans for the invasion, but Nazi war strategists became uneasy when they took a closer look at Switzerland's defense. Although the Swiss had only a part–time militia, the Nazi war strategists estimated that the Third Reich would suffer a catastrophic 200,000 or more casualties, should they attack. Unlike people in the rest of Europe, every able–bodied Swiss male was armed to the teeth and would fight to the death, even if trapped behind enemy lines. Fearing that each Alpine valley and passageway would become a Thermopylae, Hitler ordered his army to invade France instead, even though it had a larger standing army and greater number of artillery pieces, plus more and better tanks.[4] Furthermore, the British had stationed over 500,000 men in France by May of 1940.

One story about Swiss fortitude tells it all. When, prior to World War I, Kaiser Wilhelm II traveled to Switzerland to observe military exercises, he asked a Swiss militiaman: "You are 500,000 and you shoot well, but if we attack with 1,000,000 men what will you do?" The smiling soldier replied: "We will shoot twice and go home."[5]

Obviously, decentralization has some distinct advantages over larger military operations, something United States military forces learned the hard way, when dealing with vanishing and reappearing terrorist cells in the second Iraq War. Likewise, the Russian military was humbled by the evasive Mujahideen during their unsuccessful occupation of Afghanistan.

Similar historical examples are common. Why? Because when power is exercised from the bottom up, it is hard to stamp out a determined fighting force. There is no one person who could order an end to hostilities. According to Stephen P. Halbrook in *Target Switzerland*, "Switzerland was the only country in Europe that had no single political leader with the authority to surrender the people to the Nazis."[6] If Switzerland had been invaded, the fighting would have continued, even if the capital city had been captured. The Swiss were set up for a protracted guerrilla war.

Switzerland's backing of decentralization was uncommon to the European continent. According to Halbrook, "Other European nations were characterized by centralized governments often headed by elites with the power to surrender their sovereignty to Hitler, either with a short (even token) resistance or no fight at all. By contrast, Switzerland's sovereignty began with the individual, not the central authorities."[7]

Hitler's generals correctly surmised that if the French government surrendered, most resistance would stop immediately. And that is exactly what happened. The German invasion of France lasted a little over six weeks. After that, few Frenchmen were willing to fight the Nazis without their government's approval. Instead, the collectively minded and more government–trusting French citizens dutifully followed the dictates of the puppet government installed by their Nazi occupiers in the town of Vichy.

Even if a smattering of French citizens had wanted to resist the Nazis, they had no weapons. At the time, most European governments did not trust their own citizens with guns and made it nearly impossible for them to purchase small arms.

Yet Switzerland, a nation no larger than Maryland, with a prewar population of fewer than 4 million, was able to deter invasion by one of the most powerful totalitarian war machines that history had ever witnessed. With a population of 80 million citizens in 1939, Germany had over 4 million men under arms.

Interestingly, even the Roman Republic, for much of its early existence, had no standing army. From the overthrow of the monarchy in 509 B.C., to the Marian reforms in 107 B.C., the army was composed mainly of volunteers who were called up from Rome and surrounding colonies. These landowning farmers were recruited to fight in specific wars for which they had been activated, after which their units were disbanded and they were sent back to civilian life. Only Roman landowners could join the militias, ensuring that the Legions would fight to protect their own property and defend the nation.

War and Decentralization

Decentralized systems tend to produce better results, because they let individuals make independent choices on the level at which they are most relevant. Errors and mistakes can be quickly handled, on the spot. There is nothing better than firsthand knowledge to draw a brutal picture of reality.

On June 6, 1944, during the early hours of the Normandy Invasion, two strong German panzer divisions under Field Marshal Gerd Von Rundstedt waited at just inland of the Normandy coastline. They sat and watched the Allies invade Normandy with history's greatest naval armada. In short order, nearly 200,000 Allied soldiers landed on French beaches, accompanied by massive air attacks and naval bombardments. But Marshal Von Rundstedt had to twiddle his thumbs and sigh—Hitler had given explicit orders for the German forces to stay put, unless otherwise ordered.

Fortunately for the Allies, Hitler had taken over the day-to-day operations of the war, long before the Normandy Invasion. He believed he could "micromanage" the war from an underground bunker in Berlin's Chancellery. By the time he realized that Normandy was the Allies' intended invasion point, it was too late to act—the beachhead had already been secured.

As the war slowly turned against the Axis nations, Hitler had less and less contact with his generals and field commanders. He regularly issued commands without knowing much about battlefield conditions or the players. In fact, Hitler did not trust his generals, so he often put loyal Nazi party members into military positions for which they had no training. Infatuated with his own genius, Hitler produced battle plans that came with one common demand: do not deviate. According to James Lucas in *World War Two Through German Eyes*, "No unit could be moved without his knowledge or approval, a situation which led to Field Marshal von Rundstedt's bitter comment, 'I cannot even have the guard changed outside my room without referring the matter to the

Fuhrer.'"[8]

On the American side, General George Patton's spectacular victories are often attributed to his shoot–from–the–hip, stay–near–the–battlefront approach to warfare. He had inadvertently decentralized the battlefield by ignoring many orders given by rear–line generals, quipping, "No good decision was ever made in a swivel chair." He had a bird's–eye view of the combat zone, and was quick to take advantage of German weaknesses as they presented themselves. He understood that the rear–line centralized pecking order had no special powers of observation, and he hated to retake the same real estate twice.

Although viewed by the U.S. military establishment as a loose cannon, Patton was able to puncture the enemy line and break the German stranglehold in the weeks after the Normandy invasion. With his U.S. Third Army, he confounded the German High Command with daring initiative, lightning–fast maneuvers, and a relatively free hand that was unknown to an enemy taught to obey orders, at any cost. In one campaign in France, Patton captured 600 miles in two weeks. To him, flexibility and pliability were his greatest assets.

A concentration of power can inflict damage on any government's war effort, including that of the United States. In his memoir, *At the Center of the Storm*, George Tenet, the CIA director for seven years (1997–2004), contended that the Bush administration had two options for running Iraq during the American occupation. The first one, favored by the CIA and NSA, pressed for a "more inclusive and transparent approach, in which Iraqis representing the many tribes, sects, and interest groups in the country would be brought together to consult and put together some sort of rough constituent assembly that might then select an advisory council and a group of ministers to govern the country." In sharp contrast, the other option, represented by Vice President Dick Cheney and Pentagon civilians, sought a more controlled environment. Tenet wrote: "Rather than risking an open–ended political process that Americans could influence but not control, they wanted to be able to limit the Iraqis' power and handpick those Iraqis who would participate."

According to Tenet, Cheney had sized up the dilemma succinctly. "The choice he said was between 'control and legitimacy.'" The Bush administration believed they could make Iraqi exiles appear legitimate in the eyes of the people, through "economic assistance" and "good governance." Of course, America's power–hoarding occupation of Iraq instead turned out to unleash pent–up ethnic furies, intercommunal violence, and an increased flow of terrorist activities.[9]

Single Point of Failure

The citadel of centralization is far more fragile than most are willing to admit. That weakness was first explored by early evolutionary biologists concerned with the origin and descent of species. Because these researchers considered genetic diversity to be the key to survival in biological systems, they increasingly saw the mechanics of centralization as harmful to evolutionary development. The main drawback was that uniformity quashes the climate of competitive alternatives, by excluding all others. In the field of biology, the less genetic diversity in a species, the greater the risk of its extinction if the environment changes.

The shortcomings of centralization were largely ignored until the advent of the computer age. Computing power gave scientists the capability to quantify the fatal flaws underlying the tenets of centralization. The phrase that computer technicians coined to describe these inherent defects is "single point of failure."

The "single point of failure" principle refers to a system such that, if that one component were to fail, the entire system would grind to a halt. It is a sort of performance bottleneck occurring at any point in a hardware or software component. In socioeconomics, it means that one single error by a government agency could invoke a devastating outcome to society and its citizens. One error could crash a centralized system, leading to total systemic failure. But under a decentralized system, operating on open–ended mechanics similar to the Internet, the same error would not crash the entire system. The flux of traffic would find alternatives routes, and by-pass the error or blockage.

The remedy generally cited is to perform "reliability engineering," which is to add extra safety or redundant backups. But even the addition of multiple safeguards is questionable, since many layers of redundancy could clog up a system faster than a single component's failure.

To the frustration of computer engineers, extra redundancy can make a system vulnerable to what has been coined "Byzantine failure." Mimicking the effects of overarching and unreliable bureaucracies, such "crash failures" occur because components are unable to behave consistently when interacting with multiple other components. Instead of making a system more reliable, extra layers of redundancy can make a system unnecessarily complex, and therefore lead to greater insufficiency. This is why most political systems and their policies fail, especially when they refuse to incorporate power–sharing at the local level.

Decentralization and Simplicity

During World War II, Byzantine complexity dogged Germany's war production from the start. Production was not increasing fast enough to offset the higher levels being achieved by the Allies. In 1942, Hitler appointed his chief architect, Albert Speer, as the Minister of Armaments and War Production. By the time of Speer's appointment, Allied aircraft were just starting to invade German airspace, with bombing raids over vital war factories and railroad lines. But increased Allied bombing missions were not Speer's only impediment. Nazi party politics and reliance on a dense bureaucracy hindered his ability to do his job. Nonetheless, he succeeded in expanding war production by a factor of four, reaching its peak during the height of the Allied bombing campaign in 1944.

How was this possible? Allied bombing had destroyed much of Germany's crucial roads, railway lines, and manufacturing plants. The destruction of one facility—a ball bearing factory, for instance—could set off a single–point–of–failure domino effect across the entire war production line. According to Dan van der Vat in *The Good Nazi*, "The key to the Speer system for arms production was improvisation, for which flexibility, initiative and minimal bureaucracy were required—along with freedom of action, which was asking a lot, not to say the ultimate, in a totalitarian state."[10] In fact, from 1941 to 1944, Speer was able to increase production of medium– and heavyweight battle–tanks six–fold (from 2,875 to 17,328).

Ironically, as Speer was lifting controls and increasing combat aircraft production, England had adopted more of a "command economy" approach for its war production, and by 1944 was being outproduced by Germany. In 1941, England had produced 20,100 combat aircraft to Germany's 11,030, but by 1944, that had changed to 26,500 for Britain and 37,950 for Germany (the United States produced 110,752 that year). The point is obvious. Decentralization and decision–making flexibility had allowed Germany to produce more wartime goods during difficult times, compared to unbombed Germany under the "over-organized," state–centric structure.

The early computer and information industry faced similar challenges, from systems built on top–down hierarchies of one–track circuit switching and large mainframe computers. As the complexity increased, so did the number of system–crashing failures, which were often tracked to small errors. Technicians and scientists attempted to improve reliability, to prevent single points of failure. Along the way, they inadvertently came across the principles of decentralization and devolution.

In the 1960s, scientists working for the U.S. Defense Department searched for ways to ensure the survival of communication networks after a nuclear attack. That quest led computer engineers directly to the demassification of information. By decentralizing the decision–making process, the informational highway could run without one pothole impeding traffic, or shutting down an entire system. This meant that communication networks could survive a nuclear attack even on multiple American cities and military bases. Half of the United States could be blasted to the moon, but communications would still be up and operating. With this goal in mind, researchers pushed information technology toward multiplexing, accessibility, and openness—everything needed to create a network of networks: the Internet.

The early Internet, or the Advanced Research Projects Agency Network (ARPANET), was established along decentralized lines in order to fulfill the requirement of fail–safe resiliency. But such new capabilities came with a price. Under the laws of complexity, it was discovered that nobody could actually control the entire system as a cohesive unit. Although decentralization was deemed necessary, it meant that those on the top tier of the political bleachers had to give up most of their control to bottom–level users. This is a serious drawback for those firmly lodged in the traditional camp of concentrated power. To delegate power is to relinquish control, something that most political controlaholics are loathe to do.

Fortunately, most innovators of new technology are naïve about political affairs and endgames. When scientists were instructed to create an indestructible data and voice communication system, they arrived at a technology that would do the trick. They were not concerned about the political ramifications, or about preserving "second–strike" capability for the U.S. military during the Cold War years. They were interested only in solving a scientific problem. And in their process of discovery, they stumbled upon a revolutionary protocol process that would optimize the use of channel capacity in networks: "packet switching." This process provides subunits with greater autonomy and closer participation at the local level, allowing each element to make its own decision.

The founder and former editor of *Wired* magazine, Louis Rossetto, often referred to as the popularizer of cyberspace, warned that the Internet is extremely difficult to control or censor. He wrote: "Instead of opening a single line between two points to send a message, the Internet breaks the message into small parts—packets—and sends them out individually to find their way over what could be many different lines to their final destination, where they are recombined. Take out a node—or multiple nodes—along the way, and the message still gets through. The same with censorship."[11]

Often disdainful of political authority, Rossetto has argued that governments are clueless concerning the decentralization of information that resulted from the digital revolution. Speaking at the 1996 World Economic Forum (WEF) in Davos, Switzerland, Rossetto cited the antics of a French legislator who had had his feathers ruffled during a session whose speaker pondered whether the nation-state was as becoming obsolete due to new technology. The French legislator stood up, and proudly proclaimed that he knew nothing of the Internet, and didn't need to, because that was the very nature of democracy— nonexpert representatives making laws. In later musings over the politician's outburst, Rossetto observed: "What legislators don't realize is that they are like illiterates trying to tell the literate what to read."

Despite anachronistic flak from political leaders, decentralization spawned the digital and cyberspace revolution. Alvin Toffler, the American futurist and author of *The Third Wave*, saw this digital revolution as integral to a post–industrial society. He came to believe that this self-autonomous paradigm shift would not only empower the individual, but bring about the eventual obsolescence of the nation-state itself. To Toffler, the rising Information Age would come at the expense of state–centric bureaucracies and hierarchies.

Transcending class, age, nationalities, and other demographic characteristics, the technology of the Internet has the potential to enable people to peacefully overthrow the current social establishment and stifling status quo, as Timothy Leary suggested in the late 1970s. Who would have thought that a military effort to prevent failures in systems would free up future systems?

The Soviet Colossus

When a system is small and simple, with few people dependent on its performance, fiascos are merely inconvenient, the butt of humorous anecdotes. But when a system is large and intricate, constipated with a sticky diet of heavy regimentation, failures no longer incite howls of laughter.

The legacy of the Soviet colossus is replete with nightmarish ordeals that only a killjoy could appreciate. With its total dependency on statism, the Soviet system dehumanized individuals as if they were interchangeable parts of a machine, insignificant and ephemeral. Stalin's "revolution from above" crafted a totalitarian archetype so finely carved that it marred every fragment of society. The old Soviet Union's centralization of functions is felt even today, in the elusiveness of the simple pleasure of a hot shower. During summer months, Moscow residents are left with few options other than to take cold showers and let the dinner dishes pile up in the sink. It all started back in the late 1940s, with a city–wide system of central heating for hot water and steam–heating radiators. Forget about controlling and maintaining your own private heating unit. Instead, Russian authorities constructed a labyrinthine network of large boilers, connected by 5,600 miles of underground pipes.

Naturally, quality was sacrificed for quantity, which is why both housing and heating systems in Moscow are decaying rapidly. In an attempt to repair decrepit pipes, rolling cutoffs of hot water have become an annual summer ritual.[12] A few residents have tried to buck the system and install shoe carton-sized water heaters to provide some relief.

But even though motivated residents will wake up an hour early to boil water for their shower, the central heating system has other shortcomings that have Muscovites shivering with goose bumps every season. Without individual heating units, the central system can't entertain individual requests, exemptions, or alterations. Believing that they are getting the cold shoulder, Muscovites have increasingly groused that the city government is acting like a selfish landlord, carefully watching the energy meter and clenching the thermostat with a skinflint hand. The problem is obvious. Whether the outside weather is cold or warm, the state has strict timetables for switching the heat on. The situation is worse in other Moscow suburbs, like Pushkino, where hot water is often turned off in the middle of Siberia–like winters.

In a nation that had once withheld local street maps and phone books from public view, the Soviet Union was plagued by phony prices, statistics, and data. The lack of accurate information endangered its economy and caused resources to be misallocated. Russian factories routinely under-produced consumer goods in demand, while overproducing bombers and tanks. With technocrats running the system, output had only to satisfy the top–level statisticians measuring it. In an attempt to save socialism, Mikhail Gorbachev opened the information–monopoly spigot, by an amount meant to be just enough to allow "managed freedom" to spill out, in a plan to catch up with American information technology. Instead he opened the floodgates.

A correspondent in Moscow for the *Baltimore Sun*, Scott Shane experienced firsthand the disintegration of the Soviet Union. In his 1994 book, *Dismantling Utopia: How Information Ended the Soviet Union*, Shane contends that "information slew the totalitarian giant." Taking a chaologist's approach, he explains in the chapter called "What Price Socialism?" that planning a successful economy from the top down, is "as hopeless as if a human being tried consciously to control all the muscles directing his breathing, blood circulation, and digestion, deciding just when to contract his right ventricle and how much insulin should be released by his pancreas."[13]

The Soviet Union's centralization illustrates the self–destructive behavior caused by the lack of open information, competition, and choice. When centralization is in the driver's seat, nobody can change course. Citizens become unwilling passengers in politically-rigged vehicles that refrain from yielding any meaningful control. When systems are left to the mercy of political expediency, integrity is tossed aside.

Some of that expediency was plainly visible in Leningrad's state fishing industry. Local fisherman would routinely steal fish from state–operated fishing vessels and ride through town on bicycles to sell their ill–gotten catch. Everyone knew about the practice, yet it continued despite the threat of serious jail time for violators. Why? Because most Russian consumers hated waiting in hour–long lines at the state fish stores, for a few rationed fish of questionable quality. They were willing to pay higher prices for faster service, better quality, and convenience. But it was difficult for the rogue fish peddlers. They constantly had to change their routes and schedules, to avoid detection by the authorities. At random intervals, a peddler would stop and pretend his bicycle had broken down. As he feigned the repair of his bike, potential customers would ask if he had anything to sell. Of course, they knew he did.

All Russian industries suffered similar maladies, including the mining industry in the Ukraine. Kevin Klose, president of National Public Radio and former president of Radio Free Europe/Radio Liberty, detailed the corruption and goldbricking in the coal mining community of Donetsk, in *Russia and the Russians: Inside the Closed Society*. There, the miners suspected that the mining directorate, the local Communist party chief, and the police were conspiring to get rich by "illegally speculating with the extra coal they had cheated from the state and workers."[14] Eventually, it was discovered that the local authorities were siphoning off money, by underestimating the production of coal to the Communist Central Committee in Moscow. They secretly sold the surplus coal at inflated prices to other mine directorates.

In another accounting trick, "weed–covered mountains of coal in remote parts of the city were said to be moved around on paper like the pea in a shell game." At other times, when directorates feared falling short of projections, they would overstate their need for equipment, workers, and raw materials, distorting economic information even more, for central planners in Moscow.

Few miners were willing to demand an investigation, since the police appeared to be part of the illicit scheme.

Even if the Central Committee of the Communist Party of the Soviet Union and the USSR Council of Ministers had truly wanted to gain a clear overview of the economy, they had no way of drawing an accurate picture. Most directorates hid their true production figures—because they received rewards for meeting or exceeding five–year plan targets. Distortions were permanently built into the economic structure. "Planned shortcomings" was the mantra of the day.

Spontaneous Decentralization

Decentralism is not normative. It does not say how things will organize, only that they will. The defining nexus of decentralization is that things will spontaneously arrange themselves in unimaginable ways. For instance, the government of Niger struggled to stop the dust–choked desert from claiming more farmland. For decades, African politicians, anti–deforestation groups, and large–scale plantings were unable to stop the problem. Most experts were resigned to the fact that the deforestation was an unsolvable problem and nothing more could be done. Then in 2007, independent researchers issued a shocking report. Through satellite imagery and on–the–ground inventories, the researchers had discovered that somehow, Niger had increased tree coverage by "at least 7.4 million acres."

Political leaders and environmentalists were astounded. How could this have occurred without their knowledge? Niger was considered a sun–baked land in the throes of hunger and poverty. The report stated that Niger had "added millions of new trees and is now far greener than it was 30 years ago." When the government officials searched for answers, they found that it was attributable in large part to "poor farmers whose simple methods cost little or nothing at all."[15]

So what happened? Niger's population was exploding, which should have compounded the problem and led to greater loss of trees and increased deforestation. But researchers revealed that vegetation is often the densest within areas of population concentrations. What occurred is that individual farmers realized that by having foolishly cut down trees, their farms had become vulnerable to strong deserts winds, which carried away productive topsoil, allowing sand dunes to swallow their fields and villages in a desertification process. Farmers took radical measures. When they plowed and planted their fields, they would stop clearing young saplings. They decided to grow their crops around the trees, something that went against traditional farming principles.

But the farmers' success story is far more complicated. Historically, the major reason cited for the destruction of trees in Niger was the law. From colonial times, Nigerians had undervalued trees because by law they were public property. According to the *New York Times,* all trees in Niger "had been regarded as the property of the state, which gave farmers little incentives to protect them."

With no right to own trees, farmers and citizens alike would hastily chop them down for firewood and housing, giving little thought to the wholesale environmental damage (a dilemmatic outcome known as "the tragedy of the commons"). Once the farmers recognized the environmental problem, they began pressuring the government to allow them to own the trees in their own fields. The authorities resisted, but gradually government officials listened and changed the law. As a result, the farmers started to quietly plant new trees, and they prevented outsiders from tearing them down. Before anyone knew it, the grassroots effect had brought the community together and served the common good.

Although the government had foresters and detailed policies to stop deforestation, they had been unable to prevent the poor from poaching state-owned vegetation. Not until farmers and citizens began to treat the government–owned trees as their own property did the situation turn around. Not only were Niger's antiquated laws destroying the environment, but they were sabotaging the economic interests of the farmers.

Decentralized Decision Making

Decentralized decision making is not about mobocracy, demagoguery, or group actions manipulated by political provocateurs with hidden agendas. Rather, this decision–making process is structured, driven by consensus and sharing of knowledge, and activated by spontaneous order. It is not "the manufacture of consent," journalist Walter Lippmann's catchphrase that warns about the manipulation of a naïve public by partisan powerbrokers. Another journalist, H. L. Mencken, gleaned similar insights about the nature of mob–inspired demagogues, and described a demagogue as "one who will preach doctrines he knows to be untrue to men he knows to be idiots."

Inadvertently, Mencken was describing a phenomenon known as "informational cascading." Behavioral economists have long recognized that groups are prone to making bad choices, even when the majority of their individuals know better. Under the theory of informational cascading, groups of people can easily be swayed into arriving at mistaken conclusions, after having heard the first person expound wrong or biased information. Because most people are unsure of what they know, they assume that the first few confident–sounding persons to utter opinions are better informed than they are.

Similar to herds of animals, with their instinct for clustering, people often ignore their own standpoint. Instead, they trust the conclusions of others and conform to the prevailing wisdom of self-proclaimed experts. When someone with an underlying agenda speaks first and spews biased conjecture, priming the information pump with misleading claims, the crowd has a tendency to follow along, uncritically. Political systems and their manipulative surrogates routinely use this modus operandi to sway crowds, while dominating the spotlight, marginalizing the opposition, and monopolizing society with one–sided data. However, if people make their decisions and judgments in silence, without any outside, dominating influence, there is a great chance that the consensus will be correct. As *New Yorker* columnist, James Surowiecki wrote in *The Wisdom of Crowds*, "Groups do not need to be dominated by exceptionally intelligent people in order to be smart."[16]

But informational cascading is not the only way to manipulate society. In some cases, truthful information and skepticism can be blocked or delayed by culturally induced means. By using the techniques of "agnotology," the study of ignorance, a deliberate production of biased information can be used to silence potential adversaries, through the release of volumes of authoritative–sounding information. For instance, one way to "construct ignorance" is to have purveyors of disinformation produce reams of state–approved data that confuse or disillusion the citizenry, thereby neutralizing the opposition before it can organize.

Conversely, decentralized decision making is a natural procedure for distributing power throughout a larger but generally anonymous group, minus the influence of political hucksters and propaganda campaigns. A cascading mobocracy predisposed to controlling society would never consider the devolution of power or localized decision making. As with open–source software, decisions normally reserved for top–level designers can instead be engaged by end–level users. In this way, people actually run society, not the government.

Daniel Klein, a professor of economics at George Mason University, touched upon the tenets of decentralized decision making using skating as a metaphor. Terming the phenomenon "rinkonomics," he observed that when people skate around in a roller or ice rink, they do so without guidance or direction yet rarely bump into each other. Klein argues that nobody directs the overall order or traffic in rinks; there are no signs, no traffic cops. Nonetheless, the flow spontaneously becomes orderly. He points to "the coincidence of interest" as the main reason for this. When people look out for themselves, trying to avoid an injurious crash with another, everybody's interests are unintentionally promoted.[17]

When John Stossel, in a segment for the ABC–TV news show 20/20, attempted to test Klein's theory, he moved to the center of an ice rink and began shouting orders with a bullhorn (go right here, go left there), expecting greater coordination. Instead, the skaters collided more often. Somewhat perplexed, Stossel brought in a skating expert, convinced he needed smarter leadership to govern the rink and synchronize all skaters. But with bullhorn and vast experience in hand, Olympic gold medalist Brian Boitano did no better. Skaters appeared distracted, paying more attention to the amplified overseer and less to what was happening all around them.[18]

Klein concluded that life is governed by a spontaneous order that requires no choreographer. People plan, but it is a "decentral planning." Individual skaters in the ice rink know more about their condition than does the smartest central planner. This fact alone puts people in the driver's seat, giving them direct, moment–by–moment control that nobody else could satisfy. In reality, only these individual skaters can make on–the–spot, intelligent, and generally successful decisions.

The biggest advantage of decentralized decision making is the way groups work together to solve problems. Deliberating, groups can often outsmart the smartest individuals. With their "collective intelligence" or "group intelligence," groups have clearly demonstrated that they can make better decisions than one person—no matter how brilliant, important, or erudite a political leader or congressional staffer may be.

So what is the secret? It appears that within large groups, each individual is able to bring his or her own specific bits of knowledge to the table. Simply, such a process allows a host of minds to work simultaneously on the same problem. Similar to swarm intelligence, shared knowledge creates a cross–fertilization of information that would be impossible if placed under flat hierarchies manned by a few omniscient planners or so-called experts. In the television game show *Who Wants to Be a Millionaire?*, stumped contestants are permitted to ask the audience for assistance. When polled for the answer, the audience will give the correct answer 91 percent of the time, compared with the "experts," who achieve a rate of only 65 percent correct.[19]

But group intelligence comes with serious handicaps. The group often gets the wrong answer when acting en masse, if critical parameters are not applied. James Surowiecki warns, in *The Wisdom of Crowds*, that group intelligence requires independence of thought, diversity, and decentralization. If any of these ingredients is absent, a herd mentality takes over, causing the masses to be swayed toward collective hysteria, peer pressure, and conformity. These circumstances can easily trump superior judgment and cause a panic-inspired stampede—the perfect ambiance for political systems. Although the many may be smarter than the few, the many can still be misled by a deceitful few.

In the animal kingdom, there are numerous examples of species that will display decentralized decision making, spontaneously. When Larissa Conradt and Tim Roper, biologists at the University of Sussex, studied decision making in herd animals, they broke new ground. The assumption was that grazing herds, like most animals, obey the dictates of the alpha male or alpha female. Conradt and Roper wanted to see whether this was accurate. With high–speed cameras, they watched the red deer of England for any indication of why the herd would, for instance, visit a water hole. At first, the animals glanced in all directions, but once over 51 percent of the herd oriented themselves toward the waterhole, they all darted over for a drink. The alpha animal often tagged along in the rear, clearly not having been the one imposing the decision.

As for times of danger, when, for example, the herd suspected a predator lurking in the shrubs, the deer required a two–thirds' supermajority pointing at the waterhole, before any animal would move.[20]

Many experts now believe that most animals, from ants to zebras, participate in some form of cooperative decision making, also known as "quorum sensing." In fact, Bonnie L. Bassler, professor of molecular biology at Princeton University, discovered that even bacteria can communicate with each other. Many species of bacteria use decentralized decision–making sensing to coordinate group behavior.[21] Nonetheless, some animal species do rely on strong organizational hierarchies and pecking orders, during feeding and mating. But the shared–consensus behavior of the red deer mimics the self–governing autonomy and power sharing found in many open societies.

In a political context, Conradt's and Roper's surprising findings could be interpreted as a stochastic process in which a leader's duty is unrelated to his being the supreme decision maker. Under Jeffersonian democracy, it was believed that power should always remain in the hands of the people—decen-

Decentralization and Simplicity

tralized, equally dispersed, eschewing any upper–level encroachment. Civil servants were seen as barriers to the ambitions of the ruling stratum. Unfortunately, as it turned out, civil servants failed to assume the role of an alert watchdog dedicated to guarding society from the intrusion of power-seekers. The supposed public watchdogs of the people became the lap dog of the political elite.

Few governments have ever decentralized their political or economic structures from the inside, or stood up to discouraged demagogic intruders. In reality, any civil servant willing to take the role of public watchdog is more likely to be put to sleep.

The Decentralization of City–States

It was Benjamin Franklin who observed that large states tend to become tyrannical, while small ones are more prone to corruption. Smallness has drawbacks for budding overseers with expansionist dreams. When a nation's geographic boundaries are small and limited, so are the powers available within it. After all, small ponds yield small waves. And when ripples spread out from disturbances in the pond's center, backwashing has little lasting effect on others. Decentralization has same calming effect on society.

Operating under a "less is more" dictum, dispersed authority has been credited with initiating some of the greatest and most creative eras in human history, most noticeably during periods of autonomous city–states. One of the earliest examples is the Golden Age of Greece. More than 150 thriving city–states (polis) maintained their relative independence for centuries. Most historians attributed this feat to the de facto decentralization that resulted from the rugged Greek geography. Eighty percent of the Greek landscape is mountainous, separating municipalities by almost impassable terrain and narrow valleys. This steep, harsh topography led to geopolitical stalemates, by preventing regional consolidation by neighboring city–states and foreign invaders alike, thus thwarting creation of a large–scale nation–state — at least

until the reign of Philip II of Macedon, the father of Alexander the Great.

The independence of the ancient Greek city–states was unique during the Golden Age. Most populated and civilized lands had been gobbled up by large–scale systems overseen by distant kings. But what made Greek society remarkable was citizens' attitude toward systems of governance. If they were to become alarmed over the sordid exploits of governmental leaders, they would either replace them with new leaders or institute an entirely different ruling system. Some city–states even devolved their ruling authority to the lowest level possible: governance by the common citizenry.

The ancient Greek city–states became breeding grounds for experimentation in self–governance. Every imaginable form of government was put to the test: large assemblies, oligarchies, plutocracies, kings, and tyrants. But one particular Greek city–state pushed decentralization and political pluralism beyond historical norms. That city was Athens.

Widely accepted as the cradle of Western civilization and the birthplace of democracy, Athens had been ruled by a series of kings and tyrants, until the nobleman Cleisthenes radically reformed this city–state. After becoming an archon, a high–level magistrate, he opened the political floodgates to give all Athenian citizens a voice in politics.

Cleisthenes split Athens' main four tribes into ten, and separated them again, into even smaller *demes* (municipalities). This popular policy was put in place to prevent the aristocratic families from reorganizing into powerful political factions. The results were stunning. In no time, the city exploded into a world–class economy and was recognized as a hotbed of influential philosophers.

A similar efflorescence occurred during the Italian Renaissance. Developing first among northern Italian city–states in the fourteenth century, this rebirth of ancient Greek and Roman knowledge gradually spread throughout Europe. These enclaves of "merchant republics," especially Florence, and later Venice, are often cited as the origin of the Renaissance. Regarded as intellectual crossroads, these city–states were bastions of quasi-open market economies that had developed profitable trade routes in the Far East. Poised between partial democracy and plutocracy, they were ruled by wealthy families who had to jockey for political, social, and economic influence. Nonetheless, the citizenry experienced tremendous political, academic, and artistic freedom, compared with people in the rest of the world.

But the Renaissance did not develop in a vacuum. Its long roots took hold during the Holy Roman Empire, which produced more than 75 free cities that acted like sovereign nations. For instance, the imperial free city of Strasbourg, located in what is now France, gained its independence after the Battle of Oberhausbergen in 1262, when citizens were victorious against the city's bishop. After its people kicked out the ecclesiastical overseers, Strasbourg's fame and fortunes grew. Centuries later in 1605, the city became the first community in human history to establish a weekly newspaper. Strasbourg had turned into the center for humanist scholarship. No doubt also influenced by the earlier work of one–time resident Johannes Gutenberg, who had spearheaded the use of movable–type printing, the city also became Europe's center for book printing.

The Dutch experienced similar expansion of wealth and art during its golden period, in the seventeenth century. Many Dutch cities, especially Amsterdam, acted like independent city–states, establishing their own militias and navies while pursuing their own foreign and commercial politics, without regard to the other provinces.

The European free cities and peasant–farmer republics managed to secure self–governance or a charter, by gift, battle, neglect, or money. In a number of cases, city leaders would circumvent politics by simply purchasing their independence from cash–poor princes. But the overwhelming effect of greater citizen participation was to saddle with constraints ambitious leaders who attempted to emulate Caesar's insatiable lust for power.

Without a large power base or large geographical area, unpopular political leaders are vulnerable to an angry citizenry. Decentralized systems deprive political megalomaniacs of their main source of power: armed enforcers of their imprudent and detrimental policies. Without an extensive military at their beck and call, overseers are likely to be more responsive to their citizens' wishes. Local military units are reluctant to fire on agitated citizens, since many of them might be relatives and friends of the soldiers. As we saw with the Tiananmen Square incident, the Red Chinese government eventually had to truck in troops from outside provinces to get the People's Liberation Army to assault student dissenters.

But how did such disparity of power surface in Europe? After the tremendous implosion of the Roman Empire and its iron–handed regimentation, most of Europe plunged into the early medieval period. People tended to be more concerned with religion and the afterlife than with urbanization, education, and commerce. Although not considered "dark" by current historians, this period witnessed a gradual breakdown in infrastructure, trade links, and social cohesion. So when Carolus Magnus, better known as Charlemagne, came to the Frankish throne in 768, he had no working model of government. Instead, he had to improvise.

Charlemagne appointed regional governors, called "counts," to rule separate localities, granting them enormous independence and authority. Almost all the centralized functions of the state, such as raising revenue and maintaining a military, fell exclusively to the administration of the diverse counts. Eventually, the revenue and military functions were divided further: among the nobility, the count was responsible for revenue and finances, while the "duke" took responsibility for the maintenance of a military.

The obvious problem was how to monitor the counts and dukes. While it made sense to decentralize authority over a vast area, there was no means to ensure those local authorities' loyalty so far away from the physical presence of the monarch. To bring some semblance of structured authority to this system, Charlemagne instituted the office of the *missi dominici* ("envoys of the ruler," from the Latin root *missus*, meaning "to send"). The *missi* would travel around the kingdom and check up on the counts, dukes, and other local officials.

The Carolingian power–sharing model of government was innovative, establishing a balanced partnership between national and local entities. Some have referred to Charlemagne's model as an early version of the federalism that was later developed in United States.

They Who Would Decide

While lecturing in Eastern Europe in the 1980s, John Hospers, (1918-2011) professor emeritus of philosophy at the University of Southern California, touched on the inefficiencies of state–owned businesses. After one lecture, an aggravated listener told the professor that he disliked walking about barefooted. Hospers was baffled by this remark, as he had not broached the subject of footwear. The agitated man finally explained that only the government produced shoes in his nation, and that if that situation changed, every citizen would go shoeless. This man could not imagine that any other entity could design, manufacture, and distribute shoes.

Whenever the advantages of decentralization are mentioned, skeptics sound the warning bells, leery over how agents of government could implement policy without neither certainty nor far–reaching power.

Practitioners of monolithic-based economics always demand precise details of how society will operate in the future. Who will be assigned to watch over food production? Who will make sure that the nation has plenty of energy? Who will keep the economy humming smoothly? Actually, in many ways, the answer approaches that of a riddle: nobody and everybody. As with chaos itself, decentralization and open–ended systems permit anything and anybody to participate. That's the beauty of a flexible system over a single–point–of–failure system. Until a new idea is put out for public inspection, there is no certainty. The great French Enlightenment writer Voltaire recognized this fact, writing: "Doubt is not a pleasant condition, but certainty is absurd."

Certainty is absurd because order is revealed only when recognizable patterns arise. Yet, any attempt to codify newly discovered patterns is fraught with pitfalls. Iterative processes are the mother of order, but they also contain the seeds of periodic and nonperiodic subpatterns, hidden connections, and the intermixing of scalable parts, which can easily dissolve into an unrecognizable soup. Spending billions of dollars on socioeconomic policies based on attempts at correctly predicting future patterns is like trying to capture a moonbeam in your hand.

Ilya Prigogine, in his remarkable 1997 book, *The End of Certainty*, explained, that certainty and determinism always lose out to the "perpetual construction" found in a universe drenched in irreversibility and instability. Not only is life uncertain; it's akin to thrusting an introvert on stage without a script.[22]

Before the American Civil War, Southerners complained bitterly to the abolitionists, worrying about the problem of how to acquire cheap, dependable labor, if slavery were to be abolished. Their battle cry intensified with a shrill challenge: "Who's going to pick the cotton?" That was a legitimate question. Most abolitionists admitted that they could not point to any explicit person or group who would willingly harvest cotton under a hot sun. This was a vital question for Southerners. They feared that, if freed, black workers would abandon the plantations. Nobody knew what to expect if unpaid labor were no longer available. Many Southerners envisioned an economic meltdown. Some economists had a brighter outlook. They understood that economies are always reconfiguring themselves to navigate in uncharted waters. Some even granted the possibility that life is always in flux, and that few people know beforehand what is going to happen at any given time. So the question of who's going to pick the cotton is mostly irrelevant. Somebody will become involved, if a product is deemed desirable. If people want to purchase cotton, farmers and workers will not be far behind in creating some type of working structure to satisfy those demands.

Typically, central authorities try to outguess and over-control human activities, especially the unfamiliar ones. This is not a difficult assignment, since many human endeavors appear patternless and untested, providing political opportunists with a spate of easy targets on which to impose. This type of meddling is universal and ageless. In 1820, the Swiss–born author and politician Benjamin Constant remarked, "Every time the government attempts to handle our affairs, it costs more and the results are worse than if we had handled them ourselves."[23]

Central systems assume that with the right information and sufficient force, society can be pushed in the "right" direction. But natural systems operate more by vague consensus—by simple rule of thumb. Many argue that human society, if left to itself, is no different.

Peter Miller, in *National Geographic*, took on the mysteries of swarm dynamics, writing that ant colonies do amazing things, despite the fact that is no one in charge. "No generals command ant warriors. No managers boss ant workers.... Even with half a million ants, a colony functions just fine with no management at all—at least none that we would recognize."[24] So how do large insect societies operate so efficiently, especially when no single ant is very smart? Researchers often point to the role of self-organization as the main factor in which the collective behavior of ants imparts a collective intelligence. Experts argue that no one decision causes the ants to take a particular action. Rather, it is a "pattern of decisions" that motivates individual ants. Although the ant colony adheres to simple rules, the result often is complex and sophisticated behavior.

But how is it done? If, as Miller maintains, "no ant tells any other ant what to do," who runs the show? And if every individual ant is anonymous, blind to the whole process, never seeing the big picture, how could anything be coordinated? The insight from researchers is impressive. They contend that countless interactions of individual ants forge a decentralized network that has no need for a cumbersome, time–consuming bureaucracy. With almost instant feedback, the insects can make fast but individual decisions that are extremely accurate. Some refer to this phenomenon as "complexity without design," an accretion built upon by the "process of evolution."

When looking for food, ant colonies calculate how many foragers they require each morning, depending on changing conditions. According to entomologists, the ants do so through touch and smell. Such contacts stimulate ants to perform particular tasks. The more food found, the more ants move out to bring it back. In fact, collective behavior of insects has inspired computer scientists to create artificial intelligence software based on swarm intelligence. Many ant–based strategies have been invented to manage business problems, for a host of companies. The software uses mathematical procedures to solve complex problems and find the most efficient way to route vehicles, schedule airline flights, or forecast customer demand.

Decentralization and Simplicity

As for human collective intelligence, Miller underlines an important truth: "Crowds tend to be wise only if individual members act responsibly and make their own decisions. A group won't be smart if its members imitate one another, slavishly follow fads, or wait for someone to tell them what to do."

Human society has much in common with swarm dynamics. Within open societies, people have constructed freestyle structures, nearly invisible, empowered by almost mysterious powers that can feed and clothe entire nations on a daily basis without relying on the state-driven economics of *dirigisme*. These swarms of economic forces are neither superimposed from above nor predesigned. They operate by simple rules. They provide coffee–hounds with hot drinks at Starbucks, students with yellow pencils and red markers at school. They build houses, sow wheat fields, and operate hotels for weary travelers. These people work silently, outside of public view, gratified to be part of a group effort to provide needed services. And hardly anybody really notices them. Why? Because nobody looks for problems when there is already a solution.

Invisible Systems and Patterns

During the early years of the computer industry, each computer company would develop its own operating systems. For many, this situation was hunky–dory, since computers were a novelty, and exciting. Only a few computer nerds clamored for a software system that could communicate with other computers. That quickly spread. Computer users and computing professionals soon realized that compatibility would have the advantage of easing the sharing of data. Without any central planning or government mandates, users sought out more standardized systems that could easily communicate with each other. In the beginning, no single person or agency led the scramble toward uniformity. Rather, a disorganized array of computer geeks and entrepreneurs assembled personal computers in garages and dingy workshops. Most of these compatible systems were IBM clones, cobbled together by the thousands and loaded with Microsoft's disk operating system (DOS). Of course, the decision by IBM officials to let anyone reproduce its proprietary architecture had a major role in advancing hardware and software compatibility. Nonetheless, because of the demand for compatibility, one of the DOS–based systems would eventually become dominant.

The dynamics of systems consistently take skeptics down a peg or two. By early 2001, the great retail empire of Montgomery Ward was coming to an end, with the decision to close down all of their department stores, for good. But Montgomery Ward had not always been thought of as a giant department store chain. Starting as a mail–order house in 1872, the company had no stores, and would not build any until fifty years later. Because America was a rural country, Montgomery Ward mailed merchandise by the most cost–effective means: railway. And in doing so, it beat out all its competitors, who were using more expensive delivery systems. By the late nineteenth century, Montgomery Ward had become the largest retailer in the world. But then a young railroad agent who sold watches came onto the scene: Richard Sears.

Sears also started a mail–order powerhouse, which eventually surpassed Montgomery Ward. But American demographics were changing. By the 1920s, most people were living in urban areas instead of remote rural areas. So the most effective means to deliver merchandise to customers was to build centers of distribution—that is, stores.

Neither Montgomery Ward nor Sears had originally desired or planned to build massive stores to display and sell merchandise. Doing so was considered impractical. They had grown quite wealthy, and complacent, from the mail–order business. Why change? In fact, one of Montgomery Ward's executives, who suggested building retail outlets, was fired. As economist Thomas Sowell wrote, "The greatness of a free–market economy is that it does not depend upon the wisdom of those who happen to be on top at the moment."[25] Sears and Montgomery Ward were not at the top for long. A man named James Cash Penney, a one–third owner of a small retail store in Wyoming, was soon to challenge the marketplace.

Having been raised in poverty, J. C. Penney shepherded to a retail empire of over 300 stores by 1950. During this time, both Montgomery Ward and Sears were losing millions of dollars per year, so were forced to begin a desperate bid to catch up with Penney.

Following World War II, the population distribution of the United States shifted again, inspiring some managers at Montgomery Ward to propose building retail stores in suburban shopping malls. Again, these visionaries were fired. But the management at Sears took another approach and began to build the first stores in malls. Montgomery Ward finally followed suit, but was never able to overtake Sears. Instead, the retail marketplace shifted again as the result of innovations by a man who worked for J. C. Penney: Sam Walton. He came up with new ideas on how to sell merchandise on a massive scale, eventually founding the Walmart chain, earning sales larger than those of Sears and J. C. Penney combined, causing Dr. Sowell to observe: "Those who complain

Decentralization and Simplicity 219

that some are 'left behind' amid growing prosperity do not understand that leaving some behind is the way the country moves ahead."

The greatest strength of diffuse systems lies in their ability to reach down to the lowest level of decision making. The meteoric rise of Apple Computer is ample proof of the "butterfly effect": results (output) are often out of proportion to their causes (input). Apple originated in Steve Jobs' (1955-2011) garage, at a time when the conventional wisdom was that consumers would never purchase a computer for home use. Actually, Jobs and his partner, Stephen Wozniak, only wanted to sell circuit boards to members of the Homebrew Club and a local electronics store: Paul Terrell's Byte Shop. However, Terrell wanted only fully built computers, not circuit boards, arguing that there was too much additional work to putting a computer together.

Although Terrell's clients were mostly computer hobbyists, some parts of the computer—BASIC software, storage systems, keyboards, monitor—were difficult to locate and assemble into a fully integrated system. Neither Jobs nor Wozniak had anticipated this turn of events, but they realized they could make good money by taking up Terrell's offer to build fifty computers for $489 to $589 each. Despite their enthusiasm in receiving the order, "Neither Jobs nor Wozniak thought they would sell more than one hundred a year."[26]

Actually, Wozniak had attempted to sell his computer invention to his employer, Hewlett—Packard (HP), before establishing Apple with Jobs. But the offer was rejected, because HP saw no future in microcomputers, and neither did other high–tech companies in and around Silicon Valley. Years later, Robert Noyce of Intel said that a number of companies could have built a personal computer in the 1970s, but nobody thought there was a market. Even Wozniak wanted only to be an engineer. It was Jobs who had the vision.

When William Hewlett, who also started a business out of his one-car garage, wanted to design, manufacture, and market an electronic calculator that would fit into his pocket, most of his employees opposed the idea. His own marketing department told Hewlett that only a hundred or fewer would be sold monthly, which would have made it impossible to turn a profit. Nevertheless, he had a hunch that such a product might do well with consumers. Despite warnings of doom, Hewlett took a gamble; soon Hewlett–Packard could not produce enough pocket calculators to fill consumer demand.

The question about centralization becomes fundamental: Could a highly organized authority have foreseen, encouraged, or promoted high–tech products—personal computers, pocket calculators, wireless phones, DVD players, etc.? The answer is, "unlikely." The nature of a centralized system favors top–down decision making, over any meaningful emphasis on "user requirements." Basically, central authorities are ignorant of what people might find useful. Even if centralists suspected a useful trend, they would be unlikely to risk promoting what might prove an unpopular and fringe notion. On the other hand, the general public has similar anxieties; they usually balk at revolutionary ideas. For instance, almost nobody had the faintest idea of how helpful personal computers would be, until a scattering of computer nerds applied them in ways that cut costs and saved time. If the public has little imagination, mired in fickle and fleeting attention spans, how could government officials ever be expected to roll up their sleeves and dive into risky, avant-garde startups?

In 42 B.C., Publilius Syrus remarked, "It is easy for men to talk one thing and think another." This maxim was invoked during the clash of new Coke versus original Coke, in 1985. For twenty years, Coca–Cola had been losing market share to Pepsi–Cola, slipping a full one percent in 1984 alone. In 190,000 blind taste–tests commissioned by The Coca—Cola Company, participants overwhelmingly preferred the taste of the new Coke formula—61 percent to 39 percent. However, when New Coke was introduced, consumers refused to purchase it and demanded the return of the original formula. By June of 1985, over 8,000 calls per day were coming in, along with over 40,000 letters of protest by the end of summer. Coca-Cola complied, and rebranded its original formula as "Classic Coke."

Although the participants in the blind taste–tests had given high marks to the new taste, consumers were upset over the loss of the old taste—some arguing that it was like losing an old friend. It seemed that nobody had realized how important the old Coke had become in the lives of Americans. One letter by an angry consumer read: "My dearest Coke. You have betrayed me. We went out just last week, as we had so often, and when we kissed I knew our love affair was over...." Even Cuba's Fidel Castro, according to the book *For God, Country and Coca–Cola*, "could not resist taking pot shots at Coke quipping that the death of the Real Thing was symptomatic of American decay."[27]

Beyond the Reaches of the Authorities

One of the most fascinating periods of American history was when waves of settlers navigated the Overland Trails to California and Oregon. These settlers had to travel for months through untamed lands to reach the west coast. They were under no governing jurisdiction, far beyond the reach of the law, jails, sheriffs, and courts. So what happened? Did they become savage outlaws?

In *Law for the Elephant*, John Phillip Reid of New York University School of Law debunked the pulp–fiction myth of wagon trains loused up with lawless behavior. He maintains that the emigrants were keenly aware of the law, especially regarding property rights, and rarely used violence to remedy critical shortages of supplies. Reid stated: "Instead, they respected the rights of property owners much as if still back east in the midst of plenty. By respect for their neighbor, and their neighbor's property, they were, more than not, adhering to a morality of law."[28]

With all of the hardship, one would expect there to have been widespread theft, murder, and mayhem, to secure desperately needed supplies. But after surveying hundreds of the pioneers' diaries and letters, Reid discovered that settlers' social behavior did not break down. There was little thievery by the have–nots; honesty reigned supreme. People settled differences peacefully, including respecting property claims by Indians.

Despite the separation from civil society, the wagon–train pioneers self–organized to provide for security, and crafted plans in a more lateral decision–making process. This is the legacy of decentralization, which, if left to itself, can provide a wider span of control with better insight, efficiency, and transparency.

Decentralized systems are the quintessential patrons of simplicity. They allow complexity to rise to a level at which it is sustainable, and no higher. This point can never be overstated. Without a simple building–block matrix, the rising tide of complexity can foment self–destructive behavior, eventually forcing systems to collapse under their own weight. In a futile attempt to impose order from above, centralization causes systems to over–organize, while ignoring the elements of simplicity from below. Only decentralization can serve as a check against disequilibrium and prevent socioeconomic systems from falling apart.

1 Bill Venners, "The Simplest Thing that Could Possibly Work," interview with Ward Cunningham, *Artima*, Jan. 19, 2004.

2 Linda Melvern, *Conspiracy to Murder: The Rwanda Genocide and the International Community* (New York: Verso, 2004).

3 Gérard Prunier, *The Rwanda Crisis: History of a Genocide*, New York: Columbia University Press, 1995.

4 Some historical revisionists have argued that Germany spared Switzerland because of its need to conduct banking transactions. But Germany was already making such transactions through Sweden, Portugal, Turkey, Argentina, and prewar United States.

5 Carlo Stagnaro, "Interview with Stephen P. Halbrook," posted on Lewrockwell.com, Dec. 2, 2002.

6 Stephen P. Halbrook, *Target Switzerland: Swiss Armed Neutrality in World War II*, Rockville Centre, New York,: Sarpedon Publishers, 1998, p. ix in the preface.

7 Ibid., Stephen P. Halbrook,

8 James Lucas, *World War Two Through German Eyes*, London: Arms & Armour Press, 1991.

9 "Tenet Strikes Back," excerpts from George Tenet's book *At the Center of the Storm: My Years at the CIA*. Time, July 14, 2007.

10 Dan van der Vat, *The Good Nazi: The Life and Lies of Albert Speer*, Boston: Houghton Mifflin Harcourt, 1997, p. 126.

11 "Cyberspace vs. the State," *Cato Policy Report*, May/June/June 1996.

12 Erika Niedowski, "In Russia's Capital, Summer Flowers Means Cold Showers," *Houston Chronicle*, July 24, 2006.

13 Scott Shane, *Dismantling Utopia: How Information Ended the Soviet Union*, Chicago: Ivan R. Dee, 1994, p. 83.

14 Kevin Klose, *Russia and the Russians: Inside the Closed Society*, New York: W.W. Norton, 1984.

15 Lydia Polgreen, "In Niger, Trees and Crops Turn Back the Desert," *New York Times*, Feb. 11, 2007.

16 James Surowiecki, *The Wisdom of Crowds: Why the Many Are Smarter Than the Few and How Collective Wisdom Shapes Business, Economies, Societies and Nation*, New York: Random House, 2005, p. xiii.

17 Daniel B. Klein, "Rinkonomics: A Window on Spontaneous Order," Library of Economics and Liberty, May 1, 2006.

18 John Stossel's "Political Incorrect Guide to Politics," 20/20, ABC–TV, Oct. 17, 2008.

19 Jeff Howe, *Crowdsourcing: Why the Power of the Crowd Is Driving the Future of Business*, New York: Crown Business, 2008, p 144.

20 Larissa Conradt and Tim Roper, "Group Decision–Making in Animals," *Nature*, Jan. 9, 2003, pp. 155–158.

21 Bonnie L. Bassler, "The Language of Bacteria," *Genes & Development*, June

Decentralization and Simplicity

15, 2001; B. L. Bassler, "Small Talk: Cell–to–Cell Communication in Bacteria," Cell, 109 (May 17, 2002), 421–424.

22 Ilya Prigogine, *The End of Certainty: Time, Chaos, and the New Laws of Nature*, New York, NY: Free Press, 1997.

23 Benjamin Constant, *Cours De Politique Constitutionnelle* (European political thought), Paris: Didier, Libraire–Editeur, 1830. He was a French author and politician.

24 Peter Miller, "Swarm Theory," *National Geographic*, July 9, 2007.

25 Thomas Sowell, "Greatness of a Free–Market Economy? It Does Not Depend Upon the 'Wisdom' of Those Momentarily at Top," *Jewish World Review*, Jan. 2, 2001. More details on this subject can be found in Thomas Sowell's book *Basic Economics: A Citizen's Guide to the Economy*, Rev. Ed., New York: Basic Books, 2003, pp. 53–77.

26 Lee Butcher, *Accidental Millionaire: The Rise and Fall of Steve Jobs at Apple Computer*, New York: Paragon House, 1st ed., 1987.

27 Mark Pendergrast, *For God, Country and Coca–Cola: The Definitive History of the Great American Soft Drink and the Company that Makes It*, New York: Basic Books, 2000.

28 John Phillip Reid, *Law for the Elephant: Property and Social Behavior on the Overland Trail* (San Marino, CA: Huntington Library Press, 1996), p. 364. First published in 1980.

9

Self-Organizing Systems

Realistically, an organization of the unknown is only achievable by inducing its self-organization. —Friedrich Hayek

Good order results spontaneously when things are let alone. —Chuang–tzu

Failure is the health of the state. —Butler Shaffer

Some have likened it to the force of gravity. Others have taken a more spiritual interpretation, suggesting that emergent properties might originate from the finger of God. Whatever the cause, self–organizing phenomena do amazing and unexplainable things.

So what is a self–organizing system? It is a seemingly insignificant cluster of units that amass and interact through the processes of attraction and repulsion. But the real kicker is that it operates without outside guidance or control. That is, a self–organizing system acts autonomously, as if the interconnecting components had a single mind. And as these components spontaneously march to the beat of their own drummer, they organize, adapt, and evolve toward a greater complexity than one would ever expect by just looking at the parts by themselves. Scientists have referred to this phenomenon as "self–organizing systems" (SOS), and as "complex adaptive systems" (CAS).

The term "complex adaptive systems" was originated by John H. Holland and Murray Gell–Mann (the winner of the 1969 Nobel Prize in physics) of the Santa Fe Institute. Whichever term is used, these highly interdisciplinary systems involve theories and models based, essentially, on evolutionary processes. Holland describes complex adaptive systems as a "dynamic network of many agents (which may represent cells, species, individuals, firms, nations) acting in parallel, constantly acting and reacting to what the other agents are doing."[1]

When chaos theory came into prominence in the 1980s, scientists began to search for principles to explain the chaotic behavior of systems where, as Kevin Dooley, a professor of supply chain management at Arizona State University describes it, "Order is emergent as opposed to predetermined."[2]

By the 1990s, this new offshoot became known as "complexity science," or "complexity theory." Unlike chaos theory, complexity science is nondeterministic and extremely unpredictable, and posits that simple causes can result in complex outcomes.

But researchers needed a new way to model this self–directed emergence of systems. With the assistance of high–speed computers, complexity scientists developed a rather unconventional way to test their theories: a methodology that became known as "agent–based modeling" (ABM). As a computational software tool, agent–based modeling became the best way to study how individual agents (people, insects, organizations, and so forth) interact with each other and their environment. During computer simulations, entities called agents individually assess their situations and make decisions appropriate within a set of loosely established parameters. The process is revolutionary compared to standard mathematical techniques, such as statistical modeling and differential equations, which are now often cited as imposing restrictive assumptions which, for many problems, limit their use.

When researchers delved deeper into complex systems, they found themselves gravitating toward the diverse realms of biology and sociology. This development led to a number of controversial conclusions. One involves the very nature of complexity itself—that within very complex systems, even high–powered computers are unable to unravel effects or provide predictable outcomes. This means that both human observations and computer modeling are subjective, and that nobody can ever make a fully integrated decision. Freeman Dyson, the eminent Princeton physicist, once pointed out that researchers can easily overestimate their models, asserting, "They come to believe models are real and forget they are only models."[3]

Complexity scientists concluded that there are just too many factors—both concordant and contrarian—to understand. And with so many potential gaps in information, almost nobody can see the whole picture. Complex systems have severe limits, not only to predictability but also to measurability. Some complexity theorists argue that modeling, while useful for thinking and for studying the complexities of the world, is a particularly poor tool for predicting what will happen.

This shocking revelation has had far–reaching implications, especially in the fields of social and political science. Without the ability to validate the potential success or failure of a political course of action, agenda–driven advocates have found themselves promoting a weak case for reengineering society toward a particular orientation. The dilemma is fairly obvious. No single human being could ever comprehend or acquire the full knowledge needed to mastermind all–encompassing events. This means that sociopolitical systems can never find the perfect leader or perfect management system to fine–tune society. The inherent nature of complexity is to doubt certainty and any pretense to finite and flawless data. Put another way, under uncertainty principles, any attempt by political systems to "impose order" has an equal chance to instead "impose disorder."

A number of economists have suggested this for decades. Austrian economist Friedrich Hayek (1899-1992) pondered this heady issue during his 1974 Nobel Memorial Lecture on "The Pretense of Knowledge." Hayek remarked: "If man is not to do more harm than good in his efforts to improve the social order, he will have to learn that in this, as in all other fields where essential complexity of an organized kind prevails, he cannot acquire the full knowledge which would make mastery of the events possible."[4]

History of Self–Organizing Systems

In the beginning, the concept of self–organization was generally based on the universal laws of physics and chemistry that govern biological systems. The seventeenth–century philosopher René Descartes argued that ordinary laws of nature tend to create organization. In the following century, the naturalist movement stressed the importance of living organisms and universal natural laws. The naturalists, along with the deists, broke with the religious notion that God micromanages the world on a day–to–day basis. Many early scientists, including Newton, believed in a world organized from the heavenly top, likening it to a wonderful precision machine with predictable performance. The naturalists disagreed. They saw it more like a clock that, once wound by God, would operate on its own without further tinkering.

The term "self–organizing systems," coined by psychiatrist W. Ross Ashly in 1947, has invaded every major field of science—and then some. The field of physics is often credited as the first discipline to comprehend this new science by advancing distinct theorems for chaos and complexity. But in recent years, some have pointed to economists as perhaps the trailblazers in grasping self–organizing principles. Adam Smith, the father of modern economics, recognized the self–direction of human behavior, illustrated by his statement about the superior, though enigmatic, benefits of the "invisible hand." He argued that under "enlightened self–interest," the whole community would benefit, even though the process would be neither coordinated nor concerned with actual outcome. Smith actively observed that commerce is often conducted by individual agents who were unaware of the bigger picture, similar to the "integrated–partition" that is found among individual agents in swarm dynamics.

Later in the twentieth century, Friedrich Hayek continued Adam Smith's line of reasoning and concluded that local, decentralized economic systems are more prosperous when operating within their own self–directing protocols. Hayek coined the term "catallaxy" to explain the "self–organizing system of voluntary co–operation" that exemplifies "spontaneous order."

Hayek was one of the first modern–day economists to delve deeply into the working mechanics of economic coordination. Through the ideas of "public choice theory," Hayek took the position that local decision–making thresholds trump any type of centralized, command–based economy.[5] In his way of thinking, top–down planners could never muster enough relevant information to carry out the allocation of resources in any reliable or sustainable manner. Even if they could, the information compiled would have changed during its gathering, making judgments dependent on the almost impossible task of chasing a moving target. "Economists," Hayek concluded, "happily proceed on the fiction that the factors which they can measure are the only ones that are relevant."[6]

Mathematician John L. Casti echoed similar concerns over drawbacks in understanding human action, writing, "Complexity theory shows that even if we were capable of having a complete understanding of the factors affecting individual action, this would be still insufficient to predict group or institutional behaviour."[7] All too often, the validity of a system is predicated on its predictive powers. But in nonlinear systems, which encompass most systems, "It is impossible to find a set of equations that can be solved in order to predict the characteristics of the system."[8]

Hayek's spontaneous order resides in a system's ability to drive itself without external restraints or planned orientation. He asserted that society evolves through human action, not human design. The key word is "design." Although distinctly favorable to chaos and complexity theories, the Austrian school of economics takes a dubious view of chaos's "sensitivity to initial conditions," believing that such a concept may give too much design prejudice to something that can only be spontaneous. Economist Ludwig von Mises, in *Human Action*, clearly states: "There is no such thing as quantitative economics."[9] That is, past economic data could provide a wide range of historical frequencies from which to extrapolate future expectations, but there is no pre-designed constant. Economic activities by humans are chaotic with or without mathematical analysis. Economic modeling seldom comes close to real–life behavior of a system, because political systems routinely base decisions on incomplete knowledge.

In their study of human behavior, the Austrians perceived unpredictability as coming from infinite and unknown factors that are not necessarily tied to sensitive dependence on initial condition. They fear that technocratic planners will embrace and co–opt the science of chaos to promote planned societies. To do so, planners would misrepresent the data in a way to make them definable and tractable within the scope of their own self–serving analyses. In many ways, the Austrians were keenly aware of the danger of economic equations that presume knowledge of every fact and figure that could sway a dynamic system. Unfortunately, many mathematical systems are biased, their proponents searching endlessly for any means to justify a linear equation that will neatly manufacture a well-expected prediction.

Former Federal Reserve Bank Chairman Alan Greenspan recognized many of Smith's and Hayek's ideas. Sometimes called the "economy's maestro" for his record of over eighteen years at the financial helm, Greenspan once acknowledged to the Fed's policymaking committee, "We really do not know how this system works." In fact, he remarked in 1984, "A surprising problem is that a number of economists are not able to distinguish between the economic models we construct and the real world."[10] That is because "Greenspan abhorred rules, was skeptical about economic models.... If [he] stood for anything, it was flexibility and the freedom from dogma," according to Edward L. Andrews, New York Times economics reporter.[11] Greenspan realized that the economy can change in a heartbeat and do it with the complexity of countless pulsating microprocessors, pixel by pixel. He also insisted that the economy cannot be managed by "a single policy or predictable with any single economic model."[12]

Greenspan's critics argued that by refusing to institutionalize steadfast policies for the Federal Reserve, he was making up his own rules as he went along. But Greenspan understood that he could not know what he could not know, and operated accordingly. During his promotional tour for his book *The Age of Turbulence*, Greenspan admitted to Jon Stewart on *The Daily Show* that even with all of the complex mathematical models available, nobody has anything close to an infallible forecasting method. Greenspan confessed, "I've been in the forecasting business for fifty years, and I'm no better than I ever was, and nobody else is either."[13]

The Living Organism of Economics

The economy is more than a myriad of consumer demands, unlimited free–roaming capital, and hundreds of factories pumping out products and services. Instead, it might best be described as a self–directing organism with elaborate and interacting behaviors. In *Butterfly Economics*, Paul Ormerod became one of the first economists to view the economy as a "living organism—a living creature, whose behavior can only be understood by looking at the complex interactions of its individual parts." He maintained that the interaction of millions of individual agents constitutes something beyond the mere parts, to the point where economic systems learn and adapt—similar to artificial intelligence.

Ormerod further contended that the conventional view of economics presupposes that action by one individual does not alter others' behavior directly. For example, when consumers started purchasing the first Apple computers in the mid–1970s, few would have predicted that it would have had such an effect on the world, let alone start a billion–dollar personal computer industry. But of course, market chaologists disagree; they see strong feedback loops that crisscross the economic landscape. W. Brian Arthur explained it this way: "Behavior creates pattern; and pattern in turn influences behavior."[14]

Historically, classical economists have used linear equations to model economic phenomena and predict future events. This mathematization of economic systems was popular, since it was easy to manipulate the numbers. Ormerod took these theorists to task, implying that they were being imprisoned by their own theory. He wrote: "Economists who stick to linear models because they're more tractable are like drunks who look for their car keys under the street lamp because the light is better there."[15]

To show how inadequate economic modeling can be, Ormerod cited a remarkable experiment with an ordinary, garden–variety ant colony. In the 1980s, entomologists began a series of experiments to gain insight into ant decision making. The preliminary results caused perplexity, and later, excitement. In the experiment, two identical food piles were place at equal distances from the anthill. The food was being replenished, so that the piles remained equal. Logically, it was assumed that in the long term, the food piles would be visited equally; the probability rate that would be found from a series of coin tosses. However, the opposite occurred: the ants vacillated between the two food sources. After one pile was randomly discovered, the discoverer stimulated other ants to return to the first pile. Despite their seemingly methodical

Self-Organizing Systems 231

nature, the behavior of the ants was influenced by the decision of the first ant. This has important economic consequences, in that situations can be directly influenced by the behavior of one lone participant.

Next, the entomologists theorized that some type of pattern must eventually develop—that the ants must favor one pile of food over the other. Again, predictions were wrong. Even over longer periods, no pattern developed. Visits to the two food sites "fluctuated in an apparently random fashion." And "constant changes, often small but occasionally rapid and large, were entirely unexpected according to the biologists' theory."[16] This experiment led Alan Kirman, a pioneer in interacting agent models in economics, to suggest that interaction between individuals and the dynamics that that interaction creates can influence overall outcomes.

The ant experiments attest to the fact that mathematical constructs of economic modeling are very limited, and as such, tinkering with or attempting to fine–tune human or economic action by force is doomed to failure. Essentially, human society is not controllable. There have been numerous attempts to control it, through countless and terrifying means, but in the long term, they have all been futile. As during the alcohol Prohibition era in the United States, the populace will simply continue in their naturally peaceful ways by circumventing restrictive laws, or they will go underground. Perhaps one reason for this human behavior is that economic activity does not truly represent a fixed system. Instead, it might be argued that economics is an "anti–system system."

Similar to the non-cooperative aspects of John Nash's work in game theory, in which no outside authority makes players stick to the same predetermined rules, market–based systems have no central command post; they phase in and out of chaos and order, often without rhyme or reason. Once some type of system is detected, it often metamorphoses into something completely unrecognizable. Left to themselves, markets act in a way that makes them impossible to control.

In the final analysis, market–based economies are simply aggregates of countless decisions and non-proactive decisions made by a fickle public. This contrasts sharply with military operations, in which groups of soldiers are directed precisely, by a strict hierarchical organization. Soldiers march as one integral unit with a single purpose. Consumers, however, meander to a different drumbeat, on a field of diverse tastes. There is no particular direction or commander. Each consumer is one, but the marketplace is made up of millions.

The inner workings of market–based economics are a recursive enigma. Self–organizing systems emerge like new organisms—under a transitory cloud of randomness, operating more as an evolution of probability distribution than as a single trajectory. They are not designed, but emerge a result of decentralized decision making by purchasers and providers. Borrowing from Adam Smith's notion of the "invisible hand," the people in these systems are often unaware of their own importance to the larger picture, and are loosely tied together by unrelated events and arrangements. Market economies just sort of happens—created by an unborn nothingness, a far-from-equilibrium condition where the process of discovery never reaches a final resting point or goal.

"Capitalism just happened," asserted Michael Rothschild in *Bionomics: Economy as Business Ecosystem.* "Capitalism flourishes whenever it is not suppressed, because it is a naturally occurring phenomenon."[17] Rothschild saw economic activity as an "evolving ecosystem," similar to the evolutionary processes that Darwin recounted while observing various species on the Galapagos Islands.

Like recessive genes, market–based systems tend to appear whenever there is nothing to oppose them. For instance, a number of early civilizations in the Mediterranean were relatively free, wealthy, and practically warless. During the era of Minoan civilization on the island of Crete (3000 to1450 B.C.), for example, war did not appear to be of any concern. A highly advanced nation of free–trading merchants, it had no military fortification and few weapons. Archaeologists have been unable to find any trace of the type of military bureaucracy that characterized later civilizations. The inhabitants of the island of Minoa, considered by some to be the lost continent of Atlantis, even had indoor plumbing. Apparently, Minoan citizens were in an environment where they could trade, and live life as they saw fit. That changed when outsiders—the Myceneans—invaded and imposed a militarist regime.

Stateless and Self–Organizing Societies

Many early tribal societies were based on democratic practices with consensus overtones. In the Anglo–Saxon tradition, Norsemen elected their leaders and kings. The Vikings allowed both men and women to participate in their system of governance and included almost everyone except slaves and those outside the law (outlaws). The early Icelandic society (the Saga Age) and medieval Ireland had no centralized authority to make mandatory decisions, and lacked the fiat power to enforce them, had they been made. In the Americas, the Iroquois Confederacy used consensus decision–making procedures, along with federalism, self–government, and balance–of–power restraints, which all three influenced the U.S. Constitution. Whenever an emergency arose, the Iroquois Great Council, under its constitution, "had to 'submit the matter to the decision of their people' in a kind of referendum open to both men and women."[18]

Some of the early American colonies had no active government. For instance, the Quaker colony of Pennsylvania lived for the greater part of "seven years in de facto anarchism" and, according to economist Murray Rothbard, did not suffer from the experience.[19] In fact, colonial leaders elected to the Pennsylvania Privy Council extended the principles of liberty far beyond what Governor William Penn had ever imagined. Considered, in Penn's absence, a self–governing entity with full executive powers, the Council seemed determined not to hold meetings, impose levies, or comply with Penn's wishes. The state had withered away, and Penn found it difficult to reestablish a government. He complained bitterly that no one wanted to rule others. With his fortune dwindling, Penn appointed John Blackwell as Deputy Governor in a last–ditch effort to get colonial leaders to impose taxes and collect quitrents. As the lord of a feudal fiefdom, Penn wanted what he was entitled to, by virtue of his proprietary charter with King James II: income and power. Unfortunately for Penn, the Council refused to recognize Blackwell's appointment.[20]

Before European colonization, millions of Africans lived in a stateless environment. Some were pastoral and nomadic societies, such as the Nuer of Sudan, the Karamojong of Uganda, and the Masai of Kenya. Others had settled agricultural societies, such as the Kikuyu of Kenya, Ibo of Nigeria, Baule of Ivory Coast, Kru of Liberia, and Dogon of Mali.

Even earlier, the Jewish people of Israel had started out without a king—meaning that they had only charismatic tribal leaders who often denigrated the office of king. Contributors to *The Oxford History of the Biblical World,* interpreting a Biblical passage, characterized this era as a time when "social and political anarchy are summed up with 'in those days there was no king in Israel' (Judg. 17.6; 18.1; 19.1; 21.25), twice followed by the remark that 'everyone did as he wished....'"[21] In the book of Judges, Israelites' free and stateless lifestyle is documented "Everyone did what was right in his own eyes" (Judg. 17:6).

But without governmental scaffolding, how can a society deal with lawlessness and with those who would take advantage of others? Historically, most stateless societies had a digest of well–established laws, long before forming a permanent governing structure. According to Roderick T. Long, a professor of philosophy at Auburn University, "the overwhelming preponderance of historical and anthropological evidence verifies that law is far older than the state. Until recently, states were the exception, not the norm, in human society; and stateless societies have enjoyed quite sophisticated and long-lasting legal codes."[22]

Pirate Societies and Autonomous Zones

What happens when certain areas elude the formal structures of hierarchical control, allowing the populace to attain a high level of autonomy? Political writer Hakim Bey explored this concept, and dubbed these uncontrolled areas "temporary autonomous zones." He cautioned that such zones are precarious—so sensitive, in fact, that if they were to become permanent beyond the moment, the structure could collapse and stifle the freewheeling autonomy it had created.

One of Bey's examples is that of seafaring bandits during the golden era of piracy (1650–1720). Most scholars have ignored the spontaneous self-organizing nature of pirate societies. Although piracy was a criminal activity, sea rovers were often no more criminally inclined than the monarchs and tyrants of the day. But what makes these plunderers so fascinating is the open-ended, consensual structure that evolved as the result of economic realities.

One of the first to recognize these economic characteristics was Peter T. Leeson, a professor of economics at George Mason University. According to Leeson in *The Invisible Hook: The Hidden Economics of Pirates*, buccaneers were more interested in maximizing their profits than in assuming the role of unrelenting rebels obsessed with bucking the establishment. Leeson's book reveals a hidden order among pirate societies, although many writers still engage in pop-culture stereotypes of pirates as bloodthirsty mad dogs, averse to order. But Leeson, along with other historians, revealed a far different picture. Before any country had democratic systems of governance, pirate captains were democratically elected and replaced. Each pirate had one vote, and election processes were used regularly in referendums to determine what to do aboard their vessel, including whether to attack another ship. They shared the plunder equally (except for the captain and some officers), worked under a system of checks and balances, and had a written constitution and a list of rights, including freedom of expression and due process, long before the U.S. Constitution was penned. For the most part, floggings and most forms of punishment were forbidden; quarrels were often resolved by vote. Under pirate democracy, the crew voted to regulate smoking and drinking, and even had a crude form of workers' compensation for their injured, as well as a retirement program. As for racial integration, some pirate ships were forty percent black. Everybody, no matter what race or creed, had the same rights and responsibilities.

Leeson maintains that economics played a leading role in this radical shift from a harsh, authoritarian hierarchy to a bottom–up, democratically friendly structure. Perhaps this is what happens when the authorities make life so difficult that there is no honest way to make a decent living. Thus, criminality is often born of necessity. In such an autocratic atmosphere, most profit–seeking activities are driven underground, especially when upstarts compete too well against state–sanctioned and subsidized enterprises. But to be outside established law, one must develop some semblance of self–imposed rules to govern the activities of the whole body. Like any organization or business, pirate sailors discovered that cooperative behavior under a consensual structure proved to be the best way to accomplish their stated goals. Moreover, when this happens, as Leeson suggests, a spontaneous order will naturally arise, through a phenomenon he dubs the "invisible hook."[23]

Modern Stateless Societies and Somalia

Amazingly, a few stateless societies survived to the middle of the twentieth century. In the 1950s, anthropologist Leopold Popisil studied the Kapauku of New Guinea, a tribal society of 45,000 people that had no governmental structure. Like the Minoans, the Kapauku enjoyed a prosperous and generally warless existence, based on horticulture. Even in the soggy and ever–changing rainforest, the Kapauku tribes treated all property as private. Individual rights were respected, and disputes were settled by prominent wise men called *tonowi*, who had no authority except respect from the community.[24]

The only area without any central government today is the African nation of Somalia. It was ruled by a ruthless dictator, Mohamed Siad Barre, until the government fell during a civil war and coup d'état that started in 1991. Oddly, the political vacuum that ensued remained unfilled after Barre was overthrown, disproving the old political axiom that when a predatory government tumbles, it is swiftly replaced with another. Nonetheless, Somalia retains a strong tribal and ethnic structure. Several attempts have been made by local warlords, adjacent foreign powers, and the international community to restore a central government, but they have largely failed.

Economists and researchers have taken a keen interest in Somalia. The region provides a unique opportunity to study a stateless and decentralized society, self-organizing under difficult conditions. Most political pundits have written off the region, convinced that Somalia is the poster child for the indispensability of a central government. Others have argued that without someone commanding the top tiers of Somalia, the social welfare of the people would decline. But reports coming out of Somalia are the opposite of what experts and pundits have predicted.

According to a report by Peter Leeson, the chaotic situation in Somalia has produced a higher level of well-being than had the former centralized government. He wrote: "The data suggest that while the state of this development remains low, on nearly all of 18 key indicators that allow pre– and post–stateless welfare comparisons, Somalis are better off under anarchy than they were under government."[25] Nonetheless, Leeson warned: "Although a properly constrained government may be superior to statelessness, it is not true that *any* government is superior to no government at all."

Some of the improvements in Somalia since the central authorities collapsed include a growing private sector, according to a 2003 report by the World Bank.[26] In transportation, before the government fell, there was only one airplane. By 2007 approximately 15 airline companies with over 60 aircraft were flying domestic and international routes in Somalia. The United Nations reported in 2007 that Somalia's service industry was thriving.[27] There were 600 primary schools before the civil war, but by 2005 that number had increased to 1,172.[28]

As for telecommunications, *The Economist* noted that mobile phone calls in Somalia are "generally cheaper and clearer than a call from anywhere else in Africa." The article attributed this curious oddity to the fact that "No government means no state telecom company to worry about, no corrupt ministry officials to pay off (there is no ministry), and the freedom to choose the best-value equipment.... It is a vivid illustration of the way in which governments, for all their lip service to extending communications, can often be more of a hindrance than a help."[29]

While trying to avoid romanticizing Somalia improvements, Leeson concluded that the results indicated that "statelessness has substantially improved Somalia development." Other academics have agreed, including Benjamin Powell, a professor of economics at Suffolk University, who suggested that "Somalia's living standards have often improved, not just in absolute terms, but also relative to other African countries since the collapse of the Somali central government."[30]

The country is not lawless. According to social anthropologist Spencer MacCallum, Somalia has a complex system of customary laws that provide protection for both the individual and the community. Based on a strong sense of property rights and trade, this rule of law is known as the Xeer. Under the Xeer, the criminal justice system is compensatory rather than punitive, which means it needs no legislation or legislators to keep it operational. Detailed in Michael van Notten's *The Law of the Somalis*, the "customary laws" of Somalia provide no imprisonment, and fines are rarely imposed. All compensation goes directly to the victim or the victim's heirs. Further, the Xeer does not recognize victimless crimes. If there is no victim or family member to make a tort–like claim, there can be no trial. Moreover, no court has the authority to initiate an investigation without a complainant.[31]

Unfortunately, an Ethiopian proxy army invaded Somalia in 2006. With the backing of the United States, the military force was determined to set up a centralized government and instill order. It has done neither. Millions have left Mogadishu and other regional cities and relocated in tent cities, to escape the intense fighting. By 2008, at least 2.6 million Somalis were facing famine, mostly due to foreign intervention.

Agriculture, City-States and the Roman Republic

Somalia's surprising recovery before the neighboring Ethiopian army invasion is not unique. Before the dawn of agriculture, human society revolved around small clusters of tribal groups of nomadic hunter–gatherers. A lack of dependable food supplies kept both populations and those aspiring to the role of emperor down. With the domestication of wild grasslands some 10,000 years ago, tribal societies found it more fruitful to cultivate food, rather than to gather it haphazardly. As agriculture became more intense, farmers developed better tools and more successful ways to work the land. However the real revolution was more than the presence of a dependable food supply. The remarkable consequence of farming was its revolutionary by–product: large surpluses.

With the advent of surpluses, farmers now had valuable commodities with which to barter across city–state boundaries. Thriving trade centers sprouted, along with a cottage industry of artisans and merchants. People prospered; trade flourished; villages expanded; but the political structure remained stunted, caught in the crosshairs of tribal traditions that expected leadership to arise through ability or democratic processes, rather than by birthright. But the wealthy elite were at odds with these long–honored traditions, searching for power not to defend society from invading outsiders, but to assault weaker neighbors. Unknown to these early chieftains, the economy of surpluses had evolved from a freewheeling system of nomadic pastoralism to a static system of premeditated statecraft.

As city–states expanded in population and wealth, their governing systems centralized and gradually consolidated under the weight of agenda–driven insiders. Democratic traditions were found to be antiquated and either faded or were pushed away, especially during so–called emergencies. Before long, the larger and more aggressive city–states assembled large armies and found it profitable to go on invasion sprees, hell–bent on building empires.

However, one city–state fought back, and deposed its monarchy and the privileged few. That was Rome. It reshaped itself into a full–fledged republic by 509 B.C., and vested its supreme power into a number of assemblies, including the Assembly of Centuries (*comitia centuriata*) and the Assembly of Tribes (*comitia tributa*). These assemblies comprised most citizens within the city proper and had the power to declare war, change laws, appoint magistrates, and confirm the leader elected by the Senate.

Similar to what occurred to most city–states, the political tug–of–war in Rome was always between the privileged few—the "patricians"—and the underprivileged many—the "plebeians." The Roman patricians held a monopoly of political and economic power, despite their small numbers, with the Senate as its epicenter. The plebeian class comprised common citizens, farmers, merchants, and even wealthy landowners lacking political connections.

In 494 B.C., the plebeians, angered at having been double-crossed by the authorities, threatened to leave Rome and establish their own independent city–state. In an effort to prevent civil war, the Roman constitution was modified, creating for the plebeians the position of Tribune, which was considered the most powerful position in the city of Rome. The common citizen had won, for the moment, but the patricians continued to chip away at their rights.

By 275 B.C., the Senate had usurped most of the people's authority. The Assemblies were rarely called upon to decide either internal or external matters. Rome and its provinces were being ruled by Senatorial decrees, with little public participation. Nevertheless, according to the Roman constitution, the people still had the legal right to govern themselves. In this sense, the Senate had little constitutional authority, but few magistrates were willing to remind the public of their legal rights. One dauntless citizen, Tiberius Gracchus, finally did, and for his efforts he was propelled into the crossfire between the privileged and the underprivileged. Elected to the position of Tribune, Tiberius attempted to pare down the power of the senatorial class. For his noble effort, in 133 B.C. he was assassinated by the Senate and dumped into the Tiber River.

Shortly after the coup d'état, Gaius Gracchus was elected Tribune, and took over where his brother had left off. With nearly total support from the Plebeian Tribal Assembly he was determined to exert more restraints on the Senate. To stop Gaius's proposals, the Senate declared martial law. During the ensuing riots, Gaius was captured and beheaded, along with 3,000 supporters. Historian Finley Hooper wrote: "As the wise Solon of Athens once observed, the rich are not inherently any more greedy or corruptible than their poorer fellow citizens. At Rome, their powerful positions, overseas commands, and inside information had simply given them the first chance."[32]

Not long after it had established complete control over Rome and its expanding territories, the Senate, too, found itself emasculated. The Assemblies fared worse. It lost all voice and disappeared entirely. As power was consolidated into fewer hands, and into the military, Rome's decay became more pronounced. It began to feed on itself, with those in power micromanaging the economy in a way that magnified and deepened each successive crisis.

Unable to raise revenues from an already overtaxed public, emperors routinely debased their currency, by lowering the silver content of their coin—from 90 percent during Nero's rule, to just 0.02 percent during the reign of Claudius II Gothicus. The result was inflation skyrocketing to over 15,000 percent during the Third Century A.D. Farmers soon abandoned their land, unable to pay the tax collector. The middle class disappeared. To stop inflation, the emperors often resorted to disastrous wage and price controls. To make their point painfully clear, they often instituted the death penalty for any violator. According to Lactantius, an acclaimed writer of the day, much blood was spilled over "small and cheap items" while the marketplace lay bare of goods.

All through this period of economic decline, the Roman emperors blamed the merchants, speculators, and hoarders for Rome's economic problems. It never occurred to the Roman administrators that they themselves were responsible for the malaise that plagued, and finally overwhelmed, the Roman economy.

Throughout history, societies have witnessed the privileged few extending manifold options for themselves while simultaneously restricting the privileges of everyone else. Thomas Jefferson recognized this problem, observing that "the natural progress of things is for liberty to yield and government to gain ground."[33]

The Over–organizing Gene

Within all life is the seed of death. Self–organizing mechanisms have this same defective tendency. Age is the culprit in human mortality, and an "over–organizing gene" is the bane of human civilization.

After emergence, all organisms have a natural urge to do more than just survive; they want to expand. This characteristic causes societies to transfer power to the few from the many who perform various services, through the so–called "social contract." In doing so, individuals surrender some authority, in order to pool resources and achieve common goals—similar to the evolutionary process of single and multicelled organisms operating for the sake of the larger body. But political busybodies can easily succumb to the impulse to over–organize, over–think, and over–plan. They muddy the water, bog down innovation, and stifle creativity. They can install so many bells and whistles into a system that nobody can hear the music clearly. In essence, the politicos overload the system in an endless quest to be a solution in search of a problem.

The twentieth century is littered with examples of overbearing potentates determined to run roughshod over those who prefer to be let alone. Instead of providing security and protection for the citizenry, these domineering politicos feed on their host, soon becoming the problem they were created to abolish.

The primary reason, according to controlaholics, that a government must monopolize society is that nobody would voluntarily self–organize to provide public services. On the contrary, history has celebrated many noteworthy examples of people who disputed the soundness of imposed order—individuals who made personal sacrifices to improve society. One such man was Benjamin Franklin.

Dedicated to "good citizenship" and self–improvement, Benjamin Franklin exemplified the best of American character, in devoting time and energy to provide services to the public, with minimal help from the authorities. With the assistance of the *Junto*, or "Leather Apron Club", an organization for mutual improvements, Franklin established the nation's first lending library, volunteer fire department, insurance company, and free city hospital, as well as the privately funded University of Pennsylvania. He was responsible for getting the city streets of Philadelphia paved, lighted, and cleaned, and he organized a Night Watch and Militia to keep the peace. All of these public services were based on voluntary, community cooperation. And many of these private orga-

Self-Organizing Systems 241

nizations which he created in the 1700s—the library, insurance company, and so forth—still thrive in Philadelphia today.

Not only was Franklin tireless in his community work, but he freely gave away his inventions to the public—bifocals, the lightning rod, the Franklin stove—by refusing to patent them. Treating his inventions like open–source software, he wanted the opportunity to share his good fortune with others and serve the needs of society.

Unfortunately, self–directing systems are susceptible to predators. They are easily co–opted by power brokers and the unscrupulous political elite with hidden agendas. Noble ideals tend to become corrupted when systems disown voluntary means for mandatory ends.

During the early years of the labor movement in the United States, workers were able to acquire, through negotiation, the right to bargain collectively. Their organizations were manned by volunteers eager to improve working conditions and pay. They relied on the support of fellow workers, and the populace at large, to obtain the right of association. Some major labor leaders, such as Warren S. Stone, were adamant that union membership remain voluntary, believing that if a worker "wants to join a union, all right, but it is contrary to the principles of free government and the Constitution of the United States... to make him join."[34]

In their frantic struggle to completely control the workplace, labor unions sought privileges from government to make union membership mandatory. They pressured Congress to pass the National Labor Relations Act of 1935. The Act gave labor unions the legal right to set up, with a simple majority vote by the employees, "closed shops," thus creating a workplace where every employee is required to join the union and pay union dues. Like all other systems that owe their structure to coercion, mandatory union laws have become failures fraught with unintended consequences.

With compulsory unionism came rampant corruption. Finding mandatory union dues irresistible, organized crime soon dominated many of the largest unions, causing a devastating decline in public support. Further, the Supreme Court ruling of *U.S. v. Enmons* in 1973 gave labor unions the legal ability to perpetrate intimidation and violence when pursuing better wages or benefits. Soon labor had the image of a nefarious, thug–infested system, and that image hurt union membership. Peaking at nearly 36 percent of all American workers in 1945, union membership (in the private sector) declined, to in the range of 7–8 percent of the workforce by 2005. To put this in perspective, union membership had been around 8 percent of the workforce in 1900. It had come full circle.

What the labor union leaders failed to understand was that with a system using or threatening violence, they risked losing solidarity among their members and with the public. If violence can be used in one area, it can obviously be used in another. Members can easily become inanimate objects prone to be milked for "the greater good" of the system. The systemic whole becomes more important than its individual parts. Recalcitrant members can be silenced or fired. The system begins to feed on itself and, eventually, becomes but a shadow of its former self.

Even more interesting is the hypocritical nature of systems, when they demand that everyone join their cause. Although labor unions' primary objective is to unionize every employee, they do not hesitate to hire nonunion workers for their own purposes. For instance, to keep costs down, the carpenters' union in the city of Monterey, California, picketed DMC Construction for eighteen months, but employed nonunion workers to promote unionism.[35]

Most civilizations stumble before reaching any noteworthy level of greatness. Their own system obstructs further growth, like dry–rot in the heartwood of trees. During the final years of a declining civilization, the damage to society becomes more visible, especially when it is confronted by catastrophic failures. Such repeated failures frustrate the political body, to the point at which leaders are unwilling to defend what they had once cherished. In essence, this over–organizing gene causes society to be undone by its own devices and "hoisted by its own petard." When the hordes of Germanic tribes finally entered the imperial gates of Rome, many citizens welcomed them "as saviors from the onerous tax burden."[36]

Fleeing to Virgin Lands—Westward Ho

Like animals fleeing that which causes pain, disheartened people migrate to freer, less populated lands, generally meandering westward. Throughout the centuries, Western civilization has ventured away from established populated centers inhabited by overbearing magistrates and punitive taxes, settling in new, sparsely inhabited lands with undeveloped or no government. This is no accident.

Civilizations are like young biological cells that mature, grow old, and finally, die. When a civilization reaches its senior years, the youth and entrepreneurs become frustrated. There is little opportunity in a moribund system that is atrophying into a hopelessly corrupted and privilege–run environment.

The only alternative for intrepid citizens is to vote with their feet and migrate to unrestrictive lands.

Nobody knows exactly why Hellenic tribes slowly migrated from the Caucasus and settled in a region known as Greece, but presumably they were looking for a better life and warmer climates. Their migration patterns suggest that they were unorganized and had wandered for centuries, but their legacy became the foundation of Western civilization.

The hallmark of the ancient Greek civilization was its unique decentralized structure of over 150 independent *poleis*, or city–states, fiercely autonomous and relatively free, compared to the despotic empires to the east. Not only had the Greeks organized into well–coordinated trading communities, but many had forged constitutions and embraced an odd patchwork of monarchy, oligarchy, and democracy.

At first ruled by kings and tyrants, the city of Athens rebelled against the aristocratic elite, and invented a system of self–governance by ordinary people, now considered to have been the world's first democracy (around 508 B.C.) Athens entrusted its governing structure to a Council of 500 and an Assembly of 6,000. But this "ruled-by-the-people" system was not an electoral democracy in the modern sense. Fearful that the wealthy and famous would have an unfair advantage over the common man in an election, the Athenians instead selected their representatives by lot. The Athenians believed that elections would create a privileged class of rulers and could reestablish the much–hated oligarchies.

Before the rise of democracy in Athens, the city had been considered a relatively modest seafaring city–state. By the fifth century B.C., it had become the preeminent Greek superpower—one of the largest and wealthiest city–states in all of Greece, and the birthplace of Western Civilization's most celebrated ideals of art, science, and philosophy. Speech was freely tolerated; trade was encouraged; and liberty was defined as "living as one pleases."[37] In short order, other city–states attempted to imitate Athens' experiment, to varying degrees of success, including the early Roman Republic and Carthage.

But why did the city–states of Greece remain decentralized and independent for centuries? Why were these self–assembling communities not gobbled up by neighboring empires? Most historians point to the geopolitical culture of those living in mountainous terrain. Isolated by almost impregnable mountains, and often located miles away from the ocean to prevent attacks by sea, Greek city–states were almost invulnerable to foreign invaders. Although they were involved in numerous civil wars, the feisty Greeks allied together in 480

B.C., to defeat an invading Persian army forty times larger than their own, during the Greco–Persian War.

Eventually, the Greek city–states were unified into a large empire under the control of Philip II of Macedon, and later, under his son, Alexander the Great. After Alexander's death, Greece was ruled by a series of Macedonian kings, and its importance declined sharply, never to return to its former glory. By 146 B.C., a younger Roman Republic had conquered Greece and made it a province.

The westward movement of people to underpopulated land is not the only way for them to achieve a superpower status. After World War II, both Germany and Japan experienced a booming economy that some have labeled an "economic miracle." Economists and historians have cited a number of reasons for this phenomenon. One of the favorites is Ludwig Erhard's currency reform and price decontrols of 1948 Germany. Others have pointed to foreign aid under the U.S. Marshall Plan. However, according to David R. Henderson, a professor of economics at the Naval Postgraduate School in Monterey, California, during the peak of United States aid to war–torn Germany, "Marshall Plan aid was less than 5 percent of German national income. Other countries that received substantial Marshall Plan aid had lower growth than Germany."[38]

However, one fact is usually missing — glaringly so — from the "economic miracle" equation. During the war, Germany and Japan were bombed virtually into the Stone Age. Century–old bureaucracies had been completely destroyed — buildings, records, and personnel, everything. These nations had no choice but to start over from scratch, slowly emerging into new nations as if they had located in unspoiled, virgin lands.

Self–Healing and Biological Uniqueness

As any good doctor would explain to his patients, the body has a natural, self–healing process with which to fight disease and infection. The human body is a self–correcting, biological system that automatically seeks to survive. For instance, after a stroke, a body with blocked carotid arteries will often develop new blood vessels, creating a fresh flow of blood to the brain. Without outside instruction, the body finds ways to regenerate itself. Entities that want to survive find ways to do just that, as well as upgrading their ability to improve.

But not only is the body a self–healing system; each body is also unique. How unique? There are over 106,000 deaths and 2.2 million injuries per year from the side effects of prescription drugs in the United States. Why? Medical scientists have long understood that one type of medicine does not fit all. The same drug that might save one life could also destroy another. By mapping the human genome (the sum of all information in the DNA), biomedical researchers will be able, someday, to predict how a person will respond, individually, to a particular drug, paving the way for customization of medicines. These so-called "designer drugs" will be able to target a specific molecule in the body, to treat a specific condition or disease. It is hoped that eventually, designer drugs will eliminate dangerous side effects.

But the point remains: people are not carbon copies of each other. Despite impressive advances in medicine and biology, science is often at a loss in trying to understand the dynamics of a particular drug. "We really don't understand very much about drugs," remarked Dr. Micheline Piquette–Miller in *MedHunters*. "Most medications are—to put it bluntly—discovered, tested and used essentially by trial and error."[39] In fact, William Osler, often referred to as the father of modern medicine, recognized the inherent uncertainty found in his own discipline back in 1904, arguing that "medicine is a science of uncertainty and an art of probability."

This biological uniqueness points to one significant conclusion: The array of interactive factors causing complexity has a high probability of overwhelming a single–minded command structure. Shoes don't come in one size, because neither do human feet. Staunchly applying one method is unlikely to solve a problem, as there is more than one pathway to a destination. Like the deadly side effects of a particular drug, the probability of hitting the correct biological sequence to improve a particular patient's health may be impossible to calculate. Even with designer drugs, other factors may still allow for side effects, since all information about a particular patient can never be fully known. But command–based structures have neither the mechanism nor the inclination to allow those at the front line to use alternative methods. It is one pathway or none.

Nonlinear systems are embedded with internal controls, although scientists may never be able to uncover all of them. That is because systems under the spell of chaos are so sensitive to measurement that their output appears random. Nonetheless, whether or not all patterns of order will ever be revealed, self–organizing systems will find ways to circumvent or adjust to the duress of outside obtrusions' poking and prodding. And if these reactions create political and economic disruptions, command structures will prey on self–organizing systems as proof that their *raisons d'être* have failed. In economics, this type of calamity is referred to as "market failure."

Market Failure and "Succeeding by Failing"

It is widely believed that command–based structures should intervene when market–based systems do not bring about enough efficiency or equality. Because command structures possess neither of these characteristics, it would seem highly unlikely they could be the entities to spur such activity. So, when markets do fail, there is a good probability that their failure is tied governmental actions fed on a diet low in requirements for success.

In reality, government succeeds by failing: the more incompetence, the greater the potential reward in the arena of the public sector. Success is usually a political liability, since good results equate with unwanted financial repercussions. Those in entrenched bureaucracy realize the difficulty of acquiring more authority and funding, if the political "wars" on drugs, terror, poverty, climate change, disease, and illiteracy actually were to be won. This "must–lose–to–win" mindset is astounding; for political taskmasters, the situation has to get worse before it can get better. The village must be destroyed before it can be saved. The beatings must continue until morale improves. True success is not an option for a system that requires failure in order to thrive. And when considering the properties of power–law distribution, the bigger the entity, the greater the probability that it will become "too big to succeed."

In the mid–1970s, the city of Orange, California, decided to experiment with a program to lower crime. City Hall offered incentives to each policeman if the crime rate were lowered in four categories: burglary, robbery, rape, and auto theft. The deal was simple and unprecedented. For every three percentage points' drop in the crime rate, the officers would get a pay raise of one percent. Enthusiastically, many of the policemen and detectives volunteered their own time to attend civic meetings to instruct citizens on methods to fight crime, for example, how to secure their homes from burglars. The results were stunning. Crime in the four categories went down 17.6 percent.[40]

The program was deemed so successful that it was terminated within a few years. Obviously, if the crime rate continued to plunge, city administrators would be pressured to radically reduce the seemingly unneeded police force and their law–enforcement budget. For a government agency, that is equivalent to suicide. Orange's innovative strategy to deter crime had been an unprecedented success, but such achievements are not the real goal of a job–sensitive bureaucracy. Full employment and job creation always rank higher than efficiency. After all, as a former sheriff of Graham County, Arizona, Richard Mack, once confessed: "Police do very little to prevent violent crime. We in-

Self-Organizing Systems 247

vestigate crime after the fact."[41]

It is not just that policing agencies can't protect the citizenry. Across most localities in United States, the police do not even have a legal obligation to come when someone calls 911 in an emergency. Richard W. Stevens, a Washington, D.C. attorney and author of *Dial 911 and Die*, points out that "the police in most localities owe no legal duty to protect individuals from criminal attack."[42] Because of costly liability lawsuits, most states have legislated "no–duty" laws. For instance, an appellate court in California ruled: "Police officers have no affirmative statutory duty to do anything."[43] In Massachusetts, a statute makes it abundantly clear: "Authorities have no legal responsibility "to provide adequate police protection, prevent the commission of crimes, investigate, detect or solve crimes, identify or apprehend criminals or suspects, arrest or detain suspects, or enforce any law."[44] This is why law enforcement officers often explain to citizens that they are ultimately responsible for their own personal safety.

Command–based systems have few incentives to mitigate failing programs. The chaos arising from political shortcomings presents politicians with a way to abdicate their responsibilities, by saying they never have enough resources to do the job. Simply put, government failure is the perfect storm in which to undermine economic activity, alarm the public, and cry out for more authority and funding.

Government Failure

Failure is unavoidable; it is how we learn. The consequence of failure is an important mechanism, as important as success. It tells us we are doing something wrong, just as success tells us we are doing something right. When markets gyrate and sputter, shifting back and forth in their volatility, looking as though they might collapse, many experts look toward governmental bodies for help as if the latter possessed superhuman powers with which to stabilize the natural force of fluctuations. But what happens when governments themselves fail? After all, they are the highest legal authority. They are supposedly running the show. Perhaps this is what humorist Will Rogers was referring to, when he joked, "Things run in this country in spite of government, not because of it."

Any individual enterprise can get caught in downturns, varying business cycles, and bankruptcy, but the market bazaar remains open and ready for business, every day. Everyone trades to survive: even the Unabomber, a radical neo–Luddite who scratched out a living in a remote cabin, bought merchandise at a local store. People self–organize to optimize what they subjectively consider important in their lives. They know they must correct their habits as conditions change, as would most successful business entrepreneurs. Self–correction is a reality of life. But generally, governmental bodies have few virtuoso performances. As Peter Koslowski, a professor of philosophy at Vrije Universiteit Amsterdam, expressed it, "market failure is correctible, government failure is not."[45]

"Government failure" is more than chronic shortcomings, bad planning, or aggrandized public services minus the promised quality. Command–based systems engage in self–destructive behavior, snatching failure from the jaws of success by relying on gear–grinding linearization and resistance to self–correction. Political systems fail because they are prevented from providing an efficient solution from within their own organizational ranks. They are dysfunctional, weighed under by "bureaucratic management" instead of market–based "profit management," as denoted by Ludwig von Mises in his 1944 book *Bureaucracy*.

One example of government failure was revealed in the unpublished 513–page federal report that highlights the blunders of the American–led reconstruction of Iraq. The 2008 report depicts the botched efforts by the Pentagon planners who became embroiled in "a $100 billion failure by bureaucratic turf wars, spiraling violence and ignorance of the basic elements of Iraqi society and infrastructure."[46] Amazingly, the report acknowledges that government planners "kept inventing numbers" and "put out inflated measures of progress to cover up failures."

Markets can suffer financial calamities, but entrepreneurs worship efficiency, as their accountants scream for profitability. But systems based on coercive practices have a basketful of strategies to misdirect the allocation of goods and resources. For instance, government spending can "crowd out" private spending and prevent the new from rising. In other cases, political systems can engage in "rent seeking," where lobbyist–rich organizations and businesses seek to make money by manipulating the legislative process, rather than by producing goods and services. Or, under "regulatory capture," former industry members appointed to regulatory agencies act to advance commercial or special interests, instead of advancing the public good. This crony capitalism can result in inefficient allocation of goods and resources, while distorting market economics. Efficiency can be completely thrown out the window when an industry is beholden to politicalization, especially when businesses "too big to fail" are bailed out at taxpayers' expense. As Austrian economists have often framed it, inefficiency arises when means are chosen that are inconsistent with desired goals.[47]

In the private sector, markets are frequently not allowed to work. In the public sector, government policies have a built–in bias not to succeed. Usually drenched in red ink, governmental bodies have a propensity to subsidize and bail out "zombie businesses" that barely have a heartbeat. They have neither the disposition nor the incentives to allow for the timeless process of "creative destruction," popularized by Joseph Schumepter in 1942. The theory of creative destruction recognizes that change is the only constant in the universe, and that market economies will naturally remove institutional deadwood, cut it up and rebuild something more innovative and efficient, if allowed. Schumpeter summarized the process as "incessantly destroying the old one, incessantly creating a new one."[48] But governments, by the mere fact of holding the power to tax, cannot go out of business or legally fail, and therefore governments provide those running the state apparatus no incentives to stay financially responsible. Governments are exempt from the ravages of bankruptcy—their machinery always remains intact, whether they are jammed, broken or outdated. Failure is integral to any active system. Like all reproductive organisms, the new will eventually overthrow the old. Yet bureaucratic structures excel at cheating their own death, by preventing others from competing too well.

When Irish banks decided to guarantee every penny of depositors' money during the mortgage meltdown in 2008, European Union "competition authorities" were called in to force them to retreat, since other nations' banks complained bitterly about having to compete, arguing that Ireland's banks were engaging in "unfair practices."[49]

Consider government–provided services that are geared for the community. Many political scientists will justify government's intervention, because of the purported benefits of collective action or because of alleged failures by markets. As the theory goes, services such as law enforcement and national defense must remain the exclusive responsibility of the state, since everybody reaps the benefit, even though some may avoid putting money into the collective kitty. This avoidance is called the "free–rider problem."

But the theory of the free–rider problem misses the mark. Far too often, lawmakers fail to ensure that citizens get the tax–supported public services they had promised. The poor are routinely taken for an expensive ride, paying for government–operated services that are substandard, minimal, or nonexistent. For example, in the slums of Rio de Janeiro, Brazil, the police have been so ineffective and corrupt that they could not provide anything remotely resembling police protection. As in most Third World nations, citizens hesitate to make contact with the police, fearing that they might abuse them with impunity. Even without the corruption factor, Rio slums have been simply too violent for local governments to provide police protection, meaning that only the rich and middle class have access to tax–supported law enforcement.

The poor in Rio had nobody to turn to. Abandoned by the government and desperate to abate violent crime, a bloc of poor neighborhood leaders took a look at the private sector. They pooled resources; agreed to pay monthly fees; and hired for–profit vigilantes from the underground economy. By 2003, not only had the vigilantes evicted the drug gangs, narco–traffickers, and violent lowlifes in 90 of Rio's 600 shantytowns, or favelas, but their success lent credence to the willingness of citizens to pay for collective protection on their own, although not everyone in the community was paying their fair share.

Consisting of former and active police officers, moonlighting prison guards, and off–duty firefighters, these so–called militias radically reduced crime, prompting the endorsement of Mayor Cesar Maia, who labeled them "community self–defense groups." Not to be outdone, a local congresswoman and former chief of intelligence for the state anti–narcotics department, Marina Maggessi, admitted that the militias are "generally welcomed by the community."[50] She acknowledged that "the militias are the security of the poor" but that they also represent the "collapse of the state."

Although some politicians and social critics lambasted the militias for displaying hard–nosed, gang–like traits, the results were stunning. Residents reported that within the militia zones, robberies and muggings became rare; delivery trucks could travel freely, without threats of carjacking; patrons could sip coffee in outdoor cafés without fear of impromptu gun battles; and parents no longer had to shield children from stray bullets hissing overhead.[51] And when drug traffickers were confronted by the small army of beefy–looking men in black dress, carrying machine guns and wearing bulletproof vests, most vanished without firing a shot. What makes this situation even more amazing is that Brazilian drug gangs are notorious for activities beyond just running and selling illegal substances. They have become heavily involved in torture, summary executions, kidnapping, and extortion.

Even Brazilian President Luiz Inácio Lula da Silva did not lash out against the private paramilitary groups when they were started. This gray area has often been tolerated, since authorities understood that government police are unable to protect poor neighborhoods. In a number of incidents, it appeared that some militias have quietly coordinated security projects with the police, mostly in the favelas that border tourist areas. This cooperation is understandable. Brazil has had a thirty–year tradition of employing private guards and companies to protect citizens. For years, the justiceiros, or "justice makers," have protected property and maintained order for a fee, under formal contracts with specific residents and small businessmen, without collecting money from the entire community.

Apparently, the poor in Rio's slums are willing to come together and pay hard–earned money to protect themselves and, inadvertently, some free riders. Although there will always be free–lunch moochers averse to paying their fair share, many more have stepped forward to freely advance the public good. Perhaps such behavior should be viewed as the "responsible resolve rider," when people volunteer to do difficult tasks themselves, thus bettering their own situation, and, ultimately, that of their community.

Actually, this issue confronts all societies: a fear that as people anonymously walk past those in need, not one of them will stop. This unshakable anxiety was captured well by the ancient Babylonian Jewish leader Hillel, who asked, "If not me, then who?" In times of trouble, there is a need for somebody to take responsibility. Fortunately, such apprehension often motivates citizens to make personal sacrifices that can benefit the community at large. After all, this precise situation occurred during the American Revolutionary War. Congress had no authority to tax or conscript, and yet thousands volunteered to fight and fund a war which, from the start, seemed to be a losing cause.

Fractalized Information

Accurate information and feedback are vital to self–organizing systems, but data are neither symmetrical nor stationary. Mark Twain once remarked: "There are three kinds of lies: lies, damned lies, and statistics."[52] This theme has had many variations, some humorous and others dead serious. It is not the numbers, but the people who play with them. If you torture the data long enough, they will confess to anything. But there is a better reason for statistics' poor track record than mere manipulation to fit someone's agenda.

Information is only as good as the relative position it rests upon. Truth is honeycombed with an assortment of contrasting passageways. If two people witness the same car accident, one might see a car deliberately swerving to hit an adjacent vehicle. Clearly, the swerving car is at fault. But the witness on the other side of the street may see the errant car veer to avoid hitting a small child who had just darted into the street—same event, different perspectives. Both are telling the truth as to what they saw, relative to their position in the event.

Beyond common misinterpretation and biased reporting, information distributed by the media is usually superficial and limited. Compare newspaper accounts of a news event to television accounts of the same event. Newspapers have greater space to report and analyze a story, while the electronic media broadcast in thirty–second sound bites. Still, most of the information on any given incident remains unreported. Only the highlights are given. But what about the less important details? Could they tell a completely different story?

In a sense, information is "fractalized." Just like the fractional dimensionality found in Mandelbrot's fractals, information can be broken down into more and more complexity of detail, compressed to a point of infinite scalability—from the general, overall view, to the most specific. Because fractals are not purely symmetrical—their borders can be as vague as those of a flame—they can be either mirrored or asymmetrical. This fuzziness is due to the nature of randomness, which can occur at every level. Such a condition would explain the contradictory nature of information and why it can accommodate opposite eyewitness accounts of the same event. Information's complexity, infinite levels, and lack of completeness make inconsistencies commonplace. Further, the more precise the information, the more complex and confusing the subject can become. On the other hand, the more general the information, the more chance the accuracy will be diminished.

When President George W. Bush boarded the U.S.S. Abraham Lincoln in 2003, he gave a speech while standing beneath a large banner proclaiming "Mission Accomplished." The world press assumed that the White House was now declaring an end to hostilities in the second Gulf War. Of course, the violence in Iraq was continuing. To many observers, this was another idiotic, contradictory statement out of the White House. But when questioned, the White House disavowed any connection to the banner. The crew had apparently created the "Mission Accomplished" banner on their own, signaling their return to home port with another assignment completed. The news story eventually faded away.

Six months later, the White House revised their story and said that there was a small link to the crew's banner. The White House had helped the seamen get the banner printed. Some argued that ingenious advance men from the president's staff must have had a hand in the slogan after all. Again, Bush disagreed, saying "they weren't that ingenious."[53]

The truth may never be known under the political realm of spin–doctoring and spirited rounds of blame–game name–calling, but the very nature of information lends it to an inexhaustible supply of contradictions.

Even in the case of hard statistics, the numbers may be completely irrelevant to the actual situation. Like the cry of Don Quixote in *Man of La Mancha*, "facts" can be "the enemy of truth." As an illustration, residents of a mid–sized Midwest town awoke one morning in the late 1980s to discover in their morning newspaper that they had a higher crime rate than the crime–infested capital of the world, New York City. Confounded, city officials pored over the FBI's numbers and reluctantly agreed that their peaceful town must be a criminal haven. And yet, by all other accounts, the town was law–abiding. Were the numbers wrong? Or was there another explanation?

Unbeknownst to the residents, the crime statistics had one major flaw: they were only as good as the facts gathered. Citizens in high–crime areas notoriously fail to report criminal wrongdoings. Peaking in 1988, New York City's crime rate had overwhelmed the police, to the point where they barely had time to write their reports, let alone solve the crimes. Because the probability of catching any particular criminal was extremely low, many crimes went unreported. In smaller, more law–abiding towns, a much higher proportion of crimes are reported and eventually solved. There is no way for crime statistics to reflect this anomaly.

Another area in which numbers become almost meaningless is a nation's level of taxation. Europeans have often accused United States citizens of being undertaxed. On paper, the numbers look convincing. In the 1970s, Europe's maximum marginal tax rate for individual income hovered in the 60 percent range, with spectacularly high tax rates of 87 percent in Sweden and 83 percent in the United Kingdom. However, by the early twenty–first century, the average percent had been reduced to the low 50s. Meanwhile, the United States' maximum marginal tax rate was 33 percent in 1990, and 35 percent in 2005. If one were to go strictly by the numbers, it would appear that U.S. citizens are indeed undertaxed and sitting on oodles of cash. Case closed.

However, the official tax data tell only one side of a story. What about other variables looming under the radar? What about the legendary underground, informal economy? Over 500 million people worldwide—over a quarter of the world's workforce—work in the informal economy. Although actual figures are difficult to approximate, a number of studies have pegged the unofficial economy of Italy at 26.2 percent of gross domestic product (GDP), and of Greece at 28.3 percent of GDP in 2002–2003. Not only that, but according to the International Monetary Fund, up to 48 percent of the Italian workforce is "engaged in shadow economy activities"—which alone could account for 27 percent of Italy's GDP. In reality, the real numbers could be far higher. Nobody really knows.

In sharp contrast, U.S. citizens are far less prone to be involved in the off–the–books, underground economy, estimated at 8.6 percent in 2002–2003.[54]

The underground economy presents policymakers with a huge handicap. How can anyone direct a nation's economy without accurate data? Far too often, authorities make wild guesses based on information they had believed to be solid, resulting in poor policies that worsen the problems they had originally sought to solve. Information is fractalized, extremely complex, and riddled with unpredictable, emergent properties. When viewing data generated by central authorities, one must always take the skeptical view that the numbers may be more in focus with a particular political agenda than with the goal of providing an accurate snapshot of reality.

* * * * *

Complexity science is beginning to take center stage in how scientists analyze the world's economic, social, and political challenges. As technology grows, this new science will flourish, providing more penetrating insights into a universe ready to astound us with each new, unexpected step.

1 M. Michael Waldrop, *Complexity: The Emerging Science at the Edge of Order and Chaos*, New York: Simon & Schuster, 1992.

2 Kevin K. Dooley, "A nominal definition of complex adaptive systems," *The Chaos Network*, 8(1): 2-3, 1996, posted on Dooley's web site: http://www.public.asu.edu/~kdooley/papers/casdef.PDF

3 Nicholas Dawidoff, "The Civil Heretic," *The New York Times*, March 29, 2009.

4 Hayek's lecture to the memory of Alfred Nobel, December 11, 1974.

5 Both Gordon Tullock and James M. Buchanan, co-authors of *The Calculus of Consent* (1962), are considered the main founders of public choice theory, which is based on methodological individualism.

6 Hayek, Ibid.

7 J. L. Casti. *Complexification: Explaining a Paradoxical World Through the Science of Surprise*, London: Abacus, 1994.

8 Ioannis D. Katerelos and Andreas G. Koulouris, "Seeking Equilibrium Leads to Chaos: Multiple Equilibria Regulation Models," *Journal of Artificial Societies and Social Simulation*, Vol. 7, No. 2 (March 31, 2004).

9 Ludwig von Mises, *Human Action*, 3rd ed., Chicago: Henry Regnery Company, 1966, p. 351.

10 Edmund L. Andrews, "The Greenspan Effect: The Doctrine Was Not to Have One," *New York Times*, Aug. 26, 2005.

11 Ibid., Edmund L. Andrews.

12 Edmund L. Andrews, "News Analysis: 'Maestro' Is Leaving a Stellar Record But Murky Legacy," *New York Times*, Aug. 27, 2005.

13 *The Daily Show with Jon Stewart*, broadcast Sept. 18, 2007.

14 W. Brian Arthur, "Out-of-Equilibrium Economics and Agent-Based Modeling," Chapter 32, Amsterdam, The Netherlands: North-Holland, imprint of Elsevier, 2006, pp. 1551-1564, published in the *Handbook of Computational Economics: Agent-Based Computational Economics*, Vol. 2, editors: Leigh Tesfatsion and Kenneth L. Judd.

15 Paul Ormerod, *Butterfly Economics: A New General Theory of Social and Economic Behavior*, New York: Basic Books, 2001.

16 Ibid.

17 Michael Rothschild, *Bionomics: Economy as Business Ecosystem*, Frederick, Maryland: Beard Books, 1990, p. xi.

18 Charles C. Mann, "The Founding Sachems," *New York Times*, July 4, 2005.

19 Murray Rothbard, "The Origins of Individualist Anarchism in America," *Libertarian Analysis*, Winter 1970, Vol. 1, No. 1, pp. 14–28. More detailed information can be found about this time period in Rothbard's 4-volume history of Colonial America, *Conceived in Liberty*.

20 Murray Rothbard, "The Origins of Individual Anarchism in America," *Libertarian Analysis*, Vol. 1, No. 1 (Winter 1970), 14-28.

21 Michael D. Coogan, editor, *The Oxford History of the Biblical World*, New York: Oxford University Press, paperback, page 143, 2001.
22 Roderick T. Long, "Why Objective Law Requires Anarchy," *Formulations*, Autumn 1998.
23 Peter Leeson, *The Invisible Hook: The Hidden Economics of Pirates*, Princeton, NJ: Princeton University Press, 2009.
24 Bruce L. Benson, *The Enterprise of Law: Justice Without the State*, San Francisco, CA: Pacific Research Institute, 1990.
25 Peter T. Leeson, "Better Off Stateless: Somalia Before and After Government Collapse," *Journal of Comparative Economics*, Vol. 35, No. 4, 2007. Retrieved from www.PeterLeeson.com/Better_Off_Stateless.pdf
26 World Bank Advisory Committee for Somalia Country Re-Engagement Note, 2003.
27 The Somali Democratic Republic, U.N. Office for the Coordination of Humanitarian Affairs.
28 Noel Ihebuzor, "EC and UNICEF join hands to support education in Somalia," United Nations Children's Fund (UNICEF). Jan. 1, 2005.
29 "Somalia Calling: An Unlikely Success Story," *The Economist*, Dec. 20, 2005.
30 Benjamin Powell, "Somalia After State Collapse: Chaos or Improvement?" Independent Institute, policy number 64, Nov. 30, 2006.
31 Michael van Notten, (editor: Spencer Heath MacCallum), *The Law of the Somalis: A Stable Foundation for Economic Development in the Horn of Africa*, Lawrenceville, NJ: The Red Sea Press, Inc., 2005.
32 Finley Allison Hooper, *Roman Realities*, Detroit, Michigan: Wayne State University Press, 1979), p. 176.
33 Quote by Thomas Jefferson, letter to Colonel Carrington, May 27, 1788.
34 Len De Caux, *Labor Radical: From the Wobblies to the CIO* (Boston: Beacon Press, 1970), p. 145; original source: "Labor Leader Out for the Open Shop; Un–American to Force Workers Into the Union, Says President Stone of the Engineers," *New York Times*, April 7, 1910.
35 "After 18 Months, Carpenters Union Picketers Are No More," *The Carmel Pine Cone*, Feb. 16, 2007, page 4A.
36 Bruce Bartlett, "How Excessive Government Killed Ancient Rome," *The Cato Journal*, Fall 1994.
37 Roderick T. Long, "The Athenian Constitution: Government by Jury and Referendum," issue of *Formulations*—Libertarian Nation Foundation, Autumn 1996.
38 David R. Henderson, "German Economic Miracle," *The Concise Encyclopedia of Economics*, Indianapolis, IN.: Liberty Fund, Inc., 2002.
39 Michael Smith, "En Route to Designer Drugs? - Medhunters Medical Community," *MedHunters*, Spring 2002.
40 National Center for Policy Analysis, "Using the Private Sector to Deter Crime," March 1994.

41 Richard W. Stevens, "Just Dial 911? The Myth of Police Protection," *The Freeman: Ideas on Liberty*, April 2000.
42 Richard W. Stevens, *Dial 911 and Die*, Hartford, Wisconsin: Mazel Freedom Press, 1999.
43 *Souza v. City of Antioch*, 62 California Reporter, 2d 909, 916 (Cal. App. 1997).
44 Massachusetts General Laws Ann. Ch. 258 § 10(h).
45 Peter Koslowski, "Editor's Introduction," *Individual Liberty and Democratic Decision-Making: The ethics, economics, and politics of democracy, Germany*, J.C.B. Mohr (Paul Siebeck), 1987, p. 3.
46 James Glanz and Christian T. Miller, "Official History Spotlights Iraq Rebuilding Blunders, *New York Times*, Dec. 12, 2008.
47 Roy E. Cordato, "The Austrian Theory of Efficiency and the Role of Government," *The Journal of Libertarian Studies*, 4 (4), 393-403, 1980.
48 Joseph A. Schumpeter, *Capitalism, Socialism, and Democracy*. 3d ed. 1942. New York: Harper and Brothers, 1950, p. 83.
49 Shawn Pogatchnik, "Ireland Bank Guarantee Under Fire," *Monterey Herald*—Associated Press, Oct. 2, 2008.
50 Luke McLeod-Roberts, "Paramilitary Games," *NaclaNews*, July 10, 2007.
51 Peter Muello, "Militias clean up Rio slums," *Miami Herald,* posted April 30, 2007.
52 Mark Twain attributed this saying to Benjamin Disraeli.
53 Jarret Murphy, "'Mission Accomplished' Whodunit," *CBS News*, Oct. 29, 2003.
54 Friedrich Schneider and Roberto Dell' Anno, "The Shadow Economy of Italy and other OEDC Countries: What do we Know," *Journal of Public Finance and Public Choice*, Vol. 21, 2003.

10 Swarm Intelligence and Dynamics

... although the swarm of ants seems organized and directed, its morphology depends not on leadership but on the individual behaviors of the ants, often with little communication among them. —Jon Gerhart and Marc Kirschner, Cells, Embryos, and Evolution

Intelligences take many forms, but the particular ways in which social animals—ants, bees, wasps, termites, birds, fish, and so forth—network into highly coordinated units without supervision has always mystified and fascinated scientists. As it turns out, the unfolding patterns of insect and bird behavior have provided far greater scientific insights than a mere collection of dead bugs in a display case could.

Despite their interest in the behavior of insects, early researchers were not too keen on studying the bugs up close. So when scientists grudgingly pulled out their magnifying glasses to scrutinize the world of "swarmettes," it was to improve the properties of artificial intelligence. Originated in 1989 by Gerardo Beni, Suzanne Hackwood, and Jin Wang, the field of *swarm intelligence* sought to study self–organizing agents in cellular robotic systems. The objective was to design unintelligent robots capable of performing intelligent tasks, inside swarmlike groups. The discipline soon gained popularity and became an integral part of complexity science.

Eventually, swarm researchers took a serious look at the creatures they were trying to emulate. They found that the science of swarm intelligence offered a powerful computational methodology, something that could compare the actions of animals, humans, and robots to how decentralized, self–organizing structures emerge. For instance, computer models based on swarm dynamics have predicted the behavior of vehicular traffic and the movement of pedestrians on streets by looking at how army ants conduct raids. Similar studies showed how communal goals are achieved by purely decentralized means, where dumb individuals cooperate to accomplish complex, difficult tasks. In other cases, scientists had found that swarms engage in "stigmergic assemblies," a condition in which participants communicate with each other mostly by indirect means. Swarm intelligence was getting complicated.

Complexity with No Central Processor

The pressing question for early chaologists was obvious: How could mind–numbing complexity arise from social species imprisoned by limited intelligence and capabilities? After all, insects are barely conscious. Jesper Hoffmeyer, a biosemiotic researcher at the University of Copenhagen, broached this subject when he examined the swarmlike behavior of cells and tissues in the human body. He drew parallels between the intelligence manifesting itself in insect swarms and the cognitive workings of the human mind. Defining swarm intelligence as a "distributed problem–solving capacity," Hoffmeyer entertained the idea that, when it comes to intelligence, the brain works like a "swarm of swarms" that overlaps within a "hierarchy of swarms," sometimes likened to a "floating brain." In this way, swarm dynamics might help solve what Hoffmeyer calls the "ever–returning homunculus problem," which holds that "there seems to be nobody—no homunculus—inside our brain who does the thinking, there just is no central processor to control the activities of the mind."[1]

If, as biologists claim, the human brain has no central processor, then what is controlling what? Could swarm entities, in a sort of networked–mind intelligence, be setting all the rules? Could higher order emerge from mindless voids—similar to how evolutionary processes might operate? These questions elevated the importance of swarm dynamics, putting it on the front burner. Most researchers now subscribe to the theory that the aggregate actions of dumb ants responding to local stimuli lead to completion of complex tasks, making many human endeavors appear almost simple–minded. Christian Jacobs, associate professor of Bioinformatics at the University of Calgary, Canada, detected an impressive decentralized intelligence within swarms. He wrote: "For some types of applications, a collection of small, simple agents with limited intelligence, local decision–making capability, and a communication path to nearby peers can outperform a large centralized processor."[2]

One scientist who believes that humans could learn a thing or two from biologically inspired systems is Eric Bonabeau. In his judgment, swarm intelligence is an evocative modeling tool that could help human beings better organize themselves and society—which could help in developing optimization algorithms and problem–solving methods. A theoretical physicist from Paris–Sud University in France and author of *Swarm Intelligence: From Natural to Artificial Systems*, Bonabeau became obsessed with complexity theory and adaptive problem solving by watching insect colonies in the Rocky Mountains. From those observations, he came to the conclusion that "swarm intelligence offers an alternative way of designing 'intelligent' systems in which autonomy, emergence, and distributedness replace control, preprogramming, and centralization."[3]

In a 2003 interview, Bonabeau was unabashed about what he had observed. He had noticed that concentration of authority is a poor organizational technique. He commented: "Human beings suffer from a 'centralized mindset'; they would like to assign the coordination of activities to a central command."[4] Bonabeau contended that simple systems can reach high levels of complexity without taking big, deliberate steps.

Like genes, social animals do not respond consciously. And yet, the ant colonies Bonabeau had scrutinized operated seamlessly and efficiently with no central command whatsoever. "There's no individual in charge," explained Bonabeau. There's no top–down supervision. Yet these insect colonies have arranged coordinated activities of extraordinary achievement, which also serves the best interest of their whole community.

So the next question becomes this: How do dumb units—in this case, bees and ants—respond so quickly, accurately, and uniformly? For many researchers, this is where dumbness becomes an advantage. Lower life forms are too simple–minded to alter reality toward a particular bias. In sharp contrast, human behavior is more complex—the smarter the person, the greater the temptation to lie and cheat in order to achieve imagined goals.

The dumbness–versus–high–intelligence disparity cannot be overstated. Dumbness prevents social insects from distorting reality; they are too dumb to deliberately lie. In contrast, humans are too smart not to. Since human intelligence is based on abstract thought, this mental capability allows people to reshape reality. This gives humans the ability to rationalize and theorize in which ways to disregard the truth, imaging reality not as it is but as it should or could be.

Socially organized insects (eusociality) don't have the intelligence to make up falsehoods. They all witness what is actually happening, which allows a colony instantly to react as one. In their world, truth has no agenda, but for highly evolved life forms, agendas are geared to override the truth.

But could the principles of swarm dynamics work in human society? Kevin Kelly, the founding executive editor of *Wired* magazine and an expert on the digital culture, has given a high–five affirmation. In *New Rules for the New Economy*, Kelly went to great lengths to exhibit the incredible nature and accomplishments of swarms. First he jumped on the self–organization bandwagon and stated, "Dumb parts, properly connected into a swarm, yield better results."[5] Next he equated unintelligent computer chips and personal computers with the hive–mind intelligence that has been so successful with networked systems, suggesting that the "surest way to smartness is through massive dumbness."[6]

As a concrete example, he pointed to the human body, where dumb cells swarm together to propagate a smart immune system—still somewhat of a mystery to medical doctors. Obviously, swarm intelligence has established the fact that individual parts do not need to be sophisticated for their system to work well. But Kelly envisions a worldwide interconnectivity of cooperation that will liberate mankind by creating a real–time networked society.

Given recent advances in wireless technology and real–time GPS location signals, Kelly predicted a well–connected and coordinated society, robust in prosperity, attributable to the wonders of swarm dynamics and unguided learning. Examples of wide–ranging applications are everywhere. For instance, robotic arms at a GM auto–paint factory in Fort Wayne, Indiana, operating independently with tiny brainlets, beckon unpainted cars to come to their station if they need a particular color, saving time and money. The robots effect their own scheduling, without a central system telling them what to do. Japan uses the same, decentralized, mini–brain swarming system to schedule its famous, high–speed, bullet trains. Other applications include routing optimization, traffic signal control systems, communication networks, simulated crowd scenes in animated movies, military applications for controlling unmanned vehicles, optimizing shipping schedules, Particle Swarm Optimization (PSO) algorithms, NASA's planetary mapping, and possible methods for medical "nanobots" to seek out and destroy cancer cells.

Now consider an even more intriguing finding. At the University of Florida in 2004, researcher Thomas DeMarse put together a collection of 25,000 living rat neurons, or nerve cells, inside a glass dish, and tried an experiment

Swarm Intelligence and Dynamics 263

to produce a sort of "living computer." The experiment was originally set up to study neural disorders, such as epilepsy, but instead, DeMarse arranged 60 electrodes in a grid to see whether this experimental brain could fly a simulated F–22 fighter jet. Amazingly, it could—and did.

The team of researchers discovered that the cortical neurons were self–organizing and connecting inside the glass dish, creating a living neural network. Next, through a specially designed multielectrode array, DeMarse was able to communicate with the living network. At first, the cluster of neurons made the aircraft drift randomly, but eventually modified the use of the data and gradually learned how to operate the aircraft. The maneuvering was limited, basically controlling the pitch and roll of the simulated flight. But DeMarse's experiment with neural cooperation showed how swarm dynamics operates on the micro level.[7]

Medical scientists have realized that both chaos and swarmlike dynamics can drive the human brain. In a revealing article in *New Science*, David Robson concluded that "Disorder is essential to the brain's ability to transmit information and solve problems."[8]

A number of neuroscientists now recognize that near–chaotic states are vital to how the brain stores memory. Although the brain mostly appears orderly, it can unpredictably lurch "into a blizzard of noise." And it is this swarm of disorder perched on the edge of chaos that is responsible for sparking man's intelligence.

Researchers point to a clustering effect known as *self–organized criticality*, which somehow activates spontaneous avalanches of instability in a healthy brain. But nobody can figure out how the brain reaches its critical tipping point, where order bursts into chaos. Scientists did discover that collapse of order is tied to the power law of distribution—which says that bigger avalanches happen less often than smaller avalanches." Yet the triggering device for the neural avalanche remained elusive.

When computational models were applied to mimic the brain under early theories of chaos, researchers were unable to imitate the behavior of the brain. Something was missing.

The problem lay with chaos theory itself. In the1980s, most chaologists were convinced that dynamic, nonlinear systems were simply hiding order from within—"deterministic chaos." Most systems were not viewed as being dependent on randomness. Rather, complexity was seen as too deeply elaborate to understand, at the moment. But that mindset changed by the 1990s, when scientists discovered that the brain generates random "noise." This fact alone made researchers realize that the brain depends on random fluctuations, meaning that the brain's network of neurons requires both "stable phase–lock states and the unstable phase–shifting states." In fact, there appears to be higher intelligence among brains that spend a good deal of time in a balancing act at the edge of chaos.

In this sense, the human brain represents the emergence of collective intelligence, with dumb neurons and synapses swarming in self–organizing clusters, to create intelligence.

Swarming Birds of Precision

Insect–based modeling is not the only area of study for swarm intelligence. The mysterious behavior of flocking birds baffled researchers for years. Without verbal communication, flocks were accomplishing feats of aerodynamic magic that would put the U.S. Navy's Blue Angels to shame. When ornithologists couldn't explain this phenomenon, physicists took over and examined the problem through the lens of chaology.

At first, the problem seemed unsolvable. How could hundreds of birds move harmoniously, without apparent leadership or external cue? How could these small–brained, unsophisticated animals create such wonderful, swirling patterns of complexity? For a time, it was thought that birds must somehow possess high intelligence, to be able to flock with such seamless, precise formations. Was there a rigorous hierarchy to the dynamics of flocking? Could there have been an alpha bird commanding the flock? And, even more bewildering, how could birds flying randomly suddenly join together and transform into a tightly unified group without sophisticated means of communication? Such capabilities would suggest higher cognitive abilities in an animal that has been the source of such pejorative terms as "birdbrain." So the mystery thickened. Somehow, hundreds of airborne units would move in precise formation without a stringent, top–down organization. How?

John Toner and Tu Yuhai came to the rescue. In their article "Flocks, Herds, and Schools: A Quantitative Theory of Flocking,"[9] they shared their finding of a simple system which explains this phenomenon. According to Toner and Yuhai, birds need only to maintain an approximate distance between each other and follow along in an "average" direction. With their natural nimbleness and ability to adapt instantly to change, birds create complex behavior from simple rules.

But then another, seemingly insurmountable problem arose. What about errors of judgment by an individual bird? It was discovered that certain birds would frequently swerve away from the flock. In theory, such misjudgments would cause the flock to become disoriented and take off in all directions, but they didn't. What is their secret?

When Tonner and Yuhai applied the principles of fluid behavior to swarm intelligence, they discovered something wondrous. The birds' delicate balancing act, the way they continuously compensate for errors, was vital. "This process actually helps keep these misjudgments under control," wrote Tonner and Yuhai, "by quickly spreading the error among many birds so that it became very diluted."

This "sharing of error" seemed to be a major factor of self–organizing systems. The state of nature being imperfect, it is routine for individual units in any group to commit errors and misjudgments. But it appears that self–organization feeds on error. The process of trial and error provides the major component, whereas the individual self–correcting mechanism helps maintain the flock's direction, which is vital in preventing it from disintegrating into inert uniformity of entropy. This self–correcting mechanism is profound. Paradoxically, errors and self–correcting processes provide balance, and keep the group unified and coordinated.

Errors, Choice, and Randomness

Apparently, errors are not as bad as one might think. Biologists have discovered that when honeybees do their "waggle dance," a coded message to guide other bees to new sources of food, approximately five to ten percent of the bees misinterpret the message. When they fly out to find the food site, they become lost. But this is a blessing in disguise. According to experts, if this sort of error did not occur, the bees would starve. Because of an error in direction, the errant bees will explore new areas, resulting in a continuous stream of new pollen supplies. In the long run, the foraging error is not only an advantage, but is in fact necessary to the system.

Some might refer to errors as simply a matter of choice. For all we know, the miscalculating bees have simply disagreed with the waggle dancers, and decided to look in another direction, hoping for a better supply of pollen. Then again, if "choice" is too strong a word, perhaps those confused honeybees are simply exhibiting randomness. The probability is that at any given time, somebody somewhere will make mistakes.

But Eric Bonabeau saw the accidents of error as creating a sort of resiliency, ensuring the colony's survival. He suggested that "in social insects, errors and randomness are not 'bugs'; rather, they contribute very strongly to their success by enabling them to discover and explore in addition to exploiting. Self–organization feeds itself upon errors to provide the colony with flexibility (the colony can adapt to a changing environment) and robustness (even when one or more individuals fail, the group can still perform its tasks)."

Accidents, errors, and failures have graced the scientific annals with great discoveries. Penicillin came to light through a series of mishaps. The right type of mold spore just happened to land on an exposed bacterial culture dish that should have been sealed. And just by chance, Alexander Fleming, a British bacteriologist, was preparing to wash a sink full of Petri dishes when he noticed that one dish showed a clear zone where the bacteria's growth had been thwarted.

Self–Organization versus Compulsion

Political systems predicated on external control are the antithesis of self–organizing groups and communities. With few exceptions, command–and–control structures are built on the backs of self–organizing systems. Envious of the resources, manpower, and goodwill of such systems, compulsionists insidiously invade them, seeking to assimilate as many self–assembled systems as possible into their strait–laced, vertical collective. Armed with legal violence, these predators bind self–assembled systems to highly centralized structures, resulting in the same debilitation that the American Indians suffered, when the U.S. government made tribal members dependent on welfare handouts.

Armed with a Hobbesian view of society, political gatekeepers see the world as a "war of all against all," a struggle where controls supersede co-operation; compulsion overrides accountability; and expediency obstructs integrity. And when confronted with overwhelming complexity, these statists systems often find themselves in crisis mode, unwilling to set free the flexibility required to compensate for any self–made errors and misjudgments. In fact, many nations are so dysfunctional that they can't even perform the most basic tasks. According to the 2007 Failed States Index put out by the Fund for Peace, governments in 129 countries are at, or are approaching, the brink of collapse.[10]

Illustrating how out of touch with reality governmental systems can become, in 2007 the Chinese government officially "banned Buddhist monks in

Tibet from reincarnating without government permission."[11] Not to be outdone, Saudi Arabian authorities have banned the celebration of Valentine's Day. The religious police, the *muttawa*, will routinely confiscate any clothing, bags, pen holders, ribbons, or flowers colored in red during the holiday. Red roses and heart–shaped symbols are considered particularly offensive.[12]

Big Things Fail in a Big Way

In swarm intelligence of birds, the whole flock is involved in determining its direction. This "collective feedback" system — a sort of causality loop — allows each bird to feel the movement of the others. This situation provides instant, real–time response, since there are no layers of hierarchy to impede the process. Such horizontal, free — flowing, ad hoc mobility provides the nesting influence for collective grouping, without the group getting bogged down in a structural morass. The reasons are clearly exposed in swarm dynamics. Individual swarming agents must be unlimited in their ability to move, explore, and evolve. This anarchy of movement seems to empower the individual while, somewhat counterintuitively, serving as a catalyst for a sense of community. Any other way would lead to a vertical structure of deadweight loss for both individual agents and the community.

In sharp contrast, command–based systems have limited feedback and long response times. In fact, it appears that the larger the hierarchy, the less accurate the feedback and the slower the response time, and, therefore, the larger the error. The reasons are not difficult to understand. Command structures have an almost unnatural penchant to compartmentalize their fiefdom; that penchant can bolster a seemingly planned chaos. If these linear systems don't ignore unpleasant feedback, they will at least rework and spin–doctor it, to fit an exclusive political agenda. In other cases, the relevant feedback will be ignored because nobody realizes its importance at the time.

If a command–based structure needs to react to a situation, often its own hierarchy becomes a major obstruction in solving the crisis. Because of the thick layers of scaling structures, the response will not spread out evenly in a prompt manner. Rather, the reply will be routed through a series of predetermined channels, for the appropriate departments to process. As the reply moves down the ladders of command, it becomes compromised, distorted, and altered, and may no longer be the correct information or proper response. Not only have the data been corrupted by the process, but also the final decision takes far too long to carry out. And when the time comes to play the "blame game," the tendency is to find vulnerable links in the chain of command and castigate them as the underlying screw–ups. The incompetent system rarely feels the political heat, except when criticized for not having enough funding, as if increased revenues would make a large, bureaucratic system more proficient.

Poor decision making is another attribute of command–based systems. The probability that the right decision will be made at the right time is statistically low. With many options available but only one taken, the decision will likely be wrong. However, if by some miracle the appropriate decision is made, it will probably be too late to prevent a disastrous situation from mushrooming. Whatever decision is made, it will fail to anticipate fast–changing circumstances, and could itself become the major impediment to fixing the problem. It all adds up to one fact: Big things fail in a big way.

One of the biggest agencies in the federal government is the Department of Homeland Security, with an annual budget of $40 billion in 2005. After the attack on New York's Twin Towers, it folded together some 23 government agencies comprising over 181,000 employees. The Federal Emergency Management Agency (FEMA) resides under Homeland Security's wing, and was the agency responsible for coordinating emergency operations during 2005's Hurricane Katrina, which flooded 80 percent of New Orleans. As the floodwaters receded, FEMA discovered that it had more than its share of troubled waters.

From the outset, Katrina promised to be more of a human disaster than a natural one. As the Category 3 hurricane swirled to the north, it became apparent that New Orleans was sinking deeper into a bureaucratic quagmire. Despite claims of slow response, interagency power struggles, and misallocation of resources, the problem was far more basic: The system that the public had come to rely upon to save them in an hour of need simply did not work, nor could it ever. As in past natural disasters, victims were treated like cattle.

The first hint of trouble occurred the morning after the hurricane hit, when the Red Cross and other private relief agencies tried to rush into the city with supply trucks. They ran up against an impregnable wall of red tape. Incredibly, they were barred from entering the city by orders of the Louisiana governor's Office of Homeland Security. The government agency determined that relief supplies would act as a magnet and attract more evacuees to the already overcrowded Superdome— even though that is where officials had told residents to gather— well before the storm made landfall. Meanwhile, ironically, the mayor of New Orleans, Ray Nagin, was pleading across national airwaves for more food and water for his trapped citizens.

Failing to have expected the unexpected, Louisiana's Homeland Security Office erroneously thought that plenty of buses would be supplied to take everyone out in short order. None came however until the fifth day and most stood idle in city parking lots. Until then, the refugees at the Superdome and the Convention Center had to endure repeated promises of buses and supplies, giving them a false sense of hope.[13]

While disorder and violence ran amok inside the Superdome, National Guardsmen were stationed outside to prevent refugees from leaving. In fact, a number of citizens who tried to escape were chased down and dragged back into what one witness called "a hellhole."

The most astounding case of incompetence involved a 500–boat flotilla carrying 1,000 volunteers who had come from Acadiana Mall in Lafayette, expecting to rescue stranded doctors, nurses, and hospital patients in New Orleans. The flotilla of fishermen, private boaters, hunters, and others was blocked by the Louisiana Department of Wildlife and Fisheries, under the control of FEMA. The rescuers were ordered out, and told to go home.[14]

Meanwhile, over 1,000 people were still trapped inside Charity Hospital, with few medical supplies and no diesel fuel with which to run the generators. Despite the growing crisis and urgency, Dwight Landreneau, the head of Louisiana's Department of Wildlife and Fisheries, announced that the authorities had things under control, and that citizens' help was not needed. After two frustrating days, airboaters were finally allowed to conduct "renegade" boat rescues, thanks to the influence of Governor Kathleen Blanco.[15]

Consider the case of privately operated Acadian Ambulance Company. According to a *New York Times* story, "While Louisiana officials debated how to accept outside help, Acadian was directing rescues by helicopters from the military and other states." But when the company organized an evacuation plan, to fly critically ill patients from stranded New Orleans hospitals to the airport and to provide outside doctors and nurses to treat them, FEMA officials stopped them cold. Acadian had ten helicopters on the ground, waiting to bring the evacuees out from the flooded city, but the company was being stonewalled with paperwork. Finally the FEMA people said that the doctors and nurses weren't "certified members of a National Disaster Medical Team." FEMA officials kept repeating: "You're not federalized."[16]

In stark contrast, people in the French Quarter had no illusion that government help would arrive anytime soon. Feeling abandoned, citizens in this above–sea–level neighborhood decided not to wait to be rescued. They organized, and divided up chores. Some did the washing down at the river; others stayed behind to prevent looting. A number of bars, including the famous Johnny White's Sports Bar, remained open day and night. People manning these little command posts handed out water food, and medical services, a far cry from the squalor and death at the government–sponsored emergency shelters.[17]

In other nearby cities, citizens found ways to organize themselves, too. When the city–run health clinic failed to reopen in Algiers, just across the Mississippi River from New Orleans, citizens became tired of waiting and decided to do something themselves. They opened their own health clinic and a food distribution center. One frustrated community organizer commented, "If you wait on the government, you won't get nothing."[18]

Even Walmart provided relief, days before the Federal Emergency Management Agency (FEMA) got into the act. Years earlier, the company had set up its own emergency operations center for national disasters. After Katrina struck, area stores gave out tons of free merchandise: chain saws, boots, clothing, water, and ice. As one stunned shopper remarked, "I still haven't managed to get through to FEMA. It's hard to say, but you get more justice at Walmart."[19]

When the donations were tallied, Walmart had distributed $20 million in cash with 1,500 truckloads of free merchandise and enough food for 100,000 meals. In fact, at Walmart's Brookhaven, Mississippi, distribution center, the company had already loaded 45 trucks full of relief supplies before the hurricane made landfall.[20]

It would seem reasonable to assume that large, well–funded centralizing systems would pool vital information and act on it immediately. This is the widely accepted hallmark of centralization: that such systems can disseminate vast quantities of reliable data and pinpoint where to direct resources—a sort of economy of scale. It should work almost flawlessly. But again, centralizers usually dictate which information gets disseminated, and that may not always coincide with the thorny reality.

Despite extensive, round–the–clock coverage by television networks and newspapers showing desperate pleas from starving and thirsty crowds at the Superdome and Convention Center since Monday, August 29, FEMA Director Michael Brown admitted to CNN–TV that "federal officials were unaware of the crowds at the Convention Center until Thursday."[21]

Embarrassing questions haunted the disaster scene. For instance, why did police and 400–500 National Guard troops at the Superdome fail to organize citizens into work details, as volunteers had done in the French Quarter? Why did the troops fail to take the initiative once communications had been lost? And why were two U.S. Navy pilots "counseled" for having rescued 110 New Orleans hurricane victims? Although the military said the pilots were not officially reprimanded, one of the H–3 pilots was temporarily assigned to oversee a kennel. U.S. Senator Pat Roberts from Kansas was so concerned about the pilots' future military careers, that he wrote directly to U.S. Secretary of Defense, Donald Rumsfeld, on their behalf.[22]

What atrocity had the Navy pilots committed? They had taken the initiative. After delivering supplies to the Stennis Space Center, a federal facility in Mississippi, the day after the hurricane made landfall, the helicopter's crew picked up a radio message from the Coast Guard. The transmission pleaded for assistance to rescue marooned victims on the roofs of flooded homes. Out of range of radio contact with their Pensacola, Florida base, the pilots decided to respond to the distress call.

"Shocked" to see almost no rescue units in the flooded city, they lowered baskets to bring aboard two victims at a time. One of the pilots, Lieutenant Matt Udkow, said that the toughest part was watching so many people implore him to rescue them, but having to leave many behind.

Returning to base, the pilots thought they would be treated like heroes, but instead they were chided for having broken orders. They had failed to get permission to undertake a rescue mission. "Their orders were to deliver water and parts and come back," Commander Michael Holdener remarked. "We all want to be the guys who rescue people," he continued, "but they were told we have other missions we have to do right now and that is not the priority."[23]

Meanwhile, in Atlanta, some 600 to 1,400 firefighters sat on their hands, waiting to be deployed to Louisiana or Mississippi as emergency workers.[24] Many whispered: "What are we doing here?" as they sat in a Sheraton Hotel conference room attending classes on sexual harassment, equal opportunity, and customer service. Eventually, the firefighters discovered that the FEMA authorities planned to have them pass out pamphlets. Many were paramedics and were hazmat and search–and–rescue certified. Some of the firefighters were so upset that they took off their FEMA–issued shirts and refused to represent the federal agency, frustrated that people were still trapped in homes and dying along the Gulf Coast while they were doing nothing to help. Trying to restore order, one official jumped atop a chair and shouted, "You are now employees of FEMA, and you will follow orders and do what you're told."[25]

Some critics of the Hurricane Katrina fiasco argued that government agencies lack planning skills. But according to Time magazine, a simulation of a hurricane hitting New Orleans was performed in the summer of 2004. "Hundreds of regional and federal officials met in Baton Rouge for an elaborate simulation exercise. The fictional 'Hurricane Pam' left the city under 10 feet of water and looked a lot like Katrina."[26] The authorities knew it would happen again; it had happened forty years earlier, in 1965, when Hurricane Betsy (a Category 4 hurricane) roared through New Orleans, leaving three-fourths of the city under water.

A regional director of FEMA revealed that he had sent dire e–mail messages to Director Brown in Washington, warning him that victims had no food and were dying. As the only FEMA official to have arrived in New Orleans before Katrina struck, Marty Bahamonde got no response to his messages. During an October 2005 Senate Homeland Security Committee hearing, Bahamonde spoke about the government's failure to grasp the gravity of the situation: "There was a systematic failure at all levels of government to understand the magnitude of the situation. The leadership from top down in our agency is unprepared and out of touch."[27]

As the Senate hearings were being conducted—no doubt for the purpose of pinning blame on someone—the sheriff of St. Bernard Parish in the eastern side of New Orleans was reduced to begging for money. As it turned out, the use of FEMA funds to pay for ongoing operations such as police and city workers' salaries is illegal. With every single home destroyed, along with 75 percent of city infrastructure, the district was broke. The parish had had no taxable sales in 49 days and no people to send property tax notices to. It appeared that the sheriff had no other option than to break the law and use FEMA money, until Murphy Oil—one of the two oil refineries in the district—donated $2 million. Early in the month, Hibernia Bank had given an unsecured $500,000 loan so the district could make payroll. The sheriff was perplexed as to why the federal government could not do something that private businesses had done so easily.[28]

Six months after the hurricane struck, it was discovered that FEMA had 10,770 brand–new mobile homes sitting empty in an Arkansas cow pasture, while at the same time FEMA was issuing payments to 12,000 Katrina refugees living in motel rooms. Why were the mobile homes sitting vacant? It was due to a miasma of conflicting laws. Every level of government had regulations limiting the placement of temporary housing in a flood plain, and because most of Louisiana sits in a flood plain, the $367 million of mobile homes was a ghost town.

It is no mystery why command–based structures fail. They are saddled with a large, fixed, and overlapping chain of command, and the longer the chain, the higher the probability of bad decision making—the left hand not knowing that a right hand is attached, somewhere. The nature of command structures is that they often fail to see what is happening at the ground level, and, therefore, they blunder blindly yet boldly.

A postscript to Katrina: Two years after the hurricane hit, much of New Orleans still lay in ruins, with vast stretches showing little or no evidence of recovery.[29] The feeling of abandonment gave new meaning to what the city has been called since the 1930s: "The City That Care Forgot." One angry resident, Clarence Russ, summed it up: "There was supposed to be all this money, but where'd it go? None of us got any."

Within days of the 1906 San Francisco earthquake, over $5 million had been privately donated. Lloyd's of London paid out more than $50 million in claims (equivalent to $1 billion in 2005 dollars), famously telling its agents to pay all policyholder claims "without quibble."[30] With virtually no government assistance, that reconstruction of San Francisco is considered by historians to have been "swift."

During Virginia City, Nevada's Great Fire of 1875, almost 2,000 buildings burned to the ground, rendering over 10,000 people homeless. But it took only two months to rebuild the town's main street, except for two of the largest buildings—all without any government assistance. Within one year, all traces of the fire had disappeared.

Roads Gone Wild

Roads are the backbone of modern civilization. They have always represented a sort of controlled environment where every moving object—whether a burro or carriage or Lamborghini—is segregated and properly regulated. What if the principles of swarm intelligence could improve the movement of vehicles and people through city streets, providing smoother traffic flow and a significant reduction in accidents? Many would scoff. How could the reduction of centralized regulations and traffic signs lead to significantly safer roads? But again, few city planners had ever heard of Hans Monderman (1945-2008), a Dutch road traffic engineer who pioneered the concept of "shared space."

Throughout a thirty–year crusade, Monderman struggled to convince authorities to eliminate most of the traditional traffic paraphernalia that clutters roadways, allowing drivers to pay more attention to driving, and by doing so, instilling a sense of responsibility for their own driving. "We're losing our capacity for socially responsible behavior," Monderman said. "The greater the number of prescriptions, the more people's sense of personal responsibility dwindles."[31]

During Monderman's early years, many thought that he had bashed his head into a mental speed bump. Wouldn't the lack of signs, markings, and barriers spark chaos and carnage? Yet the Dutch traffic engineer persisted in his belief that traffic signals, crosswalks, warning signs, curbs, and even lines painted down the middle of the road are not just annoying, but downright dangerous to drivers and pedestrians alike. He proposed integrating vehicle and foot traffic, in order to create a more holistic driving environment. Few would listen, however Monderman was patient. By the early twenty–first century, Dutch officials finally gave him the green light to test his theories in a number of small towns there. The data astonished skeptics. Within several years, he showed statistically significant reductions in accidents and fatalities, causing his revolutionary ideas to reverberate around a traffic–clogged world.

In the town of Christianfield in Denmark, fatal accidents were reduced from three per year to zero. In Whiltshire, England, the centerline was removed for a test period. Drivers drove more "safely and had a 35 percent decrease in the number of accidents."[32] Taking a step into lawlessness, Kensington High Street in London stripped off every last vestige of traditional traffic control, rendering it, as the press called it, a "naked street."

Not surprisingly to Monderman, the street had significant and sustained reductions in pedestrian injuries. Casualties dropped by 43.7 percent over a two–year period.[33]

So what was Monderman's secret? He was using the principles of swarm dynamics, whether he knew it or not. The shared–space method works well because it parallels those successful insect–based systems. In this case, bustling motorists and pedestrians are able to self–organize and self–correct on the local level, using their own brains, rather than be locked into a sign-obeying, zombie trance.

With a paradoxical twist, Monderman averred that vehicles need to go slower to move faster. One way to do that is to get more human eye contact while on the road which equates to more self–regulated traffic flow. Further, a road that appears dangerous causes drivers to be more aware of conditions and their surroundings, overriding "automatic pilot." They must negotiate with other drivers and pedestrians for the right of way. "It works well," contended

Monderman, "because it is dangerous, which is exactly what we want. But it shifts the emphasis away from the Government taking the risk, to the driver being responsible for his or her own risk."[34]

With a subhead proclaiming "chaos equals cooperation," *Wired* magazine explained that this new approach to traffic engineering is all about understanding that building a road affects more than just the movement of vehicles. Big roads with lots of signs make drivers feel they can do anything—as long as they obey the signs. Monderman's motif suggests that the old way is "saying 'go ahead, don't worry, go as fast as you want, there's no need to pay attention to your surroundings.'" Without all the warnings and instructions, the driver must develop more responsible behavior on the road.

Monderman showed a news reporter exactly what he meant. Without so much as a glance in either direction, he deliberately walked into a busy street, an intersection that he has reworked with a roundabout. Despite the fact that the intersection accommodates 20,000 drivers daily, Dutch drivers gracefully slowed down for him—no obscenities, no honking. The reporter was overwhelmed, writing: "But in spite of the apparently anarchical layout, the traffic, a steady stream of trucks, cars, buses, motorcycles, bicycles and pedestrians, moved along fluidly and easily, as if directed by an invisible conductor."[35]

As a disclaimer, Monderman acknowledged that not every intersection was the same. Each one had to be organized in a particular way, but under the shared–space approach of "less is more." "The trouble with traffic engineers is that when there's a problem with a road, they always try to add something," Monderman said. "To my mind, it's much better to remove things."

Monderman is not alone in his assertion that having fewer traffic signs and less road capacity could lead to less congestion. There is actually a mathematical principle that addresses the dilemma of building more capacity while actually achieving less flowing movement. Known as Braess's Paradox, it was named after the German mathematician Dietrich Braess, who applied his theory to networking systems. The principle states that it is common in interactive systems for additional capacity to have a negative effect on overall performance. In other words, increased capacity can sometimes reduce the overall movement of information. This phenomenon has been observed in Internet systems when the number of routes is increased. More choice and capacity for interaction can cause systems to become overcrowded as everyone and his brother rushes toward expanded routes, which can slow things down, thus reducing efficiency.

In the Korean capital city of Seoul, Kee Yeon Hwang, an urban planner, wanted to test Braess's paradox by tearing down a major, but congested, freeway in the center of the city, known as the Cheonggyecheon. The six–lane freeway accommodated 160,000 cars per day and had traffic so gridlocked that the casual observer would've thought it was a standstill parking lot. Despite the constant gridlock, most commuters considered the roadway indispensable.[36]

When one of the three main tunnels in the city was closed, Hwang and city officials discovered to their surprise that "car volumes dropped" within the crowded city. They suspected that this puzzling phenomenon had something to do with the Braess's Paradox concluding that "by taking away space in an urban area you can actually increase the flow of traffic, and, by implication, by adding extra capacity to a road network you can reduce overall performance." Bulldozing a major freeway would appear to be far too controversial ever to get popular consensus. Interestingly, when the teardown was proposed, the greatest flak did not spring from the electorate, who eventually voted in a citywide referendum to authorize the expressway removal. The greatest opposition surfaced from Hwang's own co-workers in the urban planning department, who implied that they must "build more roads to survive."

The Cheonggyecheon freeway was demolished by 2005 and replaced with a river. Traffic congestion decreased. The predictions of traffic chaos never materialized; commuters adapted. When *The New Yorker* magazine examined this issue in 2002, they found that, "In the twenty–three American cities that added the most new roads per person during the 1990s, traffic congestion rose by more than seventy percent."[37]

*****

Swarm intelligence illustrates the complex and holistic way in which the world operates. Order is created from chaos; patterns are revealed; and systems are free to work out their errors and problems at their own level. What natural systems can teach humanity is truly amazing.

1 Jesper Hoffmeyer, "The Swarming Body," paper presented to the 5th IASS congress in Berkeley, June 1995, later published in *Semiotics Around the World, Proceedings of the Fifth Congress of the International Association for Semiotic Studies*, Berkeley 1994, Berlin/New York: Mouton de Gruyter 1997, pp. 937–940.

2 Frank Lacombe, "Modeling Swarm Behavior," Science website at the University of Calgary. Posted on Physorg.com, Feb. 21, 2006.

3 Derrick Story, "Swarm Intelligence: An Interview with Eric Bonabeau," O'Reilly Network, posted Feb. 21, 2003.

4 Story, ibid.

5 Kevin Kelly, *New Rules for the New Economy*, Chapter One: Embracing the Swarm, New York: Viking, 1998, p. 13.

6 Kelly, ibid., p. 14.

7 Ray Carson, "Brain in a dish acts as autopilot, living computer," University of Florida, Oct. 22, 2004, part of a $500,000 National Science Foundation grant.

8 David Robson, "Disorderly Genius: How chaos drives the brain," *New Science*, June 29, 2009.

9 John Toner and Tu Yuhai, "Flocks, herds, and schools: A quantitative theory of flocking," *Physical Review E*, October 1998.

10 Foreign Policy and the Fund for Peace, *2007 Failed States Index*, 2007.

11 Matthew Philips, "Beliefwatch Reincarnate," *Newsweek*, August 27, 2007, p. 14.

12 Donna Abu-Nasr, "No Red Today in Saudi Arabia: Valentine's Day Banned by Authorities," *Monterey Herald*—Associated Press, Feb. 14, 2005.

13 WorldNet Daily, "Report: Louisiana blocked Red Cross," posted Sept. 8, 2005.

14 Nancy Imperiale, "FEMA blocks 500 Florida airboat pilots from rescue work," *Sun Sentinel*, Sept. 2, 2005.

15 Janson Robideaux (Lafayette Louisiana attorney), "Citizen Flotilla Turned Back by Louisiana Department of Wildlife and Fisheries," Rense.com, Sept. 5, 2005.

16 John Tierney, "New Orleans," *The New York Times*, Sept. 17, 2005.

17 Allen G. Breed, "Survivalists of the French Quarter," *Monterey Herald*—Associated Press story, Aug. 5, 2005.

18 Ben Ehrenreich, "After the Deluge: Ice Runs," *LA Weekly*, Sept. 16-22, 2005.

19 John Tierney, "From FEMA to WEMA," *New York Times*, Sept. 20, 2005.

20 Michael Barbaro and Justin Gillis, "Wal-Mart at Forefront of Hurricane Relief," *Washington Post*, Sept. 5, 2006.

21 CNN—"Military due to move in to New Orleans," posted Sept. 2, 2005.

22 "Senator wants Pensacola rescue pilots' careers protected," *The Daytona Beach News-Journal—Associated Press*, Sept. 11, 2005.

23 David S. Cloud, "US Navy Pilots Who Rescued Hurricane Victims Are Reprimanded," *New York Times*, Sept. 7, 2005.

24 Lisa Rosetta, "Frustrated: Fire crews to hand out fliers for FEMA," *The Salt

Lake Tribune, Sept. 6, 2005.

25 "4 Places Where the System Broke Down," *Time*, Sept. 19, 2005.

26 Ibid.

27 Hope Yen, "Death in streets took a back seat to dinner," *Seattle Times*—Associated Press, Oct. 21, 2005.

28 Jay Root, "Parishes struggle to rebuild without money," *Fort Worth Star Telegram*, Oct. 22, 2005.

29 Mary Foster, "Protest marks Katrina anniversary," *Monterey Herald*—Associated Press, Aug. 30, 2007.

30 "The role of Lloyd's in the reconstruction," Lloyd's of London, Accessed, December 6, 2006.

31 Shelley Emling, "British planners take to 'naked streets,'" *Times Argus*, Feb. 13, 2005.

32 Tom McNichol, "Roads Gone Wild: No street signs. No crosswalks. No accidents. Surprise: Making driving seem more dangerous could make it safer," *Wired*, issue 12.12, December 2004.

33 "KSIs cut as borough drops guards," *Road Safety News*. LARSOA, March 3, 2006.

34 David Millward, "Is this the end of the road for traffic lights?" *Telegraph.co.uk*, April 11, 2006.

35 Sarah Lyall, "A Path to Road Safety With No Signposts," *New York Times*, Jan. 22, 2005.

36 John Vidal, "Heart and soul of the city," *The Guardian*, Nov. 1, 2006.

37 John Seabrook, "The Slow Lane: Can anyone solve the problem of traffic?" *The New Yorker*, Sept. 9, 2002.

11 Control, Order and Chaos

The more you tighten your grip, Tarkin, the more star systems will slip through your fingers.
—Princess Leia Organa, *Star Wars: Episode IV*

Govern a great nation as you would cook a small fish. Do not overdo it.
—Lao Tzu

I'm going to show these people what you don't want them to see. I'm going to show them a world without you, a world without rules and controls, without borders or boundaries, a world where anything is possible.
—Neo, The Matrix

Do we have control over our lives? *Do we have control* over anything we do? An aura of control must exist, somewhere. Otherwise, why would so many people obey or carry out harsh commands from those who think they can control heaven and earth?

Control is the golden calf of command–based systems. The ability to master events has been worshiped almost religiously as a way to remedy mankind's inadequacies. Despite the allure for control, forced change has done little to prevent nature from dropping intractable episodes regularly on humanity. Nonetheless, control is an ancient human thirst, but one that has rarely been quenched. As sages and satirists have recited throughout the centuries, the grasp for more control ultimately metes out less. In other words, this paradoxical effect is easily observable—more control gives you less, and less control gives you more. As one of the early inventors of the floppy disk and the father of the programmable logic controller, Dick Morley, wrote: "To gain control, you've got to lose control."

Still, there is a common perception that people can control the course of events in their discordant world. People can choose from a plethora of activities. They can disobey a law; speed through red traffic lights; refuse to file income taxes; flee from unhappy relationships; run naked through city streets; or simply ignore consequences. But choice is not the same as control.

Given the complexity and unpredictability of the universe, the notion of possessing any meaningful control over the world or society is unrealistic and its believer is delusional. To have fingertip control of anything is merely a fanciful intellectual exercise. Even armed with the magic of Houdini, no one could get a complete handle on the turbulence swirling wildly through most people's lives every day. Those with the tiniest grain of wisdom understand human limitations. People struggle to put their own hectic lives in some semblance of order, and realize that they have neither the time nor the aptitude to rearrange their neighbor's seemingly helter–skelter life also. They understand the sheer futility of attempting to control the uncontrollable. The Serenity Prayer sums it up best: "Lord, grant me the serenity to accept the things I cannot change, the courage to change the things I can, and the wisdom to know the difference."[1] Life is not something to control, but to understand.

Despite spontaneity and creativity being the embryonic spark that gives birth to order, humanity continuously flirts with plans to control to death anything that erupts with such an unexpected—yet vital—force.

This mindset is puzzling, since order cannot come into existence until actions become repetitive and patterns observable. But the politically savvy have come to regard order as something that can be imposed arbitrarily, a notion which is contrary to the science of complexity. The reason order cannot be artificially commanded is elementary: precise control demands precise predictability. Without precise predictability, control is impotent and almost meaningless. In other words, the lesser the predictability, the harder the entity or system is to control, and vice versa. If our universe actually operated on linear causality, with no surprises, uncertainty, or abrupt changes, all future events would be absolutely predictable in a sort of waveless orderliness.

But the scientific community discovered, decades ago, that the universe is awash in nonlinearity and uncertainty. Ergo, control is mostly illusory, because precise predictability is unattainable. And it is unattainable because of the core element of chaology: the sensitive dependence on initial condition. Since most systems depend on and are sensitive to their initial conditions, final outcomes have an annoying proclivity to have been, until then, uncertain. Even the state of perfect knowledge would not guarantee any certitude. Moreover, chaologists have often likened the spontaneous outburst of change to a tipping point at which uncertainty itself becomes uncertain.

Surprisingly, one of the most astute observations about uncertainty came from Donald Rumsfeld, the U.S. Secretary of Defense, when, in 2002, he came under intense questioning. During a Defense Department briefing about the lack of evidence linking al–Qaeda to Iraq, Rumsfeld argued that nobody could be aware of everything that is knowable. In his now famous aphorism, he declared: "There are known knowns; there are things we know we know. We also know there are known unknowns; that is to say we know there are some things we don't know. But there are also unknown unknowns—the ones we don't know we don't know."[2]

But chaotic systems are not confined to sheer randomness. Multi–layered algorithms reside deep within most complex systems, giving uncertainty the potential to hand over unknowns to secure patterns, and to establish observable structures. Some categorize this hidden order under the oxymoronic tag of "organized chaos" or "unplanned order," a condition in which things appear confusing and unorganized, yet still work out all right. Filmmaking is often considered the quintessential organized chaos: the hustle and bustle on the movie set appears unstructured, uncoordinated, and fragmented, but the work gets done. Film director Francis Ford Coppola once offered some insight into filmmaking: "Anything you build on a large scale or with intense passion invites chaos."

But unmasking the face of uncertainty is fleeting, a flash of recognition so delicate that any trespass jeopardizes detectable results. In the natural world, order perpetually rises out of chaos (*ordo ab chao*), but in the political world, the opposite is true: chaos ceaselessly spews out of state–mandated order. Imposed order disrupts natural order, triggering unwanted turmoil on a massive scale. This is why command–based systems are incapable of generating a stabilizing order; they were set up to bypass the natural process by foisting an artificially crafted, intransigent "politicalized order." Generally, the two types of order have a complete disconnect.

Immeasurable Universe

Scientists have acknowledged the difficulty in measuring an immeasurable universe. This fact became obvious during the early years of the computer age. Going as far back as the 1940s, "computers and statistical mechanics proved predicting most events theoretically impossible by the sheer number of variables."[3]

Spontaneity has few constants and a countless number of variables, making such seemingly random events and open–ended pluralism, creating an environment where control freaks and drama queens revel in contested authority. As the old adage goes, "Too many cooks spoil the broth." A gaggle of independent chefs are bound to bump into each other, as they busily work in the kitchen. But the more anal–retentive chef will be offended and eventually nitpick, bully, or marginalize anyone who refuses to follow his lead. The bossy chef will have no qualms about destroying the chefs' fellowship and their goodwill, if others refuse to champion his grand vision of "planned change." Compulsive planners feel compelled to impose a linearized order, to redirect the lives of others. And yet, it is not hard to see why planning for the future is so intoxicating. To plan is to feel as though one is in the driver's seat—that control is obtainable and justifiable. But planning and controlling are like predicting the weather in the long term: Control is fleeting, incomplete, and usually beyond anyone's ability to master it with any modicum of precision.

In Kevin Kelly's *Out of Control*, the former executive editor of *Wired* magazine opined that "no one is in control." He predicted that biology and technology will escape the bounds of human oversight, allowing complex systems to explore their own kaleidoscopic improvisation of emergent chaos. To Kelly, controls only obstruct a system's self–tuning mechanisms that rush toward "the holy grail of open–ended evolution" and toward networked consciousness. In Kelly's vision of a cybernetic world, to transcend the problem of being unable to control events, human systems will be created deliberately to be out of control. Those participating will be able to choose their own set of rules. He referred to this concept as "bio–logic" engineering.[4]

Change can't be effectively planned or controlled over the long haul; it evolves with or without detailed blueprints. But the populace is promised long–term change by high–handed doctrinaires whose only objective is to gain authority over public-sector decision making. These agenda–driven apparatchiks have come to believe that they are the ones to tame complexity and control ungovernable events. Although the majority opposes such meddling in how they run their lives, individuals are habitually shoved aside to make way for the utopian or methodical master plan.

So, when dominant, overbearing types start ordering everybody around, a system can become unwieldy and irrelevant, because the controls sought will rarely do what they were designed to do. The more one overworks society's plumbing, the more you disrupt the flow. But when it comes to living in a plugged–up society, more than enough "shit happens." Social structures become trapped in a non-homeostatic loop, where restraints fail spectacularly. That is because they are stratified on rigid hierarchical lines of overarching authority and unaccountability, ultimately they are tossed about in an unmanageable wake. The most pitiful episodes are when apologists for regimentation and governmentalism continue to "remedy" the failures of control with even stricter and more draconian doses of it.

Generally, controls do not prevent change; they merely put some limitations on wild, runaway effects—effects that are required in order for the balancing middle to be defined. When someone tries to oversee, it is at the expense of something else. All of that "Newton's-third-law-energy" must go somewhere! The only relatively effective control is that which has arisen within a system—those boundaries and controls that had been responsible for the system's very existence. This is why systems which govern the best are those that are internally based and self–directing.

Take Newton's third law of motion as a template. For every control imposed, there is an equal and opposite reaction. Maybe not an exactly equal reaction, but a little–known principle that accounts for the consequence of imposed order states that the "imposition of order equals the escalation of chaos." Known as the Law of Eristic Escalation, this principle continues: When more order is imposed by command, the longer it takes for the chaos to escalate, and the greater its magnitude.

For instance, in social situations, a shrewish wife may scream at her henpecked husband daily to perform household tasks, but the nagging typically accomplishes little more than increasing his bitterness and desire to avoid her. Absolute demands forbidding teenagers not to associate with close friends run the risk of inciting rebellious episodes. If children are prohibited from having small amounts of alcohol at family gatherings, the risk rises for abusive bingeing and alcoholism in their adult years. A mother–in–law could throw her weight around in an attempt to get her way, but would she really have control over her children and their spouses? And even if she repeatedly acts domineering, what price will she pay for exerting aggressive and pushy behavior? Will her children invite her to future social events and outings? No—she will be banished as a fun–sucking harpy.

So, where is all the control? In the business world, short–sighted pundits believe that the boss holds all the poker chips. But how much power does he have over his employees? Could he bully them? Could employees fight back and, discreetly, work less efficiently? Would unhappy employees consider resigning, if a better job offer were to come their way? In reality, company bosses have limited control over employees and how they eventually perform their duties. In most business relationships, the boss depends on the employee as much employee depends on the employer. These two opposing dynamics counterbalance each other; each needs the other in order to flourish.

Even running a dictatorship, it is difficult to control all aspects of society.

Citizens often find ways to ignore or circumvent iron–fisted rules. Many will conform—when trapped inside an information vacuum, battered by one–sided propaganda, and subjected to physical threats. But citizens are not automatons, predisposed to swallowing the authority's disinformation, hook, line, and sinker. Years prior to the Soviet Union's collapse, most citizens had already come to the conclusion that statements from Communist Party officials were virtually the exact opposite of the truth. The collapse represented the loss of the Communist state's legitimacy with Russian citizens. In a sense, the reason the government no longer had complete control was that citizens no longer believed the government was ruling in their best interest.

People can and do exert strong influence over others, especially those deficient in mental–gymnastics skills. But when control originates from private individuals, it is usually derived through the process of persuasion. If a citizen were to attempt to mimic methods commonly used by political superstars—threats of force and overt coercion—he would be condemned as a criminal, jailed, or ostracized. The ancient Greek raconteur Aesop understood this duplicity, observing: "We hang the petty thieves and appoint the great ones to public office."

In essence, control is the process by which we make systems do what we want them to do. Of course, everybody has a different take on what a system ought to do—which tends to induce single–point–of–failure debacles, but the politicalization of a system ensures intransigency. The political elite get caught up in mad stampedes to control dynamic systems they falsely believe are controllable, and when these systems fail to do as commanded, worlds collide, conflicts erupt, and wars are perpetuated. In that tarnished world, politicos are apt to swap principles for power and often end up with neither.

Spartans: Becoming a Slave to Slaves

According to psychologists, it can be a liberating experience to release the urge to control another. Some psychiatrists, such as William Glasser, author of *Choice Theory*, believe that almost all human misery can be attributed to futile attempts to make others conform to particular lifestyles. Glasser points out that individuals can control only their own behavior, nobody else's, and that they are the only ones who can make themselves sick, despondent, or blissful.

Unfortunately, many people simply can't let go of the seductive allure to control others. Acting as if they had been appointed "grand puppeteer of the universe," they determine to set the stage where every twig in the forest and every grain of sand on the beach must be in its proper place so that every actor can deliver a perfect performance. These "lineartarians" pay a heavy price for their unlimited ambitions, overmastering more than just their victims. The philosopher and novelist Ayn Rand once touched on this overbearing phenomenon, observing: "A leash is only a rope with a noose on both ends." She meant that controls are a doubled–edged sword: no matter which way the blade faces, you will get cut.

The Spartans of ancient Greece encountered such a cursed blade after having conquered the Messenians in the eighth century B.C. The Spartans had cultivated a slave–owning society so authoritarian and brutal that their culture not only abused the slaves, but irreparably traumatized the entire Spartan society.

Traditionally, most Greeks would have been satisfied with attacking a neighboring city–state, overwhelming their opponent's army, hammering out a favorable peace treaty, indulging in young women and booty, and racing back home in time for a drunken victory celebration. Yet the Spartans wanted more. After defeating the Messenians, they brutally subjugated the entire population, reducing the vanquished to state–owned slaves, or "helots."

However, the helots greatly outnumbered the Spartans, something on the order of ten to one. To deal with this threatening situation, Spartan society had to become militaristic, always on guard to fend off slave revolts. Spartans had one basic purpose in life: to defend a state dependent on slavery.

The Spartans humiliated, mistreated, and killed helots, sometimes launching wars of terror in almost ritualistic killings—thousands of unarmed helots at a time. Citizens of Sparta could freely kill any helot if they merely suspected the person of harboring a treasonous thought. Many historians attributed this practice to a general fear that the subjugated population would someday rebel and destroy Sparta. The fear was so great that Spartans always carried their spears, ready for combat, and at home they locked themselves up tightly. This dire situation caused their society to prohibit any male Spartan from pursuing a profession other than soldiery. Under these hostile conditions, a great portion of a Spartan's life had to be devoted to training for warfare. In short, the Spartans had become slaves to their slaves.

The Spartans rarely committed large military forces to fight beyond their borders, fearful of a slave revolt at home while they were gone. Some historians speculate this was the real reason that Sparta committed only 300 Spartans to the battle of Thermopylae. When Sparta did dispatch its full army of 10,000 to confront the Persians at the Battle of Plataea in 479 B.C., they took along

35,000 helots as auxiliary troops. However, once the battle was won, the Spartans beheaded many of the helots to avoid a promised emancipation.

Nevertheless, the helots revolted in a series of uprisings that were cruelly suppressed. Eventually, they did win their freedom, with foreign assistance, and became independent in the fourth century B.C.

Sparta's archenemy, Athens, took a different path. The city allowed greater openness and movement, and became a beacon of civilization. Today, tourists from around the world crowd Athens' busy streets. They marvel over the city's great works of art and literature, and take tours of the Acropolis. But what of ancient Sparta? There is little trace that it ever existed.

Gangs: Controlling the Uncontrollable

"When it comes to America's criminal justice policy, the cure is often worse than the crime."[5]

That astute observation by a senior editor of *In These Times*, Salim Muwakkil, was based on a 108–page report released by the Washington D.C.–based Justice Policy Institute in 2007. The report was blunt, asserting that heavy–handed anti–gang laws and police crackdowns were increasing gang activity instead of decreasing it. According to the report, "police dragnets that criminalize whole communities and land large numbers of nonviolent children in jail don't reduce gang involvement or gang violence."[6] One of the authors of the report, Kevin Pranis, stated: "Gangs do not drive crime rates, and aggressive suppression tactics simply make the situation worse by alienating local residents and trapping youth in the criminal justice system."

The report compared the results of anti–gang programs in three large cities—Los Angeles, Chicago, and New York—and evaluated whether the programs they developed had been successful. The study revealed that those cities engaged in aggressive gang suppression tactics had failed to stop the growing crisis of violent gang activity. Los Angeles failed miserably, with six times as many gangs and twice as many gang members as twenty years before, despite having spent billions. Although nationwide crime rates had trended downward for years, L.A. Police Chief William Bratton noted that in 2006, gang–related crimes in his city had increased 15 percent[7]. Chicago experienced the same problem. In a city where nearly half of all homicides were linked to gang members, Chicago found itself choked by a high level of violence, because of gang warfare and drug–territory disputes.

But New York City took a different approach. Law enforcement understood that they could not eliminate gangs. Their strategy was to involve the community in policing neighborhoods and to institute gang intervention programs, which centered on providing jobs, education, and counseling for gang members. "Prevention" was the key word. When the city implemented these programs, criminal activity by gangs dropped dramatically.

Yet most politicians find street gangs an easy target, especially during campaign season. Tough–on–crime measures are popular with voters who demand more protection by government. Nonetheless, according to the Muwakkil's report, "the billions of dollars spent on traditional gang suppression activities have failed to promote public safety and are often counterproductive."

Obviously, harsher controls failed to solve the problem. Stiff enforcement tactics involving gang injunctions, gang sweeps, surveillance, special task forces, more prisons, and stiffer sentencing only bolstered gang membership, strengthened their organization, and accelerated the cycle of gang violence.

What this also shows is that an over–aggressive government will tend to spawn an upside–down society. Citizens can no longer operate in the open with honesty. They are put into a situation where, in order to survive, they have no choice but to lie, cheat, and steal. The traditional above–ground society is driven to the silent depths of an underground society. When this happens, the very core of society becomes criminalized and emasculated, its citizens shackled to the chains of the political correctness of politicalization.

The Fear of Losing Control

Anxiety over losing control is one of the strongest human emotions. Most people have a need for a neat, secure, and seamless world, although such dreams rarely materialize. Uncertainty, doubt, or instability becomes the enemy, for those desperately seeking an island of order in a sea of disorder. But for those who exhibit psychoneurotic behavior, a peaceful refuge is not enough. These worrywarts will often go to extremes, and become obsessed with dominating the environment by trying to control how others think and behave. Hostile when challenged, their brains somatically prepare them for oncoming threats (similarly to how reptilian brains respond), whether real or imaginary. And as the perceived threat grows, these controlaholics conform more readily, and more rigidly to rules, orderliness, perfectionism, and inflexibility. Psychologists have a name for this: obsessive–compulsive personality disorder (OCPD).

Somewhere in the range of two to five percent of the population suffer from OCPD. Although anxiety–provoking situations are everywhere, most people manage to cope. But rule–bound neurotics cannot get over their insecurity and fear of change. One way to deal with the anxiety of losing control is to impose excessive predictability and direction on events or other people.

If it were merely a medical problem, those suffering from obsessive–compulsive behavior would mostly be found populating hospital beds or warming psychiatrists' couches. Instead, many of these anal–retentive busybodies frequent the halls of government, eager to climb the political ladder to command the fate of nations. This is a serious problem, because control freaks will gravitate toward institutions that give them what they most crave, and if they do claw their way to the political apex, lawlessness or hyper-controlling government is not far behind.

It is a basic human drive to achieve competence and be in control, but control freaks can have a self–destructive bent with an emphasis on self–righteousness, imperious procedures, and by–the–book perfectionism. This self–reinforcing behavior often pushes them to the frazzled edge, with in–your–face confrontation. It is *their way or no way.* There is only one correct method to fold socks or roll toilet paper, and if they are elected to positions of authority, they often push toward "final solutions" to systematically eradicate all imperfections.

But what makes politically deft martinets so dangerous is their readiness to convey emotions and fears to bystanders. Eager to exaggerate all sorts of catastrophic disasters, they are adept at propagating political and cultural memes to control the population. They orchestrate "phobia-fests" which overstate uncertainty, the imminence of deadly pandemics, and end–of–the–world prophecies. With religious fervor, theses manipulators roll out their doomsday evidence; proclaim their data irrefutable; hurl argumenta ad personam at doubters; and brand anyone foolish enough to be a skeptic as lower than a Holocaust denier.

During elections, these alarmists play a high–stakes game of pessimism in which political opponents attempt to "out–fear" one another. Jitters about black unrest inspired the Jim Crow laws in the Deep South. During the 1920s and 1930s, the National Socialists used the angst over Jewish influence in Germany to gain power there. The administration of President George W. Bush exploited the fear of terrorism to justify the preemptive strike on Iraq. Fear–mongering knows no bounds.

But what sets the tone is that adherence to perfectionism. Unable to tolerate imperfection, obsessive–compulsive killjoys are trapped in a closed–loop hell, where they can never achieve what they believe they must. The results are nowhere near perfect. Preoccupied with small details and strict procedures, perfectionists interfere with tasks, ultimately becoming obstructionists and saboteurs who suck the fun out of life.

The reason control freaks become proficient at controlling others is that such control allows them to quell their own anxiety. They will feel less fear if they can prevail over others. This is why they must mask their anxiety and failure with endless demands for stricter measures, while simultaneously blaming any boomeranging results on the opposition or on the incompetent. The worst part is that these stubborn and unhappy people are prepared to make everybody else's life as miserable as their own.

A Manicured World

Do we live in an orderly world, or do we just try to make it appear that way? Existentialists have framed this as a philosophical question. They delve into the uncertainty of existence, and the unlimited freedom of choice that people possess, contending that results derive more from individual choice and less from events often seen as determined by cause and effect. The definitions of "chaos" and "order" may be more of an interpretation of how man sees his environment and himself, regardless of a meaningful or absurd reality.

It is human nature to be attracted to order. Most humans crave stable structures that generate "repeatable events"—the heartwood of order. Generally, most people want tomorrow to be the same as today. They don't want anything to disturb their daily routines and rituals, which give them contentment and security.

When outside forces interrupt routines, those affected by the disruption find their minds in a state of chaos. Feathers ruffled, they replace complacency with disenchantment, and substitute barriers for openness. And yet, it is the agenda–driven disruptors who are the greatest destroyers of orderly routine that repeatable patterns often bring. Political crusaders scramble order. It's as though a stranger has come into your backyard without permission, dug up a row of roses, and replaced them with hardier, more disease–resistant plants. The outsider might have been correct, for the short term, in his or her plant selection, but a long–term, orderly process has been severed. Meddling can only upset a balance, at least for those who thought they had a well–managed garden.

Consider the shattering of order in Monterey County, California, in the 1990s, when the local District Attorney and FBI busted and imprisoned the leaders of four gangs. The authorities concentrated their efforts on ending gang violence by prosecuting the heads of gang organizations, assuming that without leadership, the criminal organizations would die. Instead, gang warfare in that county escalated rapidly. Why? Without an established leadership structure in place, lower–level gang members jockeyed for power in an utter frenzy pace. Local prosecuting attorneys referred to this unanticipated violence as a "bloodbath." The gang task force had replaced established order with a helter–skelter whirlwind of chaos, making it far more difficult to control street gangs. Of course, this result had not been the intent of the law enforcement agencies and prosecutors. They had inadvertently destroyed structures without regard to what might take their place. All too often governments routinely destroy orderly structures, only to watch worse substitutes arise, under policies that actually trigger chaotic conditions.[8]

Nonetheless, just because something is orderly does not make it virtuous. Serial killers are well known for their specific patterns, motives, and styles during their attacks. These criminals are like monsters on autopilot, inflicting harm in a repetitive, and therefore orderly, manner. Obviously, nobody sane would defend this type of systematic violence. Hence, order is neither good nor bad; it merely represents repetitive action.

So, what about man's goal of maintaining control of his physical environment? Homeowners and businesses, for example, spend considerable hours and funds to manicure their grounds, with the objective of a uniformity that gives an illusion of control over nature. The landscape architects plan identical white picket fences between the lawn and the shrubs, while the gardeners labor to trim those shrubs neatly, cut those lawns evenly, and saturate the ground with herbicides to control unruly weeds. Nothing is left to run rampant, giving the owners and passersby the warm fuzzy feeling that Mother Nature has finally been tamed.

But in reality, nature does not produce neatly mowed grass, well–pruned, disease–free trees, and clean sidewalks. Man's attempt to artificially maintain order is temporary. Without intervening human hands, lush gardens would soon transform into jungles, cluttered with overgrown ivy, thistles, weeds, and half–dead trees. Yet, despite the jungle's inherent disorder, it cultivates its own level of natural order. Windstorms prune trees; grazing animals gnaw down grasses; and wildfires burn deadwood—again, chaos blooming into order and order settling back into chaos.

Chaos and order are inextricably linked and interdependent, fluxing across the wide spectrum of phase space, switching back and forth, bifurcating at unknown points, propelling along homotopic paths in search of disequilibrium. They feed off each other with a symbiotic need to survive. But at what point can control be applied, to compensate for randomness? Phase transition, for example, water's transition from gaseous to liquid forms, or from liquid to solid, can be difficult to gauge if confronted with unlimited number of possible transitions. This is similar to what occurs in the recondite principles of the all-possible state of quantum superposition.

Control is relative to what state a system is currently occupying. If applied to the wrong phase space—where all possible states of a system are represented—controls can disrupt and destroy the repetitive order of parameters not originally targeted for control. In other words, dynamic systems have many levels, and any attempt to control something within a phase space-like system is comparable to finding an invisible needle in an unknown haystack.

The Crosswalk Principle

In the 1990s, a series of newspaper articles publicized the tragic story of a woman who was hit by a vehicle while jaywalking across a busy rural highway in northern California. Upset over the accident, the local residents petitioned the government to install a crosswalk to protect against future accidents. The request seemed simple. The cost to paint lines on the blacktop was negligible. And yet the California Department of Transportation refused to go along with the request.

Some newspaper editors were incensed. How could an agency of the government ignore grief–stricken citizens' pleas to remedy a hazardous stretch of road with an inexpensive safety feature? The California Department of Transportation rebutted with an armload of statistics. From past studies, Caltrans had discovered that when crosswalks were painted on busy rural highways, the injury rate skyrocketed. The reasons cited were fascinating. Apparently, pedestrians inside these street markings pay little attention to oncoming traffic, which might help them later in a court of law, but not in a hospital emergency room. Somehow, pedestrians feel protected, as if the painted lines are an invisible but impregnable barrier. They succumb to a false sense of control, entitlement, and groupthink. Ironically, believing that the risk of something has decreased could easily lead a person to riskier behavior (i.e., the "moral hazard" effect).

From a social chaologist's perspective, this attitude underscores a significant problem, that of people blindly delegating their authority to someone or something other than themselves. In this case, inanimate objects—painted white lines—become an entity thought to control what happens. In contrast, under self–organizing principles, self–directed agents rely on and critically interact with each other, generating insight and information that assist in the survival of the whole. In this decentralized world, authority is determined by knowledge, common sense, and function.

But to provide accurate information and knowledge and avert groupthink, the parts must avoid compartmentalization. Instead, they need to link autonomously, without specific instructions or visible structure, and cooperate in a "shared–power" approach without leadership nodes. Similar to the interconnectivity found in microorganisms and social animals, agents will partake in an integrated cluster of information–rich dynamics, which can evolve into something called "collective intelligence" or "collective creativity," although the parts may also work toward development of their own skills and in pursuit of their own interests.

This "network fishnet" node of self–organizing is learning oriented, which allows nests of insects, flocks of birds, schools of fish, and groups of human beings to navigate within a collective "smartness." But that smartness is predicated on the ability of individual agents to procure the best and most accurate information— similarly to how optimization algorithms would procure it. And that cannot be done without self–reliance, vigilance, and awareness on the part of agents who are, in essence, the ears and eyes of the whole.

Self–responsibility and reliability are antithetical to command–based systems, although the resultant, horrific policies by governmental decrees are often entirely unintentional. According to F. A. Hayek, "The knowledge essential for central planning does not exist in concentrated form."[9] Information is diffuse, diluted, decentralized, and ever changing, meaning that most political addicts do not know what they do not know. In fact, it could be argued that few people know the scope of their own ignorance. Despite the shallowness of their information, political self–seekers still lunge for the sheen of power, as *The Lord of the Rings* so vividly illustrated, in the death match over Sauron's One Ring of Power. Similarly, in their pursuit of power, public officials expose themselves to governing with biased blind spots and self–centered incentives. Public choice theory has shown that political leaders are prone to responding to incentives just like everyone else; therefore, one can't assume that altruistic passion will drive political undertakings.

Perhaps this is why autocrats focus on expropriating the self-governance and autonomy of others. If successful, the self-rulership of a citizen is transferred to upper echelons in order to concentrate power. During this power shift, centralized entities must lull the populace into a security, even if false. They need to mislead the public into believing that something bigger than themselves will guarantee their health and well–being—and everyone else's—for eternity. With such grand assurances, nobody need be responsible for his or her own actions—or mistakes.

Like wolves in sheep's clothing, political messiahs have a vested interest in hooking the general public on a risk–free life filled with guarantees. If people surrender to the illusion of a riskless society, they will stop looking out for themselves. They will forfeit whatever authority and competence they formerly possessed and become wholly unfit to recognize dangerous circumstances and unscrupulous authority figures hawking the latest flavor of snake oil. Any society that lives on a diet of idiot-proof cuisine will soon discover that somebody will concoct even better idiots and more underhanded ways to fool the public. As historical novelist Ron Burns once remarked, "You can't make anything idiot proof because idiots are so ingenious."

The most tragic consequence of protecting people from every possible risk is the loss of reliability and objectivity. If individual agents of society lose their skeptical eyes, they will not be the only ones to suffer the scourge of blindness and dysfunctional behavior. Every level of society and governance will be affected by the lack of societal integrity and fidelity.

Order Without Law

It is easy to confuse *control* with *order*. If control did equate to some semblance of order, the world would be bathing in blissful orderly serenity, as almost every scrap of land would crouch under the purview of political authority. Not only does disorder abound worldwide, but most of it can be traced back to an attempt by one political system or another to impose its definition of law and order. Assuming that every crisis must have a political solution, governing systems tighten the screws on public activities, until the ruling politicos are kicked out of office by legal measures or overthrown by force.

One federal judge had the courage to describe what happens to society when it is peppered with too many Leviathan–like proclivities. Janice R. Brown, a judge on the U.S. Court of Appeals for the District of Columbia

Circuit since 2005, explained that "where government moves in, community retreats, civil society disintegrates and our ability to control our own destiny atrophies. The result is: families under siege; war in the streets; unapologetic expropriation of property; the precipitous decline of the rule of law; the rapid rise of corruption; the loss of civility and the triumph of deceit. The result is a debased, debauched culture which finds moral depravity entertaining and virtue contemptible."[10]

But political institutions engage in more than power and forced cooperation. Many democratic nations have forged legal frameworks that prosecute crimes both with and without victims. This "mission drift" is to be expected. In many ways, constitutional governments resemble a small, household fireplace. Such hearths can provide the warmth of security, but flames of power, if not diligently kept in their proper place, could burn down the house.

Government's rate of expansion is always in proportion to its failure rate. Philosophers confronted this age–old problem, long ago. One, the English philosopher Thomas Hobbes, argued in *Leviathan* in 1660 that to have social cooperation, the public required a strong legal framework, because people cannot trust each other to cooperate. To Hobbes, a strong central authority would prevent the evil of discord and disorder. He believed that the populace is so wicked that any behavior by a governing agency is permissible—no matter how abusive.

But was Hobbes right? Are people so villainous that a monolithic legal framework is necessary, even an injuriously abusive one, to prevent one citizen from victimizing another? Is there a way to test Hobbes' hypothesis? Was there ever a period when no legal entity existed to resolve legal disputes? And if so, wouldn't social cooperation and order somehow evaporate into uncontrollable chaos? Robert Ellickson, professor of property and urban law at Yale Law School, wanted to know.

In his book, *Order Without Law*, Ellickson concentrated on Shasta County, California, ranchers and farmers, who decided that they would themselves handle any disputes over cows wandering across boundaries and causing a ruckus. Determined to avoid legal costs and entanglements, the ranchers and farmers turned to informal rules and familiar social norms to settle disputes peacefully. After poring over letters and conducting interviews, Ellickson documented creative agreements that were often contrary to formal laws, and very different from what might have resulted in a courtroom packed with law–obsessed lawyers. Without a set of official rules or judges, the ranchers were practicing self–ordering principles, piecing together legal precedent not too dissimilar from what occurred during the development of English Common Law.[11]

Combining social anthropology with microeconomic theory, Ellickson demonstrated that people are adept at resolving disputes, forming rules, and enforcing agreements. His research illustrates that controls arranged through formal laws cannot be considered a society's primary source of order. One underlying reason is that under a normal legal system, trust and moral personal character are not required, because the system relies solely on punishing lawbreakers. Nobody needs to trust anybody, but as Ellickson pointed out, social cooperation and order can function well without its players having to resort to wielding a big, punitive legal stick.

* * * * *

In the final analysis, attempts to control the personal or economic activities in a society will cause that society to suffer unintended consequences and a variety of conflicting, paradoxical conditions. Control is mostly illusory and, if yet obtained, short–lived. Order does not come from control; rather, control comes from the synchrony of spontaneous order.

1 The Serenity Prayer is often attributed to others, including St. Francis of Assisi, but without source. It is believed that Karl Paul Reinhold Niebuhr wrote the most common version in the early 1940s.

2 Donald H. Rumsfeld, Department of Defense news transcript, February 12, 2002.

3 Ainize Txopitea, "What Is The Impact of Chaos Theory on Digital Art?" London, May 2003, Internet posting: http://www.ainizetxopitea.com/link_websites/yochaos/tesis.html.

4 Kevin Kelly, *Out of Control: The New Biology of Machines, Social Systems, & the Economic World*, Reading, Mass.: Addison–Wesley, 1994.

5 Salim Muwakkil, "The Counterproductive War on Gangs," *In These Times*, August 23, 2007.

6 Judith Greene and Kevin Pranis, *"Gang Wars: The Failure of Enforcement Tactics and the Need for Effective Public Safety Strategies,"* Justice Policy Institute, July 17, 2007.

7 Personal comments by a Monterey County Deputy District Attorney and college instructor, Todd A. Hornik, Esq., September 8, 2008, during his campaign for Superior Court Judge.

8 Friedrich A. Hayek, *Individualism and Economic Order*, Chicago: University of Chicago Press: 1948, pp. 77–78.

9 Janice R. Brown, "A Whiter Shade of Pale: Sense and Nonsense—The Pursuit of Perfection in Law and Politics," speech to the Federalist Society at the University of Chicago Law School, April 20, 2000.

10 Robert Ellickson, *Order Without Law: How Neighbors Settle Disputes*, Cambridge, Mass.: Harvard University Press, 1994.

12 Paradoxes and Inconsistencies

> *Paradox is a particularly powerful device to ensnare truth because it concisely illuminates the contradictions that are at the very heart of our lives.*
> —Richard Lederer, foreword of *Oxymoronica*
>
> *Truth is always paradoxical.*
> —Lao–tzu

Why do things rarely turn out as they should? Why do plans routinely backfire? Why is life so contradictory? Is there some logical explanation or theorem that would account for so many counter–intuitive, incoherent, and contradictory phenomena? Or is the universe so mind–numbingly complex that paradoxes must permeate our time–space continuum? Whatever their causes, paradoxes have the dexterity to reveal profound truths, valuable insights, and oxymoronic contortions.

But paradoxes are more than just brawls between literal and figurative truths, semantics of grammar, or finite and infinite absurdities. Paradoxes have the quality of being infinitely divisible. They expand beyond Zeno's "the all is one" conflicts and beyond the perplexities scientists uncover in nonlinear systems. In truth, paradoxes are good at piercing the armor of long–held assumptions and shallow beliefs.

One could easily dig beneath the surface of any issue and uncover counter-intuitive findings that would better represent reality. Thorny paradoxes have a way of revealing profound patterns contrary to what one would expect. For instance, many chaologists would argue that when more order is imposed, the less stable the results. The larger the welfare program, the greater the poverty. The more spent on government education, the higher the illiteracy rate. The harsher the drug laws, the greater the use of illegal drugs. The more laws enacted, the higher the crime rate. The more public housing units built, the greater the number of people living in slums. The greater the effort by the Federal Reserve to stabilize the economy, the more turbulent roller-coaster rides of inflating and deflating bubbles. The more farm subsidies handed out to keep prices stable, the more drops in crop prices (because of the surpluses created by the subsidization). The longer unemployment benefits are provided, the longer joblessness will persist. The list seems endless.

Many of the most troublesome and least understood paradoxes relate to economics. For instance, when the jobless rate in Spain jumped to 21 percent in 2011 (nearly 45 percent for young people),[1] Spanish lawmakers and economists proposed a reform to make it easier for companies to fire workers. On a superficial level, this seems ludicrous: Wouldn't making it easier to fire workers result in more fired workers? Wrong. It has done the exact opposite. If it is legally difficult to fire a bad employee, who would want to take a chance on a new employee with questionable skills?

These types of economics-based paradoxes occur when flexibility and adaptability are banished from marketplaces. The incapacity to fire bad employees makes companies reluctant to hire more workers. Instead, they often will contract out to temporary agencies. The upshot: legislative barriers to firing workers contribute to more unemployment and temporary employment.

In the traditional sense, paradoxes are dualistic statements that appear to be both true and false, simultaneously. They are incompatible, yet compatible. They are difficult to understand, because if a paradoxical statement is false, it must then be true, and if it is true, it must be false. But what gets people excited is that many of these bizarre riddles can't be refuted. We would require a complete, unified theory of everything, in order to dispel them, but that would be impossible. What appears to be occurring is that self–contradicting phenomena are being trapped within a shifting mosaic of both opposites and infinite scaling, which together underscore underscores the complexity of the universe.

Why are paradoxes of such interest to chaologists? They illustrate that most subjects are not as simple as they were at first sight. Their many layers are deep, like an onion's, and they interlock. For instance, at first glance it would appear that the best way to ensure that every human being is well fed and clothed is simply to give them everything they could ever want—all the free food, clothing, schooling, housing, and health care possible. Spare no expense. It is only money. Governments merely need to twist people's arms and squeeze out enough cold cash to facilitate an equal redistribution of wealth. Poverty solved.

But in practice, all sorts of unwanted consequences will crop up. Complexity can be a royal pain. Destroying one system by shackling it to another ensures messy paybacks. The energy displaced must go somewhere. And when it does, counteracting forces discharge a patchwork of backlash and overlapping inconsistencies.

So what happens when political systems use brutish violence to crank open the wealth spigot? Many people would end up drowning in a sea of uncertainty and bloodshed. Interventionist policies have the capacity to tear apart the repetitive–cycle structures responsible for creating order, and to energize political chaos on a massive scale. When the political class attempts to redistribute other people's wealth, long–held societal structures become compromised.

In addition to mandating equality, governmentalists often employ spinmeisters to oversimplify and emotionalize issues so as to get their message across. Flashy charts, catchy slogans, PowerPoint presentations, and silver–tongued showmen conceal the true complexity of most socioeconomic problems. After all, they need only create a popular perception that something or someone poses a threat to the general public. With their "disaster lobby" steaming ahead at full throttle, government acolytes huff and puff about how only they have the answer. This is not a difficult feat, since usually it is they who posed the question in the first place.

But the reason paradoxes deluge the political landscape to such an overwhelming degree is the fact that logical and detailed explanations of complex issues are not emotionally satisfying to the public. Few people become excited over descriptions of the effects on price and quantity under the law of supply and demand. Politicians have learned to encourage a political culture of psychobabble and childish clichés that makes one feel euphoric and sublimely empowered. This is reinforced by political hype that focuses on inspirational tales of "human compassion," and scary caricatures of easy–to–identify but mostly fictitious villains. Although outcome–based policies may be the better tool to solve social problems, they display none of the soulful Hollywood glitter that warms the heart.

Not only are hardnosed and seemingly uncaring socioeconomic policies that attempt to balance budgets, avoid insolvency, and pay off outstanding debt boring, they are dangerous to narcissistic politicians who feel entitled to long careers in the public sector. Deft politicians—e.g., the ones who succeed in their elections—understand the power of emotional satisfaction, promises of collective salvation, and oversimplification in garnering votes. A speech chock–full of heartfelt promises usually wins in tournaments between complex self–critical logic and simple feel–good emotions. So when people and political activism butt heads over mandated change, a slew of self–contradictory logic blurs the line between rational and irrational behavior.

One such blur is the government's capacity to undermine an economy, no matter how much resources are available. In a phenomenon known as the paradox of plenty or the "resource curse," nations and regions with an abundance of natural resources tend to be bedeviled with slower economic growth compared with nations possessing fewer natural resources. Even nations awash in oil revenues can't escape these consequences. For instance, in 2007, during Hugo Chavez's second term, Venezuela's citizens, despite their country's booming oil economy, experienced severe food shortages and long waiting lines. Ironically, the price controls enacted to prevent shortages there actually made them more acute. Historically, societies based on forced equality of income have been transmogrified into beggar societies. Economies will starve and become crippled, hurting those least likely to weather hardships well—the poor, the weak, and the marginalized—despite the fact that by governmental decree, it is illegal to be unequal or poor.

In the long run, government handouts and bailouts are detrimental to the health of a society. Compulsive excesses ensure a grab bag of insecurity, unpredictability, and negative feedback loops. When government confiscates assets from certain people in order to bestow them on others, bonds are broken, releasing political chaos. It is probably safe to predict that wage earners will become upset when their hard–earned money is taken away and given to people who are less-oriented toward work or to wealthy elitists in the investment and banking industry. With such heavy–handed interference comes the inevitable sociological backlash of hostility, resentment, and acts of revenge.

Needless to say, the productive members of society will take action to offset what they consider unjust. They will flee a region, stop working, hide assets, commit sabotage, or do whatever else it takes to protect that which they value most. Paradoxes will bloom in such compromised environments. Take the Ukraine, the "breadbasket" of Europe in the 1930s, as an example of how a land of plenty can swiftly turn into one of scarcity, when political systems cause artificial famines. Some seven to ten million Ukrainians died of starvation in a socialist country, which ironically outlawed such inequalities as hunger.

Efforts to mandate change via governmental policy will serve only to drive members of society to readjust their lives accordingly, sometimes in convoluted ways. Citizens must deal with inconsistencies by acting inconsistently and with less efficiency (which economists like to call "deadweight loss"). Under such conditions, people can no longer nurture social bonds by interacting and coordinating with other members of society. Instead, the populace must react according to the dictates of a centralized system that has little knowledge about each citizen's situation. In this case, people must act as though they're irrational in order to be rational. This is the stuff of paradoxes—a world turned topsy–turvy, as if ensnared within Dr. Jekyll's and Mr. Hyde's split personalities.

Despite this nerve–wracking climate, paradoxical tensions help us better understand the nuances of reality. Yet, those who disparage unevenness as being the nemesis of humanity undervalue reality. These perpetual fixers and meddlers—"the parity pushers"—seek to change what often can't be changed. They see not what reality is, but what they want it to become. They are blinded by the fog of equilibrium and governmentalism, demanding to know why too few women rise to executive positions, or why not enough racial minorities obtain high–paying jobs. Their superficial metaphysics shields them from the prevalent injustice of the capricious, natural world. Butler Shaffer has referred to these overbearing zealots as "people–pushers" who "can be thought of as a person with a leash, in search of a dog."[2]

The parity pushers fail to see the subtle grays of complexity in all of its tortured and messy manifestations. With swords held high, they ride forth and exploit every possible weapon in the political arsenal. Equality is to be imposed, unevenness and nonlinearity banished to the nether world. Science is politicized for mass consumption, and natural laws are summarily supplanted by ideological "correctness."

The worst offenders—people–pushers on steroids—undoubtedly work in the company of governments. All too often, those who defend governmentalism and the excesses of state spending are salaried by governmental entities. They have a stake in growing the state. Bigger is better. Salaries higher. Benefits richer. Those reaping money from the state cannot help but identify with the state's interests. Money and generous benefits can easily alter a person's political outlook. Ideology follows the money.

Under a nigh–Faustian pact with power, paradoxes erupt like a runaway nuclear reactor in Chernobyl. Strange abnormalities and bizarre inconsistencies burst and shower society with seemingly unsolvable crises. As dilemmas multiply, it becomes obvious that the controls themselves are perpetrating the fraud and that direct opposites escaping from the controls would better ease most predicaments. But the predicaments can't be resolved until the social or political situations improve. And yet, these situations often can't improve until the restraining chains are unshackled—leading to a paradoxical deadlock with no way out.

What the parity pushers have done is to forge, artificially, Catch–22 quagmires that distort the natural course of events. They have whipped up surreal, convoluted crusades for every possible utopia—no matter how fantastical. Within this perverse paradise, the pendulum of unintended consequences gyrates recklessly, as political entropy takes hold. Lao–tzu observed this phenomenon over two thousand years ago, writing: "The greater the cunning with which people are ruled, the stranger the things which occur in the land."

Connections to Paradoxes

It is not difficult to understand why paradoxes and chaos theory are joined at the hip. Transition from chaos to order and back again can play havoc with differential equations. Put another way, complexity causes profound contradictions on almost every level. The unpredictable nature of the universe lends itself to a wide range of inconsistencies that emerge because of the conflict–laden nature of time, diversity, and fractal scaling. Ironically, one of the biggest discrepancies is found in chaos theory itself. Although chaotic behavior appears to be something difficult to predict or control, it is still, in principle, scientifically classified as "deterministic chaos." But in practice, chaotic systems have an unpredictability that defies most normal methods of calculation. Nonetheless, chaos theory is still tethered to deterministic formulas—a sort of Alice–in–Wonderland oddity that never ceases to amuse some chaologists. One mathematician, Ian Stewart, characterized the idiosyncrasies of chaos as something of a Pandora's box, saying that "chaos is lawless behavior governed entirely by law."[3]

Many paradoxes correspond to fractal features. Take the French proverb, "The more things change, the more they stay the same." At first glance, the statement appears devoid of sanity, but this oxymoron epitomizes the nature of fractal structures. Although every change may appear different, there is a deep symmetry among all spatiotemporal events. Among the properties of fractal scalability are competing layers of similar and dissimilar events—deviations which show that neither fractal nor Euclidean geometries are close to perfection. In the case of fractals, the geometry is described in recursive algorithms, in which sets of instructions search for ways to create fractals. But along the way, links become degraded or broken, and fractal self–similarities are exposed to evolving mutations and genetics-like drift. In this way, change appears to have a corresponding footing in both worlds: change, and status quo.

Many modern physicists see the paradox as the irreconcilable conflict between the microscopic and macroscopic worlds. The "probabilistic" nature of microscopic physics does not seem to match well with the larger, "determinist" nature of macroscopic systems. Complexity helps mitigate the conflict by describing the way systems organize themselves. But it is difficult to perceive matter as being in an indeterminate state, or to accept that scientific laws can conflict within macroscopic and microscopic realms.

Chaotic behavior possesses all sorts of double–edged swords and trade -offs. Stephen Hawking recapped Heisenberg's Uncertainty Principle as follows: "It is a no win situation; the more accurately you try to measure the position of the particle, the less accurately you can know the speed, and vice versa." Every scientific law or formula is subject to some limitations, creating cracks and holes that prevent a proper fit, as seen in Kurt Gödel's incompleteness theorems. When nonlinear behavior is applied to formulas and models, flaws become exposed, especially when the data require recursive patterns. And whether caused by the perturbation of pinballs or by planets, the slightest variation of energy can produce crosscurrents and wakes that defy uniformity and come to dominate all scientific results.

The Diversity versus Unity Paradox

One of the most salient contradictions ever to tease the brain is the *diversity versus unity paradox*. It states: "The greater the diversity, the greater the strength and the stronger the inequality." This is almost equivalent to saying that there can be no peace without conflict. After all, it can be argued that diversity pits different people, values, and skills against each other, under a competitive and polarizing backdrop. Yet, where diversity has been allowed to flower, along with opportunity and choice, personal wealth has amassed to a much larger degree, as has been demonstrated in the melting–pot society of the United States—a land that some refer to as a single nation peopled by all nations. The wealth–poverty gap is so large in many poor homogeneous nations, that the reverse principle seems to apply: There is no diversity without inequality.

The explanations for this situation vary. Some contend that a potpourri of people encourages a yin–yang synthesis, in which the interplay of opposites flows toward a state of harmonious balance. Others point to the availability of open choice and the sense of individual control that often accompanies diversity. But the pivotal premise treads on instinctive ground. When diverse people come together under their own self–organizing sphere of influence, they intuitively breed unity, trust, and collaboration. What appears to be happening is a latent entangling effect, in which great diversity fosters striking similarities and cohesion. In this sense, the cliché that "opposites attract" has some merit.

Some chaologists have argued that dichotomies and divisions provide greater resiliency than the single–mindedness of the stubbornly opinionated provides. Diversity energizes collective wisdom, instilling a deeper, more holistic order. Tensional dynamics engage society toward a more open–eyed and sophisticated level of human interaction, expanding the circle of trust beyond family and tribe via the human instinct to associate and trade.

One chaology theorist, Twila Hugley Earle, an adjunct professor at the University of Texas at Austin, lectured at the 2004 International Alliance of Holistic Attorneys conference about the "ever–changing order in human systems."[4] She argued that the old Newtonian perspective was that uncertainty and conflict were a threat to a seamless community. But Earle saw something else. From her perspective, she believed that conflict and complexity provide a diversity that inspires harmony without the side effects of mindless conformity. Her example was the vibrations found in music. She suggests that the potency of a cacophonic disturbance reflects the wisdom of Plutarch: "Music, to create harmony, must investigate discord." In *Order Out of Chaos*, Prigogine and Stengers made the same observation, writing that creativity "breaks the temporal symmetry of the objects" so that "the noise in which we live arises as music."[5]

Earle heard a symphony of unanimity. "The paradox of holism itself that lies at the heart of all modern physics is that unity and diversity are two sides of the same coin." She contended that the wellspring of a healthy community is the hard–wiring of humanity toward "an instinct to create community." And when human beings are left alone, they weave a well–crafted tapestry of cooperation, not manipulation. She wrote: "Paradoxically, conflict is essential to strengthening the fabric of community. No fabric can be woven from threads that all go the same way. The function of a loom is to hold in equal tension threads that go in counter or opposing directions."[6]

Ironically, as people become more independent and self–directed, they simultaneously gravitate toward more interdependency. Most problem-solving strategies require group involvement, thus spurring collaboration. But behavior at the other end of the spectrum is not as redeeming. If someone becomes dependent on others, subordinate and restricted, never given any meaningful responsibilities, he will begin to lose his ability to make insightful choices. Without sovereignty of action, the disempowered can become a liability to the community.

The uncertainty of being independent motivates people to accumulate resources and friends in preparation for the unknown. Fear of the unknown causes people to self-organize and spread out the risk of failure to a larger number of people. This drive to excel is not uncommon in other fields. The basic, primal emotion of fear itself has been found to be vital to mankind's survival. "Fear is a funny thing," explained Ted Abel, a fear researcher at the University of Pennsylvania. "One needs enough of it, but not too much of it."[7]

There is plenty of evidence to demonstrate how diversity in physics precipitates unity. Ilya Prigogine won a Nobel Prize for his groundbreaking work on nonlinear dynamics, contending that turbulent clashes and complexity are the primary ingredients for making sustainable order. Clearly, the energy found within turbulence is what makes self–organizing systems in society possible.

Others, like Thomas Schelling and Robert Aumann, the 2005 Nobel laureates in economics, entertained the question of how to achieve conflict resolution through the focal point of game theory. Schelling provided a host of dichotomy–based paradoxes in which a player could strengthen his position by overtly worsening his own options, or in which retaliation could be more advantageous than the capability to resist an attack. After studying game theory for years, Schelling concluded that cooperation is better for both players, far better than what found under Nash–like equilibriums. Schelling's greatest insight was his contention that under most scenarios, players will choose cooperation over conflict.[8]

When David Bohm, a quantum physicist who worked with Albert Einstein, tackled the diversity–versus–unity paradox, he examined it through the prism of wholeness and subwholes. To achieve the unity of diversity, Bohm implied that the world had to be multidimensional, with what he called "implicate order," which allowed humans to be both different and the same, simultaneously, although such awareness occurs at various levels. He framed it almost mystically, saying that the individual is universal, and the universe is individual.

Even in personal relationships, many psychologists recognized that marriage partners have a love–hate relationship, with a desire to be both emotionally connected and aloofly independent. According to Bryce Kaye, author of *The Marriage First Aid Kit* and a psychologist with years of experience in psychotherapy and marriage counseling, the reason most marriage breakups occur is not because of a lack of communication or failure to get close enough. Rather, Kaye has written, "The paradox is that most break–downs in intimacy occur because partners are not sufficiently separate." What often happens is that people in relationships lose their separate identities, become emotionally enmeshed and insecure, and feel a need to obtain a sense of worth. This condition tends to cause one of the partners to obligate the other, as if in a parent–child relationship, while correspondingly attempting to change the parent. For Kaye, the submerging of a partner's identity is the central problem, arguing that "such intrusiveness, arising from enmeshed personal identities, is far more responsible for breakups than mere communication problems."[9]

Paradox Theory

Little research has been done in formulating a particular paradox theory that encompasses nonlinear, complex systems. Still, some chaos theorists speculate that there are at least two main catalysts for paradoxes. One involves the dynamics of "opposing forces" in which entropy is suspended to allow for the emergence of self–organizing systems. Such turbulence occurs because order increases at the expense of disorder—creating a sort of "force of instability," in which matter that's becoming organized will attempt to reach a stable point, but can do so only in clumps or clusters. But even when matter comes close to stabilizing, it must eject extra matter or energy in a choppy manner, and true stability is never reached. The paradox becomes unmistakable: When matter accumulates, it fluctuates between stability and instability, which can be interpreted as saying that the closer matter–energy gets to being stable, the more unstable it gets.

The other stimulus for paradoxes concerns the unequal, irregular nature of sets and subsets that can never match up entirely. The self–similarity of fractal geometry is not the paragon of perfection. Although fractals are founded on symmetrical multiplicity, in which parts of parts reach from the infinitely big to the infinitely small, nothing is exactly identical. The parts may appear similar or even redundant, but flaws prohibit a perfectly symmetrical universe. This conflict over conformity is the prefect breeding ground for patterns to clash, because something can be false at the superficial level while true at a deeper level.

If a paradox theory could be established, it might argue that a more obscure, almost undetectable level of consistency or dimension may live within a "schema"—an underlying organizational pattern or structure. But these consistencies would be lumpy. Structures tend to organize by simultaneously holding things together and yet having the potential to pull them apart. Perhaps this phenomenon is better explained by what physicists call "quantum weirdness"—in which matter and energy at the subatomic level exist partly in all possible states, simultaneously. Under quantum superposition, everything appears to occur at the same moment in time—a ubiquitous, microcosmic world of unlimited potential, until someone takes a measurement that causes an object to be confined to a single possibility.

But what if quantum superposition is not just confined to the micro–world of atomic and subatomic particles? For the human mind, such a reality would be unthinkable. Human beings have the habit of compartmentalizing time into logical and linear frameworks, with past, present, and future separated, to better understand what is going on. Until recently, scientists slavishly obeyed mathematical formulas as if they could be used to perfectly predict reality. But what if consistency is not necessarily defined as doing the same thing all the time? Could consistency be a roller–coaster of erratic changes, a strange attractor of a higher magnitude of order that overrides simpler inconsistencies, as cause and effect become disconnected? What if most inconsistencies are superficial, merely serving to unfold changes that appear different due to time passing, but are actually consistent and archetypal? In this case, the inconsistencies or fragmented differences might be more accurate than their Euclidean counterparts.

Some have argued that existence is possible only through contradiction, and that those trained in Aristotelian logic have been blinded by the influence of a linear, one–dimensional mind. Some have argued that this is why self–contradictions and irregularity disturb the logical mind, and perhaps this is why classical scientists denied or repressed those things that didn't fit neatly into predefined, logical sequences.

Looking at it from another reference point, consider the quantum entanglement of subatomic particles. It could be argued that order and chaos are entangled—similar to the unexplainable duality of waves and particles. But such a holistic approach has its detractors. For instance, human beings tend to make structures more difficult and complex than required. They put schema over substance, and seem delighted to raise elaborate barriers to restrict what might bring parts together into wholeness. This convoluted complexity causes people to embrace black–and–white dichotomies, draw hard lines in the sand, and choose embittered sides. All too often, an over–politicized and over-complexed society finds itself defending structure over commonality. And if battle lines are clearly demarcated, it is easy to slip into an us–versus–them mindset that identifies those on the other side as subhuman monsters.

Rulers' Paradox

For political wonks, the "Rulers' Paradox" defies modern assumptions about how a democratic society operates. Under John Locke's "consent of the governed" axiom, authorities derive their power from the citizenry, under the auspices of participatory democracy.[10] The people, via the election process, transfer their authority to governing officials, who serve in the best interest of society. This transfer of power and privilege resembles the power–of–attorney that bestows the fiduciary authorization to act on another person's behalf. For instance, those in government can rightfully defend their citizens, because each person has the identical right to defend him or herself from an attacker.

But what if officials in a democratic government organize death squads to assassinate international leaders? Where does such authority to commit murder come from? What if a freely elected government takes property away from its citizens through "eminent domain" powers, incarcerates accused persons with neither due process nor *habeas corpus*, tortures suspects, kidnaps troublemakers, takes away money from citizens, or wiretaps citizens' phone lines? Where and how does a representative government acquire authority to perform such coercive acts, acts disallowed for individual citizens?

If ordinary citizens could assassinate, steal, imprison, torture, kidnap, and wiretap without incrimination, that authority could be transferred to government for its democratic arsenal of policymaking weaponry. However, in most countries, the public does not have such rights or power. And if citizens were to do what governments often have done, they would be arrested and jailed. This idea is succinctly spelled out in a quote attributed to John Locke: "The people cannot delegate to government the power to do anything which would be unlawful for them to do themselves."[11] Nonetheless, governments routinely exercise such abuse of authority on a grand scale, although most people adhere to the belief that nobody, not even their leaders, should be above the law.

But this paradox falls deeper into the rabbit hole. It is no secret that government officials concur that the people, for the most part, cannot be trusted to do the right thing. If this were not the case, legislators would abstain from passing thousands of meddlesome and nanny–like laws, confident that people are good and decent, and will behave appropriately. Yet, the ironic twist is inescapable: If people are unfit to choose the right thing, then the government agencies administered by people must also be unqualified. Thomas Jefferson noted this conundrum when he wrote: "Sometimes it is said that man cannot be trusted with the government of himself. Can he, then, be trusted with the government of others?"[12]

The most important implication of this paradox is that if the consent of the governed is violated, so is the social contract. The social contract is considered the central pillar that binds society to a legitimate state authority. Elected governments derive their authority from the consent of the governed. If the government breaks its contract with the people, then the people are no longer bound by it, and they have a right to regain their complete sovereignty.

The Political Anarchist Paradox

One would not think of powerbrokers and lawmakers as exhibiting anarchistic traits. But save–the–world prima donnas tightly gripping their scepters are eager to push for more power, and fewer checks and balances. With a craving for everything in life, they cannot resist the egotistical urge to overreach their authority and thus to become the quintessential lawbreakers.

This is no accident. As reported in *Personality and Social Psychology Bulletin*, narcissists tend to become leaders. If a group has no leader, it is the narcissist who usually steps up to the leadership plate. "They like power, they are egotistical, and they are usually charming and extroverted. But the problem is, they don't necessarily make better leaders," asserted Amy Brunell, the lead author of a study at Ohio State University at Newark.[13]

The effects of narcissism have always been a major stumbling block to peaceful society. The politically addicted always want others to follow, blindly, their intransigent agendas. They may appear to be the embodiment of absolute law and order, but beneath their badge of officialdom, they are more interested in keeping everyone else at bay for their own personal satisfaction. Arrogantly self-righteous, they don't particularly like competitors interfering with their social or economic policies. In fact, some have referred to the politically engaged as "anarchists in drag."

Narcissistic politicians feel exempt from the rule of law, and routinely violate or ignore it. For instance, President George W. Bush claimed that he had the authority to disobey more than 750 laws enacted by Congress during his terms in office, contending that they infringed on his power as commander in chief. He made that rash assertion when he got caught violating a law requiring the federal government to obtain warrants before wiretapping telephones in America.[14]

According to legal scholars, it has not been uncommon for presidents to refuse to execute some congressionally enacted laws, claiming that they were unconstitutional. During a 1977 television interview with David Frost, Richard Nixon asserted that presidents were above the law, arguing that "when the president does it, that means that it is not illegal." But the scale of President Bush's ignoring of the law was unprecedented. Bush actually violated laws he himself had signed, secretly engaging in conduct that those laws criminalized.

For political narcissists, no outside laws or authority apply, except those they agree with. An anarchist could ask for no less, except that the philosophical anarchist wants control over only his own life, while the political anarchist wants control over everybody's lives. The political anarchist is so bereft of conscience that he will twist, distort, and break any law to gain the authority he feels entitled to.

In a sense, many political leaders are identical to bomb–throwing anarchists, in that if they don't get their way with foreign leaders, they will send tanks and bombers across international boundaries. Historically, the destruction from warring nations has been far more catastrophic than anything cooked up by small bands of sophomoric anarchists.

The anarchist–tyrant mindset of narcissistic politicians allows them to defy the law while simultaneously presiding over the creation and enforcement of those very laws—an obvious conflict of interest. Authors Morris and Linda Tannehill in *The Market for Liberty* confront this anomaly, writing: "The contradiction of hiring an agency of institutional violence to protect us from violence is even more foolhardy than buying a cat to protect one's parakeet."[15] This political lawlessness represents an anarchistic duplicity, a paradoxical role that is difficult to identify, since pathological narcissists disguise their true, egotistical intentions under a law–enforcement uniform.

Obviously, political anarchists are attracted to the adrenaline rush of power, because that is where they can get the largest dose of self–gratification and audience admiration. In truth, most politicians imbibe the spirit of both anarchistic and authoritarian criminality, blending moralist and amoralist camps into a sort of schizophrenic artifice that has led to epic disasters of almost unimaginable proportion.

Paradoxes and Inconsistencies　　　　　　　　　　　　　　　　　　　311

The Paradox of Power

Power can flip–flop oddly between strength and weakness, within the political realm. James Madison was probably the first to consider seriously the "paradox of power," posing a fundamental question: How do you bestow effective authority to a leader without also giving him the authority to abuse? Madison addressed this paradox in *The Federalist Papers* (1788), writing: "In framing a government which is to be administered by men over men, the great difficulty lies in this: you must first enable a government to control the governed; and in the next place obligate it to control itself." Economist Peter Leeson stated this paradox more succinctly: "An authority strong enough to constrain itself is also strong enough to break those constraints when it's convenient."[16]

So, why can't the populace simply learn how to slap permanent handcuffs on the wrists of government, and move on? The reason is actually more psychological than political. In a nutshell, people tend to be egocentric. Because of that, there is a good chance that politicians will be lured by narcissistic temptations. This might be a shock to some, but when the powerful are entrusted with the keys to power, they often go to the supply cabinet, unlock it, and loot everything inside.

The problem is that political leaders come in many shades of self–delusion. Although they might ask for more power in order to subdue power, they must deal with their own psychological issues. After all, the very seduction of power makes the powerful fearful of losing it. Their lust for power can crowd out other important issues, giving them a blind eye to the needs of others, and in egotistical and paranoid moments motivate them to face inward while pushing others away. George Kunz, an associate professor of psychology at Seattle University, has studied such paradoxes. In *The Paradox of Power and Weakness* he wrote: "The power of power can be self–destructive. It tends to burrow into and cling to the heart, rather than expose itself to the needy claims of others."[17]

Voters are generally hostile to anyone who appears to be grasping for greater political power. They usually favor leaders who publicly proclaim their dislike for power, promising instead to empower the people. Then again, these alleged power–hating candidates would require power to accomplish these goals. To confuse matters even more, to be elected, all politicians must pretend that they have no appetite for power. This fact alone makes it nearly impossible to discover which politician is telling the truth.

But the power paradox has a deeper meaning. Power and weakness sometimes act like kissing cousins, appearing to be distant but familiar with each other—almost as if they were in a quantum entanglement state. Some experts have suggested that the best way to both defuse and gain power, simultaneously, is to distribute it widely—mimicking one of the canons of decentralization. But would this contradictory stance destroy the strength of the state? For many decades, the Soviet Union had a vast military superiority over most of its neighbors and enemies. It looked impregnable, with a war machine that seemed undefeatable. But strength can be a weakness. To build this imposing fortress, the communist U.S.S.R. had to cobble together a bone–crushing bureaucracy that ran roughshod over the populace. This policy made the Soviet government extremely centralized and expensive to maintain, disempowering and impoverishing the Russian people. The final moment arrived in 1991, when the Russian people turned down their thumbs and refused to continue supporting an unresponsive structure. In the long run, power had become the source of the Communist Party's main weakness, but lead to its ultimate defeat.

Interestingly, the business world has been aware of the power–versus–weakness paradox for years. Thomas W. Malone, professor of management at M.I.T., suggested, in *The Future of Work*, that humble people with self–effacing attitudes can be stronger than those who dictate from positions of authority. He maintains that "sometimes the best way to gain power is to give it away." In other words, Malone argues that if you give people the power to make decisions, "they will be prone to support you and more likely to donate their energy, creativity, and dedication to your cause."[18]

The Autopoietic Paradox

Autopoietic systems are self–contained, self–created, and operationally closed. But the Autopoietic Paradox argues that the more autonomous a system becomes, the higher the number of feedback loops are required for the system to remain healthy. To the skeptical inquirer, this would sound nonsensical. By definition, an independent system embodies a cloistered framework that requires no outside feedback of any kind. To be autonomous means to be free from the influence and control of others. But Professor John Briggs and physicist–philosopher Dr. David F. Peat, who pointed out this curious anomaly, proposed that most complex systems, chiefly biological ones, have symbiotic relationships that are open to outside energy and influences.[19]

This seemingly self–contradicting assertion about the emergence of a system is crucial to understanding how a self–generating system can demonstrate both independent and dependent properties. What it boils down to is that the more autonomy people acquire, the more dependent they become on the interactions of others. Without state–induced privileges, subsidies, and bailouts, people are put into a position where it is advantageous to partner with others to satisfy their needs and dreams. Under a non–welfare state, people must be responsible for their own discrete actions, since nobody is overseeing or managing their activities. Such activity is often labeled "competitive." To most collectivists, competition conjures up images of predatory sharks interested only in gobbling up rivals and prey to establish a monopoly. Ironically, it is this ubiquitous, self–governing choice to control one's destiny and its well–defined, membrane–like boundaries that breaks down the monopolies of the powerful. Independence emancipates the status quo and decentralizes structures so as to bring about co–evolutionary and interdependent networks. Trade enhances mutual dependence, while creating favorable conditions for peace. Without free, competitive actions by autonomous agents, little can be accomplished. Without cooperation, there would be little worth trying to accomplish.

Human beings are heavily dependent on each other for survival. The interplay of cooperation and competition triggers feedback loops, which not only serve as regulatory processes, but arouse outside stimulation. Since all living systems are dependent to some degree, they require synergetic autonomy of movement in order to evolve optimal ways to ensure survival. In this sense, all living systems are open, and dependent on some form of connectivity.

So where did the concept of autopoiesis come from? In 1970, before the arrival of complexity science, Chilean biologists Humberto Maturana and Francisco Varela introduced this theory in an effort to understand the complexity of living systems. They were baffled by how the cognitive, immune, and nervous systems work together so seamlessly, yet lack reciprocity. To Varela, a professor of cognitive science at the École Polytechnique in Paris, France, the key question was how "the brain configures or constitutes relevance from otherwise non–meaningful interactions."[20]

This question is fundamental for biological identity. Are living systems a mixture of subsystems, bereft of any meaningful relationships with neighboring systems and subsystems? After decades of study, these two theoretical biologists proposed that not only are living systems on the cellular level self–contained utilities, but they are "operationally closed." Herein lies the rub. How can organisms have subsystems that appear to be simultaneously closed and open? Varela himself acknowledged that his theory engenders a paradox, in that "self–organizing networks of biochemical reactions produce molecules which do something specific and unique: they create a boundary, a membrane, which constrains the network that has produced the constituents of the membrane."[21]

So, who is really running the biological show: the parts or the whole? Is it local or global? Or is it a "delocalized" system, as Varela claimed? The theory of autopoiesis quickly slid into a dilemma over the cognitive self–identity of organisms, somewhat akin to the symbolic tail–eating snake that represents no beginning or end.

Chaologists tailored this uncertainty into a classical paradox to dramatize similar quandaries faced by other disciplines. The question underscores profound principles. Within the dynamics of a structure, how can systems operate effectively with conflicting duality—one closed, miserly, separate, the other richly open and interconnected? More fundamentally, what if a system couldn't care less about selecting which one? With a fixed identity, is the overall system open or closed, independent or dependent? And more important, what decides on what is to be decided? How is "emergent coherence" possible without knowledge of exactly how the parts will mesh with other, neighboring parts? This quandary caused Varela to ask an epistemological question: *What is biological identity?*

Meanwhile, other theories came along and intruded on autopoiesis' wobbly turf. Prigogine's dissipative structures and Kauffman's autocatalytic sets explored emergent properties from simple interactive systems. But most complexity scientists have kept their distance from that and other theories that see cellular systems as "operationally closed."

Yet, to make it more confusing, many complexity theorists had to agree in principle with autopoietic systems. Many, if not most, complex system are boundary-driven, self–organized entities lacking outside control, associated with self–reference, and bootstrapped in a way that makes them unique. On the other hand, parts need not be entirely connected or aware of one another in order to play an active role in the whole. Such "detached interconnectivity" had already been observed as the phenomenon described by Adam Smith as the *invisible hand*, in which separate entities are in the dark as to what they are doing, yet still contribute to the well–being of the whole. To the more holism–inclined complexity scientists, biological subsystems can be somewhat disengaged from the main organism—where no input or output is observable—yet subsystems still are entangled in a way that benefit the entire organism.

This holistic concept is better explained under the discrete modeling of "cellular automata," which is a study of the growth of patterns on a checkerboard-like grid of cells. Introduced by John von Neumann, one of the foremost mathematicians of the twentieth century, this theory explains, mathematically, how simplicity could create complexity. In this case, cellular automata approximate evolutionary and developmental systems of nature. The way this discrete model works is by letting independent units on a grid both communicate their internal conditions and receive commensurate input from their immediate neighbors—all of which maps out the physics of cooperative emergence. This communication is comparable to the 10 trillion human neurons described as "simple switches." They are switches in the sense that neurons don't touch each other, although they fire chemical and electric signals between contact points—the synapses. But how would a heap of discrete switches accomplish anything of significance? Most people would agree that stringing together millions of Coke bottles would have little impact, and yet, neuron switches have done something miraculous. They have created something greater than what could be expected of a simple switching node: human consciousness and intelligence. The organization of human neurons has spurred the emergence properties of abstract thought, language, and culture.

In the sociopolitical realm, does autopoiesis challenge the emblematic context of rugged individualism? Many consider individualism to be the underlying cultural imprint of Americanism. It is symbolized by a breed of fiercely independent trailblazers who roamed the unexplored lands of the American West—referred to as mountain men. Hollywood has romanticized these frontier archetypes as heroic but bellicose adventurers. Although these fur–clad men were self–reliant and dauntless, many social pundits have written them off as anti–social misfits who had neither the need nor the desire to collaborate with others. Of course, this version of history is mostly a myth.

Contrary to popular perception, most mountain men traveled in groups, often employed by fur companies, and hunted in the wilderness in brigades of up to sixty men. These hunters and explorers would set up camp, then break into smaller sub-groups of two or three. They were well organized, and they knew that teamwork was superior to isolated effort. Nonetheless, there were some "free trappers"—solitary mavericks who went out alone and became hermits—but they represented a small fraction of the mountain–man population. Still, even these loners would meet up in month–long, carnival–like rendezvous in the summer to trade goods, swap stories, get drunk, and replenish supplies.

Nobody lives in a closed system, let alone a complete vacuum. What rugged self–determination brings to the table are the mechanics by which open access and uncertainty trigger teamwork and community involvement. The tension arising from the dynamics of a system provokes self–organization and growth. Without such chaos-like dynamics, social structures would trend toward a stagnant pattern of paternalism, which would provide for people's needs without expecting them to be responsible. Paternalism makes participants passive, unmotivated, and unadaptable. Such attitudes treat people as foolish children, taking the role of a father figure who makes the decisions for everyone, supposedly for their own good, even if the patriarch's actions contradict the wishes of the participants.

As discovered in the studies of swarm dynamics, independence and cooperation are synonymous, bringing together harmonious but heterogeneous unity. Dissipative systems, like social organizations, function by the spontaneous occurrence of symmetry breakup (catastrophe theory) or statistical bifurcation (anisotropy), which forge the formation of complexity structures. Such complexity is possible only through the cooperative interactions of the system's parts and subparts. Independence allows for change; dependency prevents it.

Dissipative systems maintain their identity only because they operate as completely open, network–like structures, allowing the free flow of matter, energy, and information through their environments. Individual autonomy gives everyone in a social structure an atomistic voice. That accessible voice is couched in creative, nonlinear collaboration.

In a welfare state, socio–economic problems tend to become more acute as time passes. Generally, the bigger the welfare state, the less citizens are willing to do for one another—ushering in a lethargic apathy that mirrors slow–death entropy. Why help out a neighbor or stranger? Somebody else has already been assigned to hand out funds and entitlements. If the government has the responsibility to take care of everyone, why should anyone else volunteer? Perhaps this is why Europeans, who have had a welfare state far longer than America, give far less time and money to charity.

Short–Term, Long–Term Inconsistencies

An inconsistency between the short term and the long term is not paradoxical, per se. It is the temporal outcomes from efforts toward conflicting goals that will generate contradictory results. An example: most people on di-

Paradoxes and Inconsistencies 317

ets struggle to shed their unsightly extra pounds, but the short–term enjoyment of eating fatty foods often overrides their long–term strategy of losing weight. In that sense, order is often invisible until longer periods have passed, serving to reveal recognizable patterns.

Zeno of Elea spent much of his life pointing out, within his concept of finite "instant time," what he thought were paradoxes of motion. To Zeno, motion, plurality, and change do not exist—only their illusion does. And yet, without the fluid motion of time, how could the inconsistencies of reality exist? Contradictions have the habit of developing where temporal changes cross spatial boundaries.

Temporal trespassing is dependent on relative speed, meaning that the dilation of time must "patternize" and categorize events into something recognizable. Perhaps this is the secret to why short–term fixes often fail to accomplish long–term benefits; nobody knows the outcome until someone can figure out a way to provide measurable outcomes. Of course, this suggests that a working model for short– and long–term goals is difficult to produce. For instance, short–lived events often behave randomly, but long–term results are often viewed as deterministic. The fallacy of this circular reasoning is that long–term effects are equally dependent on the randomness found in short–term outcomes. This begs the question: Does nature abhor linearity?

It is no secret that short–term and long–term tugs–of–war overspill and overlap into political boundaries. Political systems are adept at making short–term promises that have no relationship to long–term solutions. Of course, in a world addicted to the aphrodisiac of power, long–term outcomes are irrelevant. Most political leaders understand the agony of a short political shelf life. They know that even a tyrant is limited in how events will eventually play out, or how his supposedly loyal comrades will behave. Like slow–moving ocean currents, events have delayed memories that could come bubbling up at any moment, and when they do, politicos must face the consequences of their administrations' past policies. Sooner or later, their quick–fix policies will, like chickens, come home to roost, spoiling careers and reputations.

All systems need the ability to make short–term changes to ensure long–term success, but the blood sport of politics is not evolutionary by nature. Systems based on overbearing politics are static, operationally immutable, and gridlocked—meaning that political solutions are rarely practical or workable.

Paradoxes in the Economic Arena

The field of economics has no superior defense against inconsistency. Economics is well–stocked with all sorts of unpalatable realities that frighten political linearists. That is because when people engage in economic activity, they create and discard structures without regard to how things worked in the past. So, when central planners try to commandeer the cook's job, all sort of side effects bubble up and boil over.

For instance, Western democracies have enacted many laws in an effort to impose fair and open competition in the marketplace. It is true that everyone should play nice in the business sandbox, but governments have attempted to legislate virtues into business practices, practices which are unknown within their own smoke–filled, back–room chambers. The real mystery is, how can a monopoly–clad system faithfully promote open systems? By nature, command and control systems are closed–ended, single–minded, rigid, and choked–in–red–tape bureaucracies. They spawn monopolies, no–bid contracts, nationalization, unaccountable lobbyists, exclusive privileges, trickle–down cartels, secret back room deals, nepotistic interludes, and generous favors to a select few—basically, everything that is anathema to the dynamics of competitive market forces.

This particular irony is dramatic. Democratic governments regularly give lip service to a type of open competition that is verboten within their own geopolitical monopoly of power. In essence, governments are allergic to competition. The mere effort of trying to bully companies to compete in a way that a government believes to be proper will alter the outcome in unpredictable ways.

In science, this condition is referred to as the "observer effect," which posits that the mere act of observing an experiment will have an effect on the phenomenon being observed. Thus, the act of measuring a phenomenon, such as observing an electron, can alter its outcome. Perhaps this explains the long–term failure of most legal cases intended to stop so–called anticompetitive practices. When partisan gamesmanship attempts to legislate pro–competition laws, the tampering can easily flip good intentions into bad deeds. In this way, it is difficult to know for sure what is affecting what. In fact, some economists question whether anyone could ever know the exact number of competitors required to maintain what has been labeled "pure and perfect competition." For all we know, fewer competitors may be better than more, in certain circumstances. In the final analysis, observing the market is the only way to reveal what does and does not work.

Of course, most political systems are not disposed to becoming mere observers. They are eager to prescribe interventionistic and metastatic antidotes. They are more interested in static conditions than process. In its early days, the American republic refrained from interfering with the lives of its citizens, limiting itself to enforcing contracts, coining money, and organizing defenses against foreign invaders. And that was about it. In those days, leaders had little desire to right societal inequalities, impose order, legislate values, stimulate economic change, or search for foreign monsters to slay. The consensus was that it was not the duty of government proselytizers to cure any so–called evils festering beyond their limited boundaries. When it came to competition, the driving force was freewheeling innovation.

One of the more fascinating examples of the innovative and unconventional nature of competition occurred during a David and Goliath match that started in 1904. The fledging Dow Chemical Company decided to compete with a powerful chemical cartel in Germany by selling bromine lower than the costly 49 cents per pound. The German cartel Die Deutsche Bromkonvention, which had fixed worldwide bromine prices, threatened to deluge the American market with the cheap chemical if Dow should enter European markets. "Crazy Dow," as the founder was nicknamed, took the dare and sold bromine for 36 cents in Europe and Japan. The German companies retaliated and dumped the chemical on the American market for 15 cents, determined to put Dow out of business through predatory price–cutting.

Seemingly, such a blow would kill a young upstart company, but that did not happen. Instead, Herbert Dow, the quintessential opportunist, bought up the cheap, German–made bromine, repackaged it, and sold it back to Europe for 27 cents. Dow pulled out of the American markets and sent everything over to the foreign markets. The German cartel had thought they were going to put the American company out of business, and could not figure out how Dow was able to stay alive. Determined to destroy this annoying gadfly, they kept lowering the price, finally reaching 10.5 cents, but nothing seemed to be working. For some strange reason, the demand for bromine was skyrocketing in the United States. The other mystery concerned the origination of the cheaper bromine that was flooding European markets. The cartel members were in an uproar, soon accusing each other of cheating and selling the chemical below the prearranged price. According to historian Burton Folsom in *Empire Builders, The Vision and Influence of Michigan's Early Entrepreneurs*, by the time the Germans discovered what was happening, Dow had secured new markets and was becoming a chemical powerhouse. Little Dow Chemical had slain the

European giant.[22]

What is interesting to note is that historically, when an industry is accused of anti–competitive practices, especially in third–world nations, politicians routinely confiscate an entire industry, roll everything into a single, state–operated monopoly, and declare that a true competitive environment has now been achieved. Ironically, those who oppose the consolidation of the corporate entities into a monopolistic giant are often the same crowd clamoring for a monopolistic national health care system operated under the universal control of a political system. Go figure.

State monopolies make poor showcases for the virtue of free competition, despite the rants of the politically privileged class. Competition tends to flourish far better without the heavy–handedness of outside intrusions. To do otherwise is to replicate the old notion that religion and society are better off when governments control the purse strings of state–sanctioned sects.

When governments launch antitrust lawsuits to "restore competition," the results are usually unclear. In the largest antitrust case ever, the U.S. government decided to break up IBM Corporation, by force of law, in the 1960s and 1970s. Eventually, the Justice Department failed in every case filed against IBM. So, did IBM continue as an out–of–control giant with monopolistic dominance? No. Although once a behemoth with 400,000 employees, "Big Blue" is no longer considered a dominant player. The company could not keep up with fast–moving technological changes and smarter startups.

According to Thomas J. DiLorenzo, professor of economics at Loyola College in Maryland, the Sherman Antitrust Act of 1890 was actually "designed to protect incompetent businesses from superior competition, not to protect consumers from monopoly."[23] Even the renowned antitrust scholar and chief judge of the U.S. Court of Appeals for the Seventh Circuit, Richard Posner, has acknowledged that antitrust laws are generally contrary to consumer interests.

But governments have found other ways to manage competition. When the market fluctuates beyond the norm, central planners panic and attempt to handicap those involved. These regulators fail to realize that the middle can only be defined by its extremes. Occasionally, markets gyrate to extreme edges, providing helpful markers to establish a stabilizing center. This is just the natural way for systems to dissipate energy, as posited by Prigogine. But regulators have little patience with fluctuations. They find it expedient to handicap a market already reeling from past excesses, or to subsidize those that are dy-

Paradoxes and Inconsistencies 321

ing because of incompetence or bad business practices.

A good example is the scramble by American legislators, starting in 2007, to fix the crisis over bad subprime loans. Legislators rushed to shut the subprime loan gate, after the home mortgage meltdown had already left the borrowers' barn—meaning that the lending industry stopped making subprime loans once the financial crisis had hit. The industry had already been punished for its easy–credit sins—enduring record–breaking financial losses, extinction of many mortgage lenders, liquidity problems, and a quality–credit crunch. True to their political theater background, a host of lawmakers were back on center stage trying to redirect government agencies to stack more legislative controls on an industry already suffering under a heavy load. The bruised and battered monetary markets simply needed time to readjust, heal, and correct their own excesses. Never again would they dispense "no–documentation" loans like candy to children at a birthday party.

And if the political opportunists succeed, perhaps only the wealthy, with high credit scores, will be able to get home loans. This scenario harkens back to the days when the only people who could get a bank loan were those who didn't need one.

If the political opportunists succeed, perhaps only the wealthy, with high credit scores, will be able to get home loans. This scenario harkens back to the days when the only people who could get a bank loan were those who didn't need one.

The real estate speculation bubble and subsequent meltdown were set into motion by easy money, and by the low–interest loan policies of the Federal Reserve, Federal Housing Administration (FHA), Fannie Mae, Freddie Mac. As Government–Sponsored Enterprises (GSEs) that can get subsidized credit from the U.S. Department of the Treasury, both "Fannie and Freddie have blazed the way for competitive mortgage products that have helped to revolutionize the mortgage lending industry in ways that the more conservative, less innovative banks had not in the past."[24] In 1999, Fannie Mae was particularly aggressive in "easing credit requirements on loans that it will purchase from banks and other lenders."[25] Further, the Clinton administration put increased pressure on Fannie Mae "to expand mortgage loans among low and moderate income people."[26] In fact, starting in the mid–1990s, both of these government–chartered corporations—Fannie Mae and Freddie Mac—lobbied Congress for permission to buy questionable subprime loans and package them into mortgage–backed securities. Since they held the majority of the American mortgage market, other lending institutions followed suit, in order to compete.

For years, the U.S. government has initiated laws and adopted rhetoric in an effort to assist low–income, high–risk borrowers with generous mortgage programs, often enticing homebuyers into loans they could not afford. Legislation has included the American Dream Down Payment Act of 2003, which authorized the distribution of $200 million per year to help low–income families with down payments and closing costs. President Bush explicitly told federal agencies to loosen or outright eliminate regulatory barriers to affordable home ownership.

In the past, affordable–housing advocacy groups and government agencies would pressure or sue mortgage lenders for not having made loans to low–income families and minorities. When lenders argued that some of these borrowers were unqualified or had poor credit histories, the "race card" would be tossed onto the table. Affordable housing advocates, including ACORN, demanded more loans to minorities. After the lending industry finally relaxed loan qualifications for minorities, lenders were again charged with racial disparities, but this time they were condemned for making *too many loans*. In a 2008 federal lawsuit, the NAACP sued fourteen of the nation's largest lenders for having saddled bad–risk and minority borrowers with high, unaffordable interest rates.

Ironically, the rush for easy–money mortgages earmarked for low–income families contributed significantly to the collapse of the housing market. After the meltdown, new financial regulations prevented low–income borrowers from borrowing, which hastened a growing wave of home foreclosures. In fact, the subprime mortgage crisis of 2007 typifies the classic boomerang effect. The purpose for providing easy loans though various laws and quasi–public agencies had been to encourage home ownership. By the middle of 2011, the *New York Times* reported that "homeownership dropped sharply, to 66.4 percent, from a peak of 69.2 percent in 2004. The ownership rate is now back to the level of 1998, and some experts say it could decline to the level of the 1980s or even earlier."[27]

Easy credit led to unsustainable levels of private and public debt, creating a speculation bubble that put the economic train on track for a financial wreck, leading to the Great Recession. So what did President Obama's administration do? In an effort to stimulate the economy, the federal government passed a nearly trillion–dollar stimulus package crammed with massive deficit spending and debt. But wasn't too much debt the problem? ABC–TV newsman John Stossel asked the obvious question at the time: "If too much debt was a problem, why is more debt now a solution?" *Newsweek* echoed the same theme:

"The Obama administration is caught in a paradox. It must borrow and spend to fix a crisis created by too much borrowing and spending."[28] And to top it off, bailed–out banks and businesses not only were rewarded for bad business practices, but taxpayers were left on the hook to pay off these failing companies' bad gambling debts.

Other Ironies, Curiosities and Paradoxes

There are no shortages of paradoxes among Pharisees. Most people dream of becoming fabulously wealthy, but freely admit that they hate the rich. Many crave fancy new homes with modern amenities, but seek to stop greedy developers from building additional homes in their community.

Consider the case of minimum wage laws. Although most economists agree that government–mandated wage hikes tend to result in job losses for minorities and low–skilled workers—the very people the laws are intended to help—most political leaders can't wait to sponsor laws to boost so–called "living wage laws."

In another paradox, human vices are often camouflaged as virtues. When someone lambastes a depravity, it is often done to cover up the accuser's own imperfect nature. Under the licensing effect, people feel free to be two–faced and hypocritical when they criticize others for exhibiting amoral traits. For instance, those who complain the loudest about the greedy bastard next door often turn out to be some of the worst offenders when it comes to greed. The mere act of calling another person greedy allows the accuser to feel that such behavior is not within his own scope of activities. Since he was the one to point out the moral depravity, obviously, he can't be greedy, himself.

Such contradictions are deeply rooted in a mixed–signal subtext. Social commentators love to spin stories about the sins of the filthy rich, sarcastically lampooning any entrepreneur who has accumulated some wealth. These critics deplore the rich because they have too much money, while the common man goes without. But a truly ungreedy person couldn't care less about another person's wealth, no matter its size. To the nonmaterialistic man, money is merely a tool that may or may not be needed to have a contented life. So, if money is unimportant to live a full, happy life, why would anyone get upset over those who have legally gathered their own pot of gold? Could envy—another of the so–called seven deadly sins—be at play? In this case, envy over what someone else possesses is first cousin to greed.

Communist ideology is perhaps the most extreme case of self–righteousness to perform on the paradoxical stage, even denying the empirical account of human nature. The Chinese Communist Party's motto during the Cultural Revolution proclaimed: "Battle with heaven, fight with the earth, struggle with humans—therein lies endless joy."[29] Under this equality–through–force ideology, mankind is to be cleansed of his ignoble frailties, and replacing them with a flawless, classless, moneyless, altruistic society. But the violence needed to "perfect" society has a habit of backfiring. The greater the force imposed, the more the people turn away, revolt, or become isolated. By nature, people are flawed, and cannot or will not acknowledge their own vices. Nobody clearly understands the total scope of his or her own ignorance. It is difficult to eliminate that which refuses to be recognized. Contrary to what had been expected by the theorists of Marxism, generations of people living under socialism became morally corrupt in societies originally set up explicitly to eliminate all manner of corruption.

Perhaps the most contradictory tenet of Marxism is the notion of "stateless communism." It was predicted that through the administration of a socialist economy, government itself would eventually become unnecessary and wither away of its own accord. Even the Soviet Union's first constitution, in 1918, proclaimed the abolition of state authority. Of course, those nations caught under the shadow of the hammer and sickle discovered a system that was anything but stateless. "People's socialism" surged into a highly centralized institution with absolute control over almost every aspect of human life. The state was everything; the individual was subordinated to Soviet overlords. Somehow totalitarianism had replaced Marxism's espoused objective of an unstructured, utopian, workers' paradise.

Paradoxes often arise because theory routinely refuses to be subordinate to reality. If someone wished to travel to the moon, it would be highly advisable to point the spacecraft that way. If the destination is a stateless society, it would be reasonable to start removing the building blocks of statecraft instead of constructing more. Nonetheless, Marx wanted a steady–state structure in order to alter peoples' behavior, so that nobody would ever embrace greed, inequality, or money. His "logic" was to pump up governing structures to forge perfection, by liberating people from the chains of their natural inclinations. In essence, Marx was anticipating something that could not exist: a schizophrenic world where he expected to abolish government by expanding it. His delusions of ideological purity failed to take into account mankind's own complex and self–contradicting enigmas.

Paradoxes and Inconsistencies 325

Interestingly, recent theories of "organizational behavior" have impugned Marx's stateless theories, suggesting that when groups are given political power, they tend to want to preserve their privileges no matter what. This psychological urge is so strong that even groups dedicated to the destruction of privileges often reestablish a host of new advantages under a different name. In the Soviet Union, the so–called classless society had a privileged group of administrators and party members known as the "Nomenklatura." This new elite received material rewards and monopolistic privileges that outmatched those of the bourgeoisie and aristocratic classes it was designed to replace. They had their own separate and superior medical facilities, stores, and housing, all unavailable to the masses. This ruling stratum preached equality but practiced elitism; they spoke against selfishness but rode roughshod over others in order to get what they wanted—a fine touch of bitter irony that has become the legacy of equality-bent communities.

Foreign Aid Conundrum

Foreign aid is the height of irony. Critics refer to it as an international welfare program designed to make poor people in rich nations subsidize rich people in poor nations. But the real conundrum dogging foreign humanitarian aid is that it is impoverishing the African continent. International charities have concurred with African economists and journalists, alike, that foreign aid not only fails to help the poor, it increases the likelihood of starvation. This would seem impossible on the face of it, but according to CARE, one of the largest international relief organizations, the American–subsidized food programs "cause rather than reduce hunger."[30]

So what is happening? Critics argue that food aid "undermines African farmers' ability to produce food, making the most vulnerable countries of the world even more dependent on aid to avert famine." In other words, African farmers cannot compete with free or underpriced food from other nations. The aid is artificially driving down world crop prices—what some critics have portrayed as "agricultural dumping."

Complexity has the habit of screwing up even the best–laid plans. Making people completely dependent on others carries a high risk of long–term, bad side effects. Why plan for the future, if somebody else has already taken over the role? Why plant crops, if tons of food from overseas arrive free of charge, all wrapped up in nice cardboard boxes?

Time magazine author Alex Perry acknowledged this inescapable fact, writing: "Over time, sustained food aid creates dependence on handouts and shifts focus away from improving agricultural practices to increase local food supplies."[31]

Foreign aid has become an "ineffective instrument that distorts recipients' incentives" wrote Andrew Mwenda, a Ugandan radio and newspaper journalist. "For the last 40 years, Africa's been getting more, not less, aid—we've received more than $500bn. But we are getting poorer, not richer."[32] Mwenda insists that Western aid merely fuels corrupt states, sustains wars, and undermines democracy. Another journalist and the producer of the documentary *Africa: Open for Business*, Carol Pineau, confirmed the problem: "No one in Africa really believes any more that aid does any good at all."[33] The old Chinese proverb seems appropriate: "give a man a fish and you feed him for a day. Teach a man to fish and you feed him for a lifetime."

Yet foreign aid has a much longer contradictory arm. The U.S. Department of Agriculture is required to subsidize over two dozen commodities. This policy not only damages the livelihoods of African farmers, it also wreaks havoc on small–time American farmers. Small family farms are faltering, to the point where some say they are becoming a vanishing breed. The major reason cited is the generous federal farms subsidy. On the surface, this argument would seem ludicrous. The $15–$20 billion federal subsidies granted to farmers and agribusiness annually, which tend to cause overproduction, would seem to keep farmers in the lap of luxury. In actuality, "the big farms get most of the money.... Ten percent of the beneficiaries get over 70 percent of the payments...."[34] The massive payout to industrial-sized agricultural corporations lowers their overall farming costs, putting the ma–and–pa family farm at an economic disadvantage.

Farm subsidies are a testament to how such policies create problems in order to fit incompatible but predetermined solutions. One example is the mass influx of illegal immigrants into America. There is evidence that America's highly subsidized farm program is causing Mexican laborers to illegally cross the border. The artificially cheap food sold by American companies to Mexico is putting their farmers out of business and increasing unemployment. This worsening economic condition encourages Mexican farm laborers to head north to find better job opportunities.

But do the bad effects of foreign aid provide a lesson for problems found in the domestic welfare policies in America? They certainly do. Clear patterns abound. The recognition of the harm perpetrated by foreign aid practices in Africa must send a cold chill down the spine of welfare enthusiasts in the United States. If such humanitarian aid is now seen as harmful to starving Africans, causing a state of dependence for the poor and sustaining political corruption, what message does this send to poverty–stricken people in American ghettos, addicted to domestic welfare subsidies? After all, poverty levels in American have hardly budged despite the expenditure of some $5.4 trillion for anti–poverty programs (1965–1995) to mitigate wealth inequalities.

Preservation Laws That Fail to Preserve

In an ironic twist, "tree preservation" might qualify as the poster child for one of the most memorable political oxymorons, especially when lawmakers use preservation measures to control property they don't own. In many neighborhoods, such laws have actually killed trees. How has this happened? Laws enacted to protect trees on private property motivate owners not to plant trees, or to plant only the nonprotected types. Or worse, owners, mindful that small saplings frequently expand will mature into legally immune trees, chop down young trees before they reach a statutory size. Strict tree laws make trees a potential risk, if the owner wishes to make alterations to his or her property in the future. The safest route is to not plant trees at all, especially native species.

This was a lesson the Collard family of Glendale, California, learned the hard way. Asked by the Glendale Fire Department to trim their trees, the couple hired a licensed tree trimmer. Although the local tree trimmer said no permits were required, an urban forester from the city happened by, and cited the owners for failure to get a tree trimming permit for the mature trees. When the city's citation arrived in their mail, the Collards saw that the price tag was $347,600 — a sum calculated by estimating that the indigenous oak and sycamores were worth nearly $100,000 apiece.

The couple nearly passed out. The trees had not been destroyed; only about 15 percent of the foliage had been removed. Their home is situated in a high wildfire risk area, which requires them to periodically clear away vegetation on their land. What the Collard family did not know was that the tree protection ordinance first enacted in 1980 had become more restrictive, with higher fines. They soon discovered that other property owners had been hit with huge fines as well. Only after paying an attorney $1,200 and receiving a generous dose of publicity did they get City Hall to back down and promise to lower the fine.[35]

People like options as much as they like playing it safe. And they don't like being told what to do with their own property. Forced stewardship has a great potential to turn seemingly innocent laws inside out. Tree laws kill trees, because those laws ignore human behavior and the complexities inherent in society.

Sea turtles have also suffered from preservation laws originally designed to protect the species. Such rigid laws have, in fact, boomeranged and brought the species closer to extinction. Under the Convention on International Trade in Endangered Species (CITES) and the U.S. Endangered Species Act of 1973, turtle meat, even if farmed by sustainable aquaculture practices, became illegal in the United States. Most countries enacted similar restrictions in a belief that they would be protecting the animal. One company however had already started a program back in 1968, to farm green sea turtles on Grand Cayman Island. The company soon ran aground over emerging preservation laws, and became financially insolvent.

But could farming actually help an endangered species like the sea turtle? Paradoxically, a number of unconventional environmentalists have expressed the view that the best way to ensure the survival of a species is to eat it. This seems totally bizarre. But think about! There are no shortages of cows, chickens, or pigs. People will raise animals that provide a livelihood and an income. The North American bison was brought back from the brink of extinction by private ranchers.

In the case of sea turtles, the Cayman Turtle Farm (Mariculture Ltd.) had been set up to supply the market with commercially produced turtles, so as not to deplete the wild population. Through the farming of sea turtles, the supply would increase, prices would fall, and the high profit that motivated illegal poaching would diminish. But the international ban had devastating effects on the turtle farming operation, causing the venture to lose eighty percent of its market.

As so commonly happens with political advocacy, the regulations forced the Cayman Turtle Farm to file for bankruptcy in 1975. They had over 100,000 turtles to care for and feed, and no cash flow. Fortunately, a group of investors from Germany bought the assets and were eager to enter the aquaculture business. The new operation was intended to be a nonprofit research and commercial venture that would put profits back into conservation projects to protect the sea turtle. And yet the venture could not get around the international export bans. Despite good intentions, after eight years the German operation reached the point where they had to slowly downsize the operations and close the plant.

Paradoxes and Inconsistencies 329

The turtle farm was then bought by yet another group—the Cayman Islands government, which decided in 1983 to operate it as a private company. This time, the new company fared better. Not only has the company produced turtle meat for the local market, but through research and conservation programs, the facility has already released more than 30,000 turtles into the wild since 2006. Part of the cost for this program is defrayed through tourism. The farm has become one of the largest tourist attractions on the island, boasting more than 400,000 visitors in 2006.

Upside–Down Behavior

Mandatory policies often spawn upside–down behavior. For instance, laws intended to curtail illegal drugs often lead to steady growth in drug use. One reason for this inconsistency centers on the unseen link between drug pushers and tough–on–crime drug warriors. At first glance, this direct connection seems dubious. But like magnetic poles, opposites attract. In any conflict or war, both sides of the trench need the other to maintain their viability. Any Superman worth his cape requires a Lex Luthor. After all, how can someone become a hero without a villain? Leaders aspiring to greatness know that their legacy will be doomed if they cannot scare up a powerful adversary. President Bush needed Osama bin Laden as much as bin Laden needed Bush.

But the drug war's pusher–police connection runs deeper. Without punitive laws against drug use, drug lords would lose both their territorial monopolies and high profit margins to competitive forces. Similar to what occurred after the U.S. repeal of alcohol prohibition, no longer would organized crime get to call the shots by offering a product that anyone could now produce, cheaply. Crime–fighting politicians would suffer, too. They would have to give up their popular, hard–on–crime campaign slogans. Police agencies and prisons would have fewer high–paying jobs, in this environment of plummeting crime rates. Law enforcement agencies would lose a large source of revenues, with forfeiture laws now off their books. The beat cop would have to forgo his under–the–table bribes from underworld crime families.

State–imposed order has the ability to bring out unexpected and bizarre results. For instance, when the state of Hawaii mandated universal health care back in 1974, one out of every fifty Hawaiians was uninsured. But after living under a mandatory universal health care program for more than three decades, the number of people without medical insurance has worsened, to one in ten.[36]

The same phenomenon occurs when government mandates universal auto insurance. In 2007, FactCheck.org reported that "according to a study by the California Department of Insurance, between 25.5 and 30.9 percent of vehicles in that state don't have insurance."[37] Additionally, FactCheck stated that some 25 percent of drivers in California are uninsured. The same trend has developed nationwide. The 2002 AAMVA Financial Responsibility and Insurance Resource Guide reported that "between the 1989 and 1999 IRC Studies of 18 states with reporting programs in place for five years or more, 12 showed an increase in uninsured motorists and six experienced improvements."[38]

Every state requires drivers to have some minimum level of auto insurance or to show proof of financial ability to pay for possible auto accidents if found liable. Yet the proportion of uninsured motorists increased from 12.7 percent in 1988, to 14.6 percent in 2004.[39] By 2009, some reports indicated that due to the recession, the uninsured rate would soon hit 16.1 percent.[40]

Some insurance industry experts point to the human element, saying that the costs of complying with far-reaching controls, conflicting regulations, legal ambiguities, and lobbying efforts push up insurance rates, making insurance more costly for low-income families. For people with few assets to protect and nothing to lose, there is little reason to buy insurance.

* * * * *

Paradoxes are more than gag lines for late-night talk show hosts. They often conflict with what is generally accepted as possible, forcing truth to stand on its head. And yet, paradoxes go beyond misunderstandings and contradictions. Is it merely its complexity that prevents us from understanding a particular phenomenon? Or are paradoxes hiding a multitude of unknown layers that give rise to an undivided wholeness built on disjointed fragmentation? Do observers only see one kind of natural behavior, allowing the self-referential feedback loops to annihilate themselves? Could the physical world be interwoven with such complexity on every level that contradictory behavior is required for the world to function properly? Few paradoxes will ever completely reveal their true nature.

Paradoxes and Inconsistencies 331

1 Sylvia Poggoli, "Youth Protest Sweep Spain As Unemployment Soars," NPR, June 2, 2011, http://www.npr.org/2011/05/26/136683688/youth-protests-sweep-spain-as-unemployment-soars

2 Butler Shafer, "Life Is Destroying the Planet!" Lewrockwell.com blog, posted June 16, 2009.

3 Ian Stewart, *Does God Play Dice? The New Mathematics of Chaos*, New York: Penguin Books, 1989.

4 Twila Hugley Earle, "Community, Chaos Theory and the Law: A Preview of Ideas." Paper presented at the International Alliance of Holistic Lawyers, Austin, Texas, Nov. 11–14, 2004.

5 Ibid.

6 Ibid.

7 Seth Borenstein, "Science has the lowdown on fear," *Monterey Herald*—Associated Press, Oct. 31, 2007.

8 Thomas Schelling, *The Strategy of Conflict*, Cambridge, MA: Harvard University Press, 1960.

9 Bryce Kaye, Ph.D, "Paradox of Being Human," Intimacy & Boundaries Series, short Internet article from Kaye's web site, http://www.MarriageFirstAid.com/firstaid/FAarticles/paradox.htm

10 Consent of the governed was succinctly expressed in the Virginia Declaration of Rights (1776), initially drafted by George Mason, which proclaimed that "all power is vested in, and consequently derived from, the people..." The declaration also contends that the people had the right to rebel against "inadequate" government.

11 This quote is apparently a paraphrasing of Locke's ideas, since its exact wording is not found in his major works.

12 The Rulers' Paradox is my invention, formulated to highlight the contradictions in how power is routinely abused in democratic nations.

13 "Narcissistic People Most Likely to Emerge as Leaders," *Science Daily*, posted Oct. 10, 2008. http://www.ScienceDaily.com/releases/2008/10/081007155100.htm. Main source: Personality and Social Psychology Bulletin, "Leader Emergence: The Case of the Narcissistic Leaders," Sept. 15, 2008.

14 Charlie Savage, "Bush challenges hundreds of laws; President cites powers of his office," *Boston Globe*, April 30, 2006.

15 Morris and Linda Tannehill, *The Market for Liberty*, self–published in 1970, p. 41, reprinted in 1993 by Fox and Wilkes Books, Center for Independent Thought, NY: New York.

16 Peter T. Leeson, *The Invisible Hook: The Hidden Economics of Pirates*, Princeton, NJ: Princeton University Press, 2009, p. 28.

17 George Kunz, *The Paradox of Power and Weakness*, Albany: State University of New York Press, 1998, p 23.

18 Thomas W. Malone, *The Future of Work: How the New Order of Business Will Shape Your Organization, Your Management Style, and Your Life*. Cambridge, MA:

Harvard Business School Press, 2004, p. 162.

19 J. Briggs and F.D. Peat, *The Turbulent Mirror: An Illustrated Guide to Chaos Theory and the Science of Wholeness*, New York: Harper & Row, 1989.

20 John Brockman, *The Third Culture: Beyond the Scientific Revolution*, New York: Simon & Schuster, 1995, Chapter 12 by Francisco J. Varela.

21 Ibid.

22 Lawrence W. Reed, "The Predatory Bogeyman," *The Freeman*, Vol. 47, No. 7 (July 1997).

23 Thomas J. DiLorenzo, *How Capitalism Saved America: The Untold History of Our Country, from the Pilgrims to the Present*, New York: Crown Forum, 2004.

24 Kathleen Hays, "Greenspan steps up criticism of Fannie," CNNMoney.com, May 19, 2005..

25 Steven A. Holmes, "Fannie Mae Eases Credit to Aid Mortgage Lending," *New York Times*, Sept. 30, 1999.

26 Ibid.

27 David Streitfeld, "Housing Index is Expected to Show a New Low in Prices," *New York Times*, May 20, 2011.

28 Jon Meacham and Evan Thomas, "We are all socialists now," *Newsweek*, Feb. 16, 2009.

29 Nine Commentaries on the Communist Party, serialized in *The Epoch Times*, Nov. 22–27, 2007.

30 Leonard Doyle, "US food aid is 'wrecking' Africa, claims charity," *The Independent*, UK, Aug. 17, 2007.

31 Alex Perry/Kuyera, "Pain amid Plenty: Despite years of aid from the West, millions of Africans are on the brink of starvation again. Why?" *Time*, Aug. 18, 2008, pp. 33–35.

32 "Africans on Africa: Debt," BBC News, quotes by Andrew Mwenda, posted July 7, 2005, http://news.BBC.co.uk/2/hi/africa/4657139.stm.

33 Liz Dolan, "Is Foreign Aid Doing Africa More Harm than Good? Don't Try Telling Bono That," *The Huffington Post*, posted June 5, 2007, http://www.HuffingtonPost.com/liz–dolan/is–foreign–aid–doing–afri_b_50845.html.

34 Sharyl Attkisson, "Farm subsidies going to the wealthy? $20B In Tax Dollars Is Allocated To Keep Farms Afloat – And Some Lawmakers Are Benefiting," CBS: Follow the Money, Nov. 16, 2007.

35 Steve Lopez, "Out on a limb over trimming fiasco," *Los Angeles Times*, November, 28, 2007.

36 John R. Graham, "Lessons from States with 'Universal' Health Care," *Capital Ideas*, Jan. 21, 2009, Pacific Research Institute, http://www.PacificResearch.org/publications/lessons–from–states–with–universal–health–care.

37 FactCheck.org, "Dems Debating, the Sequel," Posted June 4, 2007, http://www.factcheck.org/elections-2008/dems_debating_the_sequel.html

38 Insurance Research Council and AAMVA, committee report—Resource

Paradoxes and Inconsistencies

Guide, 2002, page 14.

39 Insurance Research Council, "IRC Estimates More Than 14 Percent of Drivers are Uninsured," June 28, 2006.

40 David Pitt, "Road Hazard: uninsured driver rates climb," *Seattle Times*—Associated Press, Feb. 6, 2009.

13 *Evolution and Order Without Design*

Without order nothing can exist; without chaos nothing can evolve.
—Unknown

Evolution is chaos with feedback.
—Joseph Ford, physicist

Life is not made to order. Nature has a habit of finding ways to do what it wants. In Michael Crichton's bestselling book and blockbuster movie *Jurassic Park*, scientists were convinced that they could keep their cloned dinosaurs in check by reproducing only females. Referring to himself as a "chaotician," the character Dr. Ian Malcolm criticized the project, pointing out the unpredictable dangers of tinkering with Mother Nature. Not long into the film, Dr. Malcolm is proven more than insightful. After the security system is breeched and a slew of dinosaurs escape, a team of human survivors discovers that female dinosaurs have somehow been procreating without any male input. Nature has evolved in its own chaotic mode, validating Dr. Malcolm's foreshadowing message: "Life will find a way."

Things evolve to evolve. Evolutionary processes are the linchpin of change. These processes of discovery represent a complexity of simple systems that flux in perpetual tension as they teeter at the edge of chaos. This whirlwind of emergence is responsible for the spontaneous order and higher, organized complexity so noticeable in biological evolution—one–celled critters beefing up to become multicellular organisms. But do complex systems always allow nature to do anything it wants? For instance, would complex, adaptive systems permit large animals to evolve to the point at which females have no need of a male counterpart? Such a notion seems more befitting of the many improbabilities with which science fiction and fantasy stories bedevil their readers. But as it turns out, nature can make links, break nodes, and alter biological designs. It was discovered in 2007 that female sharks can fertilize their own eggs and give birth without the sperm from a male, a process known as parthenogenesis. The evidence was a female hammerhead shark born at Henry Doorly Zoo in Omaha, Nebraska in 2001, as reported in the journal *Biology Letters*.[1]

For years, scientists were skeptical about the shark's "virgin birth," but finally, genetic tests have conclusively confirmed that the baby shark possessed no paternal DNA. Head of Queen's University's research team and study co–author Dr. Paulo Prodöhl said, "The discovery that sharks can reproduce asexually by parthenogenesis now changes this paradigm, leaving mammals as the only major vertebrate group where this form of reproduction has not been seen." Only around seventy species, mainly insects plus several lizards, can reproduce without sex. Scientists speculate that when male sharks are unavailable, something in nature activates an ancient survival mechanism that allows females to give birth without the need for both sperm and egg to become pregnant.

Round Soap Bubbles

Why are soap bubbles round? Roundness is energy–efficient. Evolution favors such energy–saving and information-rich properties. Most scientists agree that the more efficient animals survive by developing techniques to compete with others in the same environmental niche. But some researchers' view is that organisms create the niche they occupy, as much as the niches create opportunities for the organisms. Although most evolutionary biologists contend that life forms adapt by maximizing desirable traits through natural selection, genetic drift, randomness, and mutation, some experts are beginning to doubt the predominance of efficiency in the evolution equation. Efficiency, although a major factor, is starting to be seen as only one piece in the evolution puzzle. There has been so much more to consider since the arrival of complexity science. In fact, many complexity theorists have refined their thinking, and no longer treat Darwin's theory as the best explanation for evolution.

One leading complexity scientist, Stuart Kauffman, who has expressed that Darwin's theory is of secondary importance, presented a contrarian position, writing: "Thirty years of research have convinced me that this dominant view of biology is incomplete...natural selection is important, but it has not labored alone to craft the fine architectures of the biosphere, from cell to organism to ecosystem."[2]

As the main developer of "autocatalytic set theory," Kauffman took a wide swing at natural selection, cautioning that "Darwinism is not enough. Natural selection cannot be the sole source of order in the world." Kauffman sees life arising through autocatalysis from the critical mass of diverse molecules—freestyle order arising from self–organization, and not necessarily from the result of natural selection or preset designs. After all, according to Eric J. Chaisson, a research professor of physics and astronomy at Tufts University, "There is no known agent that 'selects.' Selection is not an active force or promoter of evolution as much as a passive pruner of the misfit."[3]

A recipient of the MacArthur Fellowship, Kauffman disagrees with the neo–Darwinian suggestion that the origin of life was an accident. Under his biological paradigm, complexity theorists search for natural laws to explain the unsolved enigmas of evolution. They do not view the results of evolution as random events; life is neither a historical accident nor an improbable mishap. Kauffman maintained: "If life were bound to arise, not as an incalculably improbable accident, but as an expected fulfillment of the natural order, then we truly are at home in the universe." In order words, the order we experience is not mere happenstance, but a catalyzed reaction with a high probability of happening.[4]

Other theorists, such as German physicist and Nobel laureate Manfred Eigen, have developed a similar autocatalytic cycle, known as a "hypercycle," which seems to complement Kauffman's theories on the prebiotic origins of life. Eigen links fast chemical reactions in self–organizing systems to biological evolution. His self–reproducing, macromolecular system involves repetitive cycles of genotypes that evolve into rapidly mutating organisms or molecules. Under his "quasispecies" model, mutations develop from errors encountered during the process of copying existing DNA sequences.

But randomness still pays a leading role in evolution. According to Kauffman, his autocatalytic set is based on statistical law—probability. Under unplanned, stochastic emergence, randomly chosen elements catalyze into randomly resultant reactions. Kauffman explains that each self–organizing set of elements is part of a larger, random subset of all possible sets. For instance, if a heat wave were to dehydrate to death a particular metabolism of the first living cells on earth, the probability is good that there will be millions of other possible metabolisms that life could use. That is, no special chemicals are required for autocatalytic sets. When chemicals mix in a particular way, a passel of metabolisms are possible, meaning that self–organizing urges attest to the inevitability of life.

Order Without Design

The hallmark of evolution is its ability to process situations and generate order without relying on the crutch of a conscious designer. Most complex systems grow organically, solutions evolving through unguided and mindless forces, never reaching any final state. These homeostatic forces empower a cluster–driven complexity that defies mankind's attempts to design whatever it fancies. Why? Chaologists argue that solutions are by–products of evolutionary change—not the other way around. The freestyle dynamic of change has few direct fasteners to scripted or precalculated engineering; life is more a matter of stewardship than of mastery. Outside a narrow scope, the universe and its biochemical life forms are nonlinear, and rife with unexpected behaviors that resist predetermined order. After all, the suggestion of a designed universe implies an intentional awareness—a matrix programmed earlier for an expected outcome. This smacks of a predictable universe ruled by an all–knowing entity. If there is a universal watchmaker, he is either blind or not minding the store.

To delve into the theistic sphere for a moment, might not a god want to take a hands–on approach to entities' evolving to higher levels? If there is a supreme being, might not he conceive it more effective to deal with problems by allowing consequences to follow their natural

Evolution and Order Without Design 339

courses, instead of micromanaging heaven and earth? Wouldn't the excitement of unexpected evolutionary surprises appeal to an otherwise omniscient being?

Technically, if a certain outcome is desired, engineering a solution is vital to achieving the predicted results, but complex systems have more in common with the techniques of "reverse" engineering. One can lean more by trying to understand what actually works, than by trying to create what doesn't. For chaologists, designing a model is not as relevant as is discovering something that fits the facts they have observed. In a way, the spontaneous emergence of structures strikingly evokes Carl Sagan's astute comment: "To make apple pie from scratch, you first have to create the universe."

But it is feedback loops which underscore the mechanics of evolution. Many evolutionary chaologists recognize the feedback phenomenon as the primary force in stabilizing higher–level evolution and pushing it toward increased complexity. Spontaneous patterns emerge from interaction with other forces, chemicals, genes, and so forth. In the case of life, other genes control other genes within repetitive cycles of genetic coding. And whenever a new stimulus is added to the equation, genetic patterns can change again.

Genetic or mutational drift is simply information fed back and used to provide for the production of offspring. Strongest in small populations, such drift of genetic traits tends not to affect the reproductive fitness of populations over time. Under genetic fluctuation, chance events need to coincide with chance conditions. Genetic drift is random sampling with statistical error; it is not a copy of the gene. When packets of genetic material, alleles, are transmitted from one generation to the next, the crossover combination might not make a difference in the species' ability to survive and reproduce. Each generation is an independent event, although in a large population, a homozygous state can be reached. Complex, adaptive systems never rest, however, functioning both as explorers and exploiters of the known and the unknown. To suggest that the evolutionary process has an overall goal would amount to asserting that the future is influencing the past.

To chaologists, evolution is a form of free–flowing chaos and information exchange that co–evolve and synergize within their environment. The process is based not only on self–organizing biogenesis and autopoiesis, but on the adaptability of a species, rather than its fixed fitness level and function. Adaptation lets organisms develop slightly better skills than those of their competitors, which, in the long run, saves energy.

Some chaologists argue that a reasonable dose of inefficiency may be the most efficient way for a species to evolve. That is, a particular evolutionary path could put a species at a distinct disadvantage, but those drawbacks may prove to have little effect, because of erratic fluctuations of the environment. For instance, the human eye is poorly evolved, compared with the powerful eyes of a hawk. This handicap could have pushed mankind to the edge of extinction, but such disadvantages in evolutionary development are the norm. Evolutionary biologists acknowledge that life is full of biological inefficiencies and almost useless redundancies. In fact, many animals are replete with dysfunctional or marginal appendages and superfluous "vestigial organs." Most animals have lost past functions to evolutionary reconfigurations. The classic example is whales, which still have small hip bones embedded in the muscles of their body wall, for movement on land that was required eons ago.

Human beings are no different when it comes to vestigial organs, tissue, and behavior. According to Sydney Brenner, a South African biologist and a 2002 Nobel laureate in physiology, 97 percent of the human genome is "junk DNA." Most geneticists believe that this genetic material serves no useful purpose, and provides no instructions for protein–coding genes, although a case could be made that reduced vestigial structures exist for future restructuring. Still, most biochemical entities never reach a peak balancing point that spawns existence. The tree of life is not like a ladder; it's not linear. Organisms commonly fall away like dead branches, becoming evolutionary relics. The interlooping mazes of randomness appear to play a more significant role than does natural selection. Other geneticists argue that biological dead ends are merely evolution's way of saving energy—by reducing complexity.

Most evolutionists acknowledge that evolution has no long–term goals. Indeed, many species never evolve to a higher complexity. In fact, an overwhelming majority of species in the world are microorganisms that represent half of the world's biomass. Taking a stride toward simplicity, evolutionary endgames demonstrate that simple organisms are better equipped to form life on earth than are more complex organisms.[5]

The catechism of Darwinism faces many stumbling blocks with evolutionary chaologists. First, neither Darwin's natural selection nor the "modern evolutionary synthesis" (neo–Darwinian synthesis) from the 1930s and 1940s explains every nuance of the biology of every organism. Second, under the theories of Darwin, selection is an external choice between available options, limiting its contribution to the shaping of an organism. According to chaologist Chris Lucas, "…selection does not select 'for' a characteristic, only 'against' a disadvantageous one; all 'successful' adaptations avoid selection; as do any good, bad or indifferent changes that don't have 'selective' relevance to any particular 'culling' process." What is passed to the next generation is an "overall package, warts and all."[6]

Generally, both natural selection and complex, self–organizing systems are complementary; they mutually assist but can also oppose each other. Archaeologist Jeffrey K. McKee, in *The Riddle Chain: Chance, Coincidence, and Chaos in Human Evolution*, contended that it was a roll of the genetic dice that gave the giraffe a longer neck. Other evolutionary forces, such as natural selection, merely reinforced the giraffe's advantage over shorter–necked browsers. In fact, when it comes to the probability of emergence of intelligent life on our planet, McKee wrote: "Human evolution has been the product of many forces that together made us neither inevitable nor probable."[7]

McKee saw traditional concepts of evolution as fairly limited, because things are not so orderly. Referring to the change in genetic traits as an "autocatalytic evolution," he explained that the process is self–driven—that species can continue to alter without outside catalysts, such as changing climates.

Taking a slightly different approach, Richard J. Bird, in *Chaos and Life: Complexity and Order in Evolution and Thought*, claimed that the evolutionary processes are not disorder, but rather something that comes from infinite order. Braiding together evolutionary vision and chaos theory, Bird believes that the complexity arising from evolving species is a result of the "playing out" of chaotic systems. In order words, what appear to be random events are actually "the outcome of order."[8]

Survival of the Most Adaptable

There was a time when the concept of the "survival of the fittest" held incredible influence over the world. Social Darwinism, accredited to biologist Herbert Spencer (1820–1903), had been misconstrued by politically addicted leaders looking for any excuse to control humanity through such means as forced eugenics, sterilization, and domination. They found plenty of fodder in the competing theories of evolution.

A radical, classical liberal who opposed militarism, colonialism, and state–conferred privileges, Spencer sought to explain why things change, not just from a biological standpoint, but in the fields of psychology and sociology. Considered one of the founders of sociology, he was one of the first natural scientists to link biological evolutionary theory with social development.

With the publication of *Social Statics* in 1851, Spencer's own theory of evolution predated Darwin's, but it was overshadowed by his absence of the sort of empirical facts and figures that Darwin later provided from his research on the Galapagos Islands. Nonetheless, it was Spencer, not Darwin, who popularized the term "evolution." In fact, Spencer mentioned the "theory of evolution" in his short article, "Developmental Hypothesis," in 1852, seven years before Darwin published *On the Origin of Species*.

In his third book, *First Principles* (1860), Spencer points out what he considered to be a most fundamental law: "Evolution is an integration of matter and concomitant dissipation of motion, during which the matter passes from a relatively indefinite, incoherent homogeneity to a relatively definite, coherent heterogeneity and during which the retained motion undergoes a parallel transformation." He even argued that this "transformation is literally always towards greater complexity."

Spencer saw society as a "superorganism," intradependent with specialized structures of diverse functions, but he also acknowledged that biological organisms evolve toward self–sufficiency and individuation. Organisms have a "tendency to individuation," Spencer wrote, believing that living species, especially human beings, have a desire to preserve their lives, and that this pursuit of individual interest is the prime motive behind human interaction and its evolution. To Spencer, life forms strive in a sort of rational self–interest mold that binds the whole. He viewed human nature as merely an aggregation of "men's instincts and sentiments" that would eventually adapt to some type of greater interpersonal cooperation—a very Victorian ideal of the day. In Spencer's world, individuals were mutually dependent on each other, but not subordinate to the organism as a whole. This would explain his adamant disdain for "state–force" programs that put individuals in a subservient position.

Spencer's greatest misjudgment involved his avid support for the popular Lamarckian theory of the seventeenth century. The French naturalist Jean–Baptiste Lamarck (1744–1829) argued that the inheritance of acquired characteristics was the chief factor in the evolution of mankind. This idea of environment–shaped inheritance led to Spencer's infamous coining of the term "survival of the fittest." Ironically, a bastardized version of his theory sparked state–sanctioned programs (eugenics legislation) to re–engineer mankind to fit various preconceived notions of perfection, first appearing in the Progressive movement in the United States (1880s-1920s), and then later in the German National Socialist policies promoting creation of an Aryan race of "supermen." The common belief was that if favorable or noble characteristics could be bred onto the human race by inheritance or scientific modifications, mankind would progress to even greater heights. By the twentieth century, many statist ideological movements wrongly employed Lamarckian and Spencerian theories to justify "superior" people's extermination of "inferior" people, giving some theories of evolution a proverbial black eye.

Of course, to evolutionary chaologists, superiority is not all that it is cracked up to be. Because "superior" traits are fleeting and difficult to appraise, they see the evolutionary process as more important than its outcome. The strength of evolutionary mechanics is the overwhelming freedom they offer species, to let them adapt. Species with so-called superior traits may, for the moment, out-reproduce other species, but past performance is no guarantee of future results. Younger generations of an organism will inherit the genes of their parents, but will better traits from stronger breeding pairs increase the likelihood of greater success? Stronger men mating with stronger women might produce stronger children, but depending on the environment, bigger bones do not necessarily mean better or more adaptable offspring.

Consider the case of the mighty dinosaurs. *Tyrannosaurus rex* reigned as one of the most successful large organisms on the planet, but its rule lasted only three million years, at the very end of the Cretaceous Period. Although bigger seemed to be better, it was the small mammals who survived the massive Cretaceous–Tertiary extinction event. During the Cretaceous, small creatures had definitely been disadvantaged compared with large carnivores. More than 65 million years ago, in the flash of a moment, the environment turned more hospitable for economy-sized species, those with smaller bone structures and smaller appetites. According to many geologists and paleontologists, when an asteroid six miles in diameter hit the Yucatan Peninsula, burrowing animals found themselves at the top of the food chain. With the sun blocked by dense dust clouds, only small terrestrial vertebrates could survive in a radically altered climate of cold, dark winters.

Change being a constant and perfection being unattainable, the real trick for any species is to conserve energy while pursuing its never-ending quest for a higher order of organization. The essence of evolution is the survival of the most adaptable, and to be more adaptable, a species can get away with being suboptimal; it need only be better than its nearest competitors. There is no need for one organism to be overpoweringly better than another. That state is a waste of energy. Once an organism reaches a stable existence, it is often willing to trade efficiency for effectiveness.

Some chaologists have concluded that the effectiveness of life forms is tied to good decisions being rewarded more than bad decisions are. But even this hypothesis is problematic, since seldom do things work out as they should. A superior trait could be the death knell of a species. Peaks of fitness shift and slide. The traits that make human beings superior today—such as their tool-making ability—may be elements which, tomorrow, could destroy humanity. A predator might develop large muscles for speed, only to be confounded by prey that have evolved to cling to trees. The speed advantage the predator gained through its sole evolutionary focus on running skills would only be proven wasteful, having been negated by the adaptation of its prey. It may take the predator too long to evolve to a lighter body to chase its tree-hopping prey.

Generally, imperfections in a system can overtake and harm advantages achieved in which to gain a status of fittest. In some cases, there might be no particular "fittest" type. A niche might have several different positions equally fit for a number of species. Nonetheless, over time, those species with favorable adaptation tend to overshadow those who fail to optimize their marginal advantage.

But the ability to adapt outweighs any particular evolutionary advantage because of the shifts and uncertainties in the environment. To spend considerable energy to be far superior ignores that risk that such an overwhelming advantage could soon become an overwhelming disadvantage. The advantages—however surprising—of suboptimal states might explain why, as evolutionary biologists have identified, there exist so many vestigial organs in human beings and in other species. These organs are degenerative, imperfectly formed, or without much utility. Some of the more recognized ones are wisdom teeth, men's nipples, body hair, the coccyx (tailbone), the appendix, and tonsils. Darwin referred to them as evidence of past evolutionary history, but thought that they probably still had some minor function.

Creationists have a different point of view, sometimes convincingly, arguing that all or most vestiges have important functions. Nonetheless, the battle over vestigial organs is moot, because random drift will cause adaptation to provide both superior and inferior organs and traits. "Selection pressure" does encourage advantageous traits, but it cannot completely banish all unfavorable ones, because they may be required in the future.

Referring to all species as "transitional species," Jeffrey K. McKee contended that generalized features are more helpful for successful evolutionary adaptation and advancement. Even if one specialized trait is superior to others in the same niche, that trait might be too good for a species' own health. He explained that "the fossil record is littered with extinct primates that became too specialized."[9] In the case of humans, they were broadly diversified and had entered numerous niches, allowing them more options to evolve. Nonetheless, McKee emphasized that the dominant forces in evolution are chance, coincidence, and chaos, which make the odds of hominid evolution ever reaching a higher order questionable. Homo sapiens had "no road to follow" because too many random forces were at play.

Mindless Intelligence and Entropy

Can you have intelligence without a mind? One scientist who broached this subject was Ilya Prigogine, who saw evolution as a self–organizing system, rife with chaotic rhythms, but capable of generating a higher order in which "matter can organize itself." The concept is controversial, because a movement toward higher order in the universe violates the laws of thermodynamics. To many, a wall of incompatibility confronts those who promote self–organizing systems—especially those advancing the concept of higher–level evolution. The contradictions are formidable. The second law of thermodynamics states that systems tend to go from order to disorder, from complexity to simplicity. The principles of entropy state that all systems tend to decay, that the universe is "running down" and will eventually end in a final "heat death." This controversy has dogged evolutionists for years.

However, to be fair, many scientists argue that since outside energy from the sun shines on the earth, our planet is an "open system," and therefore higher–level evolution is relevant. One physicist took this controversy a bit deeper. Nobel laureate Erwin Schrödinger argued in 1944 that most physical laws on a large scale are attributable to chaotic behavior on a small scale. He suggested that the problem of entropy can be overcome by the principle of "order from disorder," which allows living systems to feed on "negative entropy." In his book *What is Life?* Schrödinger noted that if the number of atoms is reduced, their behavior within a system becomes more random, meaning that as density of matter increases, so can self–organizing order.[10]

Others disagree, contending that the universe is a "closed system," and that, therefore, the principle of entropy should trump any system which is attempting to increase its complexity. The point is that systems without brains do organize to higher levels, starting from a point within either biogenesis or abiogenesis. Life forms and inert matter can and do organize and cluster. They seek their own natural level of efficiency that may reach a higher order. For instance, during crystallization, structures cluster in self-replication patterns at critical points between static and chaotic regimes. They mimic cellular automation in that they evolve only through interaction with each nearest neighbor. This process is believed to represent the evolution of living organisms and minerals, and by establishing some simple rules, the evolving crystallization can form an array of complex and dazzling patterns.

Another clear example of mindless but purposeful intelligence can be seen in the volvox. A chlorophyte, the volvox is a spherical green alga that is found in ponds and lakes. In times of food shortages, separate alga cells will bind together to organize colonies. Each individual alga will connect to others by a thin strand of cytoplasm. This gives the colony the ability to move in a coordinated fashion. Similar to the movement of an octopus, the volvox colony propels itself through the water in order to trap food. And with small, red eyespots, the volvox is able to swim in the direction of light, deliberately. Operating in a unified manner, this group of cells has created a larger, far more complex organism, similar to how the higher life form created its complexity. This organism has had to achieve a greater order, to coordinate collective energy in order to live and reproduce.[11]

Another striking showcase of the impulse to cooperate intercellularly is a group of cellular slime molds known as the dictyostelids. These autonomous, soil–living amoebas subsist alone, and exist at the edge of where chemistry bumps into biology. During the life cycle of the dictyostelium discoideum, this amoeba goes through a phase that doesn't fit the classification of "alive." These solemn individual particles take on cryptobiotic (hidden life) characteristics, as put forth by University of Cambridge biologist David Keilin, who defined his discovery as: "the state of an organism when it shows no visible signs of life and when its metabolic activity becomes hardly measurable, or comes reversibly to a standstill."[12]

Still, these small individual particles can do amazing things. When a certain number of these social amoebae organize together for food and space, a strange mutation occurs. Scientists have observed them cooperating in a synergistic way, creating a large, multicelled organism in which each cell is assigned a specific function—one becomes a head, another one the digestive system. They come together to accomplish a goal that could not be accomplished by themselves. Yet with no observable DNA, they build social bonding and structure. Scientists have noticed that the dictyostelium slug will even undergo "programmed death," which some believe represents suicidal attempts to help in the group's collective survival or, at least, to maintain the new superstructure by surrendering its short, subordinate life.[13]

Evolution not Revolution

True change is evolutionary, not revolutionary. It is futile for political systems to force human beings to cooperate or construct social bonding structures. People already do that, naturally; it is evident in our evolutionary history. We are already governed by a set of hard-wired genotypes and goal-seeking parameters that deliberately seek others out, so as to forge social ties. If even little dictyostelium critters know which position to take when unifying, human beings must also possess some endogenous inkling of how to organize themselves to achieve goals. Some experts have suggested that when they cluster, these one-celled organisms might even be "choosing" their places.

The Nobel laureate and biologist Jacques Monod, in defining "living systems," settled on the fundamental characteristic of living creatures as having the capacity to set goals independently. Monod concluded that no other system has the goal–directedness of function and structure that is so overt in biological systems.[14]

The cybernetist Norbert Wiener coined the term "teleonomy" in 1943, to describe the apparent purposefulness of living systems that have been derived from their evolutionary and physiological adaptations. This concept of the teleonomic process was originated to prove that complex systems are produced without the benefit of plans or intentions, in direct contrast to "teleology." Teleology advances the notion that someone or something higher up is responsible for a design-based universe—that nothing is random or left undirected.

The collective orchestration and synchronization of living systems illustrates that human beings have a natural affinity for working together for both individual and common goals. Guns, prisons, and torture will have little long–term effect, over these physiological rhythms of complex systems. Violence for the purpose of melioristic reforms will not increase or decrease the essential, built–in feedback loops found in evolutionary properties. Order is organic; it can't just be ordered up like a bowl of ice cream or a shot of espresso.

And yet, discovering and managing order is essential to life, essential to assembling resources and talent in order to accomplish goals. Often, however, when third parties interfere and attempt to impose their own sense of order, catastrophic disorder is not far behind. This means that human beings cannot just alter their nature for the purpose of a particular political ideology or revolutionary movement. Man is who he is.

The two major constants in the universe are chaos and order. When we understand how the two work together, we will have little need to use violence for the sake of so–called change.

1 *Science Daily*, "No Sex Please, We're Female Sharks," May 23, 2007. International team of researchers came from Queen's University Belfast, the Guy Harvey Research Institute at Nova Southeastern University in Florida and the Henry Doorly Zoo in Nebraska. The paper's lead author was Dr. Demian D. Chapman. The research team's paper was published in a journal of Royal Society Publishing, "Virgin birth in a hammerhead shark," *Biology Letters*, on 23 May 2007

2 Stuart Kauffman, *At Home in the Universe: The Search for Laws of Self-Organization and Complexity*, Penguin: London, 1996, p. vii.

3 Eric J. Chaisson, "The Great Unifier," *New Scientist*, January 17, 2006, p. 38.

4 Kauffman, ibid., p. 20.

5 William B. Whitman, David C. Coleman, and William J. Wiebe, "Prokaryotes: The Unseen Majority," *National Academy of Science of the United States of America*, 95, (12), 6578–6583.

6 Chris Lucas, "Emergence and Evolution—Constraints on Form," Paper V1.8, Nov. 2004, http://www.calresco.org/emerge.htm, CALResCo Complexity Writings.

7 Jeffrey K. McKee, *The Riddled Chain: Chance, Coincidence, and Chaos in Human Evolution*, New Brunswick, NJ: Rutgers University Press, 2000, p. 18.

8 Richard J. Bird, *Chaos and Life: Complexity and Order in Evolution and Thought*, New York: Columbia University Press, 2003.

9 Jeffrey K. McKee, *The Riddled Chain: Chance, Coincidence, and Chaos in Human Evolution*, New Brunswick, NJ: Rutgers University Press, 2000, p. 126.

10 Erwin Schrödinger, *What is Life?* with *Mind and Matter* and *Autobiographical Sketches*. Cambridge University Press, 1944.

11 Vim van Egmond, "Volvox, One of the 7 Wonders of the Micro World," *Micscape Magazine*, December 2003.

12 David Keilin, The Leeuwenhoek Lecture: "The Problem of Anabiosis or Latent Life: History and Current Concept," *Proceedings of the Royal Society*, London, 150, (939), 1959, 149–191.

13 "It's a Stirring Tale of Bacteria," an initiative of Montana State University, Center for Biofilm Engineering, BioFilmsONLINE.com, Feb. 10, 2004, by Raymond Goldstein.

14 Jacques Monod, *Chance and Necessity: An Essay on the Natural Philosophy of Modern Biology*, New York: Alfred A. Knopf, 1971.

14 Chaology and Market-Based Economics

The more the state "plans," the more difficult planning becomes for the individual.
—Friedrich Hayek

Computer programs that "evolve" in ways that resemble natural selection can solve complex problems even their creators do not fully understand.
—John H. Holland

Market chaologists and complexity economists recognize Adam Smith's "invisible hand" metaphor as the earliest reference to how economic systems spontaneously emerge within society. In this way, many of the tenets of chaos theory and complexity science clearly validate the autonomous and self-assembly characteristics of market–based, laissez–faire ("let it be") economics, a term co–introduced to the English world by Benjamin Franklin in the book *Principles of Trade*.[1]

Adam Smith and a diverse array of market–based economists were on the right track when they suggested that people create the most wealth and cooperation when they are set free to act as self-governing agents. This is exactly what John H. Holland demonstrated during his search for ways to model the human brain.

One of the world's first Ph.D.'s in computer science and a predominant figurehead at the Santa Fe Institute, Holland wanted to mimic some of the processes he had observed in evolution so as to allow computers to evolve artificial intelligence. He was searching to "harness the mechanisms of evolution" and to "breed" software programs that "solved problems even when no person can fully understand their structure."[2]

When Holland set out to create his algorithms, he learned that MIT had already attempted to create a "command–and–control" computer model for an artificial intelligence project. It not only failed, but was considered completely unworkable. Thinking outside the box, Holland modified the computer program by making each digital brain "synapse" into an economic unit. "Individual synapses were paid off for solving problems, with a 'bucket brigade' to distribute the rewards to participating units."[3] The program performed extremely well. By the 1970s, Holland's "genetic algorithms" had provided scientific proof that self–interest and the profit motive are powerful self–organizing forces. But more than that, it showed that systems did best when based on bottom–up, decentralized structures in which individual agents determine their own courses of action.

Holland's key achievement was to introduce the idea of market bidding processes and cost estimates in order to generate artificial-intelligence learning. "We used competition as the vehicle for credit assignment," Holland wrote in 1986. They also treated rules as intermediates who self–organized capital, suppliers, payments, consumers, and bids.[4] With the help of cellular automata, he started with a population of random individuals. From there, every new generation was evaluated from a fitness perspective. Individual agents adapted, imitated, learned, and replicated in order to search out problems and optimize solutions. But the secret to genetic algorithms' success is that solutions are allowed to emerge and evolve, rather than being engineered or calculated. Inspired by evolutionary biology, Holland's algorithms are now used by a majority of Fortune 500 companies to solve data–fitting, trend–spotting, worker–scheduling, and budgeting problems, among others.

In his book *Adaptation in Natural and Artificial Systems*, Holland also showed that genetic algorithms strive for more than just fitness. He knew that strict competition does not always produce the best results, and he sought ways to strike a balance between exploration and exploitation.[5] He understood that an exploitation strategy carries hidden costs. To exploit is to use up resources and time that could be spent discovering truly novel strategies. Holland contended that "improvements come from trying new, risky things." So exploitative methods could actually be detrimental to success. He was looking for healthy doses of both cooperation and competition—a winning scenario, in his eyes. Even Adam Smith understood this balance over 200 years ago, writing in *The Theory of Moral Sentiment* that "nothing pleases us more than to observe in other men a fellow–feeling with all the emotions of our own breast." This is a roundabout way of saying, according to economist Daniel Klein, "man yearns for coordinated sentiment like he yearns for food in his belly."[6]

What Holland demonstrated mathematically was the concept of "spontaneous order" that was championed by economist Friedrich A. Hayek in his 1960 book, *The Constitution of Liberty*. Hayek had theorized that order would flow naturally out of a market economy separated from the state. In Hayek's view, if markets were left to themselves, they would "spontaneously optimize the wishes and desires of its participants—even though all are only pursuing their own self–interest."[7] In accordance with self–organizing principles, the pursuit of self–interest would create systems far more stable, resilient, and efficient than would any so–called scientific planning imposed by administrative fiat.

By the 1990s, other computerized scenarios with "digital organisms" yielded similar conclusions. Stuart Kauffman and John Holland worked together and in conjunction with the Santa Fe Institute, the premier center for studying complexity science. They designed a program, called "Patches," to see how groups of individuals solve problems when information is limited. The computerized landscape was set up with blind agents assigned to congregate around the highest peak. The experimental results proved successful in a one–peak world, but what about when the topography was more complex—with oddly shaped hills and irregular mountains that shifted randomly? The results: The agents were thwarted by this, and failed to reach the highest point. When the agents were allowed to exchange information, they were able to locate the highest peak.

In another computer simulation, Kauffman and Holland decided to see what would happen if only one large group of individuals was subjected to the same nonlinear, mountainous terrain. In this case, the designated group became stuck at one of the lower peaks and stayed there forever. In subsequent experiments, the group continued steadfastly in one position, failing to send out explorers to locate higher peaks. This status quo plateau was so consistent that Kauffman and Holland referred to it as the "Stalinist solution." Interestingly, if one agent was given the task to locate the peak, the information overload would render the individual ineffectual. Apparently, too much flow of data propels a system toward chaos; too little, toward rigidity.

Kauffman and Holland concluded that the best results came when individuals bunched themselves together into small clusters and exchanged information and cooperated. They could not determine how many groups would be the optimal number, only that solutions could not be engineered in advance. In other words, direction had to be discovered, not planned. The reason they gave for this outcome was that the path to higher levels kept changing its course. In simulation after simulation, a single large group could never overcome this linear handicap. The group would become paralyzed in a process that some have called "path dependence."

Realizing that linear, path–based dependency prevented innovation, Kauffman and Holland further concluded that the best strategy was to leave decision making to the players themselves. Let them choose the size and number of groups, and how to accomplish their mission. After years of study, Kauffman summed up his research like this: "In co-evolving systems, each member is only trying to pursue its own selfish advantage. Yet, as if by an invisible hand, the entire system appears magically to evolve to a poised state where, on average, the players all improve one another's performance. It's a win-win situation for everyone."[8]

These experiments affirmed the efficacy of self-organizing systems that emerge at the edge of chaos—a point "somewhere between a rigid order that is unresponsive to new information, and a system that is so overloaded with new information that it dissolves into chaos."[9]

The outcomes closely matched what the Artificial Intelligence community had also uncovered: that the brain operates mostly under a decentralizing process: competitive, but with no central processing unit (CPU) at its core.

Division of Knowledge

MIT mathematician and artificial-intelligence expert Marvin Minsky suggested that the mind has a multitude of divisions and agencies, and that knowledge itself among these divisions and agencies is compartmentalized. The partitioning aspect of the brain is important because complex systems rely on a "division of knowledge." Minsky wrote, "No higher-level agency would ever achieve a complex goal if it had to be concerned with every small detail of what each nerve and muscle does. Unless most of its work were done by other agencies, no part of society could do anything significant."[10]

Economist Daniel Klein referred to this as the "canon of local knowledge," in which the economy can be seen in terms of a chain of promises.[11] These chains have no single mind of concentrated or integrated knowledge. Like the automatic functions of the human body, they flow independently. But what if someone were to accidentally remove several links with surgical scissors? What would happen to the body whole? Obviously, an arbitrary break in a complex organism could prompt a series of cascading failures, repeating an error from layer to layer, until a general breakdown occurred—shutting down the lungs, cutting off blood flow or arresting the heart. Like the Butterfly Effect, one small event could culminate in a flatlined human body or a whole economy. This is why Adam Smith concluded that "the law ought always to trust people with the care of their own interest."[12]

According to Hayek's famous 1945 article, "The Use of Knowledge in Society," complete knowledge is never attainable in any one form, and when government attempts to centrally plan, ignorance is substituted for knowledge. To Hayek, nobody has a monopoly on truth or knowledge, and not only is most information unknowable to most people, but, when known, it is frequently contradictory. When exchanges are made, they are "based on special knowledge of circumstance of the fleeting moment not known to others." Despite Hayek's skepticism that anyone could ever possess complete, perfect knowledge, he thought there was sufficient overlap between individual agents to facilitate an interlocking cohesion, especially a type of order in which "others are allowed to pursue different ends."[13]

Further, Hayekian economists argued that market exchanges and prices would generate a better understanding of future market trends than scientific calculations could. Economist Richard Roll demonstrated this principle by researching the price of orange juice futures. Roll discovered that orange juice prices were a better predictor of future weather conditions in Florida than the National Weather Service was.[14]

The fragmented nature of knowledge makes information asymmetric, uneven—meaning that there is no such thing as perfect knowledge. Scottish economist James Mirrlees and the late Columbia University professor William Vickrey arrived at this conclusion when they studied economic theories of incentives and incomplete information. They argued, for example, that potential buyers of medical insurance are more informed about their own health than the insurance carrier is. An Oxford University professor, Mirrlees was a founder of the path–breaking field of "economics of uncertainty," which centered on the consequences of choices made with incomplete information. The two economists shared the 1996 Nobel Prize in economics for "their fundamental contributions to the economic theory of incentives under asymmetric information"—in short, information that is unequal between buyers and sellers. This concept was an important milestone for chaology. The belief in perfect knowledge had given adherents of Keynesian macroeconomics a basis for patterning society after what they perceived as precise, all–knowable, and measurable data. Without the safety net of perfect knowledge, command–and–control economics no longer had a sturdy foundation on which to stand.

Despite the unreliable and divisional nature of knowledge, the public and academia still appear to be conditioned to believe that society and human actions are under the spell of a controlling agency. The general consensus is that leadership equates to command management. But this situation does not appear in nature. For instance, the front bird in the V–shaped flock appears to be the one in charge, while the other birds play follow–the–leader. But that is not true, according to Nicholas Negroponte in his *New York Times* bestseller, *Being Digital*. He argues that no bird is really in charge. Considering the behavior of the flock, he writes, "The orderly formation is the result of a highly responsive collection of processors behaving individually and following simple harmonious rules without a conductor."[15] The Wiesner Professor of Media Technology at MIT, Negroponte believes that the non–command way of organizing is better because "a highly intercommunicating decentralized structure shows far more resilience and likelihood of survival."

In nature, there are no "conductors." Even ant colonies, most myrmecologists agree, are not as highly organized by the queen as first thought. Steven Johnson in *Emergence: the Connected Lives of Ants, Brains, Cities and Software* contends that the image of a bossy queen ant is a myth. He argues that ant queens are not authority figures. Instead, ant colonies develop solutions to changing environments through a collective intelligence. No single ant directs anything. The colony has no central directorate. Organization and cooperation are maintained by repetitive habits and scent trails laden with pheromones that instill a cumulative memory. The queen is merely an egg dispenser.[16]

To Johnson, individual ants are dumb, but they share a smart interconnectivity in a decentralized self–emergence. And, as they organize from the bottom, "They get their smarts from down below." But he warns that collective behavior does not warrant some kind of centralized authority. Even so–called sophisticated food gathering is just a series of events in which ants randomly bump into things. There are no cadres of ants with weapons orchestrating the food line back to the hive. Natalie Angier, writing for *The New York Times*, explains: "There is no top–down structure to honeybee society, no central command post or leaders with whips," and decisions are "made consensually and regionally...."[17]

Scott Camazine is a hobbyist beekeeper with a Ph.D. in biology from Cornell. Noting that all beehives are organized in pretty much the same way, he stated, "In these nests and societies, global pattern emerges without a structure imposed by an entity overseeing the system."[18] Camazine even questioned biologists' belief about the tie–in to DNA concerning the hereditary habits and instincts of bees. To Camazine this is overthinking the problem; he contends that insect societies develop a wide range of effects from the interactions of simple but basically autonomous units. Maurice Maeterlinck, author of *The Life of the Bee*, might have agreed, although his beekeeping experience was

Chaology and Market-Based Economics

honed over twenty years in the nineteenth century. He witnessed bees with their own code of morals, sometimes virtuous, other times perverse. He wrote: "a careless beekeeper will often corrupt his people, destroy their respect for the property of others, incite them to pillage, and induce in them habits of conquest and idleness, which will render them sources of danger to all the little republics around."[19]

These types of complexities are found not just in insect societies. Peter Allen, head of the Complex Systems Management Centre at Cranfield University in England, once conducted a study for the Canadian fishing industry, years before complexity science appeared on the academic radar screen. A theoretical physicist, Allen had been commissioned to make a computer model of the Chesapeake Bay ecosystem. After having input tremendous amounts of data, he discovered that the model had failed miserably. According to Allen, the model not only failed to predict the future, but also "didn't hold up long enough even to accurately describe the present."

Allen realized quickly that "you can't model biosystems by using equations for mechanical systems." The computer model omitted things related to individual diversity and the interaction between components and their subsystems. Allen went back to England and was forced to rethink how complex natural systems actually worked. Some twenty years later, he had a pretty good idea about what had gone wrong. By that time, he had upgraded his modeling system to include complexities rooted in human behavior.

By the early 2000s, Allen was swooning audiences with another simulation modeled after Canadian fishing boat captains. In this experiment he pitted two fishing-boat skippers against each other. The first captain was extremely rational, and when a report was issued highlighting the best fishing areas, he dutifully steamed to that spot. The other captain was an old, opinionated seadog, who refused to listen to any reports. He went out and looked for a nice spot to fish. The question Allen enjoyed entertaining was: Who will do best?

Quite the showman, Allen at first revealed that the rational captain did best, obviously to the disappointment of his audience. But that was not exactly true. He confessed that the level-headed fishing-boat captain did well only in the short term. In the long term, the skeptical skipper beat out the rational one. Why? As Allen explained, the rational captain did poorly because he was so involved in exploiting that he had no time to discover.

Stochastic fishermen are discoverers and become more committed to learning how to learn. In the long run, those with that particular characteristic often do spectacularly well. As Allen asserted, "Complexity allows us to under-stand our place in a creative universe where learning and transformation are key—rather than knowledge and efficiency." The simulation illustrated that long–term success is gained by discovering first, and exploiting second. The rational captain learned little from his initial successes, and was doing what market chaologists call "burning knowledge." Only through a series of failures can fisherman develop substantial knowledge about the ecological habits of fish, and where they might be located in the future.[20]

Others had trailblazed this field earlier. Friedrich Hayek had produced significant work in the fields of systems thinking and neuroscience, and he warned against treating biological systems and society under a false and simple methodology of two–variable linear relationships. He referred to this slavish, machine–driven mindset as "scientism," which seeks progress through the scientific planning of society. Proponents of scientism want to "socially engineer society in the same way that engineers design and build bridges."[21]

Of course, biological systems are not the same as mechanical or mathematical systems. The Newtonian physics of clockwork–like mechanics is a poor method for modeling human behavior or ecological systems. Bridges and roads cannot be built without engineering and design, but social and biological structures are multivariable complexities, and depend upon the evolving of spontaneous emergence. In the final analysis, scientism takes a monolithic approach, seeking to apply the same scientific methods and criteria for all disciplines. The basic problem is that measurement is imprecise; life is qualitative; and precise control is fleeting.

Open Source: A Network of Dreams

Longtime columnist and author William Tucker referred to complexity science as a theory that "explores how systems that are open to sources of energy are able to raise themselves to higher levels of self–organization." As these systems internally organize, they create an evolution-like non-equilibrium that defies entropy and the pitfalls of centralization. Those are exactly the properties of "open source" systems.[22]

In the world of business, most entrepreneurs attempt to create proprietary products and technology, to gain a slice of monopoly in their marketplace. Open competition usually makes this dream difficult, if not impossible. For a company to give away its product, and the tools to let clients alter the product themselves, would be more befitting of science fiction. But this is exactly what has occurred, with open–source software.

The open-source model freely allows anyone to modify, adapt and apply their solution to creating software. It is a decentralized system for do-it-yourselfer software geeks and even the less tech-obsessed. The most compelling feature is that it produces better software, compared to a closed system where only a few programmers are able to spot bugs and fix problems. Beyond software, open-source is a philosophy and methodology that engages in the free access and sharing of information.

Under the open-source model, the source code is freely available to anyone. One needs only to start writing code or what programmers describe as "scratching an itch." After the shell has been created, the developer usually will post it on the Internet to entice others to improve upon the code. Because the original developer has designated the program as open source, anybody can tinker with it. That is what often happens: thousands participate to improve the software by trial and error in a value–creating community. As the program slowly evolves, it often goes in many other directions, branching away to solve additional problems as well. There is no telling what form it might end up taking.

This is the heart of open structures: decentralized simplicity. There are no hierarchies, boss–induced rules, proprietary vendor, trade secrets, or monopolies. The user is as close to the system as possible. Without a direct command structure, there is nobody to slap a sleepy head, penalize bad coding, or chastise someone for hanging around the water cooler all day. If the software is disliked, nobody imposes a guilt trip or a judgment. Choice is everything.

Even the nontechnical computer users benefit greatly. They can go on line and overfill their shopping cart with software programs to download at their pleasure. In fact, many software distribution companies have sprung up to provide nontechnical users with particular software versions and customer support. But not all of these services are entirely free or noncommercial. To provide some source of revenue, many of these distributors charge for manuals and/or upgrades. Others ask for donations or take subscriptions.

Open–sourcing epitomizes the laissez–faire traits of self–organizing systems. Like a network of dreams, newly born systems offer open gateways and tools—if someone logs on, they can freely build. Of course, it is all very nebulous. Who will come? Who will build it? The answer: nobody in particular, everyone in general. Things just happen. That is the spontaneous nature of the creative process in motion. Nobody is in charge of creation. People will just drift together and create; it is not prearranged. This is the same mechanics as with any economic venture. Nobody really knows whether a new idea or product will be successful. The only way to find out is to "hang out a shingle" and see whether anyone buys. In the case of open sourcing, if the software is useful, it will continue to be popular—and it will continue to be updated. If not useful, it might just fade away. It all depends on who uses it. This is the foremost signature of open, unrestricted–access systems.

Linux: The Accidental Revolutionary

The earliest and most touted open–source software is the Unix–based operating system known as Linux. Considering himself to be an "accidental revolutionary," Linux inventor Linus Torvalds decided to share the Linux "source codes" with others, over the Internet in the early 1990s. Torvalds had simply wanted to create his own software that would have fewer crashes and enable higher productivity than competing operating systems. After posting his early versions on the Internet, he challenged the computer–geek community to make it better. They did, and it spread like wildfire, taking the world by storm.

After the Linux revolution, the commercial side of software development was never the same. Open sourcing proved that a community of people could produce high quality and evolving software for a fraction of the cost of commercial programs, and with just a few people at the helm. In sharp contrast, Microsoft Corporation employs thousands of professional software programmers and engineers to update and debug their Windows operating system (OS) software.

Another earth–shaking incident in the open–source world occurred in late 2004, when a free Internet browser hit the scene. On par with a grassroots political movement, this browser was put together with the help of thousands of computer developers across the Internet who were distressed over inferior commercial browsers. Upon release, it was hailed and praised as a savior among software programs.

Within no time, Mozilla Foundation's award-winning Firefox web browser generated over a million downloads a day—exceeding 50 million downloads as of 2005. But some of its more ardent fans did more than download the free software. They banded together and raised donations to place an advertisement in the *New York Times* to tout Firefox's superiority. The newspaper advertisement in turn raised over a quarter of a million dollars. Consumers were happy to give something back to a company that not only gave away its software but also allowed people to make changes through Firefox's open–source venture. They knew that Firefox was far better than the industry's giant, Microsoft's

Internet Explorer, which seemed to have grown too big to stay close to its clientele.

Internet Explorer and other commercial browsers had a slew of problems. Their developers had moved too slowly to fix security loopholes. Invasive spyware and unwanted commercial pop–up advertisements were invading most personal computers. These security holes were filling up, and sometimes wiping out, hard drives. Customers of most commercial browsers were paying for a service that was failing to protect them. It took a foundation a fraction of the size of Microsoft to see a need and quickly provide help. And in doing so, the consumers had taken control of a market in unprecedented ways, causing some to dub Firefox "a consumer controlled product."

Other free services combine direct reader participation in a more academic direction. Starting in 2001, the free on–line encyclopedia Wikipedia has allowed anyone to write and edit articles. Founder Jimmy Wales referred to his project as "an effort to create and distribute a free encyclopedia of the highest possible quality to every single person on the planet in their own language." Because of Wikipedia's openness, so–called "edit wars" do occur, some likening them to a social version of the Darwinian evolutionary process, although all articles are ultimately subject to oversight by Wikipedia's participating editors. To keep the site afloat, many of the participating writers and readers make monthly pledges.

The Austrian School of Economics

Only one cadre of economists has been closely aligned with chaologists: the Austrian school. Because a large part of neoclassical and mainstream economic theory is based on general equilibrium and determinism, the Austrians have mostly been ignored. Economic "linearists" model the economy as an almost changeless marketplace, feeling secure with their notion of perfect knowledge and greatly disturbed by the instability arising from market forces and price fluctuations.

According to economist W. Brian Arthur of the Santa Fe Institute, economics had regrettably turned into a branch of applied mathematics. Before becoming involved with market chaology, Arthur noticed that the "brightest young economists seemed to be devoting their careers to proving theorem after theorem—whether or not those theorems had much to do with the world."[23] Arthur was disappointed by the intensity of mathematics, especially at U.C. Berkeley. "To me, coming from applied mathematics, a theorem was a statement about everlasting mathematical truth—not the dressing up of a trivial observation in a lot of formalism."[24] Somehow neoclassical economics had reduced the richness of complexity to a narrow set of abstractions encased in pure mathematics. But Arthur was the oddball. He embraced instability, believing that it is a better prognosticator for the uncertainties of reality than are formulas written on a blackboard.

The youngest person to have held an endowed chair at Stanford University, Arthur was trying to tell economists that the economy includes outside factors: mass psychology, political passions, mood–swinging fads, general mania, and who knows what—the things that behavioral economists are now exploring. In this sense, all scientific fields are open–ended since emerging structures and patterns never quite finish unfolding, but this thought of reality being so freewheeling disturbed traditional scientists. As Arthur once observed, "Science doesn't like perpetual novelty."[25]

Unknown to Arthur until the 1980s, Austrian economists had also been belittled for their meager use of mathematics and theorems. For over a hundred years, this hardy band of dissidents had cautioned about human beings' limitations, both in knowledge and cognitive capacity. Most economists, however, were captivated by a mechanistic worldview, and the idea of a perpetually erratic world simply did not compute.

Carl Menger (1840–1921), considered the founder of the Austrian school of economics, was a classical liberal who saw economics as the science of individual choice. At the time, most economists instead saw economics as a methodical way to accumulate data that would assist the political economy of the state, treating statistics as one–dimensional historical data. A strict adherent to methodological individualism, Menger asserted that individuals, not collectives, make decisions.

To Austrian economists, there is no unified homogeneity of economic decision making. Information is scattered, uneven, and rife with uncertainty, and the economy is in a perpetual disequilibrated state of flux. Under the concept of "praxeology"—the study of human conduct—the Austrians viewed the economic world as an emerging and evolving process that provided patterns, but not predictability. According to Carole E. Scott, an economist at the State University of West Georgia, Austrian economists believed that "mathematics is useful only in understanding patterns, while neoclassical economists believe in using mathematics to make predictions."[26]

Not until Frederick Hayek had received the Nobel Prize for economics in 1974 did the Austrian economists emerge from obscurity. But even this acclaim failed to land them on the academic map. Most social–science academicians were interested in what man had attempted to design intentionally. The Austrians were looking at it the other way around. They were studying the spontaneous order that occurs when people actually took actions in the marketplace—"that which is the result of human action but not of human design."[27] However, the academic world had, much earlier, taken notice of several concepts that would later be credited as "Austrian." Benoit Mandelbrot, a French mathematician, used fractal geometry to examine the movement of cotton prices over sixty years. In 1963, he found strong evidence of recognizable and self–similarity patterns in commodity prices on a daily, weekly, monthly, and yearly basis. This finally caused traditional economists to examine chaos theory with open minds. Mandelbrot had charted seemingly random cotton prices on his computer. What he reaped from the chaotic data was a graph of clear order. Wall Street found that the Mandelbrot model offered better predictions of future prices for stocks, bonds, and exchange rates than the old "efficient market theory." Many Wall Street investment strategists agreed, such as Edgar Peters, author of *Chaos and Order in Capital Market*, who wrote that chaos and complexity theories offer a far superior analytical method for investors.

Concerned about closed systems, Hayek contended that governmental control over human behavior would always be a way–station on the road to serfdom. Like the other Austrian economists, he argued long before the collapse of the Soviet Union that complexity would overpower the capabilities of central planners. Often more interested in psychology and political science than economics, Hayek posited that there is no possible way for planners to know what is truly happening to the economy, despite socialists' claims that they can. He was critical of the abuses of "scientism" that attempted to justify inherently unknowable propositions.

In order to explain the larger chaology picture, the term "open market" must be defined. This term means more than just freewheeling economic exchange. An open market is a subset of "open systems"—where data, objects, and process *freely* move into and out of a structure. To legislate or dictate economic controls is to restrict or stop that flow. In a political context, implementing market restrictions is no different from enacting laws to prevent a person or group from expressing their opinions. Free speech operates in an open system. Likewise, the free movement of products and services is an open system. To oppose open and free markets is to endorse closed or semi–closed systems. And that is an attempt to prevent systems from evolving and changing to reach higher levels.

Moreover, Hayek contended that without detailed information, the allocation of resources could never be reliable. Only a decentralized economy, he argued, would allow economic systems to coordinate and allocate resources more to the liking of those intimately involved, on the ground level. To the Hayekian economists, this self–autonomous process would create "market order" all by itself without resorting to external controls. Interestingly, many computer programmers have come to this same understanding. They rarely create software programs that work flawlessly before or after alpha testing, even though the programmer often has complete control over his creation, and coding language is more precise than the human language. Programmers could easily see that the human language is both complex and ambiguous, and that with such an imposing drawback, it would be nearly impossible to achieve any sense of socio-economic equality or perfection.

As an example of spontaneous order, Hayekian economists often point to privately operated food distribution centers: supermarkets. Considering that most American supermarkets stock an average of over 15,000 products on their shelves (up to 45,000 for big–box stores), it would seem to be an impossible task for stores to ship, track, warehouse, and resupply every product. But they do. Even before computerization and modern inventory–control software, supermarkets rarely experienced shortages. The same could not be said for the state–owned stores in what used to be the Soviet Union, where two–hour lines and scarcity of consumer products were everyday undertakings.[28]

Although the Austrian economists hold similar views about chaos and complexity theory, the two rarely crossed paths, until a few years after the birth of the Santa Fe Institute. Under W. Brian Arthur, the Santa Fe Institute began its first research program on economics in 1988 and soon discovered that they had a great deal in common with Austrian economists.

The Strong Eat the Weak: Monopolies

Perhaps the most controversial area for market chaologists is the public fear that monopolies and oligopolies will seize control of unstructured, nonlinear economies. The fear is that night–watchman governments will be unable to prevent the strong from eating the weak, that a limited-powers government would not have the capability to stop bullies from harming the public or gobbling up smaller enterprises. The anxiety is pervasive, but historically inaccurate. During the early years of the United States, the federal government was so small that someone could have dragged it home and drowned it in a bathtub.

For almost eighty years, the U.S. government did not directly tax its citizens. The only contact most Americans had with their government was through the post office. Even in the case of law enforcement, prior to the late 1830s, cities were policed by unpaid and often unarmed marshals, sheriffs, aldermen, night watchmen, citizen volunteers, and constables. There were a handful of government–funded schools, few, if any, government regulations, no state–organized welfare "safety net," and most of the time, no standing army. Except for state laws enacted to permit slavery, government had little authority to control people's lives or the economy. If there was ever a period for monopolies and oligopolies to take total control of an allegedly frail and defenseless society, crushing the competition and suppressing the weak, this would have been the time. But despite a robust libertarian climate, business enterprises remained small to mid–size and few complained of being oppressed by captains of industry.

Not until after the Civil War, when all levels of government greatly expanded, did the situation change. By the 1880s, most states had enacted "corporate laws" that entitled corporations to special state–conferred privileges of limited liability and "personhood." Incorporated companies could now become more reckless and irresponsible (the moral hazard effect). These state–sanctioned "personhoods" gave corporations greater ability to walk away from questionable, even unethical activities, if caught. Under these laws, the corporate shell would be held mainly responsible for illegal conduct; the stockholders and corporate officers would not.

Despite corporations' state-enhanced power, they still must rely on persuasion to sell their products, to obtain their daily bread; but governments instead rely on threats and guns to enrich their bank accounts. Corporations are creatures of the state, but if privately owned, have a better record of satisfying the wants and needs of the public than any command and control system.

Corporate laws also made capital formation less risky. No longer were stockholders responsible for bad debt or abuses committed by the corporations they owned. With more money available, shadier deals became more common. Easier access to money made it possible for people with questionable character to start up all sorts of enterprises, including organized crime operations. Still, organized crime failed to establish a foothold in the American economy until stronger restrictions were imposed, in the twentieth century. During the nineteenth century, profit margins had been notoriously low, since competition was unfettered and open to everybody. Only when an activity or product became restricted or illegal did profit margins skyrocket.

This is, perhaps, why Nobel Prize–winning economist Milton Friedman (1912-2006) argued repeatedly that "business is not a friend of the free market.... It's in the self–interest of the business community to get government on their side."[29] Even *Time Magazine* writer Michael Grunwald recognized this important distinction, taking a swipe at President George W. Bush's tendency to staff governmental departments with former lobbyists. He wrote: "The capitalist idea is free markets and level playing fields; the lobbyist idea is influencing the levers of power to help clients."[30] In other words, with a consummated marriage between government and business, the tycoon groom gets safeguards from competition as a dowry. In this sense, anti–trust laws have notoriously protected competitors, not competition.

Consumer advocate Ralph Nader has been an outspoken critic of the vested–interest nature of political systems, distressed that the regulatory personnel routinely come from industry itself. He labeled this cozy relationship the "institutionalized fusion of corporate desires with public bureaucracy." In *The Monopoly Makers: Ralph Nader's Study Group Report on Regulations and Competition*, he concluded that "it is so much easier and, above all, more stable to seize the legal and administrative apparatus than to fight it, turning government agencies into licensors of private monopolies and co–conspirators against the people...."[31]

In essence, big business and big government are not antagonists; they are collaborators. John Stossel, newspaper columnist and former host of ABC's *20/20*, wrote: "Politicians like it that way because they get power and prestige, and businessmen like it because they get protection from competition."[32] This curiosity is best illustrated by economist Steven Horwitz's First Law of Political Economy: "No one hates capitalism more than a capitalist."

Peddling his book *On the Wealth of Nations* on Jon Stewart's *The Daily Show*, the provocative satirist P. J. O'Rourke summarized the works of Adam Smith with brutal honesty and humor. One of his first salvos revealed that Smith "hated corporations." In fact, the father of economics was "very suspicious of people in the marketplace." After reading over 1,800 pages of Smith's musty tomes, O'Rourke concluded that Smith viewed economics in a dim light. In Smith's view, "businessmen never get together even socially, even just to have a beer, without cheating the public." O'Rourke noted that Smith "was aware that a free market vibrates between greed and fear." When Stewart suggested that Smith believed in the goodness of people, O'Rourke retorted that Smith "believed that it is better for us all to be bad than to have one bad person in charge of us all.... The market is just to decentralize our badness."[33]

It is hardly a secret that enormous benefits come with establishing a monopoly, whether it is legal or illegal. Undermining competition and maintaining exclusive control of a commodity can be extremely profitable. With the passage of Prohibition in 1920, organized crime jumped into high gear and took advantage of sky–high profit margins by selling illegal booze. And to keep profit margins high and steady, each crime family attempted to put into place its own iron–clad monopoly, firebombing or killing any and all competitors, and establishing a direct link to government through bribery. Violent crime soared while whole police departments became mired in corruption. With gangster firepower and strict anti–liquor laws in place, an underworld boss, such as Al Capone, would have been able to amass the political power to virtually run a city from his private desk.

The Chicago underworld had existed long before Al Capone, but in small doses. In an effort to stop civic–minded reforms in the 1870s, Chicago's saloon, prostitution, and gambling interests organized and elected their own mayor, Harvey Colvin. With legitimacy and firm control of the city government, a slew of gamblers and politicians organized the first criminal syndicate in Chicago. And with control in hand, the syndicate attempted to prevent new saloons and gambling houses from competing with already established interests. However, that became a difficult proposition, because the marketplace was very competitive and the power of city government limited.

With little government structure during the early years of the United States, con men and criminal elements were impaired. They had little means to legitimize monopolistic practices and, therefore, did not rise above the status of small–time hoodlums. There were simply too many options available to people, and too few state–imposed restrictions. Anybody could compete for anything, no holds barred. Under an airy, unobstructed system, if someone sought to corner the market on alcoholic products, pushing to raise prices, no external apparatus would stop a slew of competitors from springing up and causing prices to plummet. Without laws to squelch competition, it was difficult to control the market in such a way as to ensure high profits.

When the billionaire Hunt brothers attempted to corner the silver market in 1970s, they caused silver prices to rise momentarily, but they soon got trapped in their own scheme and landed in bankruptcy court.

What the cabals of bullies and con men dislike the most is playing on a level playing field. Psychologically insecure, bullies pick only on smaller prey and, before taking on bigger projects, align themselves with muscular sidekicks. They want a clear–cut advantage over their victims. This is why street–corner thugs mug little old ladies instead of college football players. They want overwhelming muscle before they victimize someone. They want a hidden ace up their sleeve. But in the fluid private sector, there are just too many David–and–Goliath reversal of fortunes. Criminals need to go where the power is.

As the legend goes, when a reporter asked the notorious bank robber Willie Sutton why he robbed banks, he quickly replied, "That's where the money is." Of course, Sutton answered the obvious. Criminals follow the money, but the smarter ones know that it is far safer to rob the bank from the inside than the outside. Smart bullies always serve their term in office, while dumb bullies serve their time in jail, and to accomplish this skullduggery successfully, the astute lawbreaker must first gain the trust of the populace.

Obviously, crooks have little regard for regulations, laws, or ethics. Understanding their own natural aptitude to defraud, charlatans have no qualms about robbing people through hallowed institutions or state–enforced monopolies. They understand that compulsory schemes and regulatory barriers simply shield the world from competitive forces, while masking nefarious activities of slick snake–oil salesmen with savoir–faire respectability. For instance, it was only after the former NASDAQ stock exchange chairman and well–respected financier Bernard L. Madoff was turned over to the authorities by his two sons that the public discovered that his $50 to $65 billion investment fund was no more than a Ponzi scheme. But this scandal had been going on for three decades. Where were the 238,251 federal regulators? What were the 75,526 pages of mostly new regulations recorded in the *Federal Register* that year?[34]

Where was the U.S. Securities and Exchange Commission (SEC)—the agency empowered to investigate securities fraud? Apparently, the regulators were not doing their job, causing Senator Chris Dodd (D–Conn.) to condemn Madoff's fraud as a "regulatory failure of historic proportions." One reason Senator Dodd criticized the regulatory agencies was that Madoff had made little or no actual stock trades through his brokerage firm.[35] Actually, according to one state–appointed trustee, Madoff's corporation had failed to place a single trade "for more than a decade."[36] And yet the authorities had failed to detect the scam.

Whistleblowers had been trying to alert the authorities to Madoff's scheme since 1992. Harry Markopolos, a former industry executive and financial analyst, filed complaints with the SEC in 1999, asking the agency to investigate Madoff's operations. In yet another complaint to the SEC in 2005, Markopolos again warned that Madoff was involved in a "giant Ponzi scheme." All of his warnings were ignored.[37] Testifying before a House Committee in 2009, Markopolos sniped: "If you flew the entire SEC staff to Boston and sat them in Fenway Park, they wouldn't be able to find first base." After the investigation, the SEC inspector general released a "blistering report that despite five probes and having caught Madoff in 'lies and misrepresentation,' the SEC failed to follow up on inconsistencies."[38] Regulations and controls are only as good as the people who enforce them. And considering that command and control agencies are the enforcers, it is no wonder that crooks in high places rarely get caught in the regulators' crosshairs.

Perhaps this is why wealthy members of the U.S. Congress have fared far better than have the wealthy outside of the political arena. In a *New York Times* investigative piece, reporter Eric Lichtblau studied the wealth gap between lawmakers and their constituents, calling the contrast "stark," writing: "While the median net worth of members of Congress jumped 15 percent from 2004 to 2010, the net worth of the richest 10 percent of Americans remained essentially flat. For all Americans, median net worth dropped 8 percent, based on inflation–adjusted data from Moody's Analytics."[39]

Instinctively, bullies and con artists understand how and where to obtain the uppermost power and influence, and it is not stealing lunch money at the schoolyard. They realize that the "visible hand" of government offers the best opportunity to maximize shady activities and gain legitimacy. When they join forces with the political elite and insiders, they use this lucrative springboard to victimize the weak–minded with sweet–sounding promises. This alliance helps the political elite to foster monopolistic control, in order to extend their concentration of power under a corporate state. The results are disastrous to the general citizenry and economy. The economic playing field is skewed; competition is curtailed; and the bullies are provided with plenty of government–protected string—in the form of noble–sounding causes—with which to control a multitude of puppets. Inevitably, society falls helplessly into a government–driven, bureaucracy–clogged abyss of economic stagnation and hopelessness.

It is this political–bully process of outlawing competition and granting exclusive state franchises and subsidies that gave birth to the hydra of monopolies. As the economist Murray N. Rothbard noted, it was the industrial giants, like J. P. Morgan and their allies, during the Progressive Era who sought "to cartelize American business and industry." Although many of their attempts failed, these industrialists realized that they could gain a monopolist's privilege only by using the state, not through the open and unpredictable wheeling–and–dealing flurry of free–market ventures.[40]

By the middle of the twentieth century, world leaders were enthralled with government–sponsored cartels, state–sanctioned monopolies, protective tariffs, and export subsidies. Under FDR's National Recovery Administration (NRA) in 1933, large industrial companies were given monopolistic powers to restrict competition and fix prices. These government–supervised cartels were put in place during the Great Depression to stop the so–called dangers of market instability and chaotic competition. Yet there was no assurance that these policies would help consumers or lower prices. In fact, as critics had predicted, the cartel–protected companies raised their prices, which resulted in lower sales and increased unemployment, thus stalling an economic recovery.

According to Nobel laureate economist George Stigler, these large companies' legalized monopolies would, if granted special privileges, eventually impede the emergence of smaller companies. Stigler had come to understand this phenomenon as "capture," in which political stakeholders and vested interest groups would routinely use their regulatory and coercive authority to favor laws that benefited a favorable few. To combat these abuses, Stigler and other economists forged a new economic field called Public Choice Theory in the 1960s.

Whether their management is honest or shady, large companies have a vested interest in remaining big. But bigness comes with a price. Like lumbering dinosaurs with brains the size of walnuts, large organizations adapted poorly to new conditions. They are simply too bulky to swiftly change their practices and methods of doing business. They know that small, more adroit enterprises can run circles around them and, in doing so, cause loss of market share and inflict bankruptcy status. According to David Theroux of the Independent Institute, "Half of the Fortune 500 companies in 1980 fell off the list by 1990, and the trend is accelerating." In fact, of the original twelve companies listed on the Dow Jones Industrial Average (DJIA) in 1896, only one—General Electric—is still included. And even G.E. was delisted twice before regaining its status.[41]

Under a system of "state–controlled capitalism," or mixed economy, large companies can avoid normal evolutionary processes by hooking up with state power in order to direct, regulate, and micromanage the economy. And if they skirt bankruptcy, they can be declared "too big to fail," showered with billions in taxpayer bailouts, and quickly taught that bad behavior is richly rewarded. To these near monopolies, the tighter the regulations, the higher the cost to do business, and so much the better to weed out any emerging mom-and-pop

Chaology and Market-Based Economics

businesses. With less competition and legal blockades at the entry level, the big boys are now in a position to buy out or merge with midsize companies, without fear that a smaller one will suddenly make their growth strategy obsolete. This is exactly what happened to Preston Tucker and his revolutionary automobile.

The Tucker car episode is a prime example of how many find it more convenient to use the minions of the state instead of the forces of competition. Preston Tucker had engineered an innovative automobile which, if successful, would have set a new industry standard—a standard that would have truly challenged the established auto manufacturers, and would have cost them tens of millions of dollars if they'd had to retool their plants accordingly. Considered one of the best cars ever built, the 1948 Tucker was streamlined, with independent four-wheel suspension, collapsible steering column, enhanced safety features, a pop-out windshield, and a padded dashboard, and it was capable of high speed. The vehicle was, in a word, futuristic. It was the first automobile to offer seatbelts and disc brakes. The Big Three automakers, their powerful political lobbies, and the senator from Detroit, Homer Ferguson, had to find a way to stop Tucker before his car could hit the market.

In 1948, the SEC and the Justice Department prepared a report charging Preston Tucker with fraud and conspiracy, arguing that such a technologically advanced car could not be built, or, if built, would not perform as advertised. And yet, Tucker had already built seven cars, and they had performed well at speed trials in Indianapolis. Even before Tucker would see the charges against him, the *Detroit News* had run the headline, "Gigantic Tucker Fraud Charged in SEC Report." It turned out that SEC Commissioner John McDonald had illegally given the report to the newspapers, trying to convict Tucker in the public eye. Eventually, 1,600 Tucker workers were laid off; creditors demanded immediate payment. Tucker Corporation stock plunged and the company went into receivership. The auto industry was able to kill Tucker's car in the political arena, instead of fighting fair in the open marketplace.

In 1949, the case went to trial. The Federal prosecutors refused to allow the members of the jury to see Tucker's fifty vehicles, except for the hand-built "Tin–Goose" prototype. If the jury had been permitted to see the completed cars, the prosecution would have lost the sentiment of the jury, and their flimsy legal case would never have prevailed. In the end, the jury found Tucker and his associates "not guilty" on all counts, innocent of any attempt to defraud. But the verdict was a hollow victory. The Tucker Corporation had been put out of business. Instead of protecting consumers, federal regulatory agencies had protected established companies from new competition.[42]

Game Theory

Game theorists use the workings of nature to understand human behavior. It is about the exercise of options. Game theory boils down to the fact that the side with the most options has a greater probability of winning the game. In this sense, the more choices available, the greater the chance for success. On the reverse side, having fewer choices increases the likelihood of failure. This is another explanation of why a choice–driven economy is considered more resilient and fruitful.

A branch of applied mathematics, game theory compels participants to simplify their situation, since reality is far too complex to analyze with any precision. Generally, participants must make trade–offs between theory and reality. They must make certain assumptions, because they do not have the calculating power or the information at hand, with which to solve many of the game's problems. In most cases, accurate information is simply unobtainable; "perfect knowledge" is unrealistic, and the choices people make are not always rational. This is why economists and chaologists have taken a keen interest in game theory. Such modeling helps define how people interact and make decisions, and what the impact of certain decisions will be on the well–being of the other participants.

Game theory brings to the chaos–theory table the idea that generally, societies are not designed, and that most situations don't come with a rulebook. Instead, people have their own plans and designs on how things should fit together. They want to determine how the game is played, and they see societal designers as myopic busybodies who would imprison them with their theories.

Improved upon in 1950 by Princeton's John Nash, and his Nash Equilibrium, game theory does not tell a participant what a player's goal should be. Rather, it shows them how to attain a particular goal. The rules are simple, but they provide a wealth of complexity. Long–term strategy is vital, but so is a mixture of competition and cooperation. Some have likened it to the rock–paper–scissors game, but game theory participants create most of their own mutually adjusted rules across an ever–changing board.

The "prisoner's dilemma" is perhaps the most famous paradox in game theory. Two prisoners are isolated and have been accused of a crime. They can get a light sentence if both refuse to talk. But if one confesses and turns state's evidence, the confessor will get a lighter sentence, while his partner will receive a long jail term. If both confess, each will get a heavy sentence. The problem is that each wants to maximize his own well-being, but the path they take could lead to an unnecessarily bad outcome for both. Cooperation would provide the best result, but the two are being held in separate rooms. Will they succumb to their inner sense of personal gain and betray their partner, or will they cooperate and remain silent?

Interestingly, when information is sprinkled into the mix, cooperation wins out. In a 1970 study, H. A. Wichman discovered that if there was no communication between individuals in the Prisoner's Dilemma, only 41 percent of the players cooperated. When presented with the opportunity for face-to-face contact, some 87 percent decided to cooperate. When they communicated by voice but remotely, only 72% would cooperate.[43]

The Cooperation of Trade

The problem of social and economic inequalities often pits the well-to-do against the ne'er-do-well. Who is to blame? Some would like to blame the marketplace for such inequities, but to do so is to rebuke the messenger. Market activity is merely the distribution of items between participants, usually culminating in a mutually beneficial exchange. In this sense, trade is a politically neutral exchange of input, throughput, and output, based on symbiotic trade for the sake of the traders' satisfaction. It is non-ideological, concentrating on the mechanics of doing commerce.

As it turns out, the act of trading is perhaps the most stabilizing and cooperation-rich influence in the world, often credited with circumvention of prejudices, suspicions, and aggression. American explorers and trappers discovered that the best way to engage in friendly relations with the native population was to trade goods. Even with language barriers, the act of exchanging provided a peaceful language of its own. On the other hand, when trade is restricted by command and control systems, disorder and conflict are not far behind. As the nineteenth-century, French free-trade statesman Frederic Bastiat reportedly warned: "When goods do not cross borders, soldiers will."

Obviously, there is a limit on available resources in the world. This is what gave rise to economics, because economics explains how individuals can best utilize the limited resources they have; and one way is the structure of market exchange. Still, a particular trade in a poor region or nation has little to do with the overall scarcity or abundance of that region. Trade between partakers has neither a central strategy nor any binding social obligations. In many ways, trade is similar to the operation of insect colonies, where most entomologists see no reigning headmaster or conductor trying to orchestrate a grand, universal blueprint for their society. When a farmer grows wheat, he is not performing his job for some conscious, grand plan to feed the entire world. When a building contractor hammers together a new home, he has not signed up to provide universal shelter for the homeless. And yet, there are central planners who demand more food and housing for everyone, but who, themselves, have provided neither one grain of wheat nor one stud of framing for society, when the day is done.

A market economy represents the decentralized means to increase overall wealth by "negentropy"—the opposite of energy–depleting entropy. Product by product, this self–organizing economic system customizes the energy to create what individuals demand. And when the energy is exerted, and agreements are made, a wonderful wealth of peace and cooperation is produced freely.

Nonetheless, economic decisions are only as good as the psyches of the individuals involved. If there are few moral standards, the whole of society will reflect this shortcoming. If children incessantly watch violent TV programs, fingers ought to be pointing at the parents or the children, instead of reprimanding the manufacturers of television sets. Inanimate objects are neither evil nor morally praiseworthy. People choose what they do with things; things do not choose what happens to people.

Economic Systems: Marxism

Many economic systems are based on ideology and path dependence, and not on real–world actualities. Instead of deriving conclusions from observations and experimentation, many economic systems are doctrine-driven and oppose an open–ended search for truth. The "force of history" dialectic, for instance, prevents Marxists from foreseeing the consequences of their actions.

Despite Marxist platitudes about cooperation, community spirit, and social cohesion, Communist nations are the poster children for discord, holding the unofficial record for creating a culture as far from camaraderie and harmony as possible. That is because Marxist economics deals mostly with breaking and abolishing bonds, rather than establishing new ones. Under the Communist system, the means of production—capital, production facilities, natural resources—are to be confiscated, with little or no compensation to their owners. With "people's socialism" in place, worker co-ops and communes are supposed to spring up and operate the economy, although history shows they will only fuse into rigid hierarchies and bitter divisiveness.This socialization of capital is heavily centralized and collectivized in order to bring about some ill-defined equalization of people and outcomes. In practice, Marxist economics tends to foment human suffering and institutionalize disunity. As Winston Churchill once remarked, "The inherent vice of [market–based] capitalism is the unequal sharing of the blessings. The inherent blessing of socialism is the equal sharing of misery."

After the fall of the Soviet Union, hardline Marxists blamed Russia's collapse on its impure social and economic system—meaning that it never really implemented true communism. The obvious question: What would happen if a country actually did follow Marxist economics to the letter? One Communist leader attempted to do just that, in Southeast Asia. Today, this former prime minister is known as the "Butcher of Cambodia."

After being schooled in Marxist–Leninist theory in France, Pol Pot (1925-1998) returned to Cambodia in 1953 intending to create a utopian communist society. As the Vietnam War spilled over into Cambodia, Pol Pot rose to General Secretary of the Khmer Communist Party. When Prince Sihanouk engaged in a ruthless clampdown on any opposition to his regime, including Pol Pot's Khmer Rouge insurgents, the destabilization bolstered Communist activities. By 1975, the Khmer Rouge communists had captured the Cambodian capital city, Phnom Penh.

Within days, over two million Cambodians were being marched into the countryside at gunpoint, in an effort to impose a completely egalitarian society based on Mao's agrarian model and the economic works of Marxist Andre Gunder Frank. The key leaders of Pol Pot's Khmer Rouge movement had read Frank's work and believed that cities are bourgeois parasites on the countryside, and the only true value is the value of labor. To them, society needed a thorough cleansing; they argued that "what is infected must be cut out." In short order, the Khmer Rouge executed doctors, teachers, students, policemen, musicians, public servants, ethnic Vietnamese and Chinese, Muslim and Christian clergy, and anybody considered educated—even people who wore eyeglasses. State–operated radio stations boasted that they needed only one or two million people to build their new communal society. The Khmer Rouge had a saying for the other five or six million unneeded Cambodians: "To keep you is no benefit, to destroy you is no loss."[44]

Fine-tuning its uncompromising implementation of Marxist theory, the regime soon set out to abolish money and all private property. In addition, there were to be no schools, books, hospitals, or banks, no religion and no families, so as to facilitate a classless and moneyless society. Resembling a forced labor camp, everyone, including children, was forced to work 12– to 14–hour days, every day. Every former "corrupt" lifestyle or habit had to be cleansed, crushed, or consumed. There were no judges, trials, or laws. Music was forbidden. Even first–person pronouns were banned: one could speak only in collective terms of "we."

Despite the harsh social and economic controls, it was still not enough. When the results of the socialist reengineering of society came back uneven, Pol Pot, who had engaged in ethnic cleansing of Vietnamese and other minorities, began a systematic purge of his own ranks, as had Stalin and Hitler, earlier in the century. In a bout of paranoia, Pol Pot called for the death of the "hidden enemies, burrowing from within." Turning on their own ranks, the Communists in 1977 and 1978 executed over 200,000 young Khmer Rouge peasant cadres and important Khmer Rouge leaders.[45]

While the Khmer Rouge practiced total communism, the death toll grew more gruesome. After four years, the "democide"—the murder of people by their own government—stood at around two million, nearly one–third of the country's population, but the conflict and disorder would not subside.[46] Suspicious of Pol Pot's alliance with Red China, the Soviet Union–backed Vietnam invaded Cambodia in 1978, and forced the Khmer Rouge back to the mountainous countryside to continue for twenty more years of intense guerilla warfare. In response, China launched a limited invasion of northern Vietnam (the Sino–Vietnamese War). Most communist nations seemed to regularly throw out social cooperation and common goals like the proverbial baby with the bathwater.

By the late 1990s, many of the former leaders of the Khmer Rouge were being put on trial for genocide. Considered responsible for the "killing fields," Ta Mok was second–in–command of the Khmer Rouge and has been referred to by one of his country's prime ministers, Hun Sen, as the "Hitler of Cambodia." The significance of Mok is that he originally considered Cambodian nationalism as his sole ideology. Caught in an "ideological drift," Mok only vaguely understood the concepts of communism and Maoism. He enlisted as a communist guerrilla for nationalistic reasons. In an interview with Nate Thayer of *Far Eastern Economic Review* in 1997, Mok revealed: "When I joined the Communist Party of Cambodia, I did not know what communism was. They told me the party was a patriotic one. That is why I joined the party."[47]

National Socialism and Fascism

National Socialism is a political creed that absorbs systems, rather than abolishing them. A hodgepodge of socialism and nationalism, this ideology simmers in a collectivist cauldron of military prowess and racial superiority. Nationalizing some sectors of the economy such as the railroads and Jewish businesses, this command–based system permits ownership of property in name only. Legal ownership is considered secondary; what is important is that the state has the final say.

But where did this secular, anti-classical liberal, anti-capitalist and anti-democratic movement originate? In "The Mystery of Fascism," David Ramsey Steele wrote: "Fascism began as a revision of Marxism by Marxists, a revision which developed in successive stages, so that these Marxists gradually stopped thinking of themselves as Marxists, and eventually stopped thinking of themselves as socialists. They never stopped thinking of themselves as anti–liberal revolutionaries."[48]

These revisionists understood that Marx's predictions were failing to materialize. Instead of causing economic conditions to worsen, industrialization and modernization were generating more wealth, at all levels of society. Workers were becoming richer. The number of investors in capital equipment and companies was increasing. Profits were rising. But the most serious "great contradiction" of Marxism was that the better–fed and higher–paid workers were more concerned with national identity than with class struggle. By the 1890s, Marxism was in crisis. Many Marxists felt a need to embrace nationalism, in order to save socialism.

A form of "state capitalism" or "corporate state socialism," national socialism must be rigidly enforced and use extreme state intervention to control and regulate the economy. The state is seen as the administrator of all social programs, unlike in theoretical Marxism, in which the people rise up and organize the economy without the benefit of a well–defined structure.

Adolf Hitler was adamant about socializing Germany on both a massive and a personal scale. In *The Voice of Destruction*, National Socialist Hermann Rauschning, President of the Danzig Senate from 1933-1934, revealed many of his private conversations with Hitler from the mid–1930s. According to Rauschning, Hitler said:

There will be no license, no free space, in which the individual belongs to himself. This is Socialism—not such trifles as the private possession of the means of production. Of what importance is that if I range men firmly within a discipline they cannot escape? Let them own land or factories as much as they please. The decisive factor is that the State, through the party, is supreme over them regardless whether they are owners or workers. All that, you see, is unessential. Our Socialism goes far deeper.... Why need we trouble to socialize banks and factories? We socialize human beings.[49]

Hitler's anti-capitalistic bent was prominent and popular. He said of his fellow Nazis: "We are socialists, we are enemies of today's capitalistic economic system for the exploitation of the economically weak, with its unfair salaries, with its unseemly evaluation of a human being according to wealth and property instead of responsibility and performance."[50]

Generally considered the first modern welfare state in the late nineteenth century, Germany, under Hitler, expanded all sorts of social safety–net programs. Compulsory health insurance became more centralized and controlled than it had been under the system put into place by Chancellor Otto von Bismarck in the 1880s. Melchior Palyi explained, in *Compulsory Medical Care and The Welfare State* (1949), that employers' share of health care insurance in Nazi Germany increased from one–third to one–half.[51]

President Franklin D. Roosevelt copied many social programs from Hitler's Germany that had originated with Otto von Bismarck, including Social Security. The National Socialist German Workers' Party (NAZI party) had expanded medical care for the aged, including the less popular mandatory euthanasia programs. They called for full employment and good living wages. They used pro–labor rhetoric, demanding limitations on profits and the abolition of rents. Hitler expanded credit, suspended the gold standard, instituted government jobs programs, imposed unemployment insurance, imposed high tariffs to protect German industry from foreign competition, nationalized education, imposed strict wage and price controls, and eventually ran huge deficits. This should all have been expected from an ideology that proclaimed in its 25–Point Platform from 1920: "The Common Good Before the Individual Good."

Roosevelt's National Recovery Act (NRA) had its roots in Mussolini's cartelization of Italy. "Under the NRA Roosevelt established industry–wide boards with the power to set and enforce prices, wages, and other terms of employment, production, and distribution for all companies in an industry."[52] In

Chaology and Market-Based Economics

fact, Mussolini praised the economic policies of FDR's New Deal, arguing in the *New York Times*, "Your plan for coordination of industry follows precisely our lines of cooperation."[53]

Interestingly, in the 1920s, the Marxist theorist and commander of the Russian Red Army, Leon Trotsky, used the term "national socialism" as an epithet to describe Stalin's theory of "socialism in one country." He was not referring to the German version of National Socialism, but to the communist quest to infuse into Russia more nationalistic and patriotic policies, which were used very effectively, during World War II, in whipping up support among an often unsupportive citizenry.

Hitler went well beyond linearization and micromanaging of the German economy. According to Walter Laqueur in *Fascism: Past, Present, Future* Hitler exhibited obsessive–compulsive behavior.

> *A random look at the instructions emanating from his chancery shows that he [Hitler] gave orders that Wilhelm Furtwangler, the famous conductor, should not participate in the Salzburg Festival in 1938, that residents of Munich should be permitted to drink 'strong beer,' thereby opposing a planned reduction of beer's alcohol content, that a public statue at the Rhine should be illuminated by night, that the iron bars on the windows of a museum in Munich should not be painted black but bronze gold, that his aides should wear rubber soles, that the painter Gerhardinger should not be mentioned in the media, that prominent foreign visitors should not be fed canned mushrooms because of the danger of poisoning (this in May 1942!), that foreigners should not be given fishing permits, and that the monthly maximum for renting a garage should be 7 marks all over Germany.*[54]

Although it was first to gain power, Italian Fascism did not take kindly to German National Socialism at first. True to its collectivistic nature of strict conformity, Italy was suspicious of Germany's different shades of socialism and Hitler's rise to power. In fact, before the 1934 Nazi–inspired assassination of their fascist chancellor Engelbert Dollfuss, the Austrian government had sought Benito Mussolini's support against Hitler. The assassination of Dollfuss infuriated Mussolini, almost resulting in military conflict. Italian troops were deployed to the Austrian–Italian border in preparation for war against Hitler. Before his first meeting with *der Führer*, Mussolini referred to Hitler as a "silly little monkey."

The Fascism of Mussolini

Having been raised a Marxist and having close ties to Vladimir Lenin, Mussolini started his own weekly newspaper in 1910, *The Class Struggle*, and rose quickly as an influential leader in the Italian Socialist Party. Known as the "Lenin of Italy, Mussolini was a revolutionary socialist and a labor-union agitator who was arrested for advocating violence. According to David Ramsay Steele, "Mussolini was the Che Guevara of his day, a living saint of leftism. Handsome, courageous, charismatic, an erudite Marxist, a riveting speaker and writer, a dedicated class warrior to the core, he was the peerless duce of the Italian Left. He looked like the head of any future Italian socialist government, elected or revolutionary."[55]

That changed in 1914, when Mussolini joined a splinter group from the revolutionary syndicalists who supported Italy's entrance into the Great War (later known as World War I). This labor union movement metamorphosed into the Marxist–inspired *Fasci d'Azione Rivoluzionaria Internazionalista* (Union for International Revolutionary Action) in 1914—known as the Fascists—causing the infamous split between pro-war socialists and anti-war socialists. Similar breaks occurred within communist and socialist communities across Europe. Four days after Germany declared war on France, the French Communist Party (*Section Française de l'Internationale Ouvrière*—SFIO) dropped its antimilitary, internationalist stand and replaced it with French patriotism, fully supporting the war.

Boasting after the breakup that he would always remain a socialist, Mussolini tempered his view and eventually worked more closely with corporations and industrialists to gain support for his movement, while simultaneously demanding minimum–wage laws, an all–encompassing welfare state, and strong progressive taxes on capital. Such political maneuvers to widen one's political tent are not uncommon. Lenin had done the same in the early 1920s, "denationalizing" small businesses and farming communities after the Soviet Union's economy had begun to sour. When Lenin started to allow limited capitalistic activity under his New Economic Policy, he gave his famous "commanding heights speech," to defend himself against accusations of selling out his socialist principles.

Through Italian Fascism, those in power developed highly interventionist policies that sought to amplify the corporate state, in order to replace liberal, market–based economics. Creating twenty–two state–run organizations in 1926 called "corporations," Mussolini used a formula that was notoriously simple: "Everything in the state, nothing against the state, nothing outside the state."

Although Mussolini had flirted with some classical liberal policies during the early years of his regime, by 1935, he was boasting that three–quarters of Italian businesses were now under state control. By 1939 Italy had the highest percentage of state–owned enterprises outside the Soviet Union.[56] This friendship toward communist Russia was longstanding. Not only had Mussolini's government formally recognized the U.S.S.R. in 1924, but in 1933, it entered into a pact of friendship and nonaggression.

The armed conflict between the National Socialists of Germany and the Communists of Russia can be likened to two internecine street gangs, first cooperating, and then slugging it out in a contest to dominate the world. Both ideologies promoted state intervention in economic and personal affairs, but the policies they administered were of divergent structures and tactics. The NAZIS and Communists were not opposites, as some historians have attempted to argue, but two sides of the same coin. This violent rivalry between Hitler's National Socialism and Stalin's Communism was no different than what occurred after the 1917 Russian Revolution. Then, the Bolsheviks battled against many of their former socialist allies—the Socialist Revolutionaries and Mensheviks. In fact, the Socialist Revolutionaries and other leftwing groups led an armed uprising against Vladimir Lenin's Bolshevik party in many Russian cities, attacking the Kremlin with thousands of armed troops and artillery (aka Third Russian Revolution). During this turmoil between rival socialist factions, the Socialist Revolutionary Fanya Kaplan attempted to assassinate Lenin in 1918, shooting him in the arm and jaw. The climate of antagonism between the various socialist schisms in Russia was brutal and bloody. Generally, collective-minded people do not get along with each other.

Russian Bolshevism worried Fascist and National Socialist leaders. They feared that revolutionary class warfare and an economy operated by worker–controlled means of production could cause chaotic conditions to arise. To adherents of Marxism–Leninism, the working class would have to rise up and randomly, forge a fusion of factory co–ops and farming communes. And eventually, when this people's socialism reached its victorious end game, the state apparatus would wither away to nothing. This idea horrified state socialists. To them, socialism was to be molded to precise specifications and administered through a highly organized hierarchy, not by some illusive people's community that appeared to have little structure or future.

Keynesism

Named for the British economist John Maynard Keynes (1883–1946), Keynesian economics, or Keynesism, represents public policies that expand the government's authority to intervene in the economy. Many critics view Keynesianism as an attack on classical liberal economics. Some argue that his push for substantial state involvement whetted his economic appetite for some version of National Socialism. Keynes himself had written about the parallels. In the preface of the 1936 German–language edition of his book *The General Theory of Employment, Interest and Money*, Keynes told readers that his theories, like those developed by Hitler's policymakers, were much more suited to a totalitarian state than to the freer markets found in Britain.[57]

Others argue that Keynes was merely commenting that a dictator could more easily alter government policy than democratic leaders could, and yet, Hitler admired Keynes, while similarly, Keynesians admired Hitler.[58]

Keynes ultimately blamed market forces, rather than credit expansion stimulated by central banks, for the roller–coaster ride of "boom and bust" cycles. To remedy this imbalance, he suggested that during downturns, the visible hand of government grab hold of the economic reins, and then tax everyone heavily once the boom cycles returned. Keynes's chief policy proposals were to end the gold standard and to forgo balanced budgets, to allow government to print or borrow more money. Keynesians believed that government could work its way out of a recession through deficit spending. When economically good times returned, the state could simply impose heavy taxation or cut spending. What Keynes failed to predict was government's addiction to issuing unlimited blank checks, government bonds and its sugar–daddy compulsion to bail out poorly performing industries. This was not Keynes's original purpose, but his policies led to the modern welfare state, enriched the roots of central planning, and unleashed a torrent of "Vichy liberalism."

Keynes believed that markets are fundamentally unstable and that governments should supply stability, forcibly, through macroeconomic policies. From a market chaologist's perspective, economic activities will always be in flux, to sort out value, excesses, and a host of other imbalances. Market disequilibrium is not an abnormality, but Keynes wanted an economic solution that would exhibit a "continuum of equilibria."

Under the theories of "evolutionary economics," the engine of marketplaces is ever oscillating. It is impossible to maintain Keynes's "inefficient equilibrium" within the framework of Joseph Schumpeter's wavelike "creative destruction." Boom–and–bust economic cycles are self–forming and self–adjusting mechanisms that kick in to reach an average range of values. Keynes had misjudged the nonlinear nature of markets and their intractable edge–of–chaos imperfections. For market chaologists, the greatest destabilizing factor in society and the economy is command–based, etched–in–stone policies that prevent self-correction. This is probably the major reason that Roosevelt's Keynes–like policies were never able to end the Great Depression. Many economists theorize that Roosevelt's central planning policies only served to deepen and prolong America's worst economic downturn.

Keynes's theory of "demand management," once considered the cornerstone of a well—planned, mixed economy, finally faced a day of reckoning. Without sound money and with few monetary restraints, the leading nations of the Western world were brought to their financial knees. By the 1970s, most industrialized nations were experiencing high unemployment, anemic economic growth rates, staggering deficits, and runaway inflation—often referred to as "stagflation." To diehard neo–Keynesians who believed in the Phillips Curve, this situation was, theoretically, impossible.[59]

With Keynesian theories discredited, everything had come full circle. During the 1930s, Hayek's rising star in England had been eclipsed by Keynes's *General Theory*. The two had maintained a cordial relationship for decades, but because of the worldwide depression, Hayek found his own repeated calls for freer markets overshadowed by Keynes's advocacy for demand management. By the end of the twentieth century, Keynes's adversary had reclaimed the economic spotlight. Hayek was now held up as the antediluvian prophet emerging from the intellectual wilderness.

As Daniel Yergin and Joseph Stanislaw suggested in *Commanding Heights: The Battle for the World Economy* (1998), the failure of Keynesian policies and the collapse of communism redeemed Hayek and his market–based–economics ideals. The rise of chaos and complexity theories seems to have also paralleled Hayek's new superstar status, especially concerning his theory of "spontaneous order." In fact, John Cassidy in *The New Yorker* acknowledged the tremendous influence of Hayek's ideas, writing: "It is hardly an exaggeration to refer to the twentieth century as the Hayek century."[60]

Mercantilism

Defending many of the tenets of mercantilism in his book *The General Theory of Employment, Interest and Money*, Keynes contended that government intervention in the economy is necessary, although he had supported free trade during his younger years.[61] These similarities have caused some critics to refer to Keynes's theories as "neo–mercantilism."

Predominant from the 1500s to the1700s, the key doctrine of mercantilism was to limit the flow of commerce between nations. Arising out of the old, feudalistic ethos, mercantilists believed that the best way to maintain a positive balance of trade was to keep as much gold as possible in the nation's bank vaults. To accomplish this self–sufficiency policy, most nations enacted protectionist laws. As with any economic restraints, these external controls caused adverse side effects. Overall poverty increased; scarcity of particular goods became acute; and smuggling became wildly profitable. To relieve this problem, European governments discovered an ingenious way to gain a bigger share of the economic pie: They simply invaded foreign lands and took control of their natural resources.

Mercantilism fueled colonialism. This policy solved some problems at home, while creating more problems abroad. Benefiting the privileged few, state–recognized merchants now had an enforced monopoly and military troops to protect their market share. In many cases, the government would provide capital to new businesses, along with limited exemptions from taxes. At other times, top producers were rewarded with fat pensions and royal titles. The system of governance also benefited handsomely with high tariffs and kickbacks from appreciative merchants. But the overall impact of overseas possessions under imperialism had a divisive and dysfunctional effect that still haunts the Third World. For instance, Africa was commingled into fifty political nations of conflicting tribes, religions, economic classes, and ideology. Nigeria, alone, had more than a hundred ethnic groups jammed into one artificially created country, contributing to a colonial legacy that often pitted African against African, under bitter political schisms.

Eventually, mercantilism faded away, as confidence in laissez–faire and free–trade economics gained the upper hand in the late eighteenth century. Adam Smith, who had popularized the term "mercantilism," bashed its monopolistic and privileged nature in *The Wealth of Nations*. One of Smith's intellectual heirs, David Ricardo, believed, as economists still do, that both sides benefit from trade. But under mercantilism, it was presumed that the level of world wealth was fixed, and that the only way to increase one's wealth was to take it from someone else. This cutthroat game of "zero-sum" structures assumed that one party always lost, while another one gained. Classical liberal economic theory held that everyone benefits through value–for–value trading, which results in expansion of the economic pie for everyone. Since every region has its own distinct advantages and drawbacks, trading helps equalize the imbalance. For instance, there is a comparative advantage for inhabitants of the Netherlands, with its cold weather to trade their native tulips for bottles of wine produced in Italy, with its warmer climate.

Mercantilism is equivalent to "nanny–statism," in which governmental systems are viewed as useful instruments to create wealth and equality for the benefit of the impoverished. Humorist and author P. J. O'Rourke dispelled this notion, writing, "Government does not cause affluence. Citizens of totalitarian countries have plenty of government and nothing of anything else." But what if systems of governance could somehow be crafted to be efficient in providing for all sorts of services? What if they could be made to serve mankind without unintended consequences? President Harry Truman once addressed this issue. In a 1959 lecture at Columbia University, he warned, "Whenever you have an efficient government you have a dictatorship."

Adam Smith and classical economics ended the dominance of mercantilism, only to see it revived and magnified in the twentieth century under totalitarian regimes. This resurgence of government domination over economic and human life has been responsible for some of the darkest days ever experienced by humankind.

1 George Whaley and Benjamin Franklin, *Principles of Trade*, 1774. However, Franklin gave full credit to Whaley for writing a book in which they both had a hand. *Laissez-faire* is French for "Let (people) do (as they think best)." In ancient Chinese culture this noninterference concept was known as wu—wei, or "active not–doing."

2 John H. Holland, "Genetic Algorithms: Computer programs that "evolve" in ways that resemble natural selection can solve complex problems even their creators do not fully understand," *Scientific American*, July 1992, p. 66–72.

3 William Tucker, "Complex Questions." *Reason*, January 1996, pp. 34–38.

4 John H. Holland, "Escaping Brittleness: The Possibilities of General Purpose Machine Learning Algorithms Applied to Parallel Rule–Based Systems." In *Machine Learning II*, R. S. Michalski, J. G. Carbonell, and T. M. Mitchell (eds.), Los Altos, CA: Morgan Kaufmann, 1986, pp.593–623.

5 John H. Holland, *Adaptation in Natural and Artificial Systems: An Introductory Analysis with Applications to Biology, Control, and Artificial Intelligence*, Cambridge, MA: The MIT Press, 1992.

6 Daniel B. Klein, "The People's Romance: Why People Love Government," *The Independent Review*, vol. 10, no. 1, Summer 2005.

7 F.A. Hayek, *The Constitution of Liberty*, Chicago: University of Chicago Press, 1978, originally published in 1960.

8 William Tucker, "An Ownership Society Evolves," *The American Enterprise*, Vol. 16, No. 2, p. 30, March 2005.

9 Ibid.

10 Marvin Minsky, *The Society of Mind*, New York: Simon & Schuster, 1986, p. 169.

11 Daniel B. Klein, "Quality and Safety Assurance: The Division of Knowledge Does Apply to the Achieving of Trust," *The Independent Review*, Spring 1998, pp. 337–355.

12 Adam Smith, *An Inquiry into the Nature and Causes of the Wealth of Nations*, originally published in 1776, publisher, T. Nelson and Sons, Paternoster Row.

13 Friedrich Hayek, "The Use of Knowledge in Society," *The American Economic Review*, 35, No. 4; September, 1945, 519–30. One of the 12 essays in *Individualism and Economic Order*, Chicago: The University of Chicago Press, 1948.

14 Richard Roll, "Orange juice and weather," *American Economic Review*, 74, 1984, 861–880.

15 Nicholas Negroponte, *Being Digital*, New York: Vintage Books, 1996, p. 157.

16 Steven Johnson, *Emergence: The Connected Lives of Ants, Brains, Cities and Software*, New York: Scribner, 2001.

17 Natalie Angier, "In Hive or Castle, Duty Without Power," *New York Times*, May 15, 2007.

18 Trevor Rosen, "Ilya Prigogine: Mystical Science," *The Alcalde*, September/October 2004.

19 Maurice Maeterlinck, *The Life of the Bee*, New York: Dodd, Mead, and Company, 1901, p. 51.
20 Rosen, ibid.
21 Speech Panel: "The Constitution of Liberty: The Definite Edition," Prof. Bruce Caldwell, transcript of speech panel to launch the new edition of Hayek's Constitution of Liberty, April 28, 2011, sponsored by Cato Institute. www.Cato.org/events/transcripts/110428bf.html
22 William Tucker, "Complex Questions." *Reason*, January 1996, pp. 34–38.
23 Mitchell M. Waldrop, *Complexity: The Emerging Science at the Edge of Order and Chaos*, New York: Simon & Schuster, 1992, p. 22.
24 Waldrop, ibid., p. 22.
25 Joseph Jaworski, Gary Jusela, and C. Otto Scharmer, "Coming from Your Inner Self," Conversation with W. Brian Arthur, Xerox PARC, April 16, 1990.
26 Carole E. Scott, "New Science Validates Laissez–Faire and Draws Attention to Little Known School of Economics," 1996, Internet posting. Posted at: www.westga.edu/~bquest/1996/chaos.html
27 Friedrich Hayek, "The Results of Human Action but Not of Human Design," in *New Studies in Philosophy, Politics, Economics*, Chicago: University of Chicago Press, 1978, pp. 96–105.
28 Although no longer contemporary, Hedrick Smith's *The Russians* provides one of the best firsthand experiences of a failing and corrupted system.
29 Russ Roberts, "An Interview with Milton Friedman," EcoTalk, Sept. 4, 2006, sponsored by Library of Economics and Liberty.
30 Michael Grunwald, "Washington Memo—One of Their Own," *Time*, June 4, 2007.
31 Ralph Nader, *The Monopoly Makers: Ralph Nader's Study Group Report on Regulations and Competition*, New York: Grossman Publishers, 1973.
32 John Stossel, "Big Business, Government: Partners in Plunder," *Orange County Register*, Oct. 1, 2006.
33 P.J. O'Rourke, guest on the *The Daily Show* with Jon Stewart, Jan 23, 2008.
34 David R. Henderson, "Are We Ailing from Too Much Deregulation?" *Cato Policy Report*, Nov./Dec. 2008.
35 Marcy Gordon, "Madoff Fund May Have Made No Trades," *Business Week*, Jan. 16, 2009.
36 Amire Efrati and Robert Frank, "Madoff Set To Plead Guilty to 11 Felonies," *Wall Street Journal*, March 11, 2009.
37 Kara Scannell, "Perjury Charges Against Madoff?" *Wall Street Journal*, January 28, 2009.
38 Ross Kerber and Jonathan Stempel, "Blistering Report Faults SEC for Madoff Misses," *The Washington Post*, Sept. 2, 2009.
39 Eric Lichtblau, "Economic Downturn Took a Detour at Capitol Hill, *New York Times*, December 26, 2011.

40 Murray N. Rothbard, *The Case Against the Fed*, Auburn, Alabama: Ludwig von Mises Institute, 1994, p. 91.

41 David Theroux's introduction to Tom Peters' speech, "New Opportunities for Excellence in a Freer World," April 27, 1994, Independent Institute.

42 Charles T Pearson, *The Indomitable Tin Goose: The True Story of Preston Tucker and His Car*, New York: Pocket Books, 1988.

43 H. A. Wichman, "Effects of Isolation And Communications on Cooperation in a Two–Person Game," *Journal of Personality and Social Psychology* 16, 1970, 114–120.

44 Dith Pran, compiled, Kim DePaul, edited, *Children of Cambodia's Killing Fields: Memoirs by Survivors*, New Haven, CT: Yale University Press, 1997.

45 Philip Short, *Pol Pot: Anatomy of a Nightmare*, New York: Macmillan 2006, p. 368.

46 R. J. Rummel's estimates in *Death by Government*, New Brunswick: New Jersey, 1994.

47 David Lamb, "Ta Mok, 80; Key Figure in Cambodian Genocide," *Los Angeles Times*, July 21, 2006.

48 David Ramsey Steele, "The Mystery of Fascism," *Liberty*, Vol. 15, no. 11, Nov. 2001.

49 Hermann Rauschning, *The Voice of Destruction*, New York, Putnam, 1940, pp. 191–193.

50 Hitler's speech on May 1, 1927. Cited in J. Toland, *Adolf Hitler*, Garden City, NY: Doubleday, 1976, p. 306.

51 Richard M. Ebeling, "National Health Insurance and the Welfare State," chapter in *The Dangers of Socialized Medicine*, Fairfax, Virginia: Future of Freedom Foundation, 1994.

52 Sheldon Richman, "Fascism," in *The Concise Encyclopedia of Economics* (2nd ed.), compiled and edited by David R. Henderson, Chicago, Illinois: Liberty Fund, Inc., 2008.

53 Ronald Edsforth, *The New Deal: American's Response to the Great Depression*, Hoboken, New Jersey: Wiley–Backwell, 2000, p. 145.

54 Walter Laqueur, in *Fascism: Past, Present, Future*, New York: Oxford University Press, 1996, p. 31.

55 David Ramsey Steele, "The Mystery of Fascism," ibid.

56 Patricia Knight, *Mussolini and Fascism (Questions and Analysis in History)*, New York: Routledge, 2003.

57 Shawn Ritenour, "Keynes the Great?" *The Free Market*, vol. 16, no. 11, Nov. 1998.

58 George Garvy, "Keynes and the Economic Activists of Pre–Hitler Germany," *The Journal of Political Economy*, 83 (2), 1975, 391–405.

59 The Phillips Curve: when inflation is high, unemployment will be low, and vice versa.

60 John Cassidy, "The Price Prophet," *New Yorker*, February 7, 2000.
61 Leonard Gomes, *The Economics and Ideology of Free Trade: An Historical Review*, Cheltenham, U.K.: Edward Elgar, 2003, p. 5.

Index

AAMVA Financial Responsibility and Insurance Resource Guide, 330, 332
Abacha, Sani. 96
Abdussamatov, Habibullo, 40
Abel, Ted, 305
Above-ground society, 287
A Brief History of Time, 62, 77
Absolute-based Architecture, 116
Activist government surrogates, 121, 145, 175, 208
Adams, Henry, 1, 191
Adams, John, 19, 146-147
Adaptation in Nature and Artificial Systems, 24, 352, 386
Acadian Ambulance Company, 269
ACORN, 322
Aesop, 284
Afghanistan, Islamic Republic of, 55-56, 197
Africa: Open for Business, 326
African Americans, 118, 166
Agent-based modeling (ABM), 143, 226, 255
Age of Turbulence, The, 229
Agnotology, 208
Ahimsa, 161
Alabama, 165, 388
Albert, David Z., 65, 77
Alexander the Great, 211, 244
Algiers, 270
Algorithms, 6, 10, 24, 123, 261-262, 281 292, 302, 351-352, 386
Alien and Sedition Acts, 146-147
Ali, Najee, 170
Alleles, 339
Allen, Peter, 357
Al-Qaeda, 280
American Civil War, 154, 157, 215, 365
American Dream Down Payment Act, 322
American Library Association, 20
American Revolutionary War, 132, 251
Amsterdam, 143, 213, 248, 255
Amu Darya River, 47
Anarchists, 93, 98, 174, 180, 309-310
Angier, Natalie, 356, 386
Anglo-Saxon, 232
Animal Farm, 174
Anisotropy, 316
Athens, 212, 239, 243, 286
Ankara State Security Court, 166
Anti-K-mesons, 71
Antimatter, 59, 68, 71
Apollo 13, 8
Apple Computer, 13, 219, 223, 230
Aral Sea, 47
Archiphilia, 148
Aristotle, 15, 118
Arizona State University, 100, 225
Armed neutrality, 196, 222
ARPANET, 202
Arthur, W. Brian, 93-94, 112, 133, 143, 230, 255, 361-362, 364, 387
Arunga, June, 95
Aryan Man, 75, 343
Ashly. W. Ross, 227
Aspect, Alain, 65
Aspect Experiment, 65
Assembly of Centuries, 238
Assembly of 6000, 243
Assembly of Tribes, 238
Atlanta, 20, 25, 271
Atomists, 62
At the Center of the Storm, 199, 222
Auburn University, 233
Aumann, Robert, 305

Australian Communications and Media Authority, 85
Austrian school of economics, 44, 82, 86, 227-229, 249, 257. 361-364
Authoritarian Personality, The, 138, 143
Autocatalytic evolution, 10, 341
Autocatalytic set theory, 314, 337-338
Autopoiesis, 10, 31-32, 313-315, 340
Autopoietic paradox, 312, 314
Avian flu, 42
Ayittey, George, 96, 112

Bacon's Rebellion, 118
Bahamonde, Marty, 272
Baikal-Amur Mainline Railway, 47
Baltimore Sun, 204
Bandit society, 96, 106, 234
Barre, Mohamed Siad, 235
Bassler, Bonnie L., 210, 222-223
Bastiat, Frederic, 120, 373
Baton Rouge, Louisiana, 272
Baule of Ivory Coast, 233
Beard, Charles A., 181,189
Becker, Gary, 165, 187
Behr, Edward, 141, 143
Being Digital, 356, 386
Belgium, 12, 163, 193
Bell's Inequality, 65
Bell, John, 65
Belousov, Boris, 134
Belousov-Zhabotinsky (BZ) Reaction, 134
Beni, Gerardo, 259
Bentham, Jeremy, 158
Betsy, Hurricane, 272
Bey, Hakim, 234
Big Bang Theory, 35, 70, 94
Big Three, The, 371
Biogenesis, 340, 347
Bioinformatics, 260
Bio-logic engineering, 282
Biology Letters, 336, 350

Biomimicry, 126
Bionomics: Economy as Business Ecosystem, 232, 255
Biopolar feedback, 83
Bird, Richard J., 342, 350
Bismarck, Otto von, 45, 378
Black holes, 63, 65, 77, 85
Blackwell, John, 233
Blanco, Kathleen, 269
Blaug, Mark, 133, 143
Bloody Sunday, 27
Blowback, 23, 54-56, 60
Blowback: The Costs and Consequences of American Empire, 55, 60
B-mesons, 71
Bohm, David, 305
Bohr, Niels, 14, 64
Boitano, Brian, 209
Bolsheviks, 381
Bonabeau, Eric, 261, 266, 277
Boomerang effect, 23, 27, 29-33, 35, 37-59, 289, 322, 328
Bovard, James, 163
Bradbury, Michael, 108
Braess, Dietrich, 275-276
Braess's paradox, 275-276
Bratton, William, 286
Brazil, 250-251
Brenner, Sydney, 340
Bridge to nowhere, 47
Briggs, John, 312, 332
Britain, 4, 201, 382
British, 4, 41, 44-45, 48, 126, 133, 147, 152, 171, 188, 196, 266, 278, 382
British Salt Law, 152
Bromine, 319
Browne, Harry 45, 59, 164, 167,187
Brown, Janice R., 293, 296
Brown, Michael, 270, 272
Brueckner, Jan, 121-122, 142
Brunell, Amy, 309
Bryson, Reed, 39

Index

Buddhist, 266
Bureaucracy, 29, 50, 58-59, 137, 177-178, 201, 216, 232, 246, 248, 312, 366, 369
Bureau des Longitudes, 70
Burning knowledge, 358
Burns, Ron, 293
Burundi, 194
Bush, George Herbert Walker, Sr., 27
Bush, George W., 55, 199, 252-253, 288, 309-310, 322, 329, 331
Butcher of Cambodia, 375-376, 388
Butterfly Economics, 230, 255
Butterfly effect, 2, 40, 66, 71, 162, 219, 354
Byzantine failure, 200-201

Caesar, Julius,
Calculated Chaos, 35, 58
California, 4, 19, 22, 25, 38, 42, 49, 51-52, 58, 60, 73, 110, 116-117, 121, 123, 134, 138, 142-143, 171, 185, 214, 220, 242, 244, 246-247, 257, 290-291, 294, 327, 330
California Controller Office, 52, 110
California Department of Insurance, 330
California Department of Transportation (Caltrans), 291
Camazine, Scott, 356
Cambodian Communist Party,
Caplan, Arthur, 170
Capone, Al, 367
Capra, Fritjof, 115, 128, 142
Carbon dioxide, 38, 40, 59
CARE, 325
Carmel-by-the-Sea, 123
Carreras, Ben, 175
Carruthers, Martyn, 145, 186
Cassidy, John, 383, 389
Catastrophe theory, 316
Cartesian equations, 128
Casti, John L., 122-123, 142, 228, 255

Castro, Fidel, 98, 220
Catallaxy, 228
Cate, General Matthew, 38
Catholic, 130, 194
Cato Institute, 25, 112, 222, 256, 387
Catterton, James M., 109
Caucasus, 243
Cayman Islands, 328-329
Cayman Turtle Farm, 328-329
Cellular automata, 32, 315, 352
Centers for Medicare and Medicaid Services, 171
Central Intelligence Agency (CIA), 23, 54-56, 199, 222
CERN (European Organization for Nuclear Research), 68
Chaisson, Eric J., 337 350
Challenger space shuttle, 2
Chalupnicek, Pavel, 169, 188
Chamberlin, Thomas Chrowder, 1, 24
Chaos and Life: Complexity and Order in Evolution and Thought, 342, 350
Chaos and Order in Capital Market, 363
Chaos dynamics, 183-184
Chaos: Making a New Science, 3, 24, 77
Chaotician, 335
Charity Hospital, 269
Charlemagne or Carolus Magnus, 213-214
Chavez, Hugo, 300
Chemical clock, 135
Cheney, Dick, 199
Cheonggyecheon, 276
Chesapeake Bay, 357
Chhibber, Pradeep, 116
Chicago, Illinois, 186, 286, 367, 388
China, 15, 24, 96-97, 102, 112, 159, 169, 175, 181, 187, 376
Chinese, 96-97, 139, 169, 193, 213, 266, 324, 326, 375, 386
Chlorophyte, 347
Choice Theory, 228, 255, 284, 292, 370

Christianfield, Denmark, 274
Chuang-tzu, 225
Chulalongkorn, King Rama V, 157
Churchill, C. West, 27, 58   C. West Churchman?
Churchill, Winston, 7, 375
Church of England (Anglican), 131
Civil Rights movement, 53, 60, 166
Civil Rights Project, Harvard University, 25, 53, 60, 128, 159
Claremont Graduate University, 173
Classic Coke and New Coke, 81, 220
Classical liberalism, 158
Classically Liberal, 84
Class Struggle, The, 377, 380
Clear Creek fire, 75
Cleisthenes, 212
Clinton, Bill, 75, 321
Closed shops, 241
CNN-TV, 270, 277, 332
Coast Guard, 271
Coca-Cola Company, 81, 220, 223
Collard family, 327
Collective creativity, 292
Collective feedback, 125, 216, 267, 349
Collective intelligence, 35, 162, 209, 216-217, 222, 264, 292, 304, 356
Colonialism, 13, 152, 342, 384
Columbia University, 149, 186, 222, 350, 355, 385
Colvin, Harvey, 367
Command economy, 201
Commanding heights speech, 380
Commanding Heights: The Battle for the World Economy, 383
Committee on Ways and Means, 103
Common law, 149-150, 152, 295
Communists, 97, 156-157, 174, 181, 188-189, 205-206, 284, 312, 324, 332, 374-381
Communist Central Committee, 205-206
Communist Manifesto, The, 174

Complementarity, 63
Complex Adaptive Systems (CAD), 10, 45, 225, 255, 335, 339
Complexity economists, 351
Complexity Science, 3, 10-11, 31, 40, 86, 118, 124, 126, 142, 161, 226, 254, 259, 313, 336, 351, 353, 357-358
Complexity without design, 216
Compulsory Medical Care and The Welfare State, 378
Comte, Auguste, 14
Confirmation bias, 1
Congo, 194
Congo War, first and second, 194
Connecticut Courant, 147
Connell, Kathleen, 52
Conradt, Larissa, 210, 222
Conscience and Courage, 138, 143
Consent of the governed, 35, 308-309, 331
Conspiracy to Murder: The Rwanda Genocide and the International Community, 193, 222
Constant, Benjamin, 215, 223
Constitution, United States, 37, 58, 146, 233-234, 241
Constitutional Chaos, 151, 186
Constitution of Liberty, The, 112, 142, 352, 386-387
Continuum of equilibria, 382
Controlaholics, 182, 202, 240, 287
Conventicle Act, 131
Convention Center, Ernest N. Morial, 269-270
Convention on International Trade in Endangered Species (CITES), 328
Copenhagen Interpretation of Quantum Mechanics, 64
Coppola, Francis Ford, 281
Corporate law, 365
Corporate state socialism, 377
Cosmic Code, 14, 25

Index

Cosmological Constant,
Coulter, N. Arthur, 126, 142
Council of 500, 243
Counterterrorist Center, 56
Courts of Appeals for the District of Columbia Circuit, 293
Cranfield University, 357
Creative destruction, 122, 249
Cretaceous Period, 344
Crete, 232
Crichton, Michael, 9, 56, 335
Criminal Tribes Act, 48
Cronin, James W., 68, 71
Crosswalk Principle, 291
Crutchfield, Jim, 134
Cryptobiotic, 348
Crystallization, 347
Cultural Revolution, 96-97, 324
Cunningham, Ward, 191, 222
Cyberspace, 202-203, 222

Dacey, Claire, 171
Dahl, Gary, 17
Daily Show, The, 229, 255, 366, 387
Dallaire, Lieutenant General Romeo, 194
Danzig Senate, 377
Dark energy, 62, 77
Dark matter, 62, 77
Darwin, Charles, 232, 336-337, 341-342, 345, 361
Daschle, Tom, 102, 112
Davis, Gray, 51
Davis, Paul, should be Paul Davies? 1, 24, 61
Dawkins, Richard, 159, 187
Death and Life of Great American Cities, The, 124, 142
Deadweight loss, 267, 300
Death by Government, 181, 189, 388
DeCarlo, Douglas, 182, 189
Decentral planning, 209
Decentralized decision making, 27, 49, 94, 123, 125, 157, 196, 198-200, 202, 207-211, 213, 216, 221, 228, 232, 235, 243, 259-260, 262, 292, 352, 356, 359, 364, 374
Decentralized simplicity, 359
Declaration of Independence, American, 35
Deductive rationality, 93
Delocalized system, 314
Demand management, 383
DeMarse, Thomas, 262-263
Democide, 98, 181, 189, 376
Democracy Corp., 106
Democracy in America, 168, 187
Democratic mission creep, 107
Department of Agriculture (USDA), 326
Department of Energy (DOE),
Department of Drug Enforcement Administration (DEA), 109
Department of State (DoS),
Department of the Treasury, 102, 321
Descartes, René, 118, 161, 227
Designer drugs, 245, 256
Detached interconnectivity, 314
Deterministic chaos, 66, 70, 263, 302
Deterministic laws, 61, 73, 75
Deterministic predictability, 3
Detroit News, 371
Devaney, Robert, 2
"Developmental Hypothesis," 342
Devil's Footpath, The, 95
Dial 911 and Die, 247, 257
Dictator syndrome, 45
Dictocrats, 174
Dictyostelids, 347
Die Deutsche Bromkonvention, 319
Digital organisms, 353
Digital Orrery, 69
DiLorenzo, Thomas J., 320, 332
Disaster lobby, 299
Disjointed incrementalism, 93
Disk Operating System (DOS), 217

Dismantling Utopia: How Information Ended the Soviet Union, 204, 222
Disney Brothers Studio, 13
Dissipative systems, 133-134, 316 dissipative structures?
Diversity Training University International, 100
Division of knowledge, 354, 386
Dodd, Chris, 368
Dogon of Mali, 233
Dollfuss, Engelbert, 379
Dooley, Kevin, 225, 255
Double-split experiment, 68
Dow Chemical, 319
Dow, Herbert 319
Dow Jones Industrial Average (DJIA), 370
Dowlatabadi, Hadi, 41
DNA, 71, 151, 245, 336-337, 340, 348, 356
Duke University, 151
Durant, William, 21, 93
Dvorak, Lukas, 169, 188
Dynamic instability, 119
Dyson, Freeman, 27, 226

Earle, Twila Hugley, 304, 331
Ebola fever, 42
Ecole Polytechnique, 313
Economist, The, 12, 24, 236, 256
Economy as an Evolving Complex System II, The, 93, 112
Edge of Chaos, 7, 15, 94, 123, 132, 134, 175, 183-184, 263-264, 335, 354, 383
Edsel, 81
Edward, Chris, Chris Edwards? 101, 112
Eigen, Manfred, 337
Einstein, Albert, 13-14, 21, 44, 59, 61, 63-65, 70, 77, 85, 87, 89, 145, 191, 305
Ellickson, Robert, 294-295,
End of Certainty, 215, 223

Enlightenment, Age of, 3, 215
Emanuel, Rahm, 98
Emergence: From Chaos to Order, 123
Emergence: the Connected Lives of Ants, Brains, Cities and Software, 356, 386
Empire Builders, The Vision and Influence of Michigan's Early Entrepreneurs, 319
Endangered Species Act (ESA), 328
Ends justify the means, 77, 173
Entropy, 1, 11-13, 135-136, 140, 148, 182-183, 265, 302, 306, 316, 346-347, 358, 374
Environmental Protection Agency (EPA), 54
EPR Paradox, 63-65
Equalitarian, 49, 133, 159, 183
Equality of outcome, 72, 183
Erhard, Ludwig, 244
Eristic Escalation, law of, 283
Ethiopian proxy-army, 237
Euclidean geometries, 302
European Constitution, 37, 58
European Union, 120, 249
Eusociality, 262
Evolutionary biologists, 128-129, 160, 183, 200, 336, 340, 345
Evolutionary economics, 382
Existentialism, 289
Exogenous shock, 133
Exploiting versus discovery,
Extreme Project Management, 182, 189

Failed States Index, 266, 277
Fannie Mae, 321, 332
Far Eastern Economic Review, 376
Far-from-equilibrium, 11, 132-134, 232
Farm subsidies, 298, 326, 332
Fascism *(Fasci d'Azione Revolutionary International)*, 377, 379-80, 388
Fascism, Past, Present and Future, 379
Faustian pact, 301

Fawkes, Guy, 131
Federal Bureau of Investigation (FBI), 253, 290
Federal Emergency Management Agency (FEMA), 268-272, 277
Federal Housing Administration (FHA), 321
Federalists, 146-147, 296
Federalist Papers, The, 311
Federal Register, 268
Federal Reserve, 71, 229, 297, 321
Feigenbaum, Mitchell, 5-6
Ferguson, Homer, 371
Fermi National Accelerator Laboratory, 68
Feynman, Richard, 63, 68-69
Firefox, 360-361
First Principles, 342
Fitch, Val L., 68, 71
Five-Mile Act, 131
Fleming, Alexander, 266
"Flocks, Herds, and Schools: A Quantitative Theory of Flocking," 264, 277
Florence, 212
Fogelman, Eva, 138, 143
Folsom, Burton, 319
Forced busing, 53
Force of history dialectics, 374
Force of instability, 306
Ford Corporation, 81
Ford, John,
Ford, Joseph, 7, 24, 61, 335
Foreign aid, 244, 325-326, 332
Forfeiture Endangers American Rights (FEAR), 110, 113
Forfeiture laws, 108-110, 113, 329
Fort Collins, 52
Fractals, 4, 6, 80, 82, 88, 252, 302, 306
Fractalized Information, 251
Fractals: Form, Chance and Dimension, 82, 88
Franco, Francisco, 174

France, 146, 163, 165, 187, 196-197, 199, 212, 261, 313, 375, 380
Frank, Andre Gunder, 375
Frankenstein effect, 51
Franklin, Benjamin, 147, 168, 211, 240-241, 351, 386
Freeman, Walter J., 185, 189
Free rider problem, 249, 251
Freddie Mac, 321
French Communist Party (*Section Francaise de l'Internationale Ouvrière—SFIO*), 380
French National Assembly, 165
French Quarter, 269, 271, 277
Friedman, David, 155, 186
Friedman, Milton, 366, 387
Fries, John, 146
Fries Rebellion, 146
Frost, David, 310
Frost, Robert, 122
Fuller, R. Buckminster, 31, 105
Fund for Peace, 266, 277
Furtwangler, Wilhelm, 379
Future of Work, The, 312, 331
Fuzzy logic, 3

Galambos, Andrew J., 161, 187
Galapagos Islands, 232, 342
Galchen, Rivka, 65, 77
Gall, John, 28-29, 58
Game theory, 231, 305, 372
Gandhi, Mahatma, 44, 89, 115, 142, 152, 155, 161, 170, 187, 188
Gardena, 42-43, 59
Gardner, Matthew, 19
Gatto, John, 20
Geithner, Timothy, 102
Gell-Mann, Murray, 225
General Electric, 370
General Equilibrium, 133, 361
General Theory, 45, 255, 382-383
Genetic drift, 336, 339

George Mason University, 208, 234
Georgia, 20, 141, 362
Gerhart, Jon, 259
German National Socialists Workers Party (Nazis), 83, 109, 137-138, 140, 196-198, 201, 222, 288, 343, 377-379, 380-381
Germanic tribes, 149, 242
Germany, 41, 83-84, 109, 130, 138, 140, 186, 196-197, 201, 222, 244, 257, 288, 319, 328, 377-381, 388
German High Command, 196, 199
Gilley, Amy 126, 142
Gilling's Law 46, 60
Glasser, William, 284
Gleick, James, 3, 7, 24, 66-67, 77
Glendale Fire Department, 327
Global warming, 38-39, 41-42, 59-60
Gödel, Kurt, 303
Goebbels, Joseph, 83
Golden Age of Greece, 211
Golden Rule, The, 126
Good Nazi, The, 201, 222
Gorbachev, Mikhail, 204
Gordian Knot, 76
Gore, Al, 38
Gorman, Michael, 20
Gournay, Monsieur de, 36
Government failure, 247-248
Government-Sponsored Enterprise (GSE), 321
Grabbing Hand, The, 160, 187
Gracchus, Gaius, 239
Gracchus, Tiberius, 238
Grand Cayman Island, 328
Grantland, Brenda, 109, 113
Gravity's Rainbow, 33
Great Depression, 370, 383, 388
Great Recession, 322
Great Firewall, 175
Great Leap Forward, 96-97
Greco-Persian War, 244

Greece, 120, 158, 169, 180, 211, 243-244, 254, 285
Greenhut, Steven, 101, 112
Greenspan, Alan, 229, 255, 332
Greenwich Village, 146
Group intelligence, 209-210
Grunwald, Michael, 366, 387
Guevara, Che, 380
Gulf War, second, 162, 252
Gutenberg, Johannes, 213

Habeas corpus, 187, 308
Habsburg, House of, 194-195
Hackwood, Suzanne, 259
Haicheng, China, 15
Halbrook, Stephen P., 197, 222
Hamilton, Alexander, 147
Hard determinism, 67-68
Harvard University, 25, 53, 60, 128
Hatfield-McCoy feud, 157
Hawaii, 329
Hawking, Stephen, 62, 65, 77, 303
Hayek, Friedrich, 86, 99, 112, 125, 142, 225, 227-229, 255, 292, 296, 351-352, 355, 358, 362-364, 383, 386-387
Heat death, 10, 346
Heisenberg, Werner, 7, 13-15, 21, 24-25, 50, 63-64, 134, 303
Hellenic tribes, 243
Helots, 285-286
Henderson, David R., 244, 256, 387-388
Henry Doorly Zoo, 336, 350
Henry, Patrick, 131, 132
Henry VIII, King, 131
Heraclitus, 72
Hess, Karl, 17
Hewlett, Bill, 219
Hewlett-Packard Company, 219
Hibernia Bank, 272
Hightower, Jim, 16
Hillel, 251
Hindu, 161

Index

Hippocratic Oath, 105
Hirschman, A.O., 93, 112
Hitler, Adolf, 75, 99, 181, 196-198, 201, 376-379, 381-382, 388
Hitler of Cambodia, 376
Hitler-Stalin Pact,
Hobbes, Thomas, 266, 294
Hoffmeyer, Jesper, 260, 277
Holdener, Michael, 271
Holland, John H., 10, 24, 58, 123, 143, 225, 255, 351-353, 386
Holmes, Oliver Wendell Jr., 152, 186
Holy Roman Empire, 194, 212
Homebrew Club, 219
Homeland Security, 268-269, 272
Hooper, Finley, 239, 256
Horwitz, Steven, 366
Hospers, John, 214
Hot-water tax, 146
Houdini, Harry, 280
Human Action, 228, 255
Human Synergetics, 126, 142
Hunt brothers, 367
Hurricanes, 2, 31, 268, 270-273, 277
Hussein, Saddam, 55, 162
Hutchings, Robert L., 56
Hutus, 193
Hwang, Kee Yeon, 276
Hylton, Ethel, 109
Hypercycle, 337
Hyperdemocracy, 107
Hyper-social, 173

Iacocca, Lee, 137
IBM, 81, 217, 320
Ibo of Nigeria, 233
Iceland (Saga Age), 232
Ideological drift, 376
Imperial Hubris, 56, 60
Incompleteness theorems, 303
Independent Institute, 256, 370, 388
India, 12, 24, 44-45, 48, 116, 142, 152

Individualogy, 162
Inefficient equilibrium, 382
Information theory, 83, 85
Informational cascading, 207-208
Instant time, 317
Institut des Hautes Études Scientifiques (IHES), 79
Institute of Architecture and Planning at Morgan State University, 126
Institute of Optics at the University of Paris, 65
Institute on Taxation and Economic Policy, 19
Integrated-partition, 228
Intel Corporation, 110, 219
In the Wake of Chaos, 7, 24
Internal Revenue Service (IRS) 9, 37, 102-103, 108, 110
International Alliance of Holistic Attorneys, 304
Internet, 83-84, 126, 142, 200, 202-203, 276, 296, 331, 359-361, 387
In These Times, 286, 296
Inverse licensing effect, 103
Invisible hand, 227, 232, 314, 351, 354
Invisible Hook: The Hidden Economics of Pirates, The, 234, 256, 331
Iraq, 30, 55-56, 60, 197, 199, 248, 252, 257, 280, 288
Ireland, medieval, 232
Iroquois Confederacy, 232
Iroquois Great Council, 233
Ismagilov, Rustem F., 31, 58
Italian Socialist Party, 380

Jackson, Robert H., 150, 164, 186
Jacobs, Christian, 260
Jacobs, Jane, 124, 142
James II, King, 233
Jamestown, 118
Japan, 12, 17, 48-49, 244, 262, 319
Jim Crow laws, 166, 288

Jobs, Steve, 219, 233
Johnson, Chalmers, 55, 60
Johnson, Lyndon, 18
Jones, Jim, 34
Johnny White's Sports Bar, 270
Jönsson, Claus, 68
Journal of Atmospheric Sciences, 2, 59
"Journey to the Planet," PBS television show, 47
Judaism, 140
Junk DNA, 340
Junto, 240
Jurassic Park, 9, 13
Jurisprudence, 149-150, 186
Jury nullification, 151
Justice Department's Bureau of Justice Statistics, 153
Justice-makers, 251
Justice Policy Institute, 286, 296

Kalev, Alexandra, 100
Kambanda, Jean, 194
Kamin, Leon J., 128, 142
Kapauku of New Guinea, 235
Kaplan, Fanya, 381
Karamojong of Uganda, 233
Katrina, Hurricane, 268, 270, 272-273, 278
Kauffman, Stuart, 10, 24, 130, 136, 142, 314, 337-338, 350, 353-354
Kaye, Bryce, 305-306, 331
Keep It Simple, Stupid (KISS), 90
Keppler, Frank, 41
Keilin, David, 348, 350
Kellert, Stephen H., 7, 24
Kelly, Kevin, 262, 277, 282, 296
Kelly, William, 171
Kelo v. New London, 154, 186
Kentucky, 158
Ketchikan, 47
Keynes, John, 382-384, 388
Keynesism, 355, 382-383

Khmer Rouge, 375-376
Kikuyu of Kenya, 233
Killefer, Nancy, 102, 112
Killing fields, 376, 388
Kirman, Alan, 231
Kirschner, Marc, 259
Klein, Daniel, 208-209, 222, 352, 354, 386
Kleptocracies, 106
Klose, Kevin, 205, 222
K-mesons, 71
Koslowski, Peter, 248, 257
Kovalyov, Sergei, 106
Kru of Liberia, 233
Kunz, George, 311, 331
Kurdish language, 48, 166
Kyoto protocol, 41

Labor theory of value, 82-83
Lactantius, 239
Laden, Osama bin, 55-56, 329
Laissez-faire, 351, 359, 384, 386-387
Lamarckian theory, 343
Lamarck, Jean-Baptiste, 343
Landreneau, Dwight, 269
Landsbaum, Mark, 110
Langton, Christopher, 132
Laplace, Pierre-Simon, 14
Laskar, Jacques, 70, 78
Laqueur, Walter, 379, 388
Law, The, 120
Law for the Elephant, 221, 223
Law of requisite variety, 127
Law of the Somalis, The, 237, 256
Leary, Timothy, 203
Leather Apron Club, 240
Lederer, Richard, 297
Leeson, Peter, 234-236, 256, 311, 331
LeFevre, Robert, 107
Legalized violence, 98
Lenin, Vladimir, 375, 380-381
Leningrad, 48, 205

Index 401

Leviathan, 91, 293-294
Lewis, Michael, 169, 188
Lewontin, Richard C., 128, 142
Licensing effect, 99-103, 112, 323
Life of the Bee, The, 356, 387
Lifton, Robert Jay, 159, 187
Lindblom, Charles E., 93, 112
Linear Regression, 66
Lineartarians, 285
Linearists, 182, 318, 361
Linux, 360
Lister, Tim, 182
Live and Let Live, 163, 187
Living computer, 263, 277
Lloyd's of London, 273, 278
Locke, John, 35, 90, 308, 331
Lock-in systems, 86
Long, Roderick T., 233, 256
Lord of the Rings, The, 292
Lorenz, Edward, 2-3, 39, 59, 66, 80
Los Alamos National Laboratory, 5
Los Angeles, 35, 42, 170, 286
Los Angeles Sheriff Department, 108
Los Angeles Times, 58-59, 151, 171, 186-188, 332, 388
Lost, TV series, 116
Louisiana, 268-269, 271-272, 277
Louisiana Department of Wildlife and Fisheries, 269, 277
Low, David B., 56
Loyola College, 320
Lucas, Chris, 126, 142, 341, 350
Lucas, James, 198, 222
Luther, Martin, 130, 142
Luthor, Lex, 329
Lynch, Vickie, 175
Lyon, Matthew, 147

MacCallum, Spencer, 237, 256
MacArthur Fellowship, 337
MacGill, Victor, 118, 142
Machan, Tibor R., 155, 187

Machiavelli, Niccolò, 68, 77, 105, 173
Mack, Richard, 246
Madison, James, 311
Madoff, Bernard L., 368-369, 387
Maeterlinck, Maurice, 356, 387
Maggessi, Marina, 250
Magnitogorsk, Russia, 47
Maia, Mayor Cesar, 250
Malcolm, Ian, 335
Maldonado, Abel, 22, 25
Managed democracy, 107
Mandelbrot, Benoît B., 80-82, 88, 252, 363
Mandelbrot Set, 4, 80, 82
Manhattan Project, 68
Man of La Mancha, 253
Maoism, 376
Marius, Richard, 130, 142
Market chaologists, 18, 230, 351, 358, 364, 383
Market failure, 245-246, 248
Market for Liberty, The, 310, 331
Market order, 364
Markopolos, Harry, 368-369
Marriage First Aid Kit, The, 305
Mars Global Surveyor and Odyssey, NASA, 8, 40, 59, 77, 262
Marshall Plan, 244
Martin Luther King, Jr.–Harbor Hospital, 170
Martin Luther: The Christian between God and Death, 130, 142
Marx, Groucho, 38
Marx, Karl, 82-83, 173-174, 324-325, 377
Marxism, 82, 159, 160, 324, 374-376, 377, 379-381
Marxism-Leninism, 189, 375
Maryland, 2, 320
Masai of Kenya, 233
Massachusetts, 2, 19, 247, 257
Massachusetts Institute of Technology

(MIT), 2, 24, 69, 351, 354, 356, 386
Maturana, Humberto, 313
Max Planck Institute for Nuclear Physics, 41
Mazar, Nina, 101, 112
Mazzi, Eric, 41
McDonald, John, 371
McDonald, Robert M.S., 118
McKee, Jeffrey K., 341, 346, 350
MedHunters, 245, 256
Meese, Ed III, 153
Melvern, Linda, 193, 222
Mencken, H. L., 207
Menger, Carl, 82, 362
Mensheviks, 381
Mercantilism, 383-385
Merchant republics, Italy, 212
Merton, Robert K., 28, 58
Messenians, 285
Metaphysics, 118, 136, 301
Methodological individualism, 162, 255, 362
Mexico, 27, 326
Micro-organizational behavior, 162
Microsoft, 217, 360-361
Microsoft's Internet Explorer, 360-361
Microsoft Windows operating system, 360
Milgram, Stanley, 138, 143
Mill, John Stuart, 14
Miller, Dale, 99
Miller, Peter, 216-217, 223
Mindless intelligence, 7, 346
Minoans, 235
Minsky, Marvin, 354, 386
Mirrlees, James, 355
Mises, Ludwig von, 27, 44-45, 228, 248, 255
Mission accomplished, 252, 257
Mississippi, 165, 270-271
Mississippi River, 270
Mobocratical cascading,

Modern evolutionary synthesis, 341
Mok, Ta, 376, 388
Monderman, Hans, 273-275
Monod, Jacques, 348-350
Monopolies, 35, 98, 123, 131, 152, 184, 192, 204, 238, 313, 318, 320, 329, 359, 364-370, 384, 387
Monopoly Makers: Ralph Nader's Study Group Report on Regulations and Competition, The, 387
Monster curve, 80
Monterey County, 25, 242, 244, 290, 296
Montesquieu, Charles de, 150
Montgomery Ward, 217-218
Moral hazard, 365
Morgan, J.P., 369
Morgarten Pass, Battle of, 195
Moscow, Russia, 204-205
Mountain men, 315
Moyers, Bill, 96, 112
Mozilla Foundation, 360
MTBE, 54
Mujahedeen,
Municipal Mutual Insurance Company, 42
Murphy Oil, 272
Mussolini, Benito, 378-381, 388
Mutational drift, 339
Muwakkil, Salim, 286-287, 296
Mwenda, Andrew, 326, 332
Myceneans, 232
My Lai Massacre, 156, 187
Myrmecologists, 356
"Mystery of Fascism, The," 377, 388

NAACP, 322
Nader, Ralph, 366, 387
N-Body Problem, 70
Nagin, Ray, 268
Bonaparte, Napoleon, 34
Napolitano, Judge Andrew, 151, 186
NASDAQ, 368

Index 403

Nash Equilibrium, 372
Nash, John, 231, 305, 372
National Adult Literacy Survey, 20
National Aeronautics and Space Administration (NASA), 8, 40, 59, 77, 262
National Disaster Medical Team, 269
National Geographic, 59, 216, 223
National Guard, 108, 269-270
National Health Service, in United Kingdom, 171
National Intelligence Council, 56
National Labor Relations Act of 1935, 241
National Park Service, 57, 99, 108
National Public Radio, 205
National Recovery Administration (NRA), 370, 378
National Security Agency (NSA), 199
National Socialism, 377, 379, 381-382
National Socialists, 83, 109, 137-138, 140, 196-198, 201, 222, 288, 343, 377-381
Nature of Economics, The, 124
Naval Postgraduate School, 244
Negative entropy, 347
Negentropy, 374
Negroponte, Nicholas, 356, 386
Neo, alias (Thomas A. Anderson),
Neoclassical economists, 133, 361-362
Neo-Darwinism, 341
Nero, Claudius Caesar Drusus Germanicus, 91-92, 239
Neropolis, 91-92
Netherlands, 4, 143, 255, 385
Network fishnet, 292
Neumann, John von, 315
Neurons, 262-264, 315
New Deal, 379, 388
New Mexico,
New Orleans, 268-273, 277
New Rules for the New Economy, 262, 277

New Science, 2-3, 23-24, 63-64, 66, 77, 142, 189, 227, 254, 263, 277, 387
New Scientist, The, 41, 59, 350
Newton, Isaac, 3, 14-15, 55, 61, 70, 82, 118, 120, 182, 227, 283, 304, 358
New Urbanism, 124-125
New York Academy of Science, 14
New York City, 19, 124, 145, 221, 253, 268, 286-287
New Yorker, The, 208, 276, 278, 383, 389
New York Times, 20, 25, 58-59, 77, 171, 186, 188, 207, 222, 229, 255-257, 269, 277-278, 322, 332, 356, 360, 369, 379, 386-387
New York University School of Law, 221
Nifong, Mike, 151
Niger, 206-207, 222
Nigeria, 96, 233, 384
Night-watchmen government, 364
Nineteen Eighty Four – 1984, 174, 220
Nisbet, Robert A., 112, 117, 142
Nixon, Richard, 18, 102, 310
No Child Left Behind, 37, 59
No-duty laws, 247
Nomenklatura, 325
Nonequilibrium systems, 134
Non-interventionism, 196
Nonlocality Principle, 65-66
Normandy Invasion, 198-199
Norsemen, 232
North Carolina, 119, 151
Not in Our Genes, 128, 142
Notten, Michael van, 237, 256
Noyce, Robert, 219
Nuer of Sudan, 233
Neuroeconomics, 173

Oak Ridge National Laboratory, 175
Obama, Barack 22, 37, 98, 102-103, 106, 322-323
Obamacare, 22, 37
Oberhausbergen, Battle of, 212

Observer effect, 318
Obsessive-Compulsive Personality Disorder (OCPD), 117, 287-289, 379
Obstructionists, 289
Ockam's Razor, William of, 15 Ockham (c. 1288 – c. 1348), of Occam's Razor fame
Ohio State University, 309
Old Swiss Confederation, 194
Omaha, 336
On Human Nature, 159
"On the Nature of Turbulence," 79, 88
On the Wealth of Nations, 366
Open source, 122, 208, 241, 258, 358-360
Operation Ajax, 54
Orange, 246
Orange County Register, 60, 110, 112, 387
Order-from-disorder, 347
Order Out of Chaos, 11, 24, 134, 143, 304
Order Without Design, 335, 337-339, 341-349
Order Without Law, 293-294, 296
Oregon, 59, 220
Organa, Princess Leia, 279
Organizational behavior, 162, 325
Organizational free energy, 90
Organized chaos, 281
Organized crime, 36, 141, 153, 179, 241, 329, 365, 367
Origin of Species, The, 342
Orlando Sentinel, 33, 58
Ormerod, Paul, 30, 58, 230, 255
O'Rourke, P.J., 366, 385, 387
Orwell, George, 51, 174, 188
Orwellian doublespeak, 44, 51, 102
Osler, William, 245
Out of Control, 6, 9, 92, 151, 153, 193, 282, 296, 320
Outcome-based policies, 299

Overland Trail, 220, 223
Over-lawed lawlessness, 149
Over-organizing gene, 240, 242
Oxford University, 355

Packet switching, 202
Pagels, Heinz R., 14, 25
Palyi, Melchior, 378
Pandora's box, 302
Paradox of Power and Weakness, The, 311, 331
Paradox Theory, 306
Paris-Sud University, 261
Parity pushers, 301-302
Parthenogenesis, 336
Particle Swarm Optimization (PSO), 262
Patches, 353
Paternalism, 316
Path dependency, 86
Pathogenic Systems, 160
Patricians, 238
Pattern of decisions, 216
Pattern-oriented modeling, 50
Patton, George, 199
Paul, Ron, 22
Paul Terrell's Byte Shop, 219
Peasants War, 130
Peat, David F., 312, 332
Pebble-Gonsalves, Nancy, 110
Peeping Tom surveillance, 178
Pelosi, Nancy, 22
People's socialism, 324, 375, 381
Pennsylvania, 8, 131, 146, 170, 233, 240, 305
Penn, William, 131, 142, 233
Penney, J.C., 218
Pensacola, Florida,
Pentagon, 271, 277
Perfectionists, 72-73, 120, 289
"Period Three Implies Chaos," 3
Perpetual construction, 215
Perry, Alex, 326, 332

Index

Persian Gulf War, 1991, 55
Persians, 244, 285
Personality and Social Psychology Bulletin, 309, 331
Peters, Edgar, 363
Peterson, Peter G., 18, 25
Pew Research Center, 106
Phase-lock state, 264
Phase-shifting state, 116, 264
Phase space, 291
Phase state, 64
Philadelphia, 52, 240-241
Phillips Curve, 383, 388
Philip II of Macedon, 211, 244
Phnom Penh, 375
Phoenix effect, 122
Pi, 62, 73
Pineau, Carol, 326
Piquette-Miller, Micheline, 245
Pirate societies, 234-235, 256, 331
Pittsburgh, 146
Planned anarchy, 45
Planned change, 282
Planned chaos, 44-45, 96, 176, 179, 192, 267
Planned shortcomings, 206
Plante, Francis, 108
Plataea, Battle of, 285
Plebeians, 102, 238-239
Pluralism, 116, 212, 281
Podolsky, Boris, 64
Poincaré Conjecture, 71
Poincaré, Henri, 24, 70-71
Poland, 137
Political anarchist paradox, 309
Political causality, 67
Politicalization, 46, 249, 284, 287
Political flatliners, 182
Politicalized order, 281
Political reductionism, 127
Polycentric laws, 150
Popisil, Leopold, 235

Porcupine approach, 196
Positivism, 13-14
Posner, Richard, 187, 320
Post-Revolutionary War America, 132
Pot, Pol, 375-376, 388
Pournelle, Jerry, 29
Powell, Benjamin, 236, 256
Power Law Distribution, 175, 192, 246
Power Principle, 181
Pranis, Kevin, 286, 296
Pratchett, Terry, 9, 24
Pravda, 45
Praxeology, 362
Preservation laws, 327-328
"Pretense of Knowledge, The," 227
Price control, 51, 171, 239, 300, 378
Price support laws, 73-74
Prigogine, Ilya, 133-135, 143, 215, 223
Prince, The, 68, 77, 173
Princeton University, 68, 210, 226, 372
Principles of Economics, 82
Principles of Trade, 351, 386
Prisoner's dilemma, 372-373
Probability distribution, 66, 232
Prodöhl, Paulo, 336
Progressive Era, 369
Prohibition, 17, 141, 143, 153, 231, 329, 367
Prohibitions: Thirteen Years That Changed America, 141, 143
Project HOPE, 170
Protestant, 28, 130, 194
Protestant Reformation, 130
Psychological Science, 101, 112
Public Choice Theory, 228, 255, 292, 370
Public Employees' Retirement System (PERS), 102
Plutarch, 304
Pushkina. Russia,
Putin, Vladimir, 106
Pynchon, Thomas, 33

Quakers, 131
Quang Ngai hospital, 156
Quantum Electrodymanics,
Quantum Entanglement, 64-65, 307, 312
Quantum Field Theory, 65
Quantum Mechanics, 2, 13-15, 63-65, 77
Quantum Superposition, 64, 77, 291, 307
Quantum Teleportation, 66, 77
Quasispecies, 337
Quest for Community, 117, 142
Quixote, Don, 253
Quorum sensing, 210

Radio Free Europe/Radio Liberty, 205
Rand, Ayn, 112, 285
Rangel, Charles, 103
Rauschning, Hermann, 377, 388
Reactance Theory, 33, 58
Reagan administration, 153
Reagan, Ronald, 181
Red Chinese Army, 139
Red Cross, 268, 277
Red Guard, 97
Reductionism, 118, 127-129
Reese, Charley, 33, 58, 104, 113
Regulatory capture, 248
Reid, John Phillip, 221, 223
Reliability engineering, 200
Renaissance, 212
Renormalization, 63
Rent-seeking, 248
Repeatable events, 289
Repletive bonding, 161
Responsible rider problem, Free-rider problem? 249
Revolution from above, 203
Ricardo, David, 384
Riddle Chain: Chance, Coincidence and Chaos, The, 341, 346, 350
Right of initiative, in Switzerland,
Rinkonomics, 208, 222
Rio de Janeiro, Brazil, 250

Roberts, Paul Craig, 158, 187
Roberts, Pat, 271
Rodriguez, Edith, 170
Rogers, Will, 247
Roll, Richard, 355, 386
Roman Empire, 148, 150, 194, 212-213
Roman Republic, 198, 237, 243-244
Romansh,
Rome, 58, 91-92, 148-149, 198, 238-239, 242, 256
Roosevelt, Franklin D. (FDR), 48, 189, 370, 378-379, 383
Roosevelt, Teddy, 57
Roper, Tim, 210, 222
Rose, Steven, 128, 142
Rosen, Nathan, 64
Rossetto, Louis, 202-203
Rothbard, Murray N., 233, 255, 369, 388
Rothschild, Michael, 232, 255
Roundabout, 352, 275
Ruelle, David, 79-80, 88
Rulers' paradox, 308, 331
Rummel, R. J., 181, 189, 388
Rumsfeld, Donald, 271, 280, 296
Rundstedt, Marshal von, (von is not capitalized in chapter), 198
Russ, Clarence, 273
Russia (Russian Federation), 7, 34, 41, 47, 97, 106-107, 113, 181, 379, 381
Russia and the Russians: Inside the Closed Society, 205, 222
Rwandan Genocide, 193, 222
Rwanda, Republic of, 193-194
Sackellares, Chris, 185
Sacramento Bee, 52, 59-60
Sagan, Carl, 339
Saint-Exupéry, Antoine de, 90
Saint Francis of Assisi, 296
Salzburg Festival, 379
San Francisco, 58, 78, 83, 142, 172, 186, 189, 256, 273
San Francisco earthquake 273

Index 407

San Francisco Weekly, 107
Santa Fe Institute, 93, 112, 122, , 136, 225, 351, 353, 361, 364
Satyagraha, 161
Saudi Arabia, 55, 267, 277
Sauron's One Ring, 292
Seattle University, 311
Secretary of Defense, 271, 280
Seoul, 276
Schelling, Thomas, 305, 331
Scheuer, Michael, 56, 60
Schindler, Oskar, 137-138
Schrödinger, Erwin, 64, 77, 346-347, 350
Schumacher, Thomas J., 93, 112
Schumpeter, Joseph, 93, 249, 257, 382
Schumpeter Prize in Economics, 93
Schwartz, Peter, 17
Schwarzenegger, Arnold, 38
Science, 1-3, 5, 7, 9-14, 18, 21, 23-24, 27, 29, 31, 39-40, 42, 58-59, 62-66, 77-79, 85-86, 88, 101, 112, 116, 118, 123-124, 126, 128, 133, 142, 161-162, 167, 173, 186, 188-189, 226-227, 229, 243, 245, 254-255, 259, 263, 277, 280, 301, 313, 318, 331-332, 335-336, 350-351, 353, 357-358, 362-363, 386-387
Scientific American, 65, 77, 386
Scientism, 358, 363
Scott, Carole E., 362, 387
Scott, Donald, 108
Sears, Roebuck and Co., 218
Securities and Exchange Commission (SEC), 368-369, 371, 387
Selfish Gene, The, 159, 187
Self-Organizing societies, 232
Self-Organizing Systems (SOS), 10, 90, 124, 162, 225-257, 265-266, 305-306, 337, 341, 346, 354, 359
Senate Homeland Security Committee, 272
Separating School and State, 19, 25
Severe Acute Respiratory Syndrome

(SARS), 42
Shaffer, Butler, 35-36, 50, 58, 60, 225, 301, 331
Shah of Iran, 54-55
Shane, Scott, 204
Shannon, Claude, 85
Shared-power,
Sharing of error, 265
Sharp, Gene, 27
Shasta County, 294
Richman, Sheldon, 19, 25, 388
Sherman Antitrust Act, 320
Shiite, 30
Shleifer, Andrei, 160, 187
Short-term and long-term inconsistencies, 316
Sihanouk, Prince, 375
Silicon Valley, 219
Silva, Luiz Inácio Lula da, 250
Single point of failure, 16, 200-201, 214, 284
Sino-Vietnamese War, 376
60 Minutes, 109
Slavery, 118, 155, 157, 215, 285, 365
Smart Growth, 124
Smith, Adam, 173, 227-228, 314, 351-352, 354, 366, 384-386
Smith, Fred, 126
Smith, Munroe, 149, 186
Smith, Will, 99
Smoot-Hawley Tariff Act, 1930, 52-53
Social Chaology, 89-111, 113, 115-141, 143
Social Complexity, 32, 89
Social Darwinism, 342
Social Justice, 72
Social psychologists, 138, 155
Socialist Revolutionaries, 381
Social Statics, 342
Societal entropy, 148
Society Security, (could this be Social Security), 19, 136, 167, 378

Sociobiology: The New Synthesis, 159, 187
Solis, Hilda, 102
Solon of Athens, 239
Somalia, 235-237, 256
South Carolina, colony of, 141
Southwestern Law School, 35
Soviet Man—homo Sovieticus, 75
Soviet Union, 45, 47, 55, 75, 86, 169, 174, 176, 181, 189, 203-206, 222, 284, 312, 324-325, 363-364, 375-376, 380-381
Sowell, Thomas, 172, 218, 223
Space-time, 61, 63
Spaghetti Code/Loop, 76
Spaghetti Loop Effect, 75-76
Spanish Civil War, 174, 188
Sparta, Greece, 284-286
Spartans, 284-286
Special Theory of Relativity, 64
Speer, Albert, 201, 222
Spencer, Herbert, 342-343
Spontaneous order, 10, 49, 86, 130, 207, 209, 222, 228, 235, 295, 335, 352, 363-364, 383
Spooner, Lysander, 106
St. Bernard Parish, 272
Staffocracy, 29
Stagflation, 383
Stalinist solution, 353
Stalin, Joseph, 174, 181, 376
Stanford Business School, 99
Stanford Linear Accelerator Center (SLAC), 71
Stanford University, 362
Stanislaw, Joseph, 383
State-capitalism, 377
State-controlled capitalism, 370
Stateless societies, 180, 232-236, 256, 324-325
State of Fear, 56
State-sanctioned theft, 106
State University of West Georgia, 362
Steele, David Ramsay, 377, 380, 388
Stennis Space Center, 271
Stern, Itzhak, 137
Stevens, Richard W. 247, 257
Stewart, Ian, 302, 331
Stewart, Jon, 229, 255, 366, 387
Stigler, George, 370
Stigmergic assemblies, 260
Stoic philosophers, 158
Stonewall Inn, 145
Stonewall Riot, 145
Story of History, The
Stone, Warren S., 241
Stossel, John, 168, 187, 209, 322, 366, 387
Strange attractors, 80
Strasbourg, 212
St. Petersburg Pulkovo Astronomical Observatory, 41
Structured order, 91
Subjective value, 79, 81-87, 135
Suboptimal state, 344-345
Suffolk University, 236
Sukhorukov, Leonid S., 34
Sunni, 30
Supercomputer Toolkit, 69
Superdome, 268-270
Superman, 329
Superorganism, 343
Surowiecki, James, 208, 210, 222
Survival of the fittest, 342-343
Survival of the most adaptable, 342, 344
Sussman, Gerald, 69-70
Sutton, Willie, 368
Swann vs. Charlotte-Mecklenburg County Board of Education, 54
Swarm Intelligence, 121, 125 209, 216, 259-265, 267-277
Swarm Intelligence: From Natural to Artificial Systems, 261
Sweden, 84, 222, 253

Index

Swiss Confederation or Switzerland, 194-197, 203, 222
Sydney Morning Herald, 85, 88
Synapses, 94, 264, 315, 351
"Synergy and Complexity Science" 126, 142
Syr Darya River, 47
Syrus, Publilius, 220
Systemantics: How Systems Really Work and How They Fail, 28, 58

Tacitus, 92, 150
Takens, Floris, 79-80, 88
Tannehill, Morris and Linda, 310, 331
Tanqshan, China, 15
Tanzania, 194
Target Switzerland, 197, 222
Taylor, Chris Lusby, 110
Teixeira, Bob, 119
Teleology, 349
Teleonomy, 349
Ten Commandments, 150
Tenet, George, 199, 222
Temporary autonomous zones, 234
Termites, 125-126, 142, 259
Thayer, Nate, 376
Theodoric the Great, King, 158
Theory of Moral Sentiments, The, 173
Theory of Relativity, 21, 45, 64, 87
Thermopylae, 196, 285
Theroux, David, 370, 388
Third Army, of the United States, 199
Third law of motion, 55, 283
Third Reich, 196
Third Wave, 203
Thompson, Hugh Jr., 156, 187
Thoreau, Henry David, 161
Thought reforms, 159, 187
Thought Reform and the Psychology of Totalism: A Study of "Brainwashing" in China, 159, 187
Three-Body Problem, 40, 70-71

Three Mile Island, 8-9, 24
Tiananmen Square, 139, 213
Tiber River, 239
Tibet, 267
Time magazine, 37, 175, 272, 326, 366
Tin-Goose, 371
Tocqueville, Alexis de, 168, 187
Toffler, Alvin, 203
Tolstoy, Leo, 106
Toner, John, 264, 277
Tonowi, 235
Topological mixing,
Torvalds, Linus, 360
Tower of London, 131
Transitional species, 346
Transportation Equity Act,
Tragedy of the commons, 207
Tribune, 238-239
Troberman, Richard J., 109
Trotsky, Leon, 379
Truman, Harry S., 189, 385
TRW Space Technology Laboratories, 161
Tse-Tung, Mao, 96, 112, 159
Tsu, Lao, 6, 24
Tucker, Preston, 371, 388
Tucker, William, 358, 386-387
Tufts University, 337
Turkey, 48, 166, 222
Tutsis, 193
Twain, Mark, 251, 257
20/20 ABC-TV news show, 209, 222, 366
Twin Towers, 268
Tyrannosaurus rex, 344
Tyranny of Good Intentions, 158

Udkow, Matt, 271
Uganda, 194, 233, 326
Ukraine, 205, 300
Unabomber, 247
Uncaused Phenomena, 67, 69

Uncertainty Principle, 7, 13, 21, 25, 50, 63, 65, 134, 227, 303
Underground economy, 250, 254
Underground History of American Education, The 20
Underground society, 287
United Kingdom, 253
United Nations, 39, 47, 194, 236, 256
United Nations Intergovernmental Panel on Climate Change – IPCC, 39
United Nations International Criminal Tribunal for Rwanda, 194
United States concentration camps, 49
Unplanned order, 281
Unseen consequences, 120
Unstructured order, 91
U.S. v. Enmons, 241
University of Arizona, 100
University of British Columbia, 41
University of California, Berkeley, 116-117, 134, 138, 185
University of California, Irvine, 121, 142
University of Calgary, 260, 277
University of Cambridge, 348
University of Copenhagen, 260
University of Florida, 185, 189, 262, 277
University of Groningen, 79
University of Pennsylvania, 170, 240, 305
University of Texas, 304
University of Tübingen, 68
University of Wisconsin, 39
USA PATRIOT Act, 22, 37
"Use of Knowledge in Society, The," 355, 386
USS Abraham Lincoln, 252
Uzbekistan, Republic of, 47, 60

Vampire states, 96
Vat, Dan Van Der, 201, 222
Varela, Francisco, 313-314, 332
Vaughn, Bill, 100
Venezuela, 300
Venice, 212
Vestigial organs, 340, 345
Vichy, 197
Vichy liberalism, 382
Vickrey, William, 355
Victimless crimes, 153, 237
Vietnamese, 156-157, 375-376
Vietnam war, 156, 375
Vigilantes, 250
Vikings, 232
Vinci, Leonardo da, 191
Virginia, 19, 118, 131-132, 143, 158, 187, 331, 388
Virginia Act for Establishing Religious Freedom, 132
Virginia City, 273
Vishny, Robert W., 160, 187
Visible hand, 369, 382
Voice of Destruction, The, 377, 388
Volitional science, 161
Voltaire, François-Marie Arouet, 215
Voluntaryist, 157
Volvox, 347, 350
Vrije Universiteit Amsterdam, 248

Waggle dance, 265
Waldrop, M. Mitchell, 7, 24, 58, 255, 387
Wales, Jimmy, 361
Wal-Mart, 218, 270, 277 (Also spelled "Walmart")
Walras, Leon, 133
Walters, Barbara, 98, 181
Walters, Dan, 52, 60
Walton, Sam, 218
Wang, Jin, 259
Washington Association of Criminal Defense Lawyers, 109
Washington DC, 19, 27, 29, 52, 109, 147, 186, 247, 286
Washington Post, 25, 52, 60, 112, 113, 277, 387

Index

Wealth of Nations, The, 384, 386
Weatherford, Rev. John, 131
West Virginia, 158, 187
What is Life, 347, 350
Wheeler, John Archibald, 85
Whiltshire, England, 274
Whiskey Rebellion, 146
Whitehead, George, 131
White House, 98, 252
White Sea-Baltic Sea Canal, 48
Whitesides, George M., 31, 58
Who Wants to Be a Millionaire?, 209
Why Government Doesn't Work, 45, 59
Why Most Things Fail: Evolution, Extinction and Economics, 30, 58
Wichman, H.A., 373, 388
Wiener, Norbert, 349
Wikileaks, 84, 88
Wikipedia, 84, 361
Wilhelm II, Kaiser, 196
Will, George, 105
Wilson, Edward, 159-160, 187
Wired magazine, 88, 202, 262, 275, 278, 282
Wisdom, Jack, 69-70
Wisdom of Crowds, The, 208, 210, 222
Woolley, Benjamin, 80, 88
World Bank, 12, 236, 256
World Economic Forum (WEF), 203

World Trade Center, 37, 55
World War I, 163, 196, 380
World War II, 20, 49, 123, 137, 166, 196, 201, 218, 222, 244, 379
World War Two Through German Eyes, 198, 222
Wozniak, Stephen, 219

Xeer, 237

Yale Law School, 294
Yellowstone Park, 56-57
Yergin, Daniel, 383
Yorke, James A., 2-3
Your House Is Under Arrest, 109, 113
Yucatan Peninsula, 344
Yuhai, Tu, 264-265, 277

Zak, Paul, 173, 188
Zana, Leyla, 166, 187
Zeilinger, Anton, 65, 77
Zeno of Elea, 297, 317
Zero-point energy, 63
Zero-sum game, 384
Zhabotinsky, Anatoly, 134
Zhong, Chen-Bo, 101, 112
Zimbabwe, 125-126
Zionist, 137

L.K. Samuels

L.K. Samuels is editor and contributing author of *Facets of Liberty*, an anthology of political and economic writings from 1969 to 2009. His historical novel about 17th Century Ireland—*Ferret: The Reluctant King*—won "Honorable Mention" at the East of Eden Writers Conference held in Salinas in 2002. He managed the Future of Freedom Conference series for five years in Southern California during the mid 1980s. He helped found Rampart Institute with Robert LeFevre in 1984 and eventually became its president. Winner of the 2007 Karl Bray Memorial Award, he was elected Chair to the Project Area Committee (PAC) in 2008, a citizens committee to advise the Seaside Redevelopment Agency and the city of Seaside over eminent domain issues. Visit his website at www.lksamuels.com. His Wikipedia page is at http://en.wikipedia.org/wiki/L.K._Samuels.